Swords into Plowshares

NONVIOLENT DIRECT ACTION
FOR
DISARMAMENT ... PEACE ... SOCIAL JUSTICE

Revised Edition

Edited by Arthur J. Laffin and Anne Montgomery

Dedicated
to those without names,
 the disappeared, the tortured,
 the forgotten prisoners of conscience,
in gratitude for their gift to us of courage and fidelity,
and the love that unites us on the long road to peace.

WIPF & STOCK · Eugene, Oregon

Wipf and Stock Publishers
199 W 8th Ave, Suite 3
Eugene, OR 97401

Swords Into Plowshares
Nonviolent Direct Action for Disarmament, Peace and Social Justice
By Laffin, Arthur J. and Montgomery, Anne
Copyright©1996 by Catholic Worker
ISBN 13: 978-1-60899-059-7
Publication date 5/7/2010
Previously published by Fortkamp/Rose Hill Cath Worker, 1996

CREDITS

Grateful acknowledgment is made for the following: "Journey to Missouri" by Martin Holladay was first printed in April/May 1985 *Fellowship* magazine as "Letter from County Jail." Used by permission of Fellowship of Reconciliation. "Civil Disobedience as Prayer" by James Douglass, and "Obedience in the Beloved Community" and "Not Guilty" by Shelley Douglass first appeared in *Ground Zero* and are used by permission. "Where Your Income Tax Money Really Goes" (1996), published by the War Resisters League, is used by permission. "Letter From Robeson County Jail" by Philip Berrigan was first printed in the *National Catholic Reporter* on February 11, 1994 as "Imprisonment Could Hardly Be More To The Point." Used by permission of the *National Catholic Reporter*. "From Peace Army to Cry For Justice: A Short History of Nongovernmental Nonviolent Crisis Intervention," excerpted from Yeshua Moser's forthcoming book: *Recurrent Visions: A History of Citizen Peacekeeping Action.* Used by permission of Yeshua Moser. "We Have Been Guilty" by Ulf Panzer, was taken from the March 1987 edition of the *Catholic Worker* in New York. Excerpts from "Historical Overview of Nonviolence," reprinted by permission from *Engaging the Powers* by Walter Wink, copyright 1992, Augsburg Fortress Publishers. "Resistance, Jail and Parish Ministry" by Mike Palecek, reprinted with permission of the author.

Contents

Acknowledgments	v
Introduction	vii

PART I

Faith and Resistance

Divine Obedience, *Anne Montgomery*	1
Swords into Plowshares, *Dan Berrigan*	8
On Blindness and Healing, *Phil Berrigan*	19
Civil Disobedience as Prayer, *Jim Douglass*	24
Obedience in the Beloved Community, *Shelley Douglass*	29
Resistance, Jail and Parish Ministry (*Interview with Fr. Frank Cordaro*)	34
Pacifism Unrevised	38

Plowshares-Disarmament Actions

Introduction to Plowshares-Disarmament Actions, *Art Laffin*	41
Chronology of Plowshares-Disarmament Actions	48
From Ambler to AVCO, *Agnes Bauerlein*	86
Journey to Missouri, *Martin Holladay*	90
Silo Pruning Hooks Action Statement	95
For Love of the Children, *Liz McAlister*	98
Letter from Newport News City Jail, *Kathy Shields*	103
Jubilee Plowshares Action Statement	104

Confronting the Courts

Disarmament on Trial, *Elmer Maas*	107
Griffiss Plowshares Trial Brief	114
Not Guilty, *Shelley Douglass*	122
U.S. v. LaForge and Katt	125
The Necessity Defense: A Report, *Tom Lumpkin*	127

Contents

The Necessity Defense Allowed	131
Acting on Behalf of the Homeless: A Letter to the Court, *Felton Davis*	132
Opening Statement to Jury by Pax Christi - Spirit of Life Plowshares	135

Prison Witness

Letter from Robeson County Jail, *Philip Berrigan*	137
Spiritual Power Behind Bars, *Anne Montgomery*	140
Liberation in Captivity, *John Bach*	142
Exposing the Injustice, *Judith Beaumont*	145
Prison Poetry and Prose:	
Earth Day, *Art Laffin*	150
Dream, *Roger Ludwig*	151
From Alderson, Lent, 1985, *Anne Montgomery*	152
Thoughts on Deterrence, *Anne Montgomery*	153
For Martin Luther King, *Art Laffin*	154
This Paradise Earth, *Roger Ludwig*	154
For the Silo Pruning Hooks, *Helen Woodson*	155
Acts of Midwest Resisters According to Carl Kabat	156

Resistance to War Taxes

War Tax Resistance, *Bill Durland*	157
Colrain War Tax Witness, *Randy Kehler*	168
U.S. Invasion of the Western Shoshone Nation and Resistance at the Nevada Test Site	175

Local Campaigns

Faith, Hope and a Nonviolent Campaign, *Molly Rush*	177
Northern Lights Dispel Nuclear Darkness: Project ELF Resistance Campaign, *John LaForge and Mike Miles*	183
Lenten Fast and Public Witness, *Art Laffin*	187

PART II

From the Peace Army to Cry for Justice:

CONTENTS

A Short History of Nongovernmental Nonviolent Crisis Intervention, *Yeshua Moser*	193

Resistance to U.S. Massacre of Iraq

1) Reflections on the Gulf Peace Team Witness, *Anne Montgomery*	201
2) Resistance in the U.S. to Iraqi Massacre Overview of Resistance ANZUS Plowshares Yolanda Huet-Vaughn	204
3) Ground War - Whose Order? *Jeanne Clark*	207
4) Solidarity with the Victims: Return Trip to Iraq, *Anne Montgomery*	209
5) Psalter: The Second Watch, *Anne Montgomery*	212

Bosnia Peace Witness

1) Bridge Between Two Cities, *Anne Montgomery*	215
2) Sjeme Mira (Seeds of Peace) Leaflet	217

PART III

Solidarity with Latin America

Journey to Fort Benning, *Larry Rosebaugh*	221
Conspiracy of Sanctuary, *Stacey Merkt*	227
Independence for Captive States Witness	234
Peoples Fast for Peace and Justice in the Americas	237

PART IV

Human, Spiritual and Environmental Consequences of the U.S. Nuclear Weapons Build-Up and Military Policy

The Human and Environmental Cost of Nuclear Technology, Militarism and Ongoing Weapons Production, *Art Laffin*	243
The U.S. Weapons Build-Up and Nuclear and Interventionary Policy - Past and Present, *Art Laffin*	251
Idolatry, Nuclearism and the National	

Security State, *Art Laffin*	272
Collaboration in Nuclear Secrecy, *Samuel H. Day, Jr.*	281
The Moral Dilemma of Defense Workers, *Bob Aldridge*	283

Witness of Mordechai Vanunu

The Vanunu Story, *Anne Montgomery*	287
I Am Your Spy, *Mordechai Vanunu*	289

PART V

Historical Overview of Nonviolent Action	293

PART VI

Challenges Before Us, *Art Laffin*	303

APPENDICES

Appendix A   325

1) U.S. Nuclear Weapons, *Bob Aldridge*
2) Communication and Navigational Systems for Military Intervention and Nuclear War Fighting
3) Key Weapons Programs
4) Landmines
5) The Nuclear Club

Appendix B   337

1) Nuremberg Principles
2) The Nuremberg Pledge of Lawyers and Jurists
3) U.N. Resolution on the Prohibition of Nuclear Weapons
4) We Have Been Guilty, *Judge Ulf Panzer*

Appendix C   344

1) Weapons vs Human Needs
2) War Resisters League War Tax Money Chart - 1996

Appendix D   347

Groups and Organizations/Bibliography/Periodicals

Acknowledgments

We would like to express our gratitude to many special people who helped make this new edition a reality.

First, we are especially grateful to each person who contributed writings to this book as well as to those whose encouragement and support made the publishing of this book possible.

We are deeply thankful to Bruce Friedrich for his invaluable contribution of editing and proofreading. We are thankful, too, to Lois Janzen-Preheim, Stephen Kobasa, Elmer Maas, Sue Frankel-Streit, Kim Lamberty, and Jonah House friends Phil Berrigan, Michele Naar-Obed, and Gregory Boertje-Obed for their editorial assistance in various parts of this revised edition. We thank as well Paul Magno for his support and for the generous use of his computer.

We also thank in a special way Carol Bernstein Ferry and the late W.H. Ferry (we give thanks for his life), Judith Williams and Henri Nouwen, for their heartfelt support and donations to Art's peace ministry during the early preparations of this book. We also express our deep gratitude to Pat McSweeney, Tim Boylan, Art Milholland and Lucille Mostello, Fr. John Giuliani, Fr. Joe Baxer, Bishop Peter Rosazza, Janet and Martin Sheen and the Sisters of Mercy in Connecticut for their generous gifts.

We are also extremely grateful to the many dear friends in and outside our communities who have offered us strong encouragement and prayerful support, especially the Dorothy Day Catholic Worker in D.C., Jonah House, members of the Atlantic Life Community, and the Religious of the Sacred Heart. Art also expresses his love and gratitude to Margaret and Art Laffin and the entire Laffin family for their prayers and steadfast support.

We are deeply thankful, too, to Debby and Frank Fortkamp who originally agreed to publish this new edition, and to Beth Preheim and Michael Sprong at Rose Hill Books for their hard work in completing the publication of this book.

Finally, we are grateful to, and continue to be inspired by, all those whose acts of nonviolent resistance made this book possible. Deo Gratias!

INTRODUCTION

Since this book was first published in 1987, historic changes have occurred worldwide: the Berlin Wall was dismantled, the Soviet Union dissolved and the so-called Cold War ended. And in South Africa, the wall of apartheid has come down as Nelson Mandela is now president of a new South Africa.

Despite these and other breakthroughs, the rich and powerful continue to wage an unrelenting war against the poor of the world. Although the nuclear threat has seemingly diminished, nuclear weapons remain the cornerstone of a U.S. military policy designed to intimidate and dominate other nations and to protect U.S. "vital" economic interests. And with each passing day, the problem of nuclear weapons proliferation increases the likelihood of their use.

In its quest to define and control the "new world order," the U.S. has made clear that it will use whatever military force is necessary to protect its interests and to prevent another rival superpower, like the former Soviet Union, to emerge to challenge its interests. Although unprecedented prospects for a more peaceful world abound, the U.S. continues to maintain and develop nuclear and conventional weapons of mass destruction which poison the environment and are genocidal. Through its arms sales, the U.S. fuels numerous conflicts around the world, especially in the Third World. And rather than pursue vigorous nonviolent and diplomatic initiatives to avert such human disasters in the "killing fields" of our world — from the Sudan to Guatemala to Rwanda, Haiti, Bosnia, Cambodia, East Timor, and many others — the U.S., the U.N., and most of the church leadership have failed to provide the political and moral leadership necessary to bring about resolutions to these and other crises.

This book, which includes a series of new articles and many of the essays from the first edition, attempts to expose and confront the nuclear empire we live in and the violence plaguing our society and world today. It is a sharing of experience, of "experiments of truth," and of our reflections on both the discoveries and the understandings that emerge from them. It is an unfinished book, not only because the experiments continue, but because we are always striving for the truth, or rather with each tentative step we find its horizons expanding.

Since there is no one "right" way to say NO to death and YES to life, we have tried to include a variety of responses to the violent spirit of militarism that affects everyone today and has claimed countless lives in the name of "national security." In the face of this cultural addiction to violence, as

INTRODUCTION

manifested in our society by a massive array of nuclear and conventional weapons as well as by over 200 million handguns, people are working in a variety of ways for a nonviolent world without weapons and war, where the rights of all people are upheld and creation is cherished.

In recent years, a movement of people drawing on the rich biblical, Gandhian, and American traditions of nonviolent resistance have increasingly recognized the importance of engaging in acts of civil disobedience (which we prefer to call "divine obedience") as a genuine response of faith and conscience to the nuclear threat and to increasing U.S. military intervention in the Third World. Our contributors (as well as others mentioned in this book), aware of the blocking of democratic channels for change, have all spoken the truth directly and creatively with their lives. Some denied the government the means of warmaking: their money, their skills, their very bodies. Others have dismantled weapons, blocked weapons transport or have engaged in other creative actions to resist the machinery of war. Still others have protected sisters and brothers fleeing from death squads and have resisted U.S. military intervention in countries shielded by the U.S. nuclear umbrella.

These people have crossed the boundary of human law to demonstrate clearly that unless we resist the laws of an unjust system, we not only have complicity in its injustice, but we also strengthen the law's power over us, the power of love's opposite: fear. Our contributors acted (and continue to act) conscious of their own weaknesses and ordinariness, aware too that only in weakness and darkness can hope become a transforming reality.

Why is nonviolent resistance/divine obedience an imperative for bringing about disarmament? What is the connection between faith, nonviolence and resistance? How does one prepare for nonviolent acts of resistance? How does one respond to the charges brought in court? How does one view and cope with the consequences of imprisonment? How have some people nonviolently responded to U.S. intervention in Iraq and Central America and in war-torn countries like Bosnia? What are the main tenets of U.S. nuclear and foreign policy in this post-Cold War era? What is the human cost of weapons production? What does it mean to live in a national security state? What are some of the future challenges faced by people concerned about justice and peace face in the U.S.? The primary goal of this revised edition of *Swords into Plowshares* is to provide some initial answers to these and related questions.

Part I addresses the meaning and necessity of faith-based resistance and nonviolence; contains an introduction to and chronology of plowshares-

INTRODUCTION

disarmament actions as well as reflections and statements by people who have participated in these actions; examines how some resisters have responded to the courts and the consequences of jail and prison; deals with the subject of resistance to war taxes; and finally focuses on several regionally-based disarmament campaigns. **Part II** considers the issue of nonviolent intervention and solidarity with the victims of war. This section includes articles and accounts of resistance to the U.S. war against Iraq and a peace witness in Bosnia. **Part III** recounts some of the witnesses North Americans have taken to be in greater solidarity with Latin America. **Part IV** focuses on the human and environmental costs of ongoing weapons production and includes an historical overview of U.S. nuclear and military policy. It also examines the meaning of nuclearism and the national security state. This part also includes a report on the witness and imprisonment of former Israeli nuclear technician Mordechai Vanunu. **Part V** is a historical overview of how nonviolent action has been used from biblical times to now. **Part VI** offers analysis of some of the important challenges faced by individuals and the wider movement working for peace and justice. **This volume concludes** with a set of appendixes containing valuable technical information regarding existing and prospective nuclear and conventional weapons programs in the U.S.; secret weapons in the research and development stages; nations possessing and developing nuclear weapons; and the illegality of weapons of mass destruction and the legal justification for resistance. Also included are charts demonstrating how unrestrained military spending robs from us all, especially those in need; a partial listing of national and local disarmament, peace and solidarity groups; a selected bibliography; and a listing of peace and justice oriented periodicals.

We hope this book will help, in some small way, those who are seeking to clarify what nonviolent resistance/divine obedience involves and assist them in choosing what act of conscience they might take at this critical time. We must continue experimenting in truth rather than intellectualizing about it, not basing actions and decisions on our American obsession with efficiency and effectiveness. Faith assures us that the way will grow into truth, the truth that sets us free from the fears permeating our culture of violence and death. In that spirit we offer a book that its readers must continue writing.

Arthur J. Laffin
Anne Montgomery, R.S.C.J.

May 1991: Blood pouring on a Harrier Jet during a "Victory" parade on the Mall in Washington, D.C.. Protest by Atlantic Life Community.

PART I

FAITH AND RESISTANCE

DIVINE OBEDIENCE

Anne Montgomery, R.S.C.J.

Civil disobedience is, traditionally, the breaking of a civil law to obey a higher law, sometimes with the hope of changing the unjust civil law. For example, the lunch counter sit-ins in the 1950s challenged the validity of segregation laws in the South. But we should speak of such actions as divine obedience, rather than as civil disobedience.

The term "disobedience" is not appropriate because any law that does not protect and enhance human life is no real law. In particular, both divine and international law tell us that weapons of mass destruction are a crime against humanity and it is the duty of the ordinary citizen to actively oppose them. Richard Falk points out that "the international law of war has been at all stages an outgrowth of moral convictions that rested on some sense of underlying reality; a foundation for international law is often associated in the West with 'natural law.'" This natural law framework of international law "is radically inconsistent with the current postulate of strategic nuclear doctrine," and therefore, "a grave continuing series of violations of international law are taking place, causing peril to world peace and human destiny."[1]

The term "civil" has also lost its meaning since it implies faith in the system's openness to change. In reality the forces of violence are entrenched in the powers that control our "democracy," among them the Pentagon, the CIA, and large corporations.[2] "Our struggle is not against flesh and blood but the principalities and powers of this world." (Ep. 6:12) On this deeper level we need, as Jim Douglass says, much more than civility "in an act of disobedience to the coming murder of the human race. Love, the Love of God — not civility — is the power to overcome evil."[3]

And so we practice divine obedience.

Gandhi has shown us that divine obedience draws its power and, indeed, is inseparable from a nonviolent way of life, an integral living out of the loving truth that grasps us. Like divine obedience, nonviolence is an active force against rather than a passive acceptance of evil; nonviolence cannot be confused with refusing to act to change an unjust situation. Gandhi was strong on this point, adopting the term *satyagraha*, "truth-force," to describe an attitude and a style of action that is more than just a strategy to obtain a political goal. We must first open ourselves to the truth — a truth synonymous with love, a truth that is more than just an accurate judgment of an unjust situation. We must respond to the touch of God, to the inspiration that is our very strength. We speak the truth against injustice and, in our vulnerability to the very violence we oppose, hope to transform it through the greater spiritual force of love. This is the "law" of the cross, of "dying daily." Such nonviolent acts of resistance can be literally "disarming."

Therefore, in redefining terms, the emphasis is on a life empowered by truth and love as opposed to a passivity that shares in the violence of injustice by acquiescing to it. The emphasis is on obedience to the law of love and on the call to uphold it in the face of systematized divisions, enmity, and violence. To be consistent, such a life and the action flowing from it must be marked by characteristics that may appear foolish to the "wisdom belonging to this passing age" and "its governing powers." (1 Co. 2:6 *NEB*)

First and foremost, rather than the "order" fashioned by creating and then defeating enemies, peace is the work of unity, of breaking down those barriers, literal and symbolic, created by injustice and fear. It is the work Jesus offered as a sign of his authenticity and promised that anyone "who has faith in me will do ... and will do greater things still...." (Jn. 14:12 *NEB*) This unity is both source and goal of divine obedience and should, therefore, characterize its whole process, however imperfectly. The small community, be it a live-in community or one meeting at regular intervals for reflection, prayer, and action, is an effort to enflesh the command to be one, to be true to our common humanity as well as the covenant written in our hearts.

Many prospective peacemakers, feeling helpless, ask where to begin. Simple first steps to empowerment include meeting with a few others to share tensions, fears, and hopes; to reflect on Scripture and other readings on nonviolence; and to let prayer flow from this sharing and reflection. These meetings can be a focus for research and action on a local arms industry or military base. This whole meeting process requires working through layers of personal differences, inhibitions, and fears to reach a deeper level of support and strength that cannot be cheaply bought. We first begin to be peacemakers among ourselves in our local group.

Our struggles as a group remind us of our implication in the power plays and greed at the source of the violence in the larger society from which we cannot isolate ourselves. Abraham Heschel points out that although we may claim not to be guilty of the corruption in that society, we are all responsible.[4] This sense of common responsibility not only drives us to speak out, like the prophets, with our bodies as well as our words; but also enables us to see our action as a work of reconciliation rather than of conflict.

The promise of Jesus to be present where two or three are gathered in his name is thus more than a summons to liturgical prayer. The truth of our nature requires a community that, while respecting religious differences, lives a practical spirituality. Community is a reflection of the Trinitarian life built into our existence. We must be emptied if we are to discover a source of life real enough to dispel our fear of losing our own lives, in however small or great a way, for sisters and brothers. We must enflesh this life in all its poverty and power and, in so doing, discover a community of suffering and love that knows no boundaries.

Therefore, when we plan acts of divine obedience, we begin our process with community prayer, reflection, and decision making; we try to reach a harmony, deeper than differences in philosophy and style, that will maintain our spirit through the trial and prison processes which often require reaching consensus under difficult conditions. To make our prayer and action one, to reach out to the "other" in a personal way, requires that we emphasize depth and relationship rather than numbers and high-powered organization.

The power of forms of resistance like massive blockades stems from the strength of their "affinity groups" — small communities woven into a larger one. In such communities we can learn the true meaning of "conspiracy": "breathing together" the Spirit of life and being formed by that spirit into people faithful to the covenant of love — the law written in our hearts. In community we also examine our attitudes toward the arms workers, military personnel, police, and court officers we will encounter, reminding ourselves that we are bound together by our responsibility for violence as well as our desire that life be protected. We pray that in any confrontation the surfacing of fears and hopes on both sides may result in greater mutual healing and understanding. Often the anger of a guard or worker has proved to be but the "first line of defense," the wall that, broken down, opens the way to communication and the beginnings of a wider community. We need to trust without compromise. Otherwise we limit the human possibilities for conversion and growth in others as well as in ourselves.

Regarding the question of our effectiveness we have to "think small." In a real sense, our weakness is our strength, for it leaves us trusting in the power of God rather than in media power, vote power, or numbers power, however desirable these may be. Second, we believe with Gandhi that means and end are contained together in the seed our witness plants. If it is a community action, there is already more community in the world; if it is a repentant action, there is already more reconciliation; if it is a loving action, there is already more love casting out its opposite: fear.

We can only open ourselves to the free intervention of mercy in the history we live. So the real question becomes: "By whose standards are we judging effectiveness — or can we judge it at all?" The Gospel promise of "greater works" is to those who believe. We must be responsible and do our homework, research and choose our site with care, reflect and pray over the pros and cons of the action and symbols, and open up channels of support and communication. But in the end there is always a gap between faith and feasibility, and the moment of speaking the truth becomes a leap of faith that opens us to the power of that truth.

Finally, actions inspired by the "truth-force" are creative, marked by a certain empowerment and freedom. There is no one "approved" way to resist the mechanics of death that have invaded our multiple social and political structures — although some forms of noncooperation, such as draft and tax resistance, are obviously crucial. Between the lone witness, whom we hope is supported by community, and the mass blockade are a wide range of the smaller, community-inspired actions requiring various degrees of commitment and risk. Groups have climbed over or cut through fences to expose the weapons built or stored behind them and the hypocrisy of such "security." They have sat in front of trains carrying death to our new Auschwitz in Puget Sound. Some have renamed the Pentagon, White House, and arms factories, as well as the weapons produced, with death symbols and have blocked entrances by symbolically "dying." Other small groups have carried out Plowshares actions, obeying the biblical command to us, the people, "to beat swords into plowshares" and to emphasize that nuclear swords are both anti-life and anti-property.

These are all experiments in truth: the learning with our whole selves of that which our minds can grasp only partially, of what is required to be peacemakers, including the sharing not only of ideas, but of something about the experience. This sharing can take the form of banners, leaflets, songs, and liturgy, as well as dialogue with military personnel, workers, police, and onlookers. Such efforts at communication before, during, and following acts of divine obedience are crucial to the ongoing effort to transform conflict into something closer to communion.

Because of the growing gap between those who make policy decisions and ordinary citizens, symbolic actions like marking weapons with blood have grown in importance. It is almost impossible today to find a direct action like the lunch-counter sit-ins of the 1950s that directly touches those in power; for example, it is hard to break a law legitimizing a weapon except in a symbolic way. For this reason, symbolic direct action has become increasingly important. We can take symbolic direct action by blocking the doors of the factories that produce arms or the trains that transport them. We can dismantle one or two nuclear weapons as a symbol of our deeper responsibility to disarm the violence that created such weapons.

Symbols have a condensed, almost physical power and are especially important in an age when the inundation of words makes us nonlisteners. Symbols touch us on a deep, subconscious level and release memories and fears, aspirations and energies. The weapons themselves, like the ancient idols demanding the sacrifice of children, have become false symbols of protection from the very fear they inspire.

On the political level, as E.P. Thompson points out, weapons are symbols to hold our power structures together, structures that have suppressed and replaced politics with an ideology supported by the security services and the media.[5] We can go further and say that these weapons are the inevitable expressions of the violence central to the ideology of power. Because the gods of violence demand service as the price of "security," we adopt the repressive structures and strategies we condemn in others. But from our own hearts and traditions we are able to bring forth symbols that, like the two-edged sword of Scripture, divide truth from falsehood and the living from the dead.

Much of our creativity focuses on the choice of those symbols that will become our action or accompany it. Some have aroused emotions and raised serious questions of propriety, such as the pouring of blood on doors or weapons. The very "offensiveness" of bloodiness is part of the message. War is not polite; dismembered bodies are messy and nauseating. But symbols can point in many directions. Blood also speaks of human unity and of the offering of oneself, in however small a way, in a new liturgy of life and hope. Hammers, too, are a powerful and controversial symbol. We think of carpenters' hammers as creative, forgetting sometimes that building a new dwelling can require the dismantling of a dangerous structure first. When the dwelling is our unique planet and the danger both actualized and symbolized by life-threatening weapons, the "beating of swords into plowshares" becomes an urgent responsibility. Such an action is both symbolic and direct, since it carries out in a carefully defined scenario a small but real disarmament that thousands of treaties and conferences have yet to accomplish. It is a reenactment of the scriptural prophecy and serves to remind us all that the "days" referred to by Isaiah and Micah are not a future idealized time, but now.

An act of divine obedience such as entering an arms factory or military base and hammering on a missile cone or launcher is not taken lightly but requires that the process followed for other resistance actions be more intense and prolonged. In solitary and communal prayer we discern possibilities and the relationship between faith and feasibility. We examine obstacles and risks not only in the action itself, but possibly in long prison sentences and their effect on other relationships and responsibilities. We must work through our convictions and feelings concerning court and jail procedures. We must, too, face realistically the possibility of physical harm to one of us, and we must do all we can to avoid what might be more hurtful to the guard responsible than to ourselves.

Finally, when research and reasoning have reached a certain point before an action that seems "right," there is usually a moment or a series of moments, hard to describe, of "coming together": of community and action, of time and place — a moment of "seeing through a glass darkly," yet with the sureness of faith. We are not sure everything will turn out perfectly, but we are sure that it is right to go ahead. We will stop if violence threatens, but we are sure, too, that the doors meant to open will do so. Whether or not the physical ones do so, the community action itself is the opening of a door, a step into freedom, and a prayer for the intervention of mercy in history, for we refuse to believe that we are walled into fatalistic cycles of war and oppression or destined for holocaust. Above all, we are certain that the whole point of the process is our obedience and that the results are in the hands of God.

God.

Divine obedience, then, calls us not to answer threat, real or imaginary, with counterthreat, force with counterforce, but rather to break through this cycle by entering a new one on a deeper level. It is the Trinitarian life-cycle of descent into our own insecurity and emptiness, of being empowered by the Word of truth, of being freed yet bound to one another — to all our sisters and brothers — in the loving breath of the Spirit rising in us in the name of Life. It is the call to believe, in very real and desperate circumstances, here and now, that faith "gives substance to our hopes." (Heb. 1:1 *NEB*) Our response, therefore, becomes a message of hope.

NOTES

1. Richard Falk, Lee Meyrowitz, Jack Sanderson, "Nuclear Weapons and International Law," 1980. Typescript, pp. 1, 2.
2. Elizabeth McAlister, "A Community of Sanity," *Sojourners*, May 1983, p.28.
3. James Douglass, "Loving Disobedience," *Ground Zero*, May-June 1982, p. 6.
4. Abraham J. Heschel, *The Prophets* (New York: Harper Torchbooks, 1969), p. 16.
5. E. P. Thompson, "On Peace, Power and Parochialism," *Nation*, September 24, 1983, p. 244.

Swords into Plowshares

Daniel Berrigan

Editors' Note: *On September 9, 1980, the "Plowshares Eight" entered a General Electric nuclear missile plant in King of Prussia, Pennsylvania, and disarmed two nose cones of the Mark 12A reentry vehicle. Daniel Berrigan, one of the participants in this action, writes here of his reflections. These reflections first appeared in slightly different form in the October-November 1980 issue of* The Catholic Worker.

September 27, 1980, marked my first visit to the monastery at Gethsemani, Kentucky since the death of Thomas Merton in 1968. I was asked to offer the homily at morning Mass; the text was from Matthew 11:25-30 (*JB*), for the feast of St. Vincent de Paul:

> I bless you, Father of heaven and earth, for hiding these things from the learned and clever, and revealing them to the children . . .

And Matthew continues, with unexampled solemnity more typical of John:

> . . . No one knows the Son except the Father, just as no one knows the Father except the Son — and those to whom the Son chooses to reveal Him.

Then a glance descends; face to human face, he takes us in:

> Come to me all you who labor and are overburdened, and I will give you rest. Shoulder my yoke, learn from me; for I am gentle and humble in heart and you will find rest for your souls. Yes, my yoke is easy and my burden light.

In Jesus we learn of the modesty of God. I set this down in a time of promethean muscle-building, muscling in, a time of no limits, a time when literally everything is allowed: genetic splicing, abortions on demand, nuclear warheads pocking the landscape. We learn too well the sad litany of human excess; a national political campaign, for example, in which the nuclear arms race is simply not an issue, the only question being how much more how quickly. Death always inflicted elsewhere, the artificers of death presumably safe and sound in a nuclear free fire zone? We are gently driven mad.

To be alive to the future, one had best poke about in the past, at least now and then. I went to the monastery to seek a measure of light on why I had gone, some weeks before, to King of Prussia, Pennsylvania. And there, in the words of our statement,

> . . . beat swords into plowshares . . . exposed the criminality of nuclear weaponry and corporate piracy. . . . We commit civil disobedience at General Electric because this genocidal entity is the fifth leading producer of weaponry in the U.S. To maintain this position, GE drains $3 million a day from the public treasury, an enormous larceny against the poor. We wish also to challenge the lethal lie spun by GE through its motto, "We bring good things to life." As manufacturers of the Mark 12A reentry vehicle, GE actually prepares to bring good things to death. Through the Mark 12A, the threat of first-strike nuclear war grows more imminent. Thus GE advances the possible destruction of millions of innocent lives.

If a plumb line could lie horizontal, in time rather than space, then the line, tight as a bowstring, would lie between the monastery and General Electric. I do not know how to put matters more simply. Somewhere along that line we stand (if we are lucky, it is literally a lifeline). We touch it; the line is not dead at all, inert. It vibrates with the message of a living universe. At one end, a monastery, a hive of stillness and listening and strength. And at the other, an unspeakable horror, a factory of genocide. To taste death and life, you go to headquarters; you listen and learn from the experts.

No sylvan setting for General Electric, no fooling around. Austerity, efficiency, cost value, big bang for big buck. You drive into an industrial park, down a broad macadam highway; building after building, anonymous, walleyed, abstract. A campus of world experts in the science and practice of abstract death.

September 9, 1980. We rose at dawn after (to speak for myself) a mostly sleepless night. In and out of dream, in and out of nightmare. The refrain was part nuptial chant, part dirge; the latter theme dominant, the former a minor key indeed. Brasses, kettle drums, and now and again, the plaintive flute in obligato, the cry of an infant in the river reeds. . . .

We had passed several days in prayer together, an old custom indeed, as old as our first arrests in the late sixties. We were mostly vets of those years, survivors too, survivors of the culture and its pseudos and counters, survivors of courts and jails, of the American flare of conscience and its long hibernation, survivors in our religious communities, in our families (they have survived us!). By an act of God and nothing of our own, survivors of America — its mimes, grimaces, enticements, abhorrences, shifts and feints, masks, countermasks. Survivors (barely) of the demons who, challenged, shouted their name — Legion!

We knew for a fact (the fact was there for anyone who bothered to investigate) that General Electric in King of Prussia manufactures the reentry cones of Mark 12A missiles. We learned that Mark 12A is a warhead that will carry an H-bomb of 335 kilotons to its target. That three of these weapons are being attached to each of three hundred Minuteman III missiles. That because of Mark 12A accuracy and explosive power, it will be used to implement U.S. counterforce or first-strike policy.

We knew these hideous cones ("shrouds" is the GE word) were concocted in a certain building of the General Electric complex. The building is huge: we had no idea exactly where the cones could be found.

Of one thing we were sure. If we were to reach the highly classified area of shipping and delivery and were to do there what we purposed, Someone must intervene, give us a lead.

After our deed, a clamor arose among the FBI and state and county and GE (and God knows what other) police who swarmed into the building. "Did they have inside information? Was there a leak?" Our answer: Of course we had Inside Information; of course there had been a Leak. Our Informant is otherwise known in the New Testament as Advocate, Friend, Spirit. We had been at prayer for days.

And the deed was done. We eight looked at one another, exhausted, bedazzled with the ease of it all. We had been led in about two minutes, and with no interference to speak of, to the heart of the labyrinth.

They rounded us up, trundled us out in closed vans. We spent the day uncommonly cheerful in that place of penitence, in various cells of police headquarters. We underwent what I came to think of as a "forced fast," the opposite of forced feeding and undoubtedly less perilous to life and limb.

Around the corridors of the spiffy new building (we were in GE country, the local economy is 40 percent GE, GE brings good things to life) the atmosphere was one of hit-and-miss, cross-purpose, barely concealed panic. How the hell did they get into the building so easily? How about the jobs of those of us who were purportedly guarding the nuclear brews and potions?

Lines to Justice Department, Pentagon, FBI were red hot. Why can't you get your act together up there? And what are we to do with these religious doomsayers? Let them go, let them off light, let them off never? Please advise!

About noon another ploy got underway. They loaded us in vans again; back to the scene of the crime. It was like a Mack Sennett film played backward; first you were sped away in Black Maria, then you were backed freakishly into the same doorway. (It devolved later they wanted identification by the employees.) But they wouldn't talk, so we wouldn't walk.

They carried four of five of us out of the van into that big warehouse room with the bloody floor, the bloody torn blueprints stamped "Top Secret." And then the missile cones, broken, bloodied, useless. No more genocide in our name! And the wall of faces, police, employees, silent as the grave, furious, bewildered, a captive nation.

Under shrill orders from somewhere, the charade was halted. The procedure was illegal. A District Attorney said it might endanger their whole case. Indeed.

So back to durance vile. They locked us up, they kept saying: "Sure we'll feed you, presently we'll charge you." And nothing happened. By 5 P.M. the more inventive among us were ready to close their eyes, strip their shoelaces, and pretend we were eating spaghetti Rossi in the West Village.

Then something happened. One by one we were led out. Take off your shoes. And (to the six males) take off your pants.

It appeared that, these objects being stained with our blood, they were severely required as evidence.

So, like the bad little boys in the fairy tale, supperless and shoeless, we were led off to our destiny by Stepmother State.

An intuition that we and others have been pondering for a long time grows on us, presses closer.

To wit: In a time of truly massive irrationality, one had best stop playing the old academic-ecclesial game of scrabble, as though merely putting words together could make sense of moral incoherence, treachery, and meandering apathy, could break that spell.

Rationality? Reason? If these were ever in command, they had certainly fled the scene during the Vietnam War. I would be willing to venture that sanity and reason have never sat in the catbird seat again.

In the saddle of power and decision we have instead a kind of "Eichmania" analyzed by Merton, a tightly hierarchical, spiritually captivated, ideologically closed insanity. In it are caught the multi-corporations and their squads of engineers and planners, on and up to the highest responsible chairs of command — the Pentagon and White House. All, so to speak (so to doublespeak), to "bring good things to life."

And then outward into society the malaise touches all with a leprous finger; meandering apathy, at least as complex an illness as rotten power. Apathy, the natural outcome of such authority so used.

We have evidence of such indifference to moral and physical disaster in other modern societies, societies whose citizens, under whip and lash, or under a rain of bread and a politics of the circus, stood helpless to win the nod of blind, deaf fate, to speak up, to force a hearing.

Such apathy shows face today in our inability to summon resistance against nuclear annihilation. Screen out the horror; a shutter comes down. Best not to imagine what might be, best to act as though the worst could not be.

The phenomenon before the catastrophe is remarkably like the phenomenon after the catastrophe. Many of the survivors of Hiroshima, afflicted with radiation sickness, conceal their illness as long as possible, "act as though" they are not stricken. They go so far as to falsify family history, conceal the fact that they were in the orbit of death on the day of the bomb.

No wonder that today Americans find it more plausible, more conducive to sanity to ignore our nuclear plight, to fight survival in areas where the facts are less horrid, the cards less stacked. Economic woes, job layoffs, inflation — we have enough trouble drawing the next breath. And you with your little hammers and bottles of blood go out against Goliath? Thanks. Good luck. But no thank you.

Blood and hammers. The symbolic aspect of our GE action appealed to some and appalled others. But almost no one who has heard of the action lacks an opinion about it, usually a passionately stated one.

In pondering these passions, so long dormant, newly released, one learns a great deal — not about passions in a void, but about vital capacities for survival, sociability, spirituality.

Some who hear grow furious; some of the furious are Catholics; Catholics also guard us, judge us, prosecute us. This is an old story that need not long detain us.

What is of peculiar and serious interest here is the use and misuse of symbols, their seizure by secular power; then the struggle to keep the symbols in focus, to enable them to be seen, heard, tasted, smelled, lived and died for, in all their integrity, first intent.

Their misuse. How they are leveled off, made consistent with the credo of the state. Thus, to speak of King of Prussia and our symbol there: blood. Its outpouring in the death of Christ announced a gift and, by implication, set a strict boundary, a taboo. No shedding of blood, by anyone, under any circumstances, since this, my blood, is given for you. Blood as gift.

Hence the command: no killing, no war. Which is to say, above all, no nuclear weapons. And thence the imperative: Resist those who research, deploy, or justify on whatever grounds such weaponry.

Thus the drama; the symbol outpoured implies a command. Do this; so live, so die. Clear lines are drawn for public as well as personal conduct. Church and state, the "twin powers," always in danger of becoming Siamese twins, are in fact kept from a mutually destructive symbiosis by imperative and taboo. More, they are revealed for what they in fact are — radically opposed spiritual powers, as in Revelation 13. Church can never be state; state is forbidden to ape or absorb church. And this mutual opposition, this nonalignment, this friction and fraying, erupts from time to time in tragic and bloody struggle. The church resists being recast as Caesarian icon. The state, robust, in firm possession, demands that the church knuckle under, bend knee, bless war, pay taxes, shut up. Church, thy name is trouble.

The choices are not large. Toil and trouble or — capitulation. In the latter case all is lost. The symbols are seized at the altar and borne away. Now the blood of Christ, the blood of humans, is cheap indeed; for what could be cheaper than blood the church itself has declared expendable? That blood is now a commodity, a waste. When Caesar speaks, blood may be shed at will, by Christians or others; it makes no difference. Which is also to say: There exists no longer any distinction in fact between armed combatants and citizens, between soldiers and little children. Killing has become the ordinary civil method of furthering civic ends. The sacred symbol of blood, whose gift urged the command "Thou shalt not kill" — that blood is admixed, diluted, poisoned. It is lost in a secular vortex, immensely vigorous and seductive, urging a different vision. Labor is commodity, the flag is a sacred vexillum, humans are productive integers, triage rules the outcome. Finally, a peremptory secular command: "Thou shalt kill when so ordered — or else."

It seems to me that since Hiroshima, to set an arbitrary moment, this debasing of the sacred symbols into secular use and misuse has proceeded apace. To undo the blasphemy, what a labor.

We have been at this for years — dramatic events, deliberately orchestrated, arbitrary but intensely traditional, liturgical, illegal, in every case wrenching the actors out of routine and community life to face the music, face the public, face the jury.

Is it all worth it? In measure the eight who acted at King of Prussia have already answered the question. At least for themselves, and for one another. One of them said in the course of our discussion, "Even if the action went nowhere, if no one understood or followed through on it, I would still go ahead."

Worth it for ourselves. Each of us had, before the act, to plumb our motives, consult loved ones, care for the future of children, arrange professional and community responsibilities, measure in fact all good things against this "one necessary thing." And decide.

The eight so decided — yes. Such an act must be taken, even though it disrupt almost everything else, call many things in question, inflict suffering on others. The value of the act is thus measured by the sacrifice required to do it; an old and honored Christian idea, if I am not mistaken.

(For us, going as we did in fear and trembling from the Eucharist to General Electric had the feel of the last hours of Jesus, his journey from the upper room to death. We held our liturgy the night before, broke the bread, passed the cup. Light of head, heavy of heart, we nonetheless celebrated by anticipation the chancy event of the following day; and the trial to come; and the penalty. Our logic? The body was "broken for you," the cup "poured out for all."

The logic was not only our own. At one court hearing the prosecutor asked, with more than a show of contempt, under prodding from his chief, who referred to me as "this so-called priest" and "this wandering Gypsy" (sic), "And when did you last celebrate Mass?" I was obviously to be shown up as not only rootless, but faithless as well.)

But what of the larger meaning of the action, its value for the church and the public?

Here one must go slow. The value of the act for those who propose it, sweat it out, do it — this is more easily determined. Value is created, so to speak, in the breach, in a decision to gather, unite voices in an outcry, to precipitate a crisis that, at least for a time, will strip away the mask of evil.

But I know of no sure way of predicting where things will go from there, whether others will hear and respond, or how quickly or slowly. Or whether the act will fail to vitalize others, will come to a grinding halt then and there, its actors stigmatized or dismissed as fools. One swallows dry and takes a chance.

There was one sign that our action touched a nerve. A hasty attempt was made on the day of the action itself to discredit us through a dizzying list of charges. Ideology, panic, and special interests combined to barrage the media and the public with a verdict before the verdict — more violent crazies had gone on a rampage. The charges included assault, false imprisonment, reckless endangerment, criminal mischief, terroristic threats, harassment, criminal coercion, unlawful restraint. Talk about overkill! We sat in court, transfixed, gazing on our images in the crazy mirrors of the state fun house.

It takes a large measure of good sense to stand firm at such moments. People gifted with our nefarious history must remind themselves that at King of Prussia, hammers and blood in hand, we set in motion a lengthy and complex drama. One should speak perhaps of three acts.

The first act belonged in the main to us, an early morning curtain raiser, the action underway. In a sense the adversaries have not yet appeared; only a few subalterns act on their behalf, in their name: the guards and police and employees. But GE has not yet turned on its voltage. No official appears in justifying garb to bespeak the ancient myths, to invoke sacro-secular outrage at the violation of a holy place, property off bounds, the shrine accessible only to initiates. (Antigone has buried her brother's body, but Creon has not yet flogged his way to condemn her.)

Then a second act opens. It marks the marshalling of forces of law and order, the invoking of daemons of natural law, secular karma.

Anger, retaliation are in the air, the gods of property buzz furiously overhead. The actors all but tear up the script of act one; and assault is mounted on the earlier reliance on "higher law" or "conscience." Behold true conscience, behold the highest law of all, the law by which all citizens must live, the law that is our common safeguard against anarchy!

So in the manner of Shakespeare or Pirandello or Sophocles, act two is a kind of play within the play. The audience is bewildered, thrown off guard. It had read a certain kind of admirable moral truth in the face of the young woman Antigone (in the faces of a nun, of a mother of six, of a lawyer, a professor, a seminary graduate — faces like the credentials of moral worth) — now it hears another kind of truth. This is not the truth of "symbolic action," which from a legal point of view is always murky, easily discredited, and reaching troublesomely as it does into dark existence (the forbidden burial of a brother, the breaking and bloodying of icons) must be exercised, discredited — by measured, relentless argument.

The argument, of devastating force, in ancient Greece as today, I call that of the Great If.

The example of Antigone, the example of the eight, is deliberately magnified, made stark. Behold their act, performed under clerical guise, under the guise of virtue. Behold their act, as viewed by the state, the guardian and interpreter of public morality. (What an unconscious and ironic tribute is paid the defendants here, as though in the court itself, the state were erecting stone by stone a monument to the conscience it so fears — and so magnifies.)

In any case, citizens and believers, whatever divagations of spirit they were beckoned toward by the conduct of the protagonists, by their age or condition or credentials (above all, by their dark probing symbols) — all this is brought up short and abrupt. You are in court, this audience, as extensions of the jury, who are in effect extensions of the judge. You are not here to indulge in murky existential probings, but to consider the letter of the law and in your hearts to approach a verdict.

Finally, act three. Many scenes and changes; the great world, a time between events (action/trial), the agora, a courtroom, the many places where people discuss, argue, make up their minds and unmake them again, slowly or with speed come to a conclusion, the knotting of the action.

In court, the argument of the Great If is relentlessly pursued. The crime of the eight is segregated from the world; the faces of the defendants, mirrors of conscience, are hooded. The inert symbols, hammers, empty bloodied bottles, lie there, tagged, soulless, mere items of evidence. They are relics of moral defeat, emblems of legal punishment; as such, the prosecutor will refer to them with disdain and handle them with distaste. They will be compared, subtly or openly, to the tools of safecrackers, to bloodied knives and guns. What If such implements became the common tools of so-called conscience? What If all citizens, under whatever itch of notoriety, took up such tools (like the soiled hands of Antigone, heaping foul dust on her brother's body) against the law of the state? How sordid a venture!

In the course of this act, the classic Greek formula is verified; the purging of pity and fear.

These must be purged, for pity and terror get in the way of spiritual change. They are obstructive emotions; to be taken seriously, no doubt, but strictly as preliminary to the main event.

That event, in a large sense, is destined to occur neither on stage nor in the court. It is rather the unending passionate pursuit of moral good, the righting of injustice, the ousting of death, the reordering of an ethical universe and of its social and political forms.

But in order to be purged, pity and fear have first to be aroused.

How acute the Greeks were! In the first days following our action, friends invariably spoke of their forebodings, their dread of the harsh sentences that undoubtedly would befall us, their fear that our action would be ignored or misconstrued.

Pity and fear. The pity narrows emotional largesse, the fear spreads out inordinately, claims all minds. Fear of the future, fear for children bereft of parents, fear of the state and its legal savageries. . . .

One emotion is too narrow, the other too diffused. Neither finally is useful; that is to say, neither serves to heighten the truth of the universal predicament (which is not defined by prison sentences, but by nuclear annihilation) — or to grant hints and leads as to a way out.

I must inject here a message from the jails of Pennsylvania. If the eight have insisted on anything, it is that their trial and imprisonment are not the issue at stake. Pity for them gains nothing. Neither does fear for them or for their children and spouses. The eight go their way, a way meticulously chosen and after much prayer. But the issues they raise will continue to shadow their lives and vex their hearts. It is the corporate crimes of General Electric, the race toward oblivion that this monstrous entity both fuels and illustrates.

Finally, what drove us to "such extremes"?

To reach the truth, one must turn from Creon to Antigone; from the prosecutor, in our case, to the gospel.

In America, in 1980, it could hardly be called useful to the common weal or a mitigation of the common woe that a group of religious folk enter a megadeath factory — in vain proof that they are in possession of some kind of magical counterforce.

Why then?

Let us say merely because they hungered for the truth, for its embodiment, longed to offer a response to its claim on us. That even through us, an all but submerged voice might be heard, the voice of "God not of the dead, but of the living."

From our statement: "In confronting GE, we choose to obey God's law of life, rather than a corporate summons to death. Our beating of swords into plowshares is a way to enflesh this biblical call. In our action, we draw on a deep-rooted faith in Christ, who changed the course of history through his willingness to suffer rather than to kill. We are filled with hope for our world and for our children as we join this act of resistance."

ON BLINDNESS AND HEALING
Philip Berrigan

If justice comes by means of the law, Christ died in vain.
Galations 2:21 (*NEB*)

Several years ago, a few of us were discussing, with some wonderment and pain, the slow public awakening to the mounting peril of nuclear war. Even then, politicians were insanely truculent, weapons threatening from their lairs overkill on overkill, provocations constant from the superpowers, especially from the United States. Then my brother Dan brought the conversation up short with, "Well, you know, the bomb covers its tracks."

Yes, I've thought many times since, the bomb does indeed cover its tracks. As early as Hanford and Los Alamos, when scientists were laboring to make it "work," the bomb was setting up a deadly mutuality between itself and the human spirit, as though to say, "Look here! There's me and there's you. Let's make it finally unanimous!"

Consequently, what was horrifyingly obvious to a few — the high crime in building atomic bombs, deploying them, and going to the brink with them repeatedly — was not generally obvious. The bomb had covered its tracks — it had seduced us into complicity. It had no life apart from the human spirit, where it held its "high ground." Finding a welcome, it enervated, stunted, sometimes crippled the spiritual sight called understanding and the spiritual resolve called fortitude.

Very much to the point is the Gospel story of Christ curing the man born blind. That stalwart man knew and accepted certain undeniable facts: He had in fact been born blind from birth and he was now in fact healed and had received sight from Jesus, despite the prior fact that "it is unheard of that anyone ever gave sight to a person blind from birth." (Jn. 9:32 *NAB*) In contrast, the rulers of the day reacted to the cure of blindness with a blindness of their own: They resisted the man's cure because to do otherwise would be to accept the cure — cure for their lust for privilege and power, cure for their fear of losing control. They saw but one thing clearly, and it was this: Accepting the cure of the man born blind was tantamount to accepting Jesus. And accepting him meant an end to their hypocrisy, cruelty, and the patronage by the Romans.

There is a splendid pedagogy on blindness in Luke 11, a teaching on three levels moving from the mundane to the physical to the spiritual. If practical people don't hide lamps in their cellars or under bushels baskets, if they treasure eyesight to remain functional, so much more should they nourish their sight by God's truth and by truthful lives. "Take care, then, that your light is not darkness." (Luke 11:35 *NAB*) What an anomaly to encounter those who prudently light up their houses, prudently care for their eyesight, yet remain conscious of the most grievous blindness of all — the darkness of a pinched and hateful spirit?

To be sure, the bomb "covers its tracks." It embodies technological genius along with immeasurable threat and destructiveness. These combine to bludgeon and numb the spirit — why think about the unthinkable, why imagine the unimaginable, why ponder "the day after"? For our part, we cover its tracks by spoon-feeding and petting our idols. In Luke 14 Jesus expounds on three idols — family, possessions, and self, all mutually reinforcing, all obstacles to the cross which is "salvation and life." These three have innumerable progeny. Family has bloodline, ethnicity, class or caste, race (color), religious ideology, nation-state, and empire. Possessions have titles, deeds, stocks, bonds, bank accounts, wills, insurance, a wife or husband, children, and country. Self has ambition, narcissism, careerism, megalomania, prejudice, cruelty, and indifference, to mention but a few.

Idols suppress the truth; their life and livelihood is illusion, indulgence, division, violence — various faces of the lie. The bomb, being a gross, ominous, technological lie ("Peacekeeper," to use Reagan's term?) employs satellite lies to cover its tracks. These lies, our spiritual garbage, work in resonance to the Big Lie of the Bomb, creating a mutuality, a *cor ad cor*, a receptive solidarity. The bomb covers its tracks, but our idols/lies also reciprocate and brush them out. And tragic numbers remain accomplices and victims, remain in the strict sense, "bombed out."

The bomb has as well one last powerful ally, one usually unmentioned. It has the law.

(I write this in 1994 as the Clinton Administration takes tentative steps into domestic and foreign policy arenas. Inevitably, one looks for barometers characteristic of the new Presidency, and as well, justifying the hopes of millions in the U.S. and around the world. The first barometer confirms a long standing phenomenon of corporate capitalism — socialism for the rich — "millionaires were 62% of Reagan's Cabinet, 71% of Bush's and so far, 55% of Clinton's [*U.S. News and World Report*]. The second complements the first — a fiscal war chest that, with financing, hovers near $500 billion. Both betray a neo-fascist worship of the status quo; both rob the poor and condemn them to misery and desperation; both entrench war as structure and diplomacy; both prostitute law as issuing from a nuclear or interventionary gun.)

One must not think, as most legal scholars do, that the law has fallen victim to superpower belligerence or that the law has merely fallen into disrepute. The Bible offers a radically different view, exposing human law as pretender to divine law and therefore as counter to the law of love, justice and peace.

The old civil rights ballad used to ask, "Which side are you on, girl/boy? Which side are you on?" For our purposes, the question could go, "Whose law do you keep, girl/boy?"

The Word of God holds under judgment all social arrangements not in accord with the law of love and strict, definitive justice — the civil religious establishment, corporate or state capitalism, political parties and pacts, the military and the police, corporate media and education, cities, nation-states, empires (all the "civilized" foundations for competition, exploitation and war). It holds them under judgment as disobedient, unjust, and violent. Human law provides undergirding for this rebellion against God and human meaning; it is the code of the counter-Kingdom, of the old order, of a time and history terminated by Christ's incarnation. As such it enforces sanction for social (dis) order, for the bureaucratizing of sin, death, and injustice, offering an indispensable metaphysics and ethic, plus the illusion of equality through impartial treatment under the law.

The state itself, an absurd and pretentious imposter of divine sovereignty, cannot be thought of, cannot exist without law. Biblically and practically, the state and the law are one.

Paul, a Pharisee and legal scholar, converted from the "law" when he realized that officialdom, under legal fiction, has murdered the Lord of life. Paul said of the "justice" of the law: "It crucified the only person who knew no sin." (2 Co. 5:21 *NAB*) Furthermore, Paul understood that his early persecutions of Christians, all legal, continued the harassment and killing of Christ. ("Saul, Saul, why do you persecute me?" [Ac. 9:4 *NAB*]) These terrible truths led Paul to other conclusions about the law: "You have broken with Christ if you look for justice in the law; you have fallen from grace." (Ga. 5:4 *NAB*) "It is through the law that sin became sinful to the fullest extent." (Rm. 7: 13 *NAB*)

No crime can compare with official or legal crime, not even the most perverted, grisly, psychopathic assaults upon human life. No private crime can compare with the state's patronage of profitmongering and the destruction ensuing from that, or its identification with the rich and ostracism of the poor, or its military adventures with their inevitable perversion of spirit, waste, and slaughter, or its assumption of godlike qualities in the execution of alleged or real malefactors. All legal! "It is through the law that sin became sinful to its fullest extent."

No crime can compare with official, legal crime — political, corporate, systemic and now legal in threat and destructiveness. How can our government claim to have won the Cold War when its nuclear strike force and that of the CIS (Commonwealth of Independent States) maintain mutual first-strike targeting? Under their cloak of nuclear terrorism, dictators lust for the BOMB, fissionable material shifts hands on the international market, the nuclear club expands, and a nuclear Calvary beckons, one as legal as the first.

Some say, with a kind of desperate hope, that God has yet to be heard from. The statement itself is vague and slightly presumptuous. God has been heard from — in the person of Christ, and in the resisters of Greenham Common in England, of Mutlangen in West Germany, of Offutt Air Force Base, Electric Boat Company and the Pentagon.

God continues to be heard from as well in the resistance of various Plowshares witnesses. Participants in these actions have been imprisoned and those still awaiting sentencing face virtually certain conviction and jail. In every case, their obedient and lawful acts have encountered a welcome of sorts at the corporate and military hellholes — security scarce, deadly force restrained, ample time to begin conversion of the lethal hardware from its perverted and slavish state. In every case, it was as though creation "groaning in travail, awaited the salvation [justice] of God's children." (Rm. 8:22-23 *NAB*)

In every case, their testimony, whether stated at the nuclear Dachaus or in court, was a simple prayer that all might see the "tracks" and the bomb lurching on ahead. Theirs is the prayer of Bartimaeus, the blind man: "He threw aside his cloak, and jumped up and came to Jesus. Jesus asked him 'What do you want me to do for you?' 'Rabboni,' the blind man said, 'I want to see!'" (Mk. 10:50-51) *NAB*)

CIVIL DISOBEDIENCE AS PRAYER

James Douglass

One way of seeing jail today is to regard it as the new monastery. In a society preparing for nuclear war and ignoring its poor, jail is an appropriate setting in which to give one's life to prayer. In a nation that has legalized preparations for the destruction of all life on earth, going to jail for peace — through nonviolent civil disobedience — can be seen as a prayer. In reflecting today on the Lord's Prayer, I think that going to jail as a way of saying "thy kingdom come, thy will be done" may be the most basic prayer we can offer in the "nuclear security state." Because we have accepted the greatest evil conceivable as a substitute for divine security, we have become a nation of blasphemers. The nuclear security state is blasphemous by definition. As members of such a nation, we need to pray for the freedom to do God's will by noncooperating with the ultimate evil it is preparing. Civil disobedience done in a loving spirit is itself that kind of prayer.

On the other hand, civil disobedience can be done in a way that, while it is apparently not cooperating with nuclear war, still ends up cooperating with an illusion that underlies nuclear war. In any attitude of resistance to the state there is a kind of demonic underside, a power turned upside down that wishes to gain the upper hand. Civil disobedience that is not done as prayer is especially vulnerable to its underside.

A simple truth at the root of nonviolence is that we can't change an evil or an injustice from the outside. Thomas Merton states this truth at the conclusion of one of his last books, *Mystics and Zen Masters*, as a critique of "nonviolence" as it is understood by its proponents in the Western world. Merton questions "the Western acceptance of a 'will to transform others' in terms of one's own prophetic insight accepted as a norm of pure justice." He asks:

Is there not an "optical illusion" in an eschatological spirit which, however much it may appeal to agape, seeks only to transform persons and social structures *from the outside*? Here we arrive at a basic principle, one might almost say an ontology of nonviolence, which requires further investigation.[1]

Nonviolent noncooperation with the greatest evil in history is still, according to Merton's insight, a possible way into illusion, a more subtle form of the same illusion that we encounter behind the nuclear buildup. Even in nonviolent resistance, unless we accept deeply the spirit of nonviolence, we can end up waging our own form of war and contributing to the conclusion we seek to overcome. Because the evil we resist is so great, we are inclined to overlook an illusion inherent in our own position, the will to transform others from the outside.

If one understands civil disobedience as an assertion of individual conscience over against the evil or injustice of the state, the temptation to seek an "outside solution" is already present. Conscience against the state sounds like a spiritually based or "inside solution." We are, after all, stating our willingness in conscience to go to jail at the hands of the state that threatens an unparalleled evil. But our conscience set off against the nuclear state takes an external view of people acting on behalf of the state. And ultimately such a view externalizes our own conscience.

In the acts of civil disobedience I have done, I have never met "the state." As far as my own ambition goes, that has been disappointing. I have met only people such as police, judges, and jail guards who cooperate (and sometimes noncooperate) with the evil of nuclear war in complex and often puzzling ways. I have never met a person who embodies the state or nuclear war. In their nuances of character, police, judges, and guards come from the same stew of humanity as do people who perform acts of civil disobedience.

A spiritually based nonviolence, one that truly seeks change from within, has to engage deeply the spirits of both sides of a conflict. Civil disobedience as an act of conscience against the state tends to focus exclusively on our own conscience as a source of change. Yet in the act of civil disobedience we meet particular people like ourselves, not "the state," and the most enduring thing we can achieve through such an act is, in the end, our relationship to the people we touch and who touch us. Our hope should not be for any strategic victories over such representatives of the state, but rather loving, nonviolent relationships with them in the midst of our arrests, trials, and prison sentences. The danger of seeing civil disobedience as an assertion of conscience over against the evil of the state is that it may get confused into an assertion against these particular people, so that we may never really see our relationship to them as primary. In making friends with our opponents — in the police, in the Pentagon, in the military — lies our greatest hope of overcoming nuclear war.

A more fundamental question suggested by Merton is: who is this "I," this self, that is doing the act of conscience in civil disobedience? If civil disobedience accentuates or heightens this sense of self — if it gives it a sense of power — is that necessarily a good thing? Civil disobedience is often referred to today as a way of empowering its participants. For socially powerless people nonviolent civil disobedience can be a profoundly liberating way out of bondage, as one part of a larger revolution. But empowerment can also be used to cover a heightened sense of an individual self that may be a step into further bondage.

We who see ourselves as peacemakers — and don't we all? — would be deeply shocked if we could see the extent to which we act personally for war, not only in our more obvious faults, but even in our very peacemaking. Our intentions and actions for peace lead to war if they are based on a false self and its illusions. If the purpose of civil disobedience is to "empower" such a self, it is a personal act of war.

The nuclear arms race summarizes the history of a false, violent self — of many such false selves magnified in national egos — in an inconceivable evil. What the nuclear crisis says to us, as nothing else in history could, is that the empowering of a false self creates a crisis that has no solution, only transformation. We can't solve an arms race based on enormous national illusions, illusions that both exploit and protect an emptiness at the center of millions of lives. Those illusions can only be cracked open to the truth and fear and emptiness at the core of each national pride, then revealed as truly reconcilable with their apparent opposites in the consciousness of another people.

Civil disobedience for the sake of empowering a false self serves as the warring nation-state on a smaller scale. Civil disobedience as that kind of empowerment is an attempt to solve one's problems and frustrations by externalizing them in a theater in which innocence confronts the evil of the nuclear state. But we are not innocent.

The greatest treason, as T.S. Eliot points out in *Murder in the Cathedral*, is to do the right deed for the wrong reason. Civil disobedience in response to the greatest evil in history, done to empower a self that can't face its own emptiness, is the right deed for the wrong reason. Because of its motivation, it may also twist itself into the wrong deed. An ego-empowering act of civil disobedience will in the end empower both the self and the nuclear state, which while tactically at odds are spiritually in agreement. Such resistance, like the state itself, asserts power to cover a void. Civil disobedience, like war, can be used to mask the emptiness of a false self.

Civil disobedience as prayer is not an assertion of individual conscience over against the evil of the state. Protesting against something for which we ourselves are profoundly responsible is a futile exercise in hypocrisy. The evil of nuclear war is not external to us, so that it can be isolated in the state or in the Nuclear Train loaded with hydrogen bombs.[2] The nature of the evil lies in our cooperation with it. What Merton is suggesting is that as we cease cooperating in one way with that evil, our well-hidden tendency is to begin cooperating with it more intensely and more blindly in another way, defining the evil in a way external to us that only deepens and hardens its actual presence in ourselves.

The power of the evil of nuclear war is nothing more than the power of our cooperation with it. There is no evil exclusively out there, over against us. The evil is much more subtle than that. This is why it continues to exist. When we cease cooperating with evil at its source in ourselves, it ceases to exist. When we accept responsibility for nuclear war in the hidden dimensions of our own complicity, we will experience the miracle of seeing the arms race end. To paraphrase Harry Truman, the bomb stops here.

Civil disobedience as prayer is not an assertion of self over against an illusion but an acceptance of God's loving will because of our responsibility for evil: "Not my will but thine be done." The prayer of the Gospels, like the prayer of Gandhi, is at its heart an acceptance of what we don't want: the acceptance of our suffering out of love.

Jesus and Gandhi are precise about what is meant by God's will in a world of suffering. Gandhi in summing up Jesus' life said, "Living Christ is a living cross; without it life is a living death."

To be nonviolent means to accept our suffering out of love. The evil that causes suffering is an evil whose source is more deeply interior to ourselves than we have begun to understand. The prayer of civil disobedience that says, "Not my will but thine be done" — by sending us to death or to that sign of death that is jail — is a recognition that in truth we belong there, and that we will in any event ultimately find ourselves there.

Civil disobedience as prayer is not an act of defiance but an act of obedience to a deeper, interior will within us and within the world that is capable of transforming the world. "Thy kingdom come, thy will be done." To live out the kingdom of God through such an action is to live in a loving relationship to our brothers and sisters in the police force, in courts, and in jails, recognizing God's presence in each of us. It is also to accept responsibility for an evil that is ours: as we are, so is the nuclear state.

The two most violent places I've ever been in my life have been the Strategic Weapons Facility Pacific (SWFPAC), where nuclear weapons are stored at the heart of the Trident base, and the Los Angeles County Jail, where people are stored. I went to SWFPAC to pray for peace and forgiveness in front of enormous concrete bunkers, the tombs of humankind, a prayer that took me in turn to the L.A. County Jail (on the way to a more permanent prison) where 10,000 people are kept in tombs. The deepest experiences of peace that I have had have been in these same terrible places.

I believe that a suffering God continually calls us to be in such places for the sake of peace and justice. I believe that the Beloved Community is realized there. Civil disobedience as prayer is a way into that Beloved Community.

NOTES

1. Thomas Merton, *Mystics and Zen Masters* (New York: Dell, 1967), p. 287-288.

2. The nuclear train carried hydrogen bombs from the Pantex Plant in Amarillo, Texas to the Trident submarine base in Bangor, Washington, and to the Charleston Naval Weapons Station in Charleston, South Carolina until 1986 when it was discontinued by the Department of Energy. In the course of the train's final journey to Bangor, 146 people were arrested.

Obedience in the Beloved Community

Shelley Douglass

The trees outside my window are covered and weighed down with snow. The evergreens bear huge loads of it, the white contrasting with their dark green; the leafless alders are outlined in white, their branches making a delicate pattern against the darker green. I've been out in the cold to feed the rabbit and the wild birds and to make sure that the rabbit has unfrozen water to drink. The dogs, Loki and Sam, have been playing in the snow all morning, cavorting and raising great showers of the white stuff. Today is December 30, 1984 — almost a new year. This was the year of my 40th birthday, the year that our oldest child started college, the year that our youngest became a teenager. This has been a year of reckoning, of trying to understand where I've been and how my life is being drawn into the future.

Next year will be 1985. Twenty years ago, in 1965, I took the first steps on a path that led here, to this room surrounded by snow-covered trees, this room at the world's end. Those first steps were steps on a march, the march from Selma to Montgomery, Alabama. At the time it seemed that such a march must bring a dismantling of the structures of racism. I felt that the change must indeed have already come, a feeling that grew out of the experience of that day's walk and out of my own shallow understanding of the problem.

The experience of the walk was true. My understanding of the problem was not. Together they led me to a feeling that has remained with me: that the problems we face are urgent, must be solved yesterday and that they have already been solved, if we could only see it. The day we marched in Montgomery became for me one-half of a paradigm of nonviolence.

My experience of Montgomery began with a 48 hour bus ride from Madison, Wisconsin, down to Alabama. There were thirty-odd students on the bus, which was chartered by the University of Wisconsin Newman Club. We were going to Montgomery because a call had been given asking people who believed in the human family to come and march for equal voting rights. The call had followed days and weeks of violent repression of blacks who were trying to register to vote. Martin Luther King, Jr., had invited us to come and show our support; we felt it was the least that we could do.

As we journeyed through the South we became more and more frightened. Transistor radios brought us news reports of the violence ahead of us: police dogs and horses, fire hoses and billy clubs, and vigilante violence by the Klan and the White Citizens' Councils. Our marathon bus ride ended in the parking lot of a black Catholic church; its windows were blacked out as though in war. We found that the church had been threatened with retaliation if it hosted marchers. The black-out curtains were a prudent gesture to confuse any watchers. Curled up on the floor in our sleeping bags, we dozed uneasily through what was left of the night.

The next day, a sunny bright one, we joined a never-ending stream of people marching through downtown Montgomery. It seemed that the whole world was there — all shades and colors and shapes and sizes of people, representatives of all religious beliefs. We knew no one in that crowd, but we observed the care that was taken of each of us. If we were hungry, a stale doughnut would appear from somewhere. If we were too hot, there was someone nearby who would be grateful for the loan of a sweater. People held hands and helped each other over curbs and up hills. When we arrived at the Alabama state capitol and gathered under the Confederate flag flying there, we knew that we were the reality and that that flag and what it stood for were passing. Martin Luther King, Jr. spoke often of the beloved community. The day we marched in Montgomery brought me a taste of that community, a community at risk, a community of courage and caring, a sharing community.

Three years later the death of Martin Luther King, Jr. finished the picture for me. It was spring, near Easter. The United States had involved itself in Vietnam; now our marches were housing marches in Milwaukee, peace marches in Washington and New York. We had begun to see that racism and war had corporate roots, and students at the university were protesting recruitment on campus by corporations and organizations that profited from the war: Dow Chemical, maker of napalm, Honeywell, Rockwell, the CIA . . . an endless list. The violence on our campus had escalated. It wasn't unusual to get a whiff of tear gas between classes. Talk among student groups had turned to the question of violence versus nonviolence. We had tried nonviolence and it hadn't worked; many people in despair and anger were considering terrorism as a tactic.

A gunshot shattered what little peace existed that spring: Martin Luther King, Jr., was dead, shot outside a Memphis motel. His assassination came just as he was publicly linking racism and the Vietnam War. It seemed no accident. King's death swept us into depths of depression. He was our leader; we had never met him but we honored him; we loved what he symbolized: the beloved community.

It seemed to me at least that the community had died on that Memphis balcony.

On the day of King's funeral I sat in our kitchen peeling onions and listening to the radio broadcast of the services. Paul, who was two, and Mark, who was one, were playing around my feet as I worked and cried. Mark, our adopted interracial child, seemed especially at risk that day: What future was his now? The mourners at the funeral sang "We Shall Overcome" but I couldn't sing along with them; instead I looked around for the boys, who had suddenly become unnaturally silent. It was then that I saw the beloved community. The two boys, one dark-skinned with brown eyes and curly hair, one white-skinned with blue eyes and straight hair, stood together in the kitchen holding hands and singing along. They sang "We Shall Overcome" because that's what you do — you hold hands and sing along. It was then that I knew the other side of the beloved community: the suffering, grieving community that is united in its love and joyful because out of its suffering comes its triumph. Thank you, Martin Luther King, Jr.

Seventeen years after King's death I sit here in my corner of our room and look around me at the signs of the beloved community: seashells from the people of Belau, carved "peace chickens" from Salt Lake City, wall hangings from Central America, calligraphy from Japan, photographs of people from all over the world, part of our community. But I wonder: Paul, who was born in Madison, began college himself this year. We were concerned about the arms race, the Vietnam War, the draft, racism. He is concerned about the arms race, the Central American war, the draft, racism. For 20 years I've been following this path that began in Montgomery, and what has really changed?

I believe that a lot of things have changed, but I can be sure of one thing: I have changed. Twenty years ago I marched to change other people, and when I committed civil disobedience, it was to modify the injustices in an otherwise just system. Many of us went out to march or to act to correct others' mistakes, and then we returned to our own lives preparing for our futures as part of this society. What I have come gradually to understand since then is that such activity will not produce change. I do not believe that we have failed — we shortened the war in Vietnam, we did achieve some change for black people, we have raised awareness of oppression in many countries and of the part we play in it. We have, I believe, been largely responsible for the prevention of nuclear war so far.

But we are only beginning to look at the roots of the problem and to see how deep and embedded they are.

There is a counterpart to King's beloved community, a dark side. We could call it the uncaring community or perhaps the community of hatred. The bonds of this community are bonds of greed and oppression, and they hold the world together in an embrace of suffering and despair. The difference between the two communities lies in our acceptance or rejection of the ties that bind us, our love for or apathy toward one another. Through the civil rights movement and the Vietnam War I began to understand that the whole system was at fault; through the women's movement and the nuclear disarmament movement I have come to see that the deepest roots of the evil are in me.

It was very easy to leave my life for a while to go and change somebody else; it was a bit harder to change my lifestyle and begin to confront my own complicity in an exploitative system. It is harder still to change my attitudes: my laziness, my willingness to do the easy thing, my reluctance to be open to others, my reliance on the comfortable rut. What I've come to realize is that unless I can make that inner change — and unless we all can — the outer change I achieve will be only an adjustment in the same machine of uncaring.

Somehow I have to learn to live the beloved community that exists, and as I do that it will become more visible.

What I've come to believe is that there is no separation between actions and the rest of life. All of my life must be an action, an opening for that community to take form. If I can live with the vision of that community, some of my actions will be disobedient to the civil laws of any country I may live in. If I see the beloved community, for example, I will probably refuse to pay income tax because my money would be used to harm my brothers and sisters; if I see a train full of hydrogen bombs going by, the beloved community calls to me to stop it. Being obedient to the vision of the community of love will necessarily involve disobedience to laws that embody our division.

There is a further dimension. If I truly see the beloved community, then even those whose actions I oppose are a part of that community, and my resistance to their violation of community must simultaneously remind them that they are also part of us and invite them into the community. Only with all of us present will we be a full community, and only with all of us present can we find solutions to the injustices that beset us. The great temptation is to set up another boundary, a boundary around those of us who have a commitment to peace and justice, and to deny our community with those who run nuclear trains or serve on Trident submarines. If we succumb to that temptation then I believe we are creating the same shadow community that we attempt to resist. We have to address the denial of community in our own hearts, wherever we find it. In addressing this denial of community by our community we will find ourselves doing civil disobedience again: To be obedient to the vision of community we must be disobedient to our movement's tendency to judge and draw easy lines. We will be doubly disobedient: first, to state laws that protect instruments of death and, second, to mores and assumptions within ourselves that disunite us from those whom we resist.

Twenty years after Martin Luther King's life began to teach me about nonviolence, I return in a deeper way to his truth and vision.

I understand that we can exclude no one, not Sheriff Pritchard, not Ronald Reagan, no one can be left out of our vision of community.

I understand that we must invite ourselves and our adversaries into the loving and suffering community, and that to the extent we accept our own invitation, we will become disobedient to laws and roles that sunder us. Our disobedience will grow out of a deeper obedience, and we will become one.

RESISTANCE, JAIL, PARISH MINISTRY

Editors' Note: *Fr. Frank Cordaro, from Des Moines, Iowa, was ordained a Catholic priest in 1985. Since 1977 he has been actively involved in peace and justice work and in the Catholic Worker movement. He helped initiate a nonviolent resistance campaign at Offutt Air Force Base (near Omaha, NE), headquarters of the U.S. Strategic Command (StratCom), which controls the targeting and launching of nuclear warheads. He has been arrested 11 times at Offutt and has served 26 months in federal prisons and jails for these actions. Many others have also been arrested and have served prison sentences for "crossing the line" onto the base. This interview was conducted by Mike Palecek, shortly before Cordaro began serving his last prison sentence in December 1994. The following is an excerpt of an interview which appeared in the* National Catholic Reporter, *January 6, 1995.*

Do you like being a parish priest?

I like the work. It's a great role to play. The person who comes to help people celebrate their lives with the Lord. I love pastoring; it's a great art and craft. Most folks in the parishes, when it comes to priests, really don't care about their politics, they just want a person who cares about them and loves them, will stand with them, be with them when there are good times and bad and have a certain sense of prayer, a love for scripture and a willingness to share their faith.

Do you have a loyal opposition within the parish?

There are plenty of people who disagree with what I'm doing. If you would ask who would agree with Fr. Frank, there would be few, and there would be even fewer who would agree with the tactic of civil disobedience. However, what I've been trying to ask people to look at is that I'm a man who's trying to be honest with my understanding of Jesus and that I'm trying to be faithful to the Gospel. I ask them to accept me on those terms.

Do you know of anyone else in the United States doing this within the parish structure?

I don't know of many diocesan priests who are establishing this cycle of ministry resistance, jail, parish work. I'd like to run into some. I'd like to develop this format of priestly ministry. I think it works. It has for me.

What church documents support what you do?

Let's see: Matthew, Mark, Luke and John. And then more specifically and more current, the U.S. bishops' pastoral on peace, where they have a very important segment on nonviolence.

But do the bishops ever really lay down the sword?

No, they haven't. It's a critical flaw in Catholicism and larger Christianity. It's what I call the seventeen century heresy: the acceptance of state-sanctioned violence. It happened somewhere between Constantine the emperor and Augustine the theologian. The church simply bellied up to this key component of the need to be able to kill and run the affairs of Caesar and just kind of washed out Jesus' pacifism and nonviolence.

But I think we're in a recovery mode. Because it was only within the last 25 years that the Roman Catholic Church made an official acceptance of the positions for individual Catholics to be conscientious objectors to war.

I think it's time now, at the end of the 20th century, that the church fesses up, like it did to slavery. We done made a mistake. War is not in keeping with the spirit of the Gospel. We're simply not going to accept it anymore....

What do you say to those who might call you a grandstander or publicity seeker?

Usually folks who call me that are people who disagree with the issue. So it's easy to dismiss the messenger when they don't like the message. My best argument toward that is my consistency and faithfulness to what I say I believe in and just doing this through the years. There are a lot easier ways to get publicity and grandstand.

Were you tempted to stay on this side of the line when Clinton was elected?

Oh, no. Bill Clinton clearly showed he was capable of killing for the empire when, during the election, he went back to Arkansas to make sure he was there for an execution. I started doing my resistance when Jimmy Carter was elected so it makes no difference between the Democrats and Republicans in this regard.

Would parish ministry be too boring without this?

If I were just doing parish ministry, I think I would just shrivel up and die inside. But if all I did was resistance, I would be chaotic, hit and miss, with no grounding. I have uniquely developed a kind of ebb-and-flow cycle of my life, where doing priestly ministry helps me prepare to do speaking the truth and prophetic witness, and at the same time my prophetic witness helps authenticate my priesthood. I'm always in tension with two major institutions in my life, the church and the state, and at odds often with both. I must not be too far off the mark because that's exactly where Jesus put himself.

In 1990, when you were in jail in Sioux Falls, S.D., 18 priests visited you in the Minnehaha County Jail. Does that always happen, that outpouring of support?

What it meant was that the local bishop came and visited me. That opened the floodgates and was a mark of approval. Half of them I knew. The other half were diocesan priests to whom the bishop said, "If you have time, go visit Father Frank." When you have that kind of institutional support and affirmation, things happen.

You are very confident and self-assured. Does anything cause you angst?

I'm no great martyr or saint. I'm still a white male in the middle of the United States of America. Wherever I am, I'm still very privileged. When we act and witness we get thrown in jail; we clearly survive it, and often survive it well. That is not the case in other places of the world. I'm painfully aware that if I were in most other countries, especially developing countries, I'd be a dead man.

Are you ever lonely in the church or in Council Bluffs or in the peace movement?

Yeah. Often. But I've made great efforts to keep my sense of community beyond my parish and beyond my diocese and beyond my state. I make real efforts to keep connected with the subculture of resistance people whom I've come to know as friends now. The Jonah House folks, Atlantic Life

Community, folks in California, the Catholic Worker house people, people in between. So you have a certain kind of subculture that's really a family. It's very important to me.

What's the usual reaction of prison inmates when they find out about your crime and your profession?

You know, they are surprised. They just can't believe the federal government is sending anybody for six months for doing what I'm doing. They think it's so minor. I think there's a certain positive effect on inmates. The whole scene is degrading. It helps them to see that the government jails even priests who don't do anything but cross lines and try to speak for peace. It helps them see they're not the only problem in the prison system. The prison system itself, the government itself, is the greatest violator of human rights. They're the criminals.

You speak about establishing a Resistance Church in America.

Yes. Definitely. The point of the resistance church is to try to develop a consciousness of a militant Franciscan movement within the church, to help alter its attitudes and its spiritual center. And that's always done with a very alive and passionate minority. I've often quoted to Catholics that all we need is about one-percent of the Roman Catholics in this country to embrace the resistance-church model.[1] What could half-a-million nonviolent activist Christians living below the poverty line, identifying with the poor, living in intentional communities and in-and-out of jails and prisons, do for our churches and nation? I am certain that if this were to happen, we could help change the spirit and heart of the Christian churches of this nation, if not the course of history.[2]

NOTES

1. This Resistance Church, a church within the larger church, has four distinctive marks: 1) downward mobility, 2) direct identification with the poor and oppressed, 3) direct nonviolent resistance to existing unjust social, economic and political structures, and 4) small faith-based, intentional communities, committed to a radical biblical social justice agenda.
2. Article by Fr. Frank Cordaro, "A Call for a Resistance Church."

PACIFISM UNREVISED
NONVIOLENT LOVE BATTLES ANGUISH IN A RESHAPED WORLD

Editors' Note: *The following article was co-written and distributed by the following nine religious peace activists: Daniel Berrigan, Philip Berrigan, Shelley Douglass, Jim Douglass, Elizabeth McAlister, Fr. Emmanuel Charles McCarthy, Fr. Richard McSorley, Suzanne Belote Shanley and Brayton Shanley.*

Peter Steinfel's recent article in the *New York Times* entitled "Reshaping Pacifism to Fight Anguish" (Dec. 12, 1992), as well as others appearing in diocesan weeklies, religious and peace periodicals, have quoted some pacifists as finding "restrained police action" acceptable in Somalia. Non-pacifists and religious groups have espoused selective homicide for humanitarian reasons. As Christian Pacifists, we submit that such distortion of the pacifist position on war, primarily from a theological perspective, fails to mention gospel-based nonviolence rooted in the life of Jesus. Using some excerpts from the Steinfel's article, which have been repeated elsewhere, we hope to clarify the Christian Pacifist position.

The centrality of Christ's teaching, love of enemies, underpins the universal recognition of Jesus as nonviolent. If one chooses to justify the use of homicide, one is self-evidently no longer a pacifist. From Jesus, the Incarnation of the Divine, through apostolic Christianity to St. Francis of Assisi to contemporary expressions of nonviolence found in the Civil Rights and Catholic Worker movements, nonviolent communities throughout the country continue in this tradition.

Killing is clearly prohibited by Jesus. The humanitarian "end" of halting the nightmare of starvation induced by the United States' arming of Somalian strong-man Barre does not in nonviolent theory or practice ever justify the "means" of taking even one life to remedy the devastation and human misery induced by murder and armaments in the first instance.

So-called "pacifist reshaping" of prohibition against intervention and use of police force to "fight anguish in a reshaped world" is a semantically seductive but outrageous misrepresentation of pacifist practice which for centuries has included nonviolence as the Christian theology of Redemption. Such falsification cries out for clarification and refutation.

No temporal "re-examination of the morality of military intervention" by intellectuals, theologians or ethicists — no "reinterpretations of concepts of national sovereignty and nonintervention," will ever undermine the conviction of those who believe as an article of faith that war is evil. Nor can such revision ever "un-Jesus Jesus" to fit the changing world order. Eternal truths are not bought and sold like the armaments which blaspheme them. No humanitarian posturing with "Restore Hope" gestures from the barrel of a gun, like the ones we sold to Somalia, will ever mitigate the lie that ends justify means.

Such distortion of principal, morality, language and intent will never alter the clarity of Jesus' life in conformity to the will of God as the way to resisting systemic evil — the oppressive power structure which sacrificed Him on the altar of expediency.

The gospels teach us that one's entire life is reshaped, not by a changing world order, but by following the example of Christ. It is in this spirit of rededication to a deep interior conversion, translated into a nonviolent lifestyle which refuses to cooperate with evil wherever it occurs, that those who wish to be disciples of Jesus must embrace with all of its transforming power.

We join with the cloud of nonviolent witnesses throughout the centuries who have been committed to the Suffering Servant, Messiah Jesus, and His method of redeeming humanity from the immense mystery of evil by means of nonviolent love of friend and enemy. Christian Pacifism, nonviolent love, was shaped in the Incarnation of Jesus and cannot be reshaped by any temporal world order.

Easter 1984: Banner draped across a Patriot missile launcher during the Pershing Plowshares action at Martin Marietta plant in Orlando, Florida. Photo from Office of U.S. Attorney, Orlando, FL.

Plowshares-Disarmament Actions

An Introduction to Plowshares-Disarmament Actions

Art Laffin

In this article, I would like to give a brief background of plowshares actions, reflect on the underlying spirit and hope of these actions, address how the courts have responded, and briefly address some of the major criticisms about these actions. It is my intent here not to be exhaustive in covering all these issues in great detail, but to give the reader a general sense of what plowshares actions are about.

On September 9, 1980 the "Plowshares Eight" carried out the first plowshares action. They entered a General Electric plant in King of Prussia, Pennsylvania, where the nose cones for the Mark 12A nuclear warheads were manufactured. With hammers and blood they enacted the Biblical prophecies of Isaiah (2:4) and Micah (4:3) to "beat swords into plowshares" by hammering on two of the nose cones and pouring blood on documents. Thus the name "plowshares" has been used to identify this kind of action. They were subsequently arrested, tried by a jury, convicted and sentenced to prison terms ranging from 1 1/2 to 10 years. After a series of appeals that lasted 10 years they were resentenced to time served — from several days to 17 1/2 months.

Since the Plowshares Eight action, others, acting individually and in community, have entered military bases and weapons facilities and have symbolically (and in certain instances actually) disarmed components of U.S. first-strike nuclear weapons systems: the MX, Pershing II, Cruise, Minuteman ICBM's, Trident II missiles, Trident submarines, B-52 Bombers, P-3 Orion anti-submarine aircraft, the NAVSTAR system, the ELF communication system and nuclear-capable battleships. Combat aircraft used for military intervention, such as helicopters, the F-111 fighter bomber, the F-15E fighter, the Hawk aircraft, as well as other conventional weapons, including anti-aircraft missiles launchers, bazookas, grenade throwers and AK-5 automatic rifles, have been disarmed. Model weapons have been disarmed at an "Arms Bazaar." People who have been involved in plowshares actions have undertaken a process of intense spiritual preparation, nonviolence training and community formation, and have given careful consideration to the risks involved in such an action. Plowshares activists, accepting full responsibility for their actions, remain at the site of their action so that they can publicly explain their witness.

Resonating closely with this spirit of nonviolent direct disarmament, other people, though not seeing their action arising out of the biblical prophesy of Isaiah and Micah, have been compelled to nonviolently disarm components of nuclear and conventional weapons. Although individuals who have carried out these actions have been inspired by the biblical vision embraced by plowshares participants, they view their action as being primarily motivated by a deeply-held conscience commitment to nonviolence or by other spiritual or moral convictions.

As of January 1996, over 130 individuals have participated in 54 plowshares and related disarmament actions. Also two groups, intending to disarm nuclear weapons components, were unable to do so because of high security. Some of these people have gone on to participate in other plowshares actions. Disarmament actions have occurred in the U.S., Australia, Germany, Holland, England and Sweden. The backgrounds of plowshares activists vary widely. Parents, grandparents, veterans, former lawyers, teachers, artists, musicians, priests, sisters, house-painters, carpenters, writers, poets, health-care workers, students, advocates of the poor and homeless, and members of Catholic Worker communities have all participated in plowshares actions. Most of those who have participated in plowshares actions remain actively involved in the peace and justice movement.

In my view, the basic hope of the plowshares actions (and here I'm not attempting to speak for other disarmament actions) is to communicate from the moment of entry into a plant or base — and throughout the court process and prison witness — an underlying faith that the power of nonviolent love can overcome the forces of violence; a reverence for the sacredness of all life and creation; a plea for justice for the victims of poverty and the arms race; an acceptance of personal responsibility for the dismantling and the physical conversion of the weapons; and a spiritual conversion of the heart to the way of justice and reconciliation. Thus, plowshares participants believe that the physical dismantling of the weapon and the personal disarmament of the heart is a reciprocal process. As Phil Berrigan states: "We try to disarm ourselves by disarming the weapons."

The main symbols used in plowshares actions are hammers and blood. Hammers are used to literally begin the process of disarmament that thousands of talks and numerous treaties have failed to accomplish. The hammer is used to take apart as well as create and to point to the urgency for conversion of war production to products that enhance life. The blood symbolizes the mass killing that weapons of mass destruction can inflict, as well as the murderous cost they now impose on the poor. Blood speaks too of human unity and the willingness to give one's life rather than to take life.

Seeking to expose the violence, secrecy, and idolatry of the national security state, some plowshares defendants have tried to present a "justification" or "necessity" defense. During their defense they have tried to show, through personal and expert witness testimony, that their actions were morally and legally justified and that their intent was to protect life and prevent a crime. In most cases, the courts have shown their complicity in protecting the interests of the national security state and have disallowed this defense. Some plowshares groups have also presented a defense declaring that a state religion of "nuclearism" has been established which is unconstitutional, in violation of the First Amendment. Moreover, nuclearism is in violation of God's law which forbids the worship of "gods of metal." Plowshares defendants have moved for dismissal of all charges brought against them; for the law, as applied in these cases, is used to protect this unconstitutional state religion. Such motions have been consistently denied.

With the exception of the Aegis Plowshares and the first Australian Plowshares action, all plowshares activists have been prosecuted for their actions. While most plowshares-disarmament activists have pled not guilty and have gone to trial, several have opted to plead "no contest" or "guilty" to charges brought against them. All of the trials to date, mostly jury trials, have ended in convictions. However, members of the Epiphany Plowshares were tried an unprecedented five times with three trials ending in hung juries and mistrials. Also, Chris Cole's first trial for a plowshares action in England ended in a hung-jury.

During these trials, which have occurred in both state and federal courts, most of the defendants have represented themselves and have been assisted by legal advisers. The trial tactics by judges and government prosecutors have become increasingly repressive. A "Motion In Limine," which calls for the complete prohibition of any "affirmative" defenses, has been introduced in a number of plowshares trials. For example, prior to the third and fourth trials of the Epiphany Plowshares, the trial judge, complying with the U.S. Prosecutor's request, imposed a "gag" order forbidding any mention of such subjects as the Bible, God's law, international law, U.S. military intervention in Central America, nuclear weapons and the poor. For speaking about these subjects, two defendants were given contempt charges and 20-day jail sentences. And during their opening statement to the jury in North Carolina, members of the Pax Christi-Spirit of Life Plowshares were found in contempt of court for not complying with the judge's instruction to refrain from speaking about crimes of the national security state and their moral and legal intent.

Prison sentences have varied for each plowshares and disarmament action. These sentences have ranged from suspended sentences to 18 years. The average sentence for plowshares activists has been between one and two years.

Doing support work on behalf of plowshares activists has also been an integral part of the plowshares actions. Efforts by local support groups have been invaluable in supporting plowshares activists during trial and imprisonment and in helping to educate the public about the meaning of these actions. As people have been sentenced to long prison terms, support for prisoners and their families has been, and continues to be, crucial.

Throughout the 15-year history of the plowshares actions, questions and criticisms have been raised regarding different aspects of these actions. Some have voiced concerns that these actions are violent because property, in this case a weapon, has been damaged. Plowshares activists believe that nuclear weapons and all weapons of war are anti-God, anti-life, and therefore, are inherently evil and have no right to exist. Thus, it is the responsibility of people of faith and conscience to begin to nonviolently dismantle these weapons. In the Trident Nein plowshares action in which I participated, we hammered and poured blood on missile hatches and sonar equipment of the first-strike Trident submarine. With spray-paint we renamed the Trident

INTRODUCTION TO PLOWSHARES-DISARMAMENT ACTIONS

"USS Auschwitz," because of our belief that such a weapon has no more right to exist than the Nazi gas ovens. Would trying to take apart a gas oven be considered an act of violence or vandalism? I believe that it would not. Would it be consistent with nonviolence? I believe so. We believe that trying to dismantle a weapon of mass murder is not an act of violence even though the media and the courts characterize these acts as "vandalism" and various other crimes, rather than as an act of disarmament. The real crime, we believe, is not the hammering upon weapons, but the U.S. government's first-strike nuclear policy, its military interventionist policy, and its commitment to wage a war against the poor of the world to protect its economic interests.

People have also questioned whether these actions are truly nonviolent because of the secrecy that surrounds the action. Plowshare participants contend that no advance public notice is needed to disarm an illegal weapon that has no right to exist in the first place. (Did Jesus give advance notice when he cleansed the temple? Did abolitionists give advance notice about harboring slaves?) People have a moral and legal right to begin the disarmament process at any base or factory at any time. They possess this right because they honor and try to embody God's law, which authorities and personnel break consistently by their work. There is therefore, no moral or political duty to inform or dialogue with them about a witness beforehand. The witness is the dialogue.

Moreover, once the action occurs there is no attempt to conceal the truth of what happened. Plowshares people take full responsibility for their action by awaiting arrest, telling the story of their action in court and to the public, as well as speaking out from jail.

Also, in the past the government has charged peace activists and plowshares participants with conspiracy charges. Care is taken prior to each action to avoid exposing others to the risk of such charges. It seems to me that this approach, while different from other nonviolent actions, reflects the spirit of biblical nonviolence.

There have also been important concerns raised about the need for what disarmament activist Peter Lumsdaine calls a more "effective strategic resistance" approach to the weapons rather than the mostly symbolic approach of plowshares actions.[1] This approach, which centers on committing "maximum" damage to key weapon systems (i.e. NAVSTAR) in order to render them ineffective, has certainly provoked a meaningful dialogue — one which continues. While plowshares activists have different perspectives on this issue, most would undoubtedly agree with the following viewpoint articulated by Phil Berrigan:

> Plowshares began disarmament in 1980, doing what the government refused to do for 35 years. With equal concern, Plowshares appealed to the hearts, minds and spirits of the American people — 'You must share disarmament!' The twin goals of Plowshares — symbolic yet real disarmament and sharing disarmament — have a reciprocity. The weapons exist because our fear, violence and hatred built them. Plowshares must address both realities....
>
> The hammer is a modest tool and a potent symbol, which within the context of Isaiah's prophecy, insists upon a universal responsibility for justice and peace. But it also confines us within human limits — we are not superpeople, nor do we embody the fantasies of Hollywood or the Washington plutocrats. The imperative is to be human in an inhuman time, to act in season and out despite the prospect that the American empire might not break up in our lifetime, nor disarmament happen while we live.
>
> If that be the case, modesty of means will sustain us as another face of faith. And faith is not faith except for the long haul.[2]

Regarding this notion of faith, Liz McAlister asserts:

> There's not going to be any real disarmament until there's a disarming of hearts. And so one puts oneself on the line to symbolically, but really, disarm the weapons in a hope and a prayer that the action might be used by the Spirit of God to change minds and hearts. One puts oneself on the line — at risk and in jeopardy — to communicate the depth of commitment to that hope.[3]

Based on my experience, it is important to note that each of the plowshares participants I've met has carefully reflected on these and other important considerations prior to an action. While there does exist among plowshares participants a basic unanimity about the underlying spirit for plowshares actions, there is a diversity of opinion among plowshares participants about certain issues including defenses to use in court, the level of cooperation with court and probation authorities, and the payment of fines and restitution. Clearly, these and the other issues that I have addressed have generated important discussion among plowshares activists and the wider disarmament movement.

In the final analysis, people who do plowshares actions are *ordinary* people who, with all their weaknesses, are attempting to respond in faith to a biblical mandate which must be enacted in our violent world. These actions are not to be glamorized or taken lightly. People have taken great risks, experienced the loneliness and dehumanization of prison, and have had to cope with many difficult personal and family hardships. Building and sustaining an acting community takes extraordinary commitment and is certainly not problem-free. Yet, with all their limitations and imperfections, these actions are a powerful reminder that we *can* live in a world without weapons and war if people are willing to begin the process of disarmament by literally beating the swords (weapons) of our time into plowshares. While these actions are deemed criminal by the state, they should be considered, in light of the great evil we face, the norm. Although each plowshares action has many similarities to others, in the end each is unique, each is a learning process, each is an experiment in truth.

NOTES

1. For a more in depth explanation of the effective strategic resistance approach see article by Peter Lumsdaine in *The Nuclear Resister*, October 7, 1992.
2. Phil Berrigan, *The Nuclear Resister*, December 23, 1992.
3. Liz McAlister, *The Catholic Agitator*, November 1992.

A CHRONOLOGY OF PLOWSHARES-DISARMAMENT ACTIONS
SEPTEMBER 1980 - JANUARY 1996
Compiled by Art Laffin

This chronology briefly describes the 54 Plowshares (and two attempted Plowshares actions) and other related disarmament actions that have occurred through January 1996, and the trials and sentences each person received.

Plowshares Eight: September 9, 1980 Daniel Berrigan, Jesuit priest, author and poet from New York City; Philip Berrigan, father and co-founder of Jonah House in Baltimore, MD; Dean Hammer, member of the Covenant Peace Community in New Haven, CT; Elmer Maas, musician and former college teacher from New York City; Carl Kabat, Oblate priest and missionary; Anne Montgomery, Religious of the Sacred Heart sister and teacher from New York City; Molly Rush, mother and founder of the Thomas Merton Center in Pittsburgh and John Schuchardt, ex-marine, lawyer, father and member of Jonah House, entered the General Electric Nuclear Missile Re-entry Division in King of Prussia, PA where nose cones for the Mark 12A warheads were made. They hammered on two nose cones, poured blood on documents and offered prayers for peace. They were initially charged with over 10 different felony and misdemeanor counts.

In February 1981, they underwent a jury trial in Norristown, Pennsylvania. During their trial they were denied a "justification defense" and could not present expert testimony. Due to the Court's suppression of individual testimony about the Mark 12A and U.S. nuclear war-fighting policies, four left the trial and returned to witness at G.E. They were re-arrested and returned to court. They were convicted by a jury of burglary, conspiracy and criminal mischief and sentenced to prison terms of five to 10 years. They appealed and the Pennsylvania Superior Court reversed their conviction in February 1984. The State of

Pennsylvania then appealed that decision. Following a ruling in the fall of 1985 by the Pennsylvania Supreme Court in favor of the State on certain issues (including the exclusion of the justification defense), the case was returned to the Superior Court Appeals Panel. In December of 1987, the Superior Court of Pennsylvania refused their appeal, but ordered a re-sentencing. This ruling, however, was appealed to the Pennsylvania Supreme Court.

In February 1989, the Pennsylvania Supreme Court denied a hearing of any further issues in the case, and on October 2, 1989 the U.S. Supreme Court announced it would not hear the Plowshares Eight Appeal. On April 10, 1990 the Plowshares Eight were resentenced by the Pennsylvania Court of Common Pleas in Norristown and, with neither the prosecutor nor G.E. making any recommendations or asking reparations, were paroled for up to 23 and 1/2 months in consideration of time already served in prison. Judge James Buckingham listened attentively to statements by defendants, and by attorney Ramsey Clark, Dr. Robert J. Lifton, professors Richard Fall and Howard Zinn, which placed the "crime" in the context of the common plight of humanity, international law, America's long tradition of dissent, and the primacy of individual conscience over entrenched political systems.

Plowshares Number Two: On December 13, 1980 Peter DeMott, former seminarian and Vietnam veteran from Jonah House, entered the General Dynamics Electric Boat (EB) shipyard in Groton, Connecticut during the launch ceremony for the "USS Baltimore" fast attack submarine. Noticing an empty EB security van with keys in it, he got into the van and repeatedly rammed the Trident "USS Florida" denting the rudder. Security guards then broke into the van and arrested him. He was tried by a jury in New London Superior Court and convicted of criminal mischief and criminal trespass. He was sentenced to one year in jail.

Trident Nein: Independence Day, 1982, Judy Beaumont, a Benedictine sister and teacher from Chicago; Anne Montgomery, of the Plowshares Eight; James Cunningham, an ex-lawyer from Jonah House; George Veasey, a Vietnam Veteran also from Jonah House; Tim Quinn, expectant father and housepainter from Hartford, CT; Anne Bennis, teacher from Philadelphia; Bill Hartman, peace worker from Philadelphia; Vincent Kay, housepainter and poet from New Haven; and Art Laffin, member of the Covenant Peace Community in New Haven; entered EB to make a "declaration of independence" from the Trident submarine and all nuclear weapons. Four boarded the Trident "USS Florida" by canoe, hammered on several missile hatches, poured blood, and with spray-paint, renamed the submarine "USS Auschwitz." They were arrested within half an hour. Meanwhile, five others entered EB's south storage yard and hammered and poured blood on two Trident sonar spheres. They were apprehended after three hours. During their two-week jury trial in New London Superior Court, they were disallowed a justification defense and expert witnesses were prohibited from testifying about the dangers of the first-strike Trident. They were convicted of criminal mischief, conspiracy and criminal trespass and ordered to pay $1,386.67 in restitution to the Navy. They were sentenced to jail for up to one year.

Plowshares Number Four: November 14, 1982 — five days after the Trident Nein sentencing — John Grady, auto mechanic from Ithaca, New York; Ellen Grady, aide to an elderly woman and peace worker, also from Ithaca; Peter DeMott, of Plowshares Number Two; Jean Holladay, grandmother and nurse from Massachusetts; Roger Ludwig, a poet and musician involved in work with the poor in Washington, D.C.; Elmer Maas, of the Plowshares Eight; and Marcia Timmel, from the Dorothy Day Catholic Worker in Washington, D.C., entered EB. Three boarded the Trident "USS Georgia" and hammered and poured blood on several missile hatches. Four others entered the south storage yard and poured blood and hammered on Trident components before being quickly apprehended. Like the Trident Nein, they underwent a jury trial and were denied a justification defense. They also were convicted of criminal mischief, conspiracy and criminal trespass. They received prison sentences ranging from two months to one year.

AVCO Plowshares: July 14, 1983 Agnes Bauerlein, mother and grandmother from Ambler, PA; Macy Morse, mother and grandmother from Nashua, NH; Mary Lyons, mother, grandmother and teacher from Hartford, CT; Frank Panopoulos, member of the Cor Jesu community from New York City; Jean Holladay, of the Plowshares Number Four; John Pendleton, member of Jonah House; and John Schuchardt, of the Plowshares Eight; entered the AVCO Systems Division in Wilmington, Massachusetts, where MX and Pershing II nuclear weapons components are produced. They hammered on computer equipment related to these weapons systems and poured blood on blueprints labeled MX-"Peacekeeper." They also issued an indictment against AVCO and its co-conspirators, including the "national security state" and the armed forces, with an indictment for committing crimes against God and humanity by manufacturing for profit weapons of genocide. They were apprehended within an hour. During their jury trial they were able to present a justification defense, but this defense and expert testimony was disallowed by the judge prior to jury deliberation. They were convicted of wanton destruction and trespass. They were sentenced to jail for up to 3 1/2 months. After seven years in the Massachusetts Appellate Courts, their appeal was denied on November 16, 1990. They were then sentenced to time already served which included three months for Jean and John Pendleton and nearly two weeks for the others.

Griffiss Plowshares: On Thanksgiving Day, 1983 Jackie Allen, a nursery school teacher from Hartford, CT; Clare Grady, an artist and potter from Ithaca, NY; Dean Hammer, father and member of the Plowshares Eight; Elizabeth McAlister, mother and co-founder of Jonah House; Vern Rossman, minister, father and grandfather from Boston, MA; Kathleen Rumpf, a Catholic Worker from Marlboro, NY; and Karl Smith, member of Jonah House; entered Griffiss Air Force Base in Rome, NY. They hammered and poured blood on a B-52 bomber converted to carry cruise missiles as well as on B-52 engines. They also left at the site of their witness a written indictment of Griffiss Air Force Base and the U.S. Government pointing to the war crimes of preparing for nuclear war and depicting how the new state religion of "nuclearism" denies constitutional rights and punishes acts of conscience. Unnoticed for several hours, they finally approached security guards and were arrested.

In this, the first Plowshares case to be tried in federal court, their justification defense was denied. They were acquitted by a jury of sabotage, but they were convicted of conspiracy and destruction of government property. They received prison sentences ranging from two to three years. Their appeal was denied in federal court in March 1985.

Plowshares Number Seven: On December 4, 1983 Carl Kabat, of the Plowshares Eight, and three West Germans — Herwig Jantschik, Dr. Wolfgang Sternstein and Karin Vix — entered a U.S. Army base in Schwaebisch-Gmuend, West Germany and carried out the first Plowshares action in Europe. Six weeks earlier, they publicly announced their actions, but did not disclose the exact date or place. They participated in a six-week peace march in Germany where they distributed a booklet informing the public and media about their action and previous plowshares actions. On December 4, they entered the base early in the morning and with hammers and bolt cutters disarmed a Pershing II missile launcher. They were soon apprehended by U.S. soldiers. Following their arrest, they were all released their own recognizance. Carl returned to the U.S. and did not attend the trial. During the first week of February 1985, the three Germans were tried before the three judges and two lay judges and convicted. After their conviction, the judges called the Pershing II a "bad prophesy" and characterized their action as violence. Herwig and Wolfgang were sentenced to 1800dm ($900) or 90 days in jail, while Karin was sentenced to 450dm ($225) or 60 days in jail. Karin and Herwig served their prison sentence; Wolfgang paid the fine.

Pershing Plowshares: In the season of Passover, Easter Morning, April 22, 1984 Per Herngren, a student and peace worker from Sweden; Paul Magno, from the Dorothy Day Catholic Worker in Washington, D.C.; Todd Kaplan, involved in work with the poor in Washington, D.C.; Tim Lietzke, member of Jeremiah House in Richmond, VA; Anne Montgomery, of the Plowshares Eight and Trident Nein; Patrick O'Neill, university student and peace worker from Greenville, North Carolina; Jim Perkins, teacher, father and member of Jonah House; and Christin Schmidt, university student and peace worker from Rhode Island; entered Martin Marietta in Orlando, Florida. Once inside, they hammered and poured blood on Pershing II missile components and on a Patriot missile launcher. They also served Martin Marietta with an indictment for engaging in the criminal activity of building nuclear weapons in violation of Divine, international and national law. They also displayed a banner which said: *"Violence Ends Where Love Begins."* They were apprehended after several hours. During their jury trial in federal court they were denied a justification defense. They were convicted of depredation of government property and conspiracy. They were sentenced to three years in federal prison, given five-year suspended sentences with probation, and each ordered to pay $2,900 in restitution. Both their appeal and motion for reduction of sentence were denied in federal court. Herngren, a Swedish national, was deported on August 27, 1985 after serving over a year of his sentence.

Sperry Software Pair: August 10, 1984 John LaForge and Barbara Katt, house painters and peace workers from Bemidji, MN, dressed as quality control inspectors, entered Sperry Corporation in Eagan, Minnesota. Once inside they poured blood and hammered on two prototype computers designed to provide guidance and navigation information for Trident submarines and F4G fighter bombers. In addressing Sperry's nuclear war preparations, they also served Sperry with a citizens' indictment declaring that Sperry is committing war crimes in violation of national and international law. After a two-day jury trial in federal court in which they were allowed to present a justification defense, they were convicted of destruction of government property. Judge Miles Lord imposed a six-month suspended sentence and used the occasion to criticize the arms industry and to cite Sperry's corporate corruption. He also recognized the legitimacy of the justification defense for civil disobedience trials and for the Sperry Software trial in particular.

Trident II Plowshares: October 1, 1984 William Boston, a house painter and peace worker from New Haven, CT; Jean Holladay, of the Plowshares Number Four and AVCO Plowshares; Frank Panopoulos and John Pendleton of the AVCO Plowshares; and Leo Schiff, draft registration resister and natural foods chef from Vermont; entered the EB Quonset Point facility in North Kingston, Rhode Island. They hammered and poured blood on six Trident II missile tubes and unfurled a banner which said: *"Harvest of Hope – Swords into Plowshares."* They also placed a pumpkin at the site and posted a written *"Call to Conscience"* on the missile tubes condemning these weapons under international and religious law and calling on those responsible to cease their crimes against humanity. They were arrested within half an hour and charged with possession of burglary tools, malicious damage to property and criminal trespass.

During their jury trial, expert witnesses were allowed to be qualified in the presence of the jury. However the judge ruled this and other expert testimony irrelevant and denied a justification defense. At the end of their two-week-long trial, the prosecution dropped the burglary tools charge (a felony carrying 10 years) as the defendants pled guilty to the malicious damage to property charge. (After the State's case, the judge dismissed the trespass charge). After two days of prayer and discernment, the five concluded that pleading guilty was the most nonviolent course to take. On October 18, 1985 they were each sentenced to one year and a $500 fine. Frank was given an additional two months for a contempt charge relating to his refusal to disclose to the judge who drove the group to EB.

Silo Pruning Hooks: November 12, 1984 Carl Kabat, of the Plowshares Eight and Plowshares Number Seven; Paul Kabat, an Oblate priest from Minnesota; Larry Cloud Morgan, Native American and mental health care worker from Minneapolis, MN; Helen Woodson, mother of eleven children and founder of the Gaudete Peace and Justice Center from Madison, WI; entered a Minuteman II missile silo controlled by Whiteman Air Force Base in Knob Noster, Missouri. Once inside the silo area, they used a jackhammer and air compressor to damage the silo cover lid. They then offered a Eucharist and left at the silo a Biblical and Native American indictment of the U.S. government and the institutional church for their complicity in the pending omnicide of nuclear holocaust. They were arrested close to an hour after their action by armed military guards authorized to use "deadly force" against intruders. Following their arrest, they were declared by the court to be a "threat to the community" and were thus held on "preventive detention" and denied bond.

They underwent a jury trial in federal court in February 1985 in Kansas City, Missouri. They were convicted of destruction of government property, conspiracy, intent to damage the national defense and trespass. On March 27, 1985 they received the most severe prison sentences to date of any Plowshares group: Larry — eight years; Paul — 10 years; and Carl and Helen — 18 years. They were also given three to five years probation and ordered to pay $2,932.80 each in restitution. On November 1, 1985 U.S. District Judge D. Brook Bartlett, their trial judge, reduced Helen's sentence from 18 to 12 years, including five years probation. In March 1987, Larry and Paul were released from prison following a sentence reduction hearing. Larry's sentence was reduced to 36 months and three years probation, while Paul's sentence was reduced to 40 months and four years probation. Both were required to perform 300 hours of community service and to not violate the law for the duration of their probation. All but Helen appealed. Their appeals were denied in the Spring of 1986. On April 22, 1987 the U.S. Supreme Court ruled not to consider Carl's appeal. His sentence has since been reduced to 10 years including five years probation. On April 12, 1991 Carl was released on probation with the condition that he pay restitution. For reasons of conscience he has refused to comply with this order.

On January 27, 1989 Larry was convicted of two counts of going out of the district of Minnesota, a violation of his probation, and was sentenced to prison for one year. The occasions of his departures were to attend protests at the Trident base in King's Bay Georgia. He was taken into custody by U.S. marshals at a church near the Trident base. Due to health reasons the Judge recommended that Larry be sent to the Medical Center for Federal Prisoners in Rochester, Minnesota. Larry was released on November 13, 1989.

Resistance in Captivity: On March 16, 1988 Helen Woodson walked through the main gate of Alderson Prison carrying a banner and statement protesting the nuclear arms race, pollution of the environment and prison conditions for women. She was apprehended outside the prison by a patrol vehicle. She was temporarily placed in solitary confinement and then transferred to FCI Pleasanton in California. On December 10, 1988 in honor of Gaudete (Rejoice!) Sunday, Helen carried out another resistance action, this time, at FCI Pleasanton. She walked to the rec field track bearing an athletic bag stuffed with sheets, towels and papers doused with flammable nail polish, set the bag next to the fence and ignited a "lovely Advent blaze." Then she hung a banner reading: "There is no security in the U.S. government, nuclear weapons, chemical contaminants, prisons and UNICOR — military prison industries. Fences make slaves. Tear Them Down." And then, with toenail clippers, she snipped the "security" alarm wire, severing it in four separate places. She was sent to the hole and charged with attempted escape, arson, destruction of government property and inciting to riot. In late January 1989 she was moved to MCC San Diego. Before leaving Pleasanton she learned that the evidence for her action was destroyed and she was not prosecuted. After a short stint in San Diego, she was transferred to Marianna Prison in Florida. As a result of federal appeals court ruling, Helen was released on parole on June 14, 1993. During the spring of 1993 an appeals court overturned a lower court ruling and affirmed the government's position that it could release Helen on parole. Helen had filed a civil suit asking to be held in prison until the expiration of her sentence, and then be conditionally released.

Three days after her release, she was involved in several controversial protests (which went outside the bounds of traditional nonviolent protest) focusing on the idolatry of money, corporate greed and the destruction of the earth. She was arrested and convicted for these actions and was sentenced to 202 months in prison. She is now at the Marianna Prison.

Plowshares Number Twelve: February 19, 1985 Martin Holladay, a carpenter from Sheffield, Vermont, entered another Minuteman II missile silo of Whiteman Air Force Base near Odessa, Missouri. With hammer and chisel, he damaged the silo lid and some electrical boxes. He also poured blood on the silo and spray-painted *"No More Hiroshimas."* He left at the site an indictment charging the U.S. government with committing crimes against God and international law by its nuclear war preparations. After his arrest he was denied bond and held until trial. During his four-day jury trial, he was denied the opportunity to present a justification defense. On April 25, 1985 he was convicted of destruction of government property and destruction of national defense material. He was sentenced on May 16, 1985, to eight years in federal prison and five years probation. He was also fined $1,000 and ordered to pay $2,242 in restitution. Martin was released from prison after 19 months following a sentence reduction hearing on September 24, 1986. He remained on probation through 1991 and was required to pay restitution.

Trident II Pruning Hooks: April 18, 1985 Greg Boertje, ex-army officer and peace organizer from Louisiana; John Heid, former Franciscan seminarian and social worker from Ithaca, NY; Roger Ludwig, of the Plowshares Number Four; Sheila Parks, former college teacher from Medford, MA; Suzanne Schmidt, mother, grandmother, worker with the disabled and member of Jonah House; and George Veasey, of the Trident Nein; entered the EB Quonset Point facility in North Kingston, Rhode Island — the same site where the Trident II Plowshares had acted seven months earlier. They poured blood and hammered on three Trident II missile tubes and spray-painted *"Dachau"* on them. They left there a *"Call to Conscience"* indicting General Dynamics for war crimes and preparing for a war of aggression in violation of international, constitutional and spiritual law. Arrested after a short time, they were charged with possession of burglary tools, malicious damage to property and criminal trespass.

While Sheila and Suzanne were released nearly a month after the action on a "promise to appear" (PTA) and John after five months, Greg, George and Roger remained in jail for nearly nine months, refusing to accept a PTA for reasons of conscience. Shortly before their trial date, the judge released the three unconditionally from prison. During their two-week jury trial, the judge denied their justification defense, insisting that their motives were irrelevant to the case. They were convicted of all three charges. In a special gesture of support for the group, four jurors had the judge publicly read a statement from them conveying that they were sympathetic to their cause. On March 31, 1986 they were sentenced to three years, suspended after one year, and given two years probation. John, Greg, George and Roger were released during the summer of 1986. Sheila and Suzanne were released in January 1987.

Michigan ELF Disarmament Action: May 28, 1985 Tom Hastings, a Wisconsin peace activist involved in radio work, entered a wooded area in Michigan's upper peninsula and sawed down one of the poles carrying the Navy's "Extremely Low Frequency" (ELF) transmitter antennas which are used to coordinate the communications, command, and control process of all nuclear submarines in the U.S. He remained at the site for 45 minutes, praying, singing and planting a circle of corn around the pole. The next morning, he gave a part of the pole to Congressman Bob Davis' office and turned himself in to the local sheriff. Held for 48 hours, he was released on personal recognizance. He underwent a jury trial and was convicted of malicious destruction of property. On September 27, 1985 he was sentenced to 15 days and two years probation.

Pantex Disarmament Action: July 16, 1985, Richard Miller, involved in work with the poor in Des Moines, Iowa, began dismantling a section of railroad track from the railroad spur leading from U.S. Department of Energy's Pantex Nuclear Weapons Assembly Plant in Amarillo, Texas to a main line of the Topeka and Santa Fe Railroad. After first taking extensive precautions to prevent accidental derailment and avoid personal injury, he labored with railroad tools for seven hours, removing a 39-foot section of rail. Pointing out the connection between the Nazi extermination camp at Auschwitz and the Pantex factory, which is the final assembly point for *every* nuclear weapon made in the U.S., he put up a banner that read: *"Pantex=Auschwitz – Stop the Trains."* He further stated: "At Auschwitz the trains carried the people to the crematoria; at Pantex the trains carry the crematoria to the people." Charged with "wrecking trains" and destruction of national defense materials, he underwent a jury trial in federal court and was convicted. On November 8, 1985 he was sentenced to two four-year sentences to run concurrently. He was released from prison in February 1989 upon completing his sentence.

Wisconsin ELF Disarmament Action: August 14, 1985 Jeff Leys, a draft registration resister and peace worker from St. Paul, Minnesota, continued the process of disarming ELF (see Michigan ELF action) by sawing two deep notches in an ELF pole hoping to weaken it and leaving the rest to natural forces. (Unlike the Michigan ELF still under construction, the 56-mile Wisconsin ELF system is fully operational, with 1.5 million watts flowing through it). In a statement he carried with him to the site he explained: "I act today in accordance with the teachings of Gandhi, Christ and the Indians — and in accordance with the basic underpinnings of humanity, as expressed in the various world religions . . . and international laws." After an hour, Jeff walked to a transmitter site to turn himself in. Jailed after his arrest, he was tried by a jury on September 30, 1985 and was convicted of criminal damage to property. On October 29, 1985 Jeff was sentenced to five months in jail and given a three-year suspended sentence with three years probation. He was also ordered to pay $4,775 in restitution. In April of 1986 Jeff began serving his three-year sentence because of his refusal to pay restitution for reasons of conscience. His appeal was denied in September 1986. He was released in August 1987.

Martin Marietta MX Witness: September 27, 1985 Al Zook, father and grandfather active with the Catholic Worker in Denver, CO; Mary Sprunger-Froese, member of the Bijou Community and involved in hospitality work in Colorado Springs, CO; and Marie Nord, a Minnesota Franciscan sister involved in hospitality work for women; entered Martin Marietta's Denver,

Colorado plant. (Martin Marietta has a $2 billion contract for building and testing the MX missile). With the intent of disarming components of the MX missile, they carried blood and hammers into the MX work area. Finding the area highly secured by employees wearing "peacekeeper" security badges, the three were not able to enter areas where MX work is done and directly disarm any MX components. They were, however, able to pour blood on large interior windows overlooking the work areas and unfurled their banner: *"Swords into Plowshares."* They were quickly arrested and each charged with felony burglary and criminal mischief. The burglary charge was eventually dropped, however the criminal mischief charge was changed from a misdemeanor to a felony. They were imprisoned for one month before they were released on their own recognizance. On March 5, 1986 they were found guilty by a jury of criminal mischief exceeding $300. During their trial the judge refused to hear their justification defense. On May 1, 1986 they were sentenced to two months in prison.

Al and Marie appealed their case and the Colorado Court of Appeals recently reversed their convictions. The appeal was based on the judge's denial of their motion to proceed *in forma pauperis*, after his determination that their indigence was voluntary. The state had petitioned for a review of the case before deciding to retry Al and Marie.

Silo Plowshares: Good Friday, March 28, 1986 Darla Bradley and Larry Morlan of the Davenport Catholic Worker in Iowa; Jean Gump, a mother of 12 and grandmother from Morton Grove, Illinois; Ken Rippetoe, a member of the Catholic Worker in Rock Island, Illinois; and John Volpe, father, former employee at the Rock Island Arsenal and member of the Davenport Catholic Worker; entered two Minuteman Missile Silos controlled by Whiteman Air Force Base near Holden, Missouri. Dividing into two groups, the first group of three went to Silo M10 while the second group went to Silo M6. Hanging banners on the silo fences, one of which read: *"Disarmament – An Act of Healing,"* they employed sledgehammers to split and disarm the geared central track used to move the 120 ton missile silo cover at the time of launch. They also cut circuits and used masonry hammers to damage electrical sensor equipment. They then poured blood on the silo covers in the form of a cross and spray-painted *"Disarm and Live"* and *"For the Children"* on the silo pad. They left at the site an indictment charging the U.S. government with committing crimes against the laws of God and humanity and indicting as well the institutional Christian church for its complicity in the arms race. They were arrested by heavily armed military police nearly 40 minutes after their action. Following their arrest they were taken into custody and then released on their own recognizance. During their five-day jury trial they presented important evidence regarding their state of mind but the jury was not allowed to consider justification as a defense. On June 27, 1986 they were convicted of destruction of government property and conspiracy. In addition, Jean, Larry and Darla were cited for contempt for refusing to answer questions about where they met prior to the action. They served seven days in jail following the trial. John and Ken were also imprisoned for refusing to cooperate with the conditions of their release so long as the others were imprisoned for contempt. They were released on July 8. On August 22, 1986 Darla, Jean, Ken and Larry were sentenced to eight years with five years probation while John was sentenced to seven years with five years probation. John and Darla were ordered to pay $1,680 in restitution while Larry, Jean and Ken were ordered to pay $424. Each was also fined $100.

In April 1987, John was released from prison following a sentence reduction hearing. His sentence was reduced to 10 months, five years probation, and he is required to pay restitution. Ken and Darla were released from prison in mid-June 1987 after their sentence was reduced to one year. They were placed on probation for five years and were ordered to pay restitution. On April 18, 1990 his $424 having been paid anonymously, Larry, who had been imprisoned since his action, went to a halfway house and was released on probation on July 20, 1990. And in October of 1990, after four years of imprisonment, Jean was released on probation.

Pershing to Plowshares: On December 12, 1986 on the seventh anniversary of the NATO decision to deploy the Cruise and the Pershing II in Europe, Heike Huschauer, a member of the city council of Neuss, West Germany; Suzanne Mauch-Fritz, a social worker from Stuttgart; Wolfgang Sternstein, Plowshares #7; and Stellan Vinthagen, an orderly from Sweden; entered a back-up U.S. Army weapons depot at Schwabisch-Gmund, West Germany and damaged the tractor-rig of a Pershing II Missile Launch box. They hammered on the crane that maneuvers the missile and on the generator that operates the launcher, and poured blood on the rig. The banner which they hung over the truck stated, *"Choose Life for the Children and Poor."* These words were also spray-painted on the roadway. They were discovered after 30 minutes, when they signalled to a nearby guard.

In a statement of intent the four said, "With awareness of our responsibility, we understand that we are the ones who make the arms race possible by not trying to stop it." Following their arrest, they were released. On October 11 through October 19, 1989 nearly three years after their disarmament action, they were tried before three professional judges and three lay judges on the charges of sabotage, damage to government property and trespassing. During their trial they were allowed to present evidence about the moral and legal justification for their action. They pleaded that if the court accepts their justification defense they must be acquitted. If not, they must be given a high sentence. The court did not accept their pleading and handed down the following sentences: Wolfgang 1200dm or 120 days in jail, Heike, Suzanne and Stellan 600dm or 60 days in jail. In addition, for a subsequent blockade action, Stellan, Heike and Wolfgang were sentenced to 20, 80 and 135 days, respectively. Suzanne paid the 600dm fine. Stellen and Wolfgang served their sentences and were released in April 1990. On March 4, 1991 Heike was ordered to serve her 101-day sentence despite her appeal for a postponement of sentence so that she could continue her organizing efforts to end the U.S. war against Iraq.

Epiphany Plowshares: On January 6, 1987, the Christian Feast of the Epiphany, Greg Boertje, of the Trident II Pruning Hooks; Rev. Dexter Lanctot and Rev. Thomas McGann, priests of the Archdiocese of Philadelphia; and Lin Romano, an advocate for the poor from Washington, D.C.; entered the Willow Grove Naval Air Station in Horsham, PA. Dividing into two groups, one group went to a Navy P-3 Orion anti-submarine aircraft — an essential part of the U.S. first-strike arsenal. Meanwhile the other group went to a Marine CH-53 Sea Stallion and an Army H-1 Huey helicopter — both integral parts of U.S. interventionary forces. Both groups hammered and poured blood on the aircraft and displayed banners which proclaimed: *"Seek the Disarmed Christ"* and *"Espadas en Arados – Swords into Plowshares."* The four left behind a statement which explained why they acted on Epiphany, the Christian feast that recalls the Three Magis' search for the Christ child, "who came in the name of Peace." Having therefore addressed the "deadly connection" between nuclear weapons and military intervention, they also left an indictment of the U.S. government for its criminal interventionary wars in Central America and the Middle East and its first-strike nuclear war-making policies. They were charged with conspiracy, destruction of government property and trespass — charges which carry up to 15 1/2 years.

On March 31, they underwent a week-long jury trial in federal court in Philadelphia and were prevented from presenting a crime prevention or necessity defense. For the first time in a Plowshares case, the trial ended in a hung jury and a mistrial. On May 11, 1987 they were retried. The defendants were once again denied their affirmative defenses, and their testimony was even more severely restricted than in the first trial. Despite the constraints of the court, their trial once again ended in a hung jury and a mistrial. In an interview following the trial, one juror stated he believed the group did not act with criminal intent and affirmed their efforts for disarmament. After the second trial the two priests, who were suspended from their priestly duties after the action, accepted a plea bargain, pled guilty to criminal trespass, and were sentenced to 100 days in federal prison plus $500 fines. Their suspensions were lifted following their release from prison.

On July 13, 1987 a third trial began for Boertje and Romano. This trial ended in a mistrial when the judge ruled that the jury had been "contaminated" by statements from the defendants and spectators. On September 21, 1987 a fourth trial began, with the judge's repressive "gag order" remaining in effect. During the trial, both defendants received two contempt charges and had lawyers appointed to represent them (defendants had been representing themselves). On September 25, 1987 they were found guilty of all three charges.

On November 17, Lin was sentenced to two years and 100 days in prison plus five years probation. For reasons of conscience, Greg chose not to appear for sentencing. In a written public statement issued at the time of sentencing, Greg stated his intention to go "underground" and eventually emerge in another nonviolent action.

Following his trial, conviction and sentencing for the Nuclear Navy Plowshares action, Greg was sentenced to 33 months for failing to appear at the original sentencing for the Epiphany action. Lin, and then Greg, appealed their case from prison on the grounds that the judge violated their "pro se" rights when he appointed lawyers to represent them. They won the appeal and each was granted individual trials. Lin was eventually released from prison after serving nine months. In November 1988 her charges were reduced to trespass, whereby she was not entitled to a jury trial. She was tried before a U.S. Magistrate, convicted, and was sentenced to two years probation even though she had already served more jail time than the maximum sentence for trespass — six months.

In April 1989 charges against Greg were dropped, though he still had to serve a 33-month sentence for failure to appear at sentencing. In July 1990, Greg was released from prison and placed on probation.

Paupers Plowshares: On Good Friday, April 17, 1987 two brothers, Fr. Pat Sieber, a Franciscan priest who works at St. Francis Inn, a shelter for the homeless and soup kitchen in Philadelphia; and Rick Sieber, a father of three who also works at St. Francis Inn; entered the Naval Air Development Center in Warminster, PA. Once inside they dug a hole and buried a foot-long coffin that listed the names of 65 homeless and poor people who have been buried in an unkept lot in northeast Philadelphia known as potters or "paupers" field since 1980. They also placed a three-foot cross bearing the same names on top of the makeshift grave. They then approached a P-3 Orion aircraft — an integral part of the U.S. first-strike arsenal — and hammered on the plane's strobe light, cut wires in the nose of the plane and poured blood on a wing and fuselage area of the aircraft. While awaiting arrest they knelt in prayer and held a banner which said: *"God Hears the Cry of the Poor."* They left at the site a statement and indictment addressing the criminality of U.S. nuclear war preparations, the priority the government gives to arms over the poor, and how these arms preparations are actually killing the poor. In addition to signing their own names to these statements, they also signed the name "Lazarus" to represent the poor for whom they acted. They were charged with unlawful entry and destruction of government property. On June 12, the charges were reduced to one misdemeanor — unlawful entry.

On August 5, 1987 after an hour-long bench trial, the pair were found guilty of unlawful entry. They were sentenced to one year's probation, fined $100 and ordered to pay $1,540 in restitution. In February 1989 their restitution was dropped and they paid their fine which went towards a victims compensation fund.

White Rose Disarmament Action: On June 2, 1987 in the early morning, Katya Komisaruk, a peace activist from the San Francisco Bay area, walked through an unlocked gate leaving cookies and a bouquet of flowers for security guards and entered a satellite control facility named "NAVSTAR" at the Vandenberg AFB in Santa Barbara County, California. ('NAVSTAR' is the U.S. global positioning system of satellites. When fully operational, this system will consist of 18 orbiting satellites which will be able to provide the navigational and guidance signals to Trident II and other nuclear missiles as well as the Star Wars system, for a first-strike nuclear attack.) Once inside, she used a hammer, crowbar and cordless electric drill to damage panels of an IBM mainframe computer and a satellite dish on top of the building. Using a crowbar she removed the computer's chip boards and danced on them. On the walls she spray-painted *"Nuremberg," "International Law,"* and statements for disarmament. After being undetected for two hours, she left the base and hitchhiked to San Francisco. The next morning she held a press conference at the Federal Building in San Francisco to explain her action whereupon she was taken into custody by the FBI. She was charged with sabotage and destruction of government property. Each charge carries a maximum penalty of 10 years in prison and/or a $250,000 fine. The day before her trial the sabotage charge was dropped in the face of a defense brief that had been earlier submitted calling upon the government to prove every element of the charge beyond a reasonable doubt.

Her trial began on November 10, 1987 in U.S. District Court in Los Angeles. Several weeks before the trial, Judge Rea ruled in favor of the U.S. prosecutor's "Motion in Limine" which would severely restrict the evidence allowed as well as Katya's personal testimony. Katya, who represented herself and was assisted by co-counsel, was not allowed to mention words like "nuclear missiles" or "first-strike." The jury found her guilty of destruction of property on November 16, 1987. On January 11, 1988 Katya was sentenced to five years in prison. In addition Judge Rea ordered her to pay $500,000 restitution because he had heard that there might be a movie or book based on her action. Katya closely identifies with Sophie Scholl, a young German woman and member of the White Rose group during World War II, who was executed by the Third Reich for publicly opposing Nazi atrocities. On February 9, 1990 Katya was released from prison and placed on probation for the duration of her sentence.

Transfiguration Plowshares (West): On August 5, 1987 at 5:15 p.m., the exact moment (8:15 a.m. in Japan) when the U.S. dropped the first atomic bomb on Hiroshima in 1945, Jerry Ebner, a member of the Catholic Worker Community of Milwaukee; Joe Gump, father of 12 and husband of the imprisoned Jean Gump of the Silo Plowshares from Morton Grove, IL.; and Helen Woodson, acting as a "co-conspirator" from Shakopee Prison in Minnesota where she was serving a 17-year sentence for the Silo Pruning Hooks action, carried out the fourth nonviolent disarmament of a Minuteman II Missile silo controlled by Whiteman AFB in Missouri. They went to silo K-9 near Butler, Mo., and once inside the silo area, Jerry and Joe used a kryptonite bicycle lock to lock themselves within the fenced area. After pouring their own blood in the shape of a cross on the concrete silo lid, they used one eight and one three pound sledge hammer on the tracks used to open the silo lid. They also hammered on electrical connectors and other apparatus and cut various electric wires with bolt cutters. They then hung disarmament banners and sang and prayed while awaiting arrest. They also left at the site their action statement and indictment, signed by the three, as well as a photo of Jerry, Joe and Helen. In the interest of 'conservation' they used the very same banners and bolt cutters used by the Silo Pruning Hooks and Silo Plowshares. A while later military police arrived in a vehicle armed with a machine gun and arrested Jerry and Joe.

Explaining her involvement in the action, Helen stated she participated "in spirit" through a "conspiracy for life." The three named themselves the *"Transfiguration Plowshares"* to commemorate the Transfiguration, the Christian feast celebrated on August 6 which recalls the revelation of Christ to his disciples as the Lord of heaven and earth and also represents a foreshadowing of Christ's resurrection.

At a mid-August court hearing they were charged with a two-count felony indictment: conspiring to damage government property and destruction of government property — both federal charges. In a relatively open trial, the two were allowed to show a video film entitled *Hiroshima/Nagasaki: 1945*. This video, which the two carried into the silo with them, contained footage of the immediate effect of the bomb dropped on the two cities. Jerry was able to sing two songs to the jury which he first sang at the silo. Judge Howard Sachs, however, made it clear in his instructions to the jury that these things were ultimately irrelevant to the case before them. On October 22, the jury found them guilty. On December 11, 1987 Jerry Ebner and Joe Gump were sentenced to 40 and 30 months respectively in prison. Joe was released in November 1989. Jerry served more than two years in prison before being paroled. After being out of prison for a period of time he was jailed once again during the summer of 1990 for not cooperating with the conditions of his parole. He was released from federal prison on April 5, 1991 and remained on probation through 1994.

Transfiguration Plowshares (East): On August 6, 1987, Hiroshima Day and the Christian feast of the Transfiguration, Margaret Brodhead, a journalist; Dan Ethier, a former computer programmer and Catholic Worker; and Tom Lewis, artist and long-time peace activist — all from Worcester, MA — entered the South Weymouth Naval Air Station near Boston at dawn. They hammered and poured blood on the bomb bay doors and bomb racks of a P-3 Orion nuclear-capable anti-submarine plane which can use nuclear depth charges and homing torpedoes to attack submarines. They also hammered on the magnetic anomaly detector of an S-H 2F LAMPS MK-1 Sea Sprite helicopter. They also hung pictures of Hiroshima victims on the aircraft as well as a *"Swords into Plowshares"* banner. In a signed statement and indictment they left at the site, they said "the blinding light of that first atomic bomb turned life into death, but the blinding light of the Transfiguration revealed that death would be turned into life in Christ's Resurrection." They further charged the "Nuclear National Security State" with contravening international and divine laws. They were taken into custody by base security shortly after their action as they knelt in prayer holding a banner that read *"Christ Transfigured – Death Into Life."*

The three were initially charged with unlawful entry, a federal misdemeanor. In December Dan pled no contest and was sentenced to six months probation and community service of 100 hours. Tom and Meg were convicted on March 4, 1988 after a six-hour bench trial in Boston, where they presented testimony on the unconstitutional status of the arms race and the aircraft's status as "instrumentalities of crime" under international law. On April 26, Meg and Tom were sentenced to six months probation and 100 hours community service.

Harmonic Disarmament for Life: On August 16, 1987 the day of Harmonic Convergence, George Ostensen, a peace activist from the Northeast, in conspiracy with plowshares prisoner Helen Woodson, enacted a Plowshares action at the ELF Communication System Transmitter Site near Clam Lake, Wisconsin. Early in the morning, George entered the North ground of the ELF Trident communication system. Using a hatchet, saw, and other tools, he proceeded to cut down three ELF poles, notched two other poles, and cut some ground wires. He poured blood over the poles, hammered on ground-well electrical control boxes, placed photos of children and planted flowers inside the boxes and near the poles, and hung peace banners.

In statements he carried to the site, George stated: "These Extremely Low Frequencies hurt our earth by subjecting all God's creatures to highly unstable electromagnetic non-ionizing radiation and giving the Trident first-strike capability to destroy all life." In reference to the Harmonic Convergence, the lining up of the planets on August 15 and 16, he stated the convergence is the beginning of the new age and harmony, according to ancient Mayan, Tibetan and Hopi calendars.

Following his action at the North ground, George, undetected, went to the Terminal Control Center to inform the security guards on duty of his action. After spray-painting on the Terminal Center *"Trident – ELF is in violation of International Law and God's Law"* and *"Swords into Plowshares"* he spoke with a security guard who asked him to leave the site. George then went to a fenced in area near the control center and manually switched off several generators used to control computers and electricity at the site. He did this three times, following warnings to security personnel that the ELF site must be shut down. Finally, the local sheriff was called and George was arrested — some nine hours after he entered the site.

On August 20, George was charged with two felony counts of sabotage — both state charges and each carrying a maximum penalty of 10 years in prison if convicted. The indictment also listed Helen as aiding and abetting in the action and noted the ELF site had to be closed for 29 hours. On January 10, 1988 following a three-day jury trial in Ashland County District Court, George was convicted of one count of sabotage and acquitted on the second count. On February 12, 1988 George was sentenced to 33 months. In July 1988 he was denied parole. On May 2, 1989 his appeal was denied by the Wisconsin Court of Appeals, and the court ruled that his sabotage conviction was valid.

He was released from prison in September 1989 after serving two-thirds of his sentence. On October 2, Gandhi's birthday, he returned to ELF with other friends and carried a *Swords into Plowshares* banner up the road to the transmitter site. He was arrested and returned to jail. He waived a parole revocation hearing and was ordered to serve the remaining 11 months of his original sentence. On January 30, 1990 he was released from prison.

Australian Plowshares Action: On December 28, 1987, the feast of the Holy Innocents, Marie Grunke, a Blessed Sacrament Sister of Newtown; Joanne Merrigan and Anthony Gwyther, both of the St. Francis House, Darlinghurst; boarded the "USS Leftwich" during a public inspection while it was anchored in Sydney Harbor. The "USS Leftwich" is a nuclear-capable destroyer of the Spruance class recently deployed in the Persian Gulf. Recalling the innocents that were killed by King Herod and those children that continue to die from war and hunger, they poured their own blood on an ASROC anti-submarine nuclear depth charge launcher and a Tomahawk cruise missile launcher, weapons of first-strike capability. They hammered on these weapons to begin their disarmament and initiate their conversion into instruments of peace. After leaving their action statement on the ship, they were escorted off without being arrested or charged.

Nuclear Navy Plowshares: On Easter Sunday, April 3, 1988, Philip Berrigan of Jonah House (and original Plowshares 8); Andrew Lawrence of the Community for Creative Nonviolence; Sr. Margaret McKenna, a Doctor of Theology and member of the Medical Mission Sisters in Philadelphia; and Greg Boertje, former Army officer and member of Trident II Pruning Hooks and Epiphany Plowshares; boarded the battleship Iowa at Norfolk Naval Station in Virginia. The four boarded the battleship as part of a public tour greeting the vessel on its return from service in the Persian Gulf. With hammers and blood, the four disarmed two armored box launchers for the Tomahawk Cruise Missile and unfurled two banners: *Seek the Disarmed Christ,* and *Tomahawks Into Plowshares.*

The four worked for two or three minutes before they were seen by security. A "security alert" was sounded and the pier was vacated of all but naval personnel. Hundreds of people had come on Easter Sunday to visit the "USS Iowa" and the "USS America" which was also on display. Tours of both vessels were shut down.

Andrew, Greg, Margaret and Phil were held for some time at the Naval Base, questioned by the FBI and then transported by the FBI to Virginia Beach. They appeared in court on April 4, were charged with criminal trespass – a charge which does not entitle defendants to a jury trial. Because of Greg's status as a fugitive (stemming from his non-appearance at the sentencing for the Epiphany Plowshares) he was held on $25,000 bond. Though the others were offered a personal recognizance bond, they refused this bond as an act of solidarity with Greg. They were tried before a U.S. Magistrate on May 19, 1988 in federal court in Norfolk Virginia and convicted of trespass.

In an effort to diffuse courtroom support, the sentencing of the four was set on different days during July 1989. Margaret was sentenced to time served (over three months), two years probation and 240 hours community service and prohibited from entering any military installation during her probation. She was then released. Andrew received a four-month sentence. Greg and Phil each received the maximum sentence of six months.

In March 1989 Margaret received a four-month jail sentence for refusing to cooperate with the conditions of her probation. However she was credited with the time she already served before trial and ordered to jail for 20 days.

Kairos Plowshares: In the pre-dawn hours of June 26, 1988 Kathleen Maire, a Franciscan sister of Allegheny, NY; Jack Marth, a member of POTS (Part of the Solution) in the Bronx, NY; Sr. Anne Montgomery, a participant in three previous plowshares actions; and Christine Mulready, member of the Sisters of St. Joseph of Brentwood, NY; approached the Trident submarine, "USS Pennsylvania" at EB in Groton, CT, with the intent of carrying out a symbolic act of disarmament. Paddling against the current in the midst of a fast approaching storm, they were spotted in their rubber rafts in the Thames River by EB security before reaching the Trident. Apprehended by EB security, they were held overnight in jail. They were arraigned on charges of trespass, conspiracy to commit criminal mischief, and criminal intent and fined $40 for failure to use a light on their raft. They were released on a PTA and the charges were eventually dropped.

Kairos Plowshares Too: On August 1, 1988 Kathleen Maire and Anne Montgomery continued the Kairos Plowshares process by entering the EB facility in Quonset Point, RI, where they hammered and poured blood on Trident submarine parts. They held a banner which read: *"Trident D-5 Into Plowshares"* and were quickly apprehended. They were charged with malicious mischief and trespass and then released on a PTA. On September 27 they were tried by a judge in S. Kingston, RI. In a trial that lasted only 90 minutes, they were convicted by the judge of the above charges. They were sentenced to six months supervised probation and ordered to pay $250 in restitution for the fence they cut. After Kathy and Anne told the judge that, for reasons of conscience, they wouldn't pay the restitution or cooperate with probation, he changed their probation to "unsupervised" and fined them $250. To date they have not paid the fine.

Credo Plowshares: On September 20, 1988 Marcia Timmel, of Plowshares #4, mother and member of the Olive Branch Catholic Worker in Washington, D.C., entered the Sheraton-Washington Hotel in D.C. — site of the Air Force Association Arms Bazaar. Once inside she hammered and poured blood on a Textron Defense System (TDS) MX missile display, thereby dismantling it, and was subsequently arrested. She left at the site a statement decrying the blasphemous theme of the Arms Bazaar, *"Freedom: A Creed To Believe In,"* and issued her own creed (credo) of life, faith and love for the human family. During her two-day jury trial in D.C. Superior Court she used promotional literature of TDS, producer of the MX, to demonstrate the clear intent of TDS and the Air Force to prevail on Congress for the deployment of 50 new MX missiles. "We've been making $200 million a year for the last 10 years on this," said a TDS employee. "She took that model down the first day of the exhibition and we couldn't use it. She probably deprived us of a chance to persuade a couple members of Congress."

Under the constraints of a jury instruction that relieved the government prosecution of the need to prove evil intent, the jury convicted Marcia on November 18, 1988 of property damage. On December 29, she was sentenced to 90 days, 83 days suspended pending completion of probation (90 days), and was ordered to serve seven days beginning January 9, 1989.

Dutch Disarmament Action: On December 8, 1988 the first anniversary of the

INF Treaty, 12 Dutch peace activists, calling themselves "INF Ploughshares," cut through fences to enter the Woensdrecht Airbase and made their way to cruise missile bunkers where they carried out the first disarmament action in Holland. In their action statement they declared: "The INF Treaty was signed to eliminate the ground launched cruise and Pershing missiles from Europe. But the amount of air and sea launched missiles for European battlefield is increasing enormously and NATO plans are ready to modernize nuclear forces in Europe. The bunkers of cruise missiles won't be destroyed but given a new military destination. We oppose these new steps in the arms race.... We have started demolishing the Cruise missile bunkers ... by beating the bunker steel into ploughshares with sledge hammers. We demand that the money destined for new arms be spent instead on producing food for the hungry, detoxifying toxic waste dumps and cleaning polluted water." They were subsequently apprehended and most were released by Dutch authorities after being held for thirty hours. Kees Koning was released after 8 days.

NF-5B Plowshares: On January 1, 1989, Kees Koning, an ex-army chaplain and priest; and Co Van Melle, a medical doctor working with homeless people and illegal refugees; both of whom participated in the INF disarmament action, entered the Woensdrecht airbase once again, and began the conversion of NF-5B fighter airplanes by beating them with sledge hammers into ploughshares. The Dutch planned to sell the NF-5B to Turkey for use against the Kurdish nationalists as part of a NATO-aid program which involves shipping of 60 fighter planes to Turkey. They were charged with trespass, sabotage and $350,000 damage. They were detained in jail through their trial and received nationwide media attention. They were tried before three judges on February 9, 1989. Among those who were allowed to testify at the trial were a Kurdish lawyer, a former Dutch air force officer, and Phil Berrigan. They were convicted and given the following sentences: Co Van Melle was sentenced to seven months in prison, three months suspended and two years probation; and Kees Koning was sentenced to eight months in prison, two months suspended and two years probation. They were released pending appeal. Their appeal was denied on November 17, 1989.

Other Dutch Plowshares-Disarmament Actions:

On February 9, 1989 Dutch activists Ad Hennen and Rolland van Hell, who were inspired by the two previous disarmament actions, entered a Dutch military base and started the conversion of Hawk missiles with axes. Ad was released pending trial, but was then detained because of his previous record. On April 5,

1989 they went to trial and were convicted. They were sentenced to six months in prison, plus a four-month suspended sentence and two years probation. Ad was released pending their appeal. Their appeal was denied on November 17, 1989.

On Good Friday, March 24, 1989 Kees Koning, who had participated in the first two Dutch disarmament actions, entered a Dutch airbase and with a pick-axe began disarming a fighter plane destined for Turkey. He was subsequently arrested and imprisoned. On May 31, 1989 Kees went to trial. The state prosecutor demanded 18 months imprisonment, but had failed to observe that Kees had disarmed the same plane he worked on January 1, 1989. The judges ruled that he could not damage something he already damaged before and released him immediately.

On July 16, 1989 the anniversary of the first nuclear explosion named "Trinity," Kees Koning entered the Valkenburg Air Base in the Netherlands and with a sledgehammer, began to disarm a P-3 Orion nuclear-capable airplane. Simultaneously, other Dutch activists entered the base and reclaimed the land by starting to cultivate it for life instead of death. Kees was arrested and imprisoned and began a fast which lasted until August 9, 1989. Following a trial, he was convicted on September 12, 1989 and sentenced to six months in prison. On November 17th, following an appeal hearing for his January 1, 1989 action, Kees began a fast to demand an end to Dutch weapons sales to Turkey. He ended his fast on December 15, 1989. In the Spring of 1990 Kees was released from prison.

Stop Weapons Exports Plowshares 2: On February 16, 1989 the first Plowshares action occurred in Sweden. Anders Grip, a truck driver who works with a group providing material aid to the Third World; and Genially Akerberg, a consultant for organic farming; entered a railroad yard in Kristinehamn where weapons waited to be shipped to an Indian boat on the west coast of Sweden. They damaged the loading mechanism of the Haubits 77B mobile anti-aircraft missile launcher with hammers. This launcher was produced by the Bofors arms company. They then displayed a banner saying: *"Disarmament has begun," "We must dare to be disobedient," "Violence and oppression depend upon our obedience and passivity."* When the police came a half-hour later, Anders and Genially had set up a dining table and invited the police to join them in a meal. They were placed under arrest. On their way to the police station several of the police expressed support for their action and advised them of another potential site for a plowshares action. They were released later that night. They were sentenced to pay $10,000 in restitution to Bofors which they refused to pay.

Thames River Plowshares: Early in the morning on Labor Day, September 4, 1989 Jackie Allen, artist and shelter worker of the Ahimsa Community in Voluntown, CT and member of Griffiss Plowshares; Kathy Boylan, mother, sanctuary worker and member of the Long Island, NY Catholic Peace Fellowship; Art Laffin, member of the Isaiah Peace Ministry and Trident Nein; and Elmer Maas, member of the Isaiah Peace Ministry and participant of two previous plowshares actions; Anne Montgomery, participant in five previous plowshares actions; Jim Reale, arborist and member of Jonah House; and Homer White, husband and member of the Caritas Community in Chapel Hill, NC; swam and canoed up the Thames River to the USS Pennsylvania Trident submarine, docked at the Naval Underwater Systems Center in New London, CT. Jackie, Anne, Kathy and Homer swam to the Trident. In full view of armed security, Jackie and Kathy hammered and poured blood on the Trident near the conning tower, while Anne was detained at the Trident dock. Jackie also carved the word "death" on the Trident. After 30 minutes Jackie and Kathy, who were fire-hosed by sailors, were taken into custody by the Coast Guard.

Heavy tidal currents forced Homer to return to shore and he was arrested upon entering the main gate of the Naval Underwater Systems Center.

Simultaneously, Art, Elmer, and Jim canoed to the tail end of the Trident and, in full view of armed security, hammered and poured their blood on the side of the sub. They boarded the Trident, hammered several more times, and prayed, sang and read from St. John's Gospel for 45 minutes. They, too, were fire-hosed before taken into custody. They left on the Trident a videotape of live footage of Hiroshima after the bombing, a Salvadoran cross, a banner, booklets documenting the nuclear arms race at sea and naval nuclear accidents, their action statement and *"Call to Confession and Captivity."* Concurrent with this action, a 96-foot-long banner was dropped over the Gold Star Bridge in New London, proclaiming *"Trident Is The Crime."*

After being held overnight in jail, they were arraigned and released the next day on a PTA. Charges were later dropped against Homer, presumably due to insufficient evidence. During their three-day trial in U.S. District Court in Hartford, they focused on their "lack of criminal intent" and on the criminality of the Trident, despite certain restrictions imposed by the court. Citing a ruling made by the Silo Pruning Hooks judge, their trial judge, Judge Nevas, instructed the jury to disregard the defendants' and their character witnesses' religious, moral and political views about the U.S. nuclear weapons policy. On December 19, they were convicted by a jury of conspiracy to enter a naval reservation for an unlawful purpose. All, except Jackie, were acquitted of trespass with intent to injure and depredate U.S. property. In addition, Jackie was the only one charged and convicted of destruction of government property less than $100. (During the trial the government entered into evidence one photo of hammer marks on the Trident, where Jackie said she hammered. Kathy claimed responsibility for some of the hammer marks in the photo. Despite each of the Thames River Plowshares conveying to the jury and the Court that they should all be treated the same way for their community act of disarmament, Jackie still was convicted of these charges. On March 6, 1990 they were given the following sentences: Jackie, Kathy, Art, Elmer, and Jim were sentenced to 60 days in prison; Anne was given a 120-day sentence. On January 7, 1991 the U.S. Court of Appeals for the Second District denied an appeal made by Jackie, Elmer, Jim and Art.

Plowshares Eskiltuna: On March 20, 1990 three Swedish peace activists, Lasse Gustavsson, Linus Brohult and Johan Hammarstedt, entered the FFV-Ordinance weapons factory in Eskilstuna, Sweden and disarmed the "Carl-Gustaf" bazooka with hammers. Their hammers were covered with pictures of their families. Seeking to stop the deadly export of Swedish weapons, the activists disarmed the "Carl-Gustaf" bazooka because it had been used in Vietnam and was smuggled to Saudi Arabia via Great Britain during the 1980s. The U.S. also buys these bazookas. In a statement distributed to employees explaining the purpose of their action, the plowshares activists write: "By living the way we do we support war and injustice. Swedish weapons are used in warfare all over the world. It is the responsibility of each and every one of us to contribute to disarmament. By disarming Swedish weapons we hope to break through paralysis and powerlessness and instead help achieve peace and justice." On March 5, 1991 they were tried and convicted in Eskiltuna's District Court. They were ordered to pay $900 in restitution which they have refused to pay.

Upper Heyford Plowshares: Early on March 21, 1990, the first day of Spring, British peace activists Stephen Hancock and Mike Hutchinson carried out the first British plowshares action. They entered the Upper Heyford U.S. Air Base and hammered on the outside of an F-111 fighter plane and then climbed into the cockpit where they also hammered on the nuclear weapons control panel. They left inside the plane a piece of the Berlin Wall and a statement that the INF treaty was a fraud because it eliminated no nuclear weapons. The F-111s, made by General Dynamics, are nuclear-capable supersonic strike fighter planes which were used in the bombing raids against Libya in 1986. Their low level navigation and weapons delivery capability allows bombing at night and in adverse weather. Both activists wore "Mickey Mouse" ears, as they explained, "to have a friendly silhouette" for Americans guarding the base and its material. They also wore sheets that said: *"Mickey Mouse Fan Club – Peace Section."* They pinned on the side of the F-111 a banner that reiterated the message of their action and the statement *"Isaiah was Here!"* The two were arrested and held by the Ministry of Defense police and charged with "suspicion of criminal damage" amounting to 200,000 pounds. They were released on bail after serving seven days in jail. On September 4, 1990 a jury found Mike and Steve guilty of damaging the aircraft and possessing mallets and fluid with intent to damage property. They were sentenced to 15 months imprisonment. They were released on parole on March 7th and were on probation through June 1991.

Doves of Peace Disarmament Action: On April 3, 1990 Susan Rodriguez, a long-time peace and community activist from Hayward, CA, entered the Physics International Laboratory on San Leandro, CA, a company which uses computers to simulate nuclear weapons explosions and research their effects on military hardware. She proceeded through several computer labs and used a small sledgehammer to disarm several computers. When finally confronted by the police, she stopped and was arrested. Susan had learned of PI's relationship to the military industry in the course of her work for a computer repair company. On December 14, 1990 she was tried and convicted by a jury of two felony counts: burglary and malicious mischief (causing more than $25,000 worth of damage).

On March 20, 1991 Susan was sentenced to one year in jail, suspended, 750 hours community service, three years probation and $1,000 restitution.

ANZUS Peace Force Plowshares: Early in the morning on January 1, 1991 Moana Cole, a Catholic Worker from New Zealand; Ciaron O'Reilly, a Catholic Worker from Australia; and Susan Frankel and Bill Streit, members of the Dorothy Day Catholic Worker in Washington, D.C.; calling themselves the ANZUS (Australia, New Zealand and U.S.) Peace Force Plowshares, entered the Griffiss Air Force Base in Rome, NY.

After cutting through several fences, Bill and Sue entered a deadly force area and hammered and poured blood on a KC-135 (a refueling plane for B-52's) and then proceeded to hammer and pour blood on the engine of a nearby cruise missile armed B-52 bomber that could be used in the Middle East. They presented their action statement and an indictment to base security who encircled them moments later. Simultaneously, Moana and Ciaron entered the base at the opposite end of the runway, and made a sign of the cross with blood on the runway, spray-painted *"Love Your Enemies – Jesus Christ," "No More Bombing of Children in Hiroshima, Vietnam, Iraq, or Anywhere!"* and *"Isaiah Strikes Again."* For approximately one hour they hammered upon the runway chipping at two sections, one being nearly five-feet in diameter, before they were detained. In their action statement they declared that they came together from three different countries to reclaim the acronym from the ANZUS Treaty and create a "new pact for peace, which is the way of the Lord." They also asserted they were acting to prevent war in the Persian Gulf and called upon people to nonviolently resist war and oppression. In their indictment they cited the U.S. government for war crimes and violations of international law. All four were indicted on January 9th on federal charges of conspiracy and property destruction and faced a maximum sentence of 15 years in prison. After being held in jail for over two months, they accepted pre-trial release on March 6th. They went to trial in federal court in Syracuse in May and were convicted by a jury. On August 20th, they were sentenced to 12 months in prison and ordered to pay $1800 in restitution. After serving 10 months Bill and Sue were released from prison in mid-June 1992. Moana and Ciaron were released in late June on bail pending a deportation hearing. In October 1992, Moana returned to New Zealand following her court-ordered voluntary deportation. Ciaron returned to Australia following his deportation hearing in March of 1993.

Arms Factory Plowshares: On March 1, 1991 three Swedish peace activists (Stefan Falk, Anders Grip and Per Herngren, of the Pershing Plowshares) entered with the morning shift at the Swedish Ordnance's armaments factory in Ekilstuna, Sweden. Once inside, they disarmed with hammers two "Carl Gustaf" grenade throwers and one AK-5 automatic rifle. Their act of disarmament was met by workers, guards, and later the police, calmly and without violence. The three were placed under arrest, charged with unlawful entry and property damage, and later released. They were tried in 1994 and found guilty. Per and Stefan were fined and Anders was sentenced to one month in jail. Swedish Ordnance also requested $11,000 in restitution. (Swedish Ordnance is a major producer of Swedish weapons and the largest share of its production is for export. The Carl Gustaf grenade thrower is distributed worldwide and was used extensively in the Persian Gulf.)

CHRONOLOGY OF PLOWSHARES-DISARMAMENT ACTIONS

AEGIS Plowshares: Before dawn on Easter, March 31, 1991 Phil Berrigan, from Jonah House and participant in two previous plowshares actions; Kathy Boylan, member of the Thames River Plowshares and the Gulf Peace Team, from Long Island, NY; Tom Lewis, participant in the Transfiguration Plowshares East action from Worcester, MA; Barry Roth, psychiatrist and peace worker from Worcester, MA; and Daniel Sicken, an Air Force veteran and war tax resister from Brattleboro, VT; boarded the "USS Gettysburg," an Aegis-equipped Cruiser docked at the Bath Iron Works in Bath, ME. (According to the Navy, Aegis is "the most capable surface launched missile system the Navy has ever put to sea.") They proceeded to hammer and pour blood on covers for vertical launching systems for cruise missiles. They also left at the site their action statement which said in part, "We witness against the American enslavement to war at the Bath Iron Works, geographically near the President's home." They also left an indictment charging President Bush, Secretary of War Cheney, the National Security Council and the Joint Chiefs of Staff with war crimes and violations of God's law and international law, including the killing of thousands of Iraqis.

They spent nearly two hours on the ship and in the yard before turning themselves into a member of the security force. After rejecting unsecured bond in court on April 1, all five were released unconditionally on April 3 pending trial by the state of Maine on charges of criminal trespass. Without explanation, the state decided against prosecuting them, and charges were dismissed one day before their scheduled jury trial.

Darwin Plowshares: Early on August 17, 1991, Anthony Gwyther, of the West End Catholic Worker in Brisbane, Australia, entered Darwin RAAF base. He poured blood on a U.S. B-52 bomber in Darwin to participate in the "Pitch Black '91" joint military exercises. He hammered on the bomb bay doors and inside the bomb bay area of the area of the aircraft beginning its conversion into implements to serve life. Anthony was then arrested by RAAF personnel to whom he gave his "Statement of Intent." He was held at Berrimah Police Headquarters for questioning and was released on bail. His hammer, bearing the inscription *"Everyone beneath their vine and fig tree, unafraid,"* his banner reading *"Beat Swords into Ploughshares,"* and a copy of the video "Nowhere To Hide," made in Iraq during the height of U.S. bombing by Ramsey Clark, were taken from him to be used as evidence in court. Anthony was charged with "criminal trespass" and "criminal damage" under the Northern Territory Criminal Code and with "trespass on Commonwealth property." He was tried and convicted in mid-December 1992 and was sentenced to three months in jail and ordered to pay a fine of $4369.

Soldier Disarms Rifle: On January 8, 1992, Magnus Eklund, a 22-year-old Swedish conscript, disarmed his AK4 automatic rifle with a household hammer. Upon completing his action, he told his officers he intended to refuse service and identified himself as a conscientious objector. He was held in the military barracks overnight before being reported to the civil police. In his statement he explained: "I want to put an end to my own violence and show my fellow soldiers that there are conscripted soldiers who don't accept militarism.... I wish we could be a little less frightened to disobey. We have to trust our own thoughts. Big structures, like militarism, do, after all, depend on single individuals." He was sentenced to four months in prison.

Good Friday Plowshares Missile Silo Witness: On Good Friday morning, April 17, 1992, about 50 people accompanied Fr. Carl Kabat and Carol Carson as they caravaned to the Missile Silo Site #N5 at Whiteman AFB in Missouri, the same silo that Carl and other members of the Silo Pruning Hooks disarmed in 1984. They cut through a fence and once inside, Carol used a sledgehammer on the concrete lid of the silo while Carl performed a rite of exorcism. A half an hour later, two Air Force security guards arrived in a jeep. They ordered Carol and Carl to leave the silo compound and to face away from their supporters and the silo. But the crowd of supporters calmly proceeded to link arms and lovingly surround Carl and Carol. When the two security guards tried to separate them, small groups of people would return to the circle for song and prayer. Eventually the police arrived and Carol and Carl were arrested. Both were jailed and held until their court appearance on April 29th. At that time, Carol and Carl made a preliminary agreement with federal prosecutors whereby Carol and Carl would plead "no contest" to trespass in exchange for the property destruction charged being dropped. On May 15th, Carl and Carol were sentenced to six and three months in a halfway house.

Harriet Tubman — Sarah Connor Brigade Disarmament Action: Before dawn on May 10, 1992, Keith Kjoller, a peace activist, graphic artist and cinema worker from Santa Cruz, CA; and Peter Lumsdaine, a father, peace worker, writer from Santa Cruz, entered a secure area of the Space Systems complex at Rockwell International in Seal Beach, CA, wearing Rockwell shirts and workclothes. They entered Building 86 where they used wood-splitting axes to break open steel-mesh reinforced windows and a door of two dust-free "clean rooms" containing nine NAVSTAR global positioning satellites, which were being readied for delivery to the U.S. Air Force. Delicate components in the seven uncompleted satellites were also exposed to potentially damaging unfiltered air as well as tiny fragments of metal and glass. One completed NAVSTAR was struck 60 times with an ax. (This satellite, awaiting shipment to the NAVSTAR launch complex at Cape Canaveral, had to be completely disassembled by Rockwell technicians to assess and repair the damage, which totaled $2.75 million). As they were about to ax another satellite, Peter was seized at gunpoint while Keith was assaulted and choked unconscious by Rockwell personnel — despite both activists declaring themselves unarmed and intending not to threaten or struggle with them. They were then taken into police custody.

The NAVSTAR GPS system is used for guiding advanced U.S. weapons and military/police assault teams to their targets — from bombers and cruise missiles during the Gulf War to counterinsurgency / search-and-destroy operations throughout the Third World. NAVSTAR is central to Pentagon preparations for launching a nuclear first-strike.

Keith and Peter named their disarmament effort "The Harriet Tubman — Sarah Connor Brigade" honoring the historical conductor of the "underground railroad" and the fictional nuclear resistance fighter of the popular movie *Terminator 2: Judgement Day*. In their action they sought to commit maximum damage, thereby challenging plowshares and the wider disarmament movement to go beyond symbolic witness in addressing the war machines key technologies. Unlike other disarmament or plowshares actions, they also intended to leave Rockwell if they were able to following their action.

Held initially on $1 million bond and "preventive detention," their case was assigned to an FBI "investigation and terrorism" agent and they were charged with damaging property manufactured for the U.S. government, a felony carrying up to 10 years. Choosing to direct resources toward resistance organizing rather than a trial by an unjust government, they entered into a "guilty" plea agreement. Their bond was reduced to $50,000 and they were released in mid-June for four weeks under electronic monitoring. On September 21, 1992, in accordance with the "guilty" plea agreement, Peter was sentenced to two years prison, and Keith to 18 months with three years probation and $15,000 restitution being ordered for each of them by U.S. Judge Gary Taylor, who acknowledged the historical legacy of civil disobedience in his court room. Keith was released on parole from Lompoc Federal Prison in late September 1993. Peter was sent to a half-way house in December 1993 and was released in the Spring of 1994.

PLOWSHARES-DISARMAMENT ACTIONS

BAe Plowshares: On January 6, 1993, feast of the Epiphany, Chris Cole, a Christian peace activist from Oxford, England, entered the British Aerospace (BAe) weapons factory in Stevenage, Herts, and used a household hammer to disarm a radar dome mold for the European Fighter Aircraft, a nose cone, a computer and the Hawk strike attack aircraft. He also poured blood on military equipment and carried two banners which said: *"Heal the World – Hammer BAe Swords into Ploughshares"* and *"Prepare the Way of the Lord – Swords into Ploughshares."* The hammer and one of the banners were also used in the "ANZUS Plowshares" action at Griffiss AFB in 1991.

In a statement he left at the site he explained: "The Epiphany remembers when three men presented gifts to the infant Jesus. My gift of disarmament is for all the infants who are threatened with BAe weapons, from Northern Ireland to East Timor." (BAe is a heavy supplier of Hawk fighter planes to Indonesia. These planes, in turn, are used against the people of East Timor). After being at the site for about an hour, during which time he entered several buildings, he was arrested and jailed. On January 7th, he was charged with having caused criminal damage in excess of 475,000 pounds (about $700,000). On October 7, 1993, Chris was tried by a jury. Following eloquent testimony by Chris concerning BAe's criminal activity and how he had tried a variety of methods to appeal to BAe to disarm, the judge instructed the jury that they must use their "conscience, common sense and common humanity" to decide their verdict. The judge also told the jury that "if what Mr. Cole says is happening in East Timor, it may amount to genocide, which is a crime against British and International law. On October 11th, the jury deliberated on the case for five hours and could not reach a verdict — at least three members of the jury thought Chris had done the right thing. Thus the trial ended in a hung jury.

Four days later Chris had a new trial. This time he was convicted and sentenced to eight months imprisonment. He was released shortly after his conviction for he had already served the required time for this sentence.

Good News Plowshares: Before dawn on Good Friday, April 9, 1993, Kathy Boylan, participant in two previous plowshares actions; Greg Boertje-Obed, participant in three other plowshares actions; and Michele Naar-Obed from Jonah House; entered the Newport News Shipbuilding in Newport News, VA wearing badges identifying themselves as "disarmers." After cutting through a fence, they proceeded to the "USS Tucson" fast attack submarine. They scaled 80 feet of scaffolding and climbed aboard. They then disarmed two Tomahawk cruise missile launchers by removing the inner metal casings and hammering on them with household hammers. They also poured blood onto these launchers as well as on a third Tomahawk launcher.

The three spray-painted *"Disarm – Christ Lives," "LOVE,"* and the sign of Christ's cross. They also displayed signs and hung banners. They left at the site a five page indictment against the government for its war preparations and asserted that fast-attack submarines, which carry vertically launched, nuclear and conventional Tomahawk cruise missiles, are being illegally constructed at Newport News Shipbuilding. These missiles, carrying conventional warheads, were used during the U.S. massacre of Iraq and were responsible for much of the slaughter of Iraqi civilians and military.

After they completed their action, they prayed, sang and explained the purpose of their action to a nearby worker whom they had encountered during their action. The worker called security and they were taken into custody and placed under arrest. They were charged with state charges of "wanton trespass," a misdemeanor, and "destruction of property," a felony which carries a five year maximum sentence, and taken to the Newport News City Jail where they were held on $1500 bond.

On May 4, 1993, they were tried by a judge on the trespass charge and given a $100 fine. Their trial was held in closed session because the judge cleared the court when supporters applauded as Greg, Michele and Kathy entered the courtroom.

On August 24th they were tried by a jury (this time on the property destruction charge), convicted, sentenced and released — all in one day. Despite attempts by the prosecutor and the judge to limit their testimony, the three were given some latitude to speak and offered eloquent testimony. However, in response to the judge trying to restrict Michele's closing statement, Greg explained to the court that they could no longer continue with the trial and invited supporters to join with them in singing "Rejoice In the Lord Always." Marshals removed the three from the courtroom, along with 15 supporters who were taken to holding cells in the courthouse. When the jury reached a decision about the verdict and the sentencing, the three returned to the courtroom. They were found guilty and sentenced to eight months and a $2,500 fine (which they refuse to pay). Supporters earlier taken into custody were released. And after serving 4 1/2 months in jail, Kathy, Greg and Michele were released for they had already served the required time for an eight-month sentence.

JAS into Plowshares: On June 22, 1993 Swedish peace activists, Pia Lundin and Igge Olsson entered a hanger at SAAB airplane factory in Linkoping, Sweden and proceeded to hammer on the bomb mountings underneath the wings of the JAS (Hunting Attack Scanning), an attack reconnaissance plane. They sowed wheat on the factory grounds and awaited their arrest. When the police arrived to arrest them, they were invited to share bread and water with them, thereby symbolizing that the resources of the earth are enough for everyone when they are shared. Authorities alleged that there was $200,000 in damages. On July 16th they were tried and convicted of "malicious damage."

On June 24th, peace activists Tomas Falk and Hans Leander entered the SAAB plant, intending to hammer on three of the four remaining JAS planes (the last plane would be left as a symbol of the need for more people to come forward to disarm it). Upon entering the factory they were apprehended, and thereby unable to carry out their action. They were charged with aiding and attempt to "sabotage" and convicted of aiding and attempting to do "malicious damage." In October 1993, the four were sentenced to one year in prison and ordered to pay $80,000 in restitution to SAAB. They were released from prison in August and November 1994.

Not wanting to give money to arms production, the group offered SAAB a deal where the group would raise the $80,000 and give it to a water well project in India instead of to SAAB. SAAB responded positively from the beginning, but when it became clear to them that the activists would not stop the resistance until the factory was converted, they ended the dialogue and handed their request over to the "Kronofogde" (corresponds to IRS in the U.S.). The group decided to resist Kronofogde and is, as of this printing, in the process of raising money for the water well project.

Pax Christi-Spirit of Life Plowshares: Early on the morning of December 7, 1993, Phil Berrigan, a participant in three previous plowshares actions; John Dear, a Jesuit priest, author, and peace activist who works with the homeless in Washington, D.C.; Lynn Fredriksson, a peace activist who works with the homeless in Baltimore; and Bruce Friedrich, a member of the Dorothy Day Catholic Worker in Washington, D.C.; entered the Seymour Johnson AFB in Goldsboro, North Carolina. Coincidentally, the base was going through special war-game exercises and maneuvers on this anniversary of Pearl Harbor. Wading through water and crossing rough terrain, the four made their way past hundreds of Air Force personnel and approached a nuclear capable F-15E fighter plane. (The F-15E, which costs $40 million, is capable of carrying both nuclear and conventional weapons and was the mainstay of the U.S.-led attack on Iraq). They hammered on bomb pylons, the main bomb guidance antenna, the cock-pit undercarriage, one guidance light, and the Lantern all-weather flight pod. Additionally, they removed the air intake covers and poured blood in the air intakes and over the side of the plane. They also placed on the ground their statement and an indictment charging the base and the U.S. government with crimes against peace and humanity along with their banner which read: *"Disarm and Live."* After several minutes, they were surrounded by hundreds of Air Force soldiers, some screaming: "This is the real world." They were charged in federal court with destruction of government property, a felony. Stating that they could not comply with a court order not to return to the base, they were held without bond.

After being denied advisory counsel by a federal judge, and after having their trial date changed three times, the four appeared in federal Court in Elizabeth City, NC on February 15th to begin their jury trial. Before the trial began, the prosecutor introduced a "Motion in Limine" which would prohibit the defendants from being able to speak about moral and political justification for their action. When they were not allowed by the judge to finish their opening statement to the jury, they turned their backs to the judge as about 20 supporters joined them in saying Lord's prayer and singing peace songs. Lynn, John and Bruce were held in contempt of court along with six supporters. David Sawyer, an African-American supporter, was assaulted by U.S. marshals and was, in turn, charged with assault. David spent three weeks in jail and his case was later resolved. Meanwhile, the other six supporters were given six-month sentences. However, five were released on March 9th and 10th and placed on one-year supervised probation. Brad Sjostrom was imprisoned for three months and then placed on one-year supervised probation. Judge Boyle later that afternoon declared a mistrial stating that the jury had been "contaminated." The four plowshares defendants were sent back to jail.

Seeking to deter possible further courtroom resistance, Judge Boyle ordered that the four be given separate jury trials. He also ordered that each defendant must have standby advisory counsel. In addition, the judge threatened the defendants in advance with contempt of court should they defy any of his rulings and the prosecutor and the judge strongly enforcing the Motion in Limine "gag order" on the defendants. With U.S. Marshals tightly restricting supporters admission into the courtroom, defendants and supporters witnessed what were perhaps the most repressive plowshares trials to date. In each of the trials the four were repeatedly objected to by vindictive prosecutors and were constantly warned by the judge that the Bible, their religious views, the role of the F-15E fighter plane used to bomb Iraq and U.S. nuclear war preparations were irrelevant. Phil was the only one of the four to take the stand to testify. And after Boyle's ruling that she could not give her opening statement to the jury because it was irrelevant, Lynn remained silent throughout her trial.

Despite the court's attempt to suppress the truth, each of the four were able to powerfully and creatively witness to the truth of their action. Each were found guilty with the juries taking one-hour for Phil, 30 minutes for John, 20 minutes for Lynn and 6 minutes for Bruce to return their verdicts. On July 6, 1994, the four were sentenced to the following:
Phil: eight months in jail, four months house confinement; John: 7 1/2 months in jail, 4 1/2 months house confinement; Lynn: 14 months in jail; Bruce: 15 months in jail. Each were given credit for time already served. They were also sentenced to three years of supervised probation and ordered to pay $2700 in restitution.

Anarchist Plowshares: On January 27, 1994 activists Calle Hoglund and Karna Rusek entered the Satenas F7 base in Sweden as exercises were being conducted. They proceeded to hammer on the nose cone of a Viggen-type military aircraft. The two were subsequently held in custody for five weeks. They were both charged and convicted of sabotage, a felony offense. Calle was sentenced to 14 months in prison and Karna to three months. On appeal, Calle's sentence was reduced to 12 months.

Ulf Lundblad, Mats Kolmisopi and Henrik Hoglung were also charged with aiding in this "act of sabotage." Ulf and Henrik were sentenced to eight months in prison and Mats, because he is under 18, was not given a prison sentence. Ulf and Calle began serving their sentence on November, 27, 1995.

Good Friday — April Fool Plowshares: At noon on April 1, 1994 (Good Friday and April Fools Day), Fr. Carl Kabat, still on parole for the Silo Pruning Hooks action and participant in three other plowshares actions, entered the Grand Forks Missile Field in North Dakota dressed as a clown. After cutting through a fence surrounding a Minuteman III missile silo (not scheduled to be deactivated under the START II agreement), he proceeded to hammer on a combination dial for the silo as well as the silo lid. He prayed, sang and hung a banner on the silo fence which said *"Stop Nuclear Weapons."* After about a half an hour, a helicopter, a tank and 10 soldiers armed with machines guns arrived at the site and held him there for two hours.

Meanwhile, Sam Day and Michael Sprong, who were outside the missile silo fence supporting Carl, were asked to leave. When they refused to do so, they too were taken into custody and charged with trespass (this charge was later dropped). Carl was taken to the Barnes County Jail in Valley City, North Dakota. In an excerpt from a statement issued at the time of his action Carl stated: "Only by taking personal responsibility for our actions and inactions can we begin to address the crime of nuclear weapons. Each of us must be like the run-away slave who refused to accept slavery, those who turned their homes into safe houses, or even the judge and jury that refused to find guilty those who broke the laws of the time in their efforts to end slavery. In one abolitionist case the jury was jailed by the judge for refusing to find the defendant guilty."

At a preliminary hearing Carl was charged in State Court with trespass and malicious destruction of property — both felony charges — and was ordered held without bond. During his arraignment on April 13, Carl pled "no contest" to the charges against him and stated that his action was on behalf of the children of the world. On May 16th, Carl was sentenced to five years in prison and ordered to pay a $7,000 fine. At this writing he is serving his sentence at the North Dakota State Penitentiary, PO Box 5521, Bismarck, ND 58502.

Jubilee Plowshares: On August 7, 1995 six religious peace activists carried out coordinated plowshares actions on the East and West coasts to commemorate the 50th anniversary of the U.S. atomic bombings of Hiroshima and Nagasaki.

Jubilee Plowshares East: Before dawn, Michele Naar-Obed of the Good News Plowshares, Philadelphia activists Rick and Erin Sieber (father and son), and Amy Moose a social worker and peace activist from New York City, entered Newport News Shipbuilding. They cut through a fence and walked to the "USS Greenville" fast attack submarine. They boarded the sub and proceeded to hammer and pour blood on the soft metal casing inside four vertical launch tubes for the Tomahawk cruise missile. They also pasted pictures of the Hiroshima victims to the submarine and laid out their statement and indictment. After a period of prayer they then spoke with a shipyard worker about their action, who in turn called security, and they were arrested. The four were jailed at Newport News City Jail and held on $6,500 bond. Rick Sieber was released on bond several hours later.

The four were charged by the State of Virginia with trespass and destruction of property (a felony). On September 19, the four were tried on the trespass charge. Despite attempts by the court to suppress the truth, especially during cross examination of Newport News personnel, the four were able to offer powerful testimony about their witness. They were convicted and immediately given the maximum sentence for this charge: one year in jail and a $2,500 fine.

The four decided to appeal and be tried again on the trespass charge during their jury trial on the charge of property destruction.

Amy, Michele, and Erin were released on bond shortly after trial. Following their release, Amy accepted a plea bargain agreement due to personal reasons.

Five days before their expected Jury trial in December, they were notified that state charges were being dropped and that they would be indicted on federal charges. On January 19, 1996 Erin, Rick, and Michele pled not guilty to the following charges: damage to national defense materials, conspiracy to damage national defense materials, damaging government property (damage to submarine and to shipyard fence) and conspiracy to damage government property. These charges carry a maximum sentence of 45 years in prison and a $1.5 million fine. During a March 13 hearing, their trial (originally scheduled for March 19) was postponed because one of the two lawyers representing the group was dismissed by the judge due to an alleged conflict of interest. Also the court ordered that each defendant be assisted by legal counsel. Their trial is expected to take place some time in April 1996.

Jubilee Plowshares West: Shortly after 8:00 a.m. Ukiah school teacher and peace activist Susan Crane, and Steve Kelly, a Jesuit priest from Oakland, walked onto Lockheed-Martin Corporation in Sunnyvale, CA, builder of the first-strike Trident II D-5 missile. They approached a large assembly building and, to their amazement, a large rolling door opened up. They walked into the building and proceeded to hammer and pour blood on missile casings. On a nearby desk, Susan found classified plans for the missile and poured blood on them. While Steve and Susan awaited their arrest, they spoke with some of the workers and displayed photos of nuclear victims.

They were both taken into custody by state authorities and then released after 48 hours. Federal authorities then ordered them back to court on August 11. They pled not guilty to felony charges of destruction of government property and conspiracy. Bond was set at $75,000 for Susan and $50,000 for Steve.

On November 28, 1995, they were tried by a jury in San Jose Federal Court. During her testimony, Susan attempted to introduce the Nuremberg Principles into evidence. When she was stopped for the third time, supporters in the courtroom successively stood up and read from the principles and read from the Bible. Federal Marshals removed eight supporters from the building. Susan was also removed from the courtroom. When Steve refused to proceed with the trial, the jury was removed from the courtroom. Eventually resuming her testimony, Susan challenged the judge: "I do not accept your authority. . . . I do not know why I am not allowed to speak the highest law of the land." Steve also offered compelling testimony and both offered character witnesses.

During cross-examination, both refused to answer questions about who drove them to the site. Each received civil contempt charges. They were both found guilty of the two felony counts — charges which carry a maximum prison sentence of 15 years. On March 13, 1996 both were sentenced 10 months in prison (with credit for time served) and $100 in court costs.

Seeds of Hope — East Timor Ploughshares: On January 29, 1996, Joanna Wilson, borough council member from Merseyside; Lotta Kronlid, a gardener from Sweden; and Andrea Needham, a nurse from Kirby, carried out the third British Ploughshares action. In the early morning they entered the British Aerospace military site at Warton, Lancashire and proceeded to disarm a Hawk warplane. They hammered on the radar nose of the plane and on the control panel. When they were finished with their work, they were able to make some phone calls from inside the South Hangar to tell their friends and the press about their witness. They were then arrested by the police.

The Hawk ground-attack airplane that they disarmed (jet number ZH 955) was part of an order destined to Indonesia. Since 1975 (when East Timor declared its independence), Indonesia has been waging a genocidal war against the people of East Timor. More than 200,000 people have been killed, which is about one-third of the pre-invasion population. The group stated that there is substantial evidence that Hawks from previous deals have been used by the Indonesian military to bomb civilians.

The arms export to Indonesia, and especially the Hawk deal, has been opposed by many people and groups all over Britain, the group says. But the government and BAe have refused to stop the sale. "These planes will soon be killing people in East Timor unless action is taken immediately to stop them," the group says.

The three women are now held in remand, charged with illegal entry and criminal damage. Their trial date is expected sometimes during the spring of 1996.

Another member of the group, Angie Zelter, an environmental campaigner from Norfolk, publicly stated she intends to carry out a future ploughshares action at BAe to continue the process of disarmament there.

FROM AMBLER TO AVCO:
A REFLECTION ON THE AVCO PLOWSHARES WITNESS

Agnes Bauerlein

The blessings of a large family were never more clear to me than on the afternoon of July 4, 1982, when we gathered for a family picnic at our home in Ambler, Pennsylvania. My grandchildren splashed playfully in the backyard swimming pool, surrounded by doting aunts and uncles. Their mothers chattered nearby under the shade of an oak tree. A volleyball game raged in the background while my husband snoozed in oblivion, the newspaper covering his face.

On that holiday I was perhaps more acutely aware of my blessings because I knew that I probably would not be part of that tranquil domestic scene for some time to come. Later on, as we gathered around the table, my heart skipped a beat at the thought of being involved in an act of civil disobedience/divine obedience that might possibly mean a long separation from my loved ones.

Slowly, over many previous months of serious thoughts and prayers, I had decided to protest the proliferation and continuation of the nuclear arms buildup in a stronger way than I had previously done. I had decided that civil disobedience would be my way of saying "no" to an insane arms race that threatens all life on our planet.

I left home on a July morning of 1983 to join my six compatriots in preparation for our symbolic disarmament action. Our time was spent in sharing, prayer and solitude. Under the theme "faith in the face of fear," we celebrated the Eucharist. We all had our own fears and anxieties, which we openly expressed with each other. We broke the bread and shared the wine in remembrance of Christ. And in faith we accepted what would come the next day.

Sleep did not come easy that night and, at 5:30 that following morning, July 14, I watched a magnificent sunrise over the ocean and saw it as a good omen. For the last time we met in a circle, prayed for guidance and, after some hurried hugs, left for our destination.

Walking into AVCO, a plant in Wilmington, Massachusetts, that manufactures components for the MX and Pershing II missiles, we carried our household hammers, our blood, photos of our families, various prayers, and statements of peace and justice. On behalf of our 37 children, 24 grandchildren, and all future generations, we also issued an indictment against AVCO and its co-conspirators, including the "national security state" and the armed forces, for committing crimes against God and humanity by manufacturing for profit weapons of mass destruction. Our intent in issuing this indictment was to show that our acts were justified under divine and international laws — laws that call upon all people to prevent crimes against humanity from occurring.

Entering the building went smoothly, contrary to our expectations. Doors were literally opened for us and we were met by greetings of "Good Morning." Once inside the building, I was overwhelmed with a feeling of oppression. This factory of mass destruction brought images of violence, death, and hell to my mind as we wandered through the vast open area, looking for a suitable place to commit our action. Fear took hold of me. It was not a fear of being caught, but a fear of not being able to express my sense of despair through this action. Still, I knew the truth must be told. Faith led us through an unfamiliar building into an assembly room filled with large crates where we found parts to the MX. We poured our blood over these and symbolically hammered this particular nuclear "sword" into a "plowshare," and prayed that our action would bear fruit. Strangely enough, we were in there for quite a while. Even our singing and hammering, sounding like a bell of justice, drew no one's attention. Eventually, though, we were discovered and apprehended by AVCO's security and local police — but not before we were able to carry out a direct act of disarmament and expose the nature of AVCO's work.

Later that day, after we were arrested and processed, we were all jailed. The men were taken to Billerica Jail in Massachusetts. The four of us women spent the next 10 days at the Framingham Jail before being released on our own recognizance at the pretrial hearing. Certainly feelings of oppression and powerlessness are very clearly dominant ones for prisoners. But had I not sensed that same oppressive factor at AVCO where workers were "free"? Had I not sensed the very subtle oppression of the kind of work being done there? Had I not sensed the powerlessness of the workers who "must work to support their families"? The atmosphere of prison kept calling me into prayer, for there the stark realities of life are strong, and brokenness is a continual reminder of our need to be in touch with the Spirit of God.

Questioning injustice has always been second nature to me. As a child living in Nazi-occupied Holland during World War II, I remember asking my father why the police didn't do something to protect the Jews who were so blatantly subject to persecution. Reading Dorothy Day in the Catholic Worker in the 1950s and 1960s, I wondered why the Roman Catholic hierarchy was not listening to her convictions of pacifism and nonviolence.

My personal acquiescent acceptance of the events that led to a war in Southeast Asia will forever remind me that commitment to family does not preclude commitment to the rest of humanity or the call of conscience. So many years of bottled-up, unanswered questions finally erupted in February 1981 when I became closely involved with supporting the Plowshares Eight during their trial. Their example showed me that I must take responsibility for the world I live in and act on my faith, regardless of the consequences. They filled me with hope for the future. To realize that I had the freedom to act on my convictions was very liberating. I now can foresee a world for my children and grandchildren. I realize that the earth doesn't have to be governed by fear and violence. I simply decided that raising and nurturing 11 children was too much of an investment to leave unguarded. In opting for a life without nuclear weapons, I decided to take action myself and not let the future of my family be decided by someone else. I also wanted my children to know that questioning authority is right and that acts of conscience should be the norm.

During our mid-December jury trial in 1983, I tried to speak about my conscience convictions. The expert testimony offered in our defense also served to communicate my belief that our actions were morally and legally right. Having myself experienced the horrifying effects of Nazism, it was deeply moving to hear the testimony of Dr. Richard Falk, who told the jury that, under the Nuremberg Accords and international law, actions like ours are required not only to prevent future crimes such as those perpetrated by the

Nazis, but also to prevent the use of weapons of indiscriminate mass destruction from ever occurring. Also in light of the imminent danger posed by nuclear weapons, Daniel Ellsberg testified that our actions were reasonable and necessary to help lessen the risk of nuclear war and initiate the process of disarmament. These witnesses and others who testified all reconfirmed for me that I have a moral and human duty to act to prevent nuclear war.

Despite hearing testimony on the justification of our acts, the judge declared that all of the expert witnesses' testimony was irrelevant to the case. He also ruled that issues of conscience and moral and international law could not be considered by the jury in rendering a verdict.

The jury found the AVCO Plowshares members guilty of trespassing and "wanton" damage to property. The seven of us were immediately taken to jail and shortly thereafter released on our own recognizance, pending an appeal for another trial.

Perhaps my youngest son Matthew, then aged 10, summed it up best of all when I questioned him on his feelings of my possible prolonged absence. His answer was thoughtful and simple. "I don't like it when you are away and I will miss you, but I know why you are doing it and the more of you that are doing it, the better it will be for us kids."

JOURNEY TO MISSOURI

Martin Holladay

This is the tale of a journey, symbolic and actual. It is a journey from Lebanon to Vermont to Missouri, where I now find myself in jail awaiting trial for hammering on the concrete lid of a nuclear missile silo.

The poets of the Old Testament referred to Lebanon as a land particularly blessed with beauty and fruitfulness: the land as an ideal, a flower of creation.

Let grain abound throughout the land;
on the tops of the hills may it sway.
Let its fruit flourish like Lebanon;
let it thrive like the grass of the field.
                              Psalm 72:16

Your plants are an orchard of pomegranates
with choice of fruits, . . .
with every kind of incense tree,
with myrrh and aloes
and all the finest spices.
You are a garden fountain,
a well of flowing water
streaming down from Lebanon.
                          Song of Songs 4:13-15

I grew up in Lebanon before the civil war. My actual memories of the country's crystalline natural beauty mingle with nostalgia to form an ache for Eden that parallels that of the poets' hymns. Anyone who traveled much in Lebanon before 1975 should be able to identify with this feeling. The orchards of Lebanon bear a cornucopia of fruit, mythic in variety and perfection of flavor; and in spring the melting snow brings forth wildflowers that carpet the hills.

The land of Lebanon is to me a land of unfailing abundance, like the waters of Afqa, which cascade as a full-formed river from the mouth of a mountain cave. The beauty and miraculous fertility of Lebanon are real manifestations of the limitless love of God.

This Lebanon belongs to my youth. Because it is now many years and thousands of miles distant, and because its hills have been transformed by war, this Lebanon of memory has become symbolic and irretrievable. From Lebanon I am banished as from the original garden.

For the last ten years, I have lived in the woods of northeast Vermont. There I am sometimes a carpenter, but chiefly a gardener. In Vermont I built my house and raise what food I can: eggs, potatoes and other vegetables, apples and berries. This is my post-Eden existence:

By the sweat of your brow
you will eat your food
until you return to the ground.
Genesis 3:19

This verse makes clear the human identification with the soil. But what are the ramifications of our sweaty bond to the land?

The ideal of the relationship between farmer and land is that of the relationship between lovers. As the farmer becomes intimate with and nourishes the land, to that degree the land responds and brings forth abundantly. The fulfilled relationship between farmer and land must nourish both. The manual labor necessary for cultivation strengthens the bond of intimacy felt by the farmer. Tenderly the farmer props up and terraces the land where it sags from the rain, makes it rich with compost where carelessness has impoverished it, restores plants to plots made barren.

As God is our lover — "even the very hairs of your head are all numbered" (Mt. 10:30) — SO the farmer becomes lover to the land, until every wrinkle and fold is known. The farmer then is grieved to see the beloved degraded, grieved to be parted from the beloved.

Everyone who has left houses or brothers or sisters or father or mother or children or fields for my sake will receive a hundred times as much and will inherit eternal life. (Mt. 19:29) This list of beloved ones — those from whom we are grieved to be parted — culminates in "fields."

As the fulfillment of the relationship between lovers is sexual, so too is that of the farmer and the land. The essential agricultural act is the planting of seed, the land swells with germination. We see why in all cultures the earth has been considered female.

As my relationship with the land in Vermont was deepening, I became aware that the government of this country is moving in a different direction. The accelerating nuclear arms race is based on a much different relationship to the land than that of the farmer.

The first requirement for the nuclear arms race is a belief in the legitimacy of violence. All violence is a revolt against God, for the murderer assumes the role of judge and kills one who was created in God's image. Our nuclear program is blasphemous, for it reflects our willingness to destroy creation. We stand ready to destroy not only our sisters and brothers who are Christ with us, but the very fertility of the soil: to destroy the mountains of Lebanon. Our sin has evolved from the tasting of fruit to setting fire to the garden.

My increasing awareness that the nuclear threat reaches every where, even to the backwoods of Vermont, brought me to a most difficult fork in the road. Eventually — not without heartache — I gave away my chickens and took leave of the land. I traveled to Missouri, to the missile fields.

In Missouri the soil is deep and black, richer and easier to farm than the thinner, stonier, steeper soil of Vermont. Here I saw farms homes and barns, cattle and hogs, and fields stubbly with last year's corn.

In the farmers' very fields are missile silos. Until one knows what they are, they are inconspicuous. One sees a level area about a hundred yards square surrounded by a chain-link fence. Inside a circular slab of concrete and a few steel poles. The surrounding farmland is plowed right up to the fence. The missile is invisible, underground.

If one drives the back roads of Missouri, the first silo one sees is followed a few miles down the road by another, and then another.

There are over a thousand Minuteman missile silos in the Midwest, and a hundred and fifty in Missouri alone. They are scattered through the countryside — like razor blades in a loaf of bread.

Part of the reason for our profound failure to deal with these nuclear weapons on a moral level is that it takes an act of the imagination to understand the reality of our huge arsenal. The traveler sees only a fenced, level area marked with a "No Trespassing" sign. But the reality of that site is a Minuteman II missile with a range of eight thousand miles, armed with a 1.2 megaton nuclear warhead, one hundred times more powerful than the Hiroshima bomb. The missile site represents an explosion beyond imagining, a rain of fire and poison such as the world has never known, a nightmare of melting cities and burning flesh.

It is my awareness of a rising tide of violence that brought me here: the violence that has now covered Lebanon; the violence of nuclearism, which now indicts all Americans, even rural Vermonters; and the violence here in the farmland of Missouri, where it is as stark as a launching site for a Minuteman missile. For each silo the earth has been excavated and replaced with concrete, steel, and plutonium. The missile is in the cornfield; our separation from the fields is now triumphant.

That our culture is moving away from an intimate relationship with the land has become a cliche. Yet the movement from making love to rape is fundamental and bespeaks a wrenching moral degradation and turning away from God. The phallic nature of our missiles is inescapable, and their deadly intent certifies that there is no beloved, only victims. The insertion of a sixty-foot nuclear missile into buried silo is a graphic image of rape. We are sowing a different crop now, and none can imagine the harvest. "They sow the wind, and reap the whirlwind." (Hos. 8:7)

On February 19, 1985, the trial of the Silo Pruning Hooks began in Kansas City. Helen Woodson, Larry Cloud Morgan, Rev. Carl Kabat, and Rev. Paul Kabat were on trial for hammering and praying on the concrete lid of a missile silo in response to the words of Isaiah 2:4, "They shall beat their swords into plowshares." That morning I expressed my support for their action by entering a different silo beating it with a hammer and chisel, and pouring blood. "The earth will disclose the blood shed upon her; she will conceal her slain no longer." (Is. 26:21) The small sound of my hammer was a farmers anguished "No."

Where do we find our hope, and how does the healing begin? Jesus gave us two great commandments. The first is: "Love the Lord your God with all your heart and with all your soul and with all your mind." (Mt. 22:37) We are grounded in this commandment by the fact that we must eat and are therefore indissolubly linked to the soil that feeds us-to the earth, God's creation. This commandment does not call us merely to make a statement of preference for God, a declaration devoid of responsibility. Our love for God requires us to love justice and therefore to implement it, to love all creation and therefore to defend it.

The second of the two great commandments is to "Love your neighbor as yourself." (Mt. 22:39) We are grounded in this commandment by the fact that we are each of woman born and therefore indissolubly linked to the human family. In our love for our neighbors, violence has no place. We are called to disarmament, a disarmament of the heart. But our love for our neighbors also calls us to protect them, to prevent harm, to intervene to save them.

Do what is just and right. Rescue from the hand of the oppressor the one who has been robbed. Do no wrong or violence to the alien, the fatherless or the widow, and do not shed innocent blood in this place. (Jr. 22:3)

Editors' Note: Martin Holladay was tried in U.S. District Court in Kansas City, Missouri April 22-25, 1985. He was convicted of destruction of government property and sentenced to eight years imprisonment. In September 1986, his sentence was reduced to the time he had already served — 19 months — and he was released.

SILO PRUNING HOOKS ACTION STATEMENT

Editors' Note: *This statement was issued by the Silo Pruning Hooks at the time of their disarmament action, November 12, 1984. Fr. Paul Kabat, O.M.I., Fr. Carl Kabat, O.M.I., Larry Cloud Morgan, and Helen Dery Woodson used a jackhammer and air compressor to begin the disarmament of a Minuteman II missile silo in Knob Noster, Missouri. See "Plowshares Chronology" for further details of action.*

War is one of the oldest facts of history. Since the beginning of time, human beings have slaughtered each other in a mindless orgy of greed, power, and national pride. Today, however, as never before in history, our vast arsenal of nuclear weapons threatens all life on earth, the very existence of God's creation. Surely, today, the words of the Lord in Genesis (4:10) echo in our ears: "Why have you done this terrible thing? The blood of your brother [and sister] cries out to me from the earth!"

In the fertile earth of Missouri, graphically depicted in the movie *The Day After*, lies a demonic force of death. Each missile silo conceals the power to destroy millions of lives, and thus our rich fields have become the final, bloody burial ground for all humanity.

Our Christian faith calls us to accept personal responsibility for ending the cycle of violence that threatens us all. In their "pastoral Letter on War and Peace," the bishops remind us: "Peacemaking is not an optional commitment. It is a requirement of our faith. We are called to be peacemakers ... by our Lord Jesus. We are called to move from discussion to witness and action." We can no longer bury weapons of mass destruction in God's earth and, with them, bury our conscience and our faith in the nonviolent Christ who proclaimed love of enemy and God's kingdom of justice and peace. Today, Christians must act as peacemakers, "beating swords into plowshares and spears into pruning hooks" (Is. 2:4 *NAB*), disarming our hearts, our lives and our nation.

Faithful to that mandate, we have come today to begin the disarmament of one missile silo. In cutting the fence, we remove the barriers of peace symbolized there. In pouring our blood, we expose the murderous intent inherent in the weapon and in our government's war policies. In hammering the silo cover and instruments, we render temporarily useless a weapon of mass murder, and in damaging the warning system, we express our intent to place our trust in the Lord of Life rather than in "gods of metal." (Lv. 19:4, *TEV*)

In so doing, we express our love for our brothers and sisters throughout the world and call upon them to act in conscience to achieve disarmament. We affirm the responsibility of each person to stand firmly in the way of the forces of death with life-giving witness and action. And we pray that, through the grace of God, our act may enflesh the total disarmament of body, mind, and spirit to which we are called.

Sow for yourselves justice and reap the blessing
Plant new ground in peace
For it is time to seek the Lord.

A Special Plea for Life

Larry Cloud Morgan, Whitefeather of the Ojibway, Grandson of Loonsfoot and Red Bird Woman, with the Silo Pruning Hooks. In the Name of the Native American People I ask the government of the United States of america, so called by the great-great-grandchildren and grand children of immigrants who came to my land 492 winters past, to take from our Mother the Earth these machines of fire that destroy earth and human life throughout the lands of all people.

I act today, as the Old Ones have said I must, to take our stand, to make our land calm once again.

The trees must remain green, the waters must be crystal, the sands are to be pure and warm once again.

The sage and sweet grass, where the deer and elk lay their heads, must once more be safe and soft for them. Where the children shall walk and grow must be peaceful and warm; no bad shall they hear, and only good things their eyes shall see.

The circle we form, which knows no color and knows no end as our feet touch our Mother the Earth, shall not feel the hurt and destruction of fire.

The winds are pure, and the Grandfathers have told us the time is now when peace must come from the North Wind, where the Old Ones have gone and only they, with the Great Spirit, know what is tomorrow.

For Love of the Children
Elizabeth McAlister

As I was sitting in the Syracuse Public Safety Building (a euphemism for jail in these quarters), some of the reality of what I and my friends had done began to well up in me. It was accompanied, as reality usually is, by terror. Probably one of the hardest things for us human creatures is facing reality. Like so many others, I don't like to think about things like death — my own death or the death of people close to me. I certainly don't like to think about war and that kind of death and, above all, I don't like to think about nuclear war and the death of all we have known.

But I found myself thinking about all of these things while in jail. Once in jail, life becomes radically stripped down; so many of the distractions are gone. It becomes a little bit harder to run away from oneself and from reality and terror. Parenthetically, this is one of the reasons I think jail is an important experience for me — and probably would also be for a lot of people who have never thought about jail in relation to themselves.

I thought about jail in relation to myself only once while growing up. While I was a postulant in a religious community in 1959, I read of the life of St. Bernard of Clairvaux. I read of Bernard as a warrior who experienced his conversion to Christ through a long period in jail, and I thought then that I would need such a jail experience for me to become "holy." But it seemed utter fantasy that such would be my lot. Reality being stranger than fantasy, I have seen the insides of a goodly number of jails, but without the experience of becoming holy.

I was in the Public Safety Building this time because I and six friends had entered Griffiss Air Force Base in Rome, New York, on Thanksgiving 1983. We went inside the building that housed, among other things, a B-52 bomber that was being outfitted to carry a full complement of cruise missiles. Some of us hammered on the bomb bay doors of that B-52, poured our own blood on the fuselage, spray-painted the phrases "320 Hiroshimas" and "Thou Shalt Not Kill" and "If I Had a Hammer" on it, and taped to it photos of our children, and a "people's indictment" of Griffiss Air Force Base that we had drawn up. The other half of the group did similar work in a nearby storage area for B-52 engines. They painted "Omnicide" and "Stop Cruise" in strategic locations.

The government responded to our acts by indicting us for sabotage, for destruction of government property, and for conspiracy. And so I was sitting in jail looking at the possibility of spending twenty-five years there. That much reality can be frightening, especially when the one facing it has three young children aged nine, eight, and two whom she loves deeply.

Into this atmosphere and these ruminations, a friend sent a cartoon. It depicted two children talking. The first asked if the second had seen "The Day After" on TV. The second child responded, "No! My parents wouldn't let me. They thought it would be too scary! Did you see it?" "Yes," responded the first. "Did you find it scary?" "Not as scary as my parents did," said the first. "Oh!" said the second. "What did they find the scariest part?" "The very end," said the first, "when I asked them what they were going to do to stop it."

I sent the cartoon to my older children, Frida and Jerome, along with the letter I was writing them that day. The Day After was televised on November 20; our action was on November 24. Their Dad and I had watched the film with them (as well as with other members of the Jonah House community) and we had talked with them afterward about the meaning of the film. We talked too about the action I was about to undertake (though not the specifics because children don't need that kind of information; they don't need to be responsible for it). We told them that I had been preparing with several others to engage in a disarmament or "Plowshares" action in the coming week. It would mean that I would probably be in jail for some time and be apart from them. Our children have grown up with these realities as part of the air they breathe; they have seen many people in the community in which we live, including their mom and dad, imprisoned for resistance to nuclear annihilation. But to have mom do something like this and to face her possible absence from their day-to-day lives for an indefinite amount of time — this was a large step.

Both of the older children said that they understood, in a new way, why this resistance was so necessary. They were willing to accept the personal sacrifice of my absence as their part in trying to stop a nuclear war from happening, as their part in trying to avoid the suffering that the movie displayed in an understated but nonetheless very clear way. They committed themselves to assume more responsibility around the house and especially to be helpful in dealing with the questions and fears of their little sister who was not able to understand as they were. It was a moment of extreme closeness for the four of us, a moment of accepting together whatever might come, and we concluded our conversation with prayer and big, big hugs.

We all back down from moments like that. The children remain(ed) querulous, somewhat selfish, lazy; they remain(ed), in short, young children. But we don't back down completely. Something of the clarity of a moment like that stays with us, enlightening a dark time. While the children fear prolonged separation, they are proud of their mom and of themselves for' offering something, for sharing something of the suffering of children in less privileged environments. They are, as we are wont to tell them, First World children but they have some consciousness of Third World children, which, we hope, will affect their lives and the choices they make in them.

Little Katie is another story. Not because she's our child do I say it; she's a beautiful little person. She is as full of life and joy and love and curiosity as any two-year-old (maybe a little more than many-but that gets too subjective). And watching her grow is watching a miracle unfold. It is hard to think about missing all that. And, for her part, I have to agonize lover the potential damage to her spirit. At the same time as she is a deterrent to this kind of risk, she is a spur to it. Nursing her as I did for almost two years — she showed no inclination to be weaned — I heard the persistent question welling up within me: "Will this child be able to grow up?"

To nurture such innocent life and know, as I do, the threat to her life, to know, as many have sought to tell us, the threat to all life on this planet means to make some choices. The options are few and clear: first, I could choose to hide somewhere, anywhere, with my children, to remain protective of them, isolated. But I know there is nowhere we can go. I guess I also know that it would not be possible for me for very long — to choose a "security" for my children that cannot be an option for other or for all parents.

Second, I could pretend that the threat is not there at all; I could live without seeing or hearing or thinking about it. That is all too possible to do.

But that would mean making my own body and soul and those of our children part of the problem-part of the numbness, indifference, and resultant selfishness that enables the machinery of war to mushroom out of all control. it would also mean surrendering the few clues I have arrived at throughout my life about what it means to be a decent, responsible, caring human being.

Or third, I can ask how I can best love my children and I can answer by working to provide for them and the millions like them a hope for the future. I cannot say that I hope for a future for them without, at the same time, being willing to do something to make that hope become a reality.

The action we took at Griffiss Air Force Base was the sixth such Plowshares action. These actions sprang from our prayerful reflection on the biblical mandate out of Isaiah and Micah to "beat swords into plowshares, and spears into pruning hooks." They sprang from our shared realization that even as the arms race has been built weapon by weapon, decision by decision, disarmament needs to occur weapon by weapon, decision by decision, or as one person expressed it, "dent by dent." Our hope in doing these Plowshares actions is not so much that we will successfully destroy a particular weapon.

Our hope is that in our effort to be obedient to the Spirit, to life, the Spirit might become more present in our world, empowering more and more people to act in whatever ways they can to say a clear "no" to such destructive weaponry, to say a clear "no" to policies that call for the use of such weaponry.

The first Plowshares action took place at the GE facility in King of Prussia, Pennsylvania, in September, 1980. The group of eight participants included my husband, Phil Berrigan, his brother Daniel, two other members of the Jonah House community, and four friends. One of the women who acted at King of Prussia is the mother of six children. The AVCO Plowshares included four grandmothers; they had collectively 37 children and 24 grandchildren. Many of the men and women who have participated in these actions have done so as parents. Each would articulate it differently, but all acted so that the children might have some hope of a future. It would be a great service if these parents' voices could be heard more in our days.

It is so clear how torn-up people are today. If we try to look squarely at what is happening in our world, we become so full of despair, of hopelessness, that we cannot live. And so we withdraw into numbness. I read a lot of Robert Lifton in the Public Safety Building and could identify with so much of what he writes. Then Dan Berrigan sent me a book called *Bringing Forth In Hope* by Denise Priestley (New York: Paulist, 1983). I devoured the book, feeling that it said things for me that I had not been able to say for myself. She writes at one point: "It is very difficult for me and for others to get a handle on how to stop this evil, and that is part of its destructiveness. Everything is presented as so interdependent that there are no longer any limits or boundaries, and the whole system becomes overwhelming.... There is no more powerful or destructive weapon than the creation of this kind of confusion in and among people.... We begin to believe that this is the only reality that exists, and the possibility and hope for a new way of being is pushed further and further out of our consciousness."

Against this ennui, the seven of us at Griffiss (as well as others who have acted for justice and peace before and since our action) felt hope as an urgent imperative calling us to enunciate (albeit in fear and in trembling) a testimony to life. We sought above all, to enunciate hope, to announce that while this is a time when death appears to reign supreme, it is also a time of hope. The promise of new life is at hand for our world if people reach out and grasp for it, if people in solidarity with one another reach out and dismantle the weapons that block our access to life.

Editors' Note: Adapted from an article that originally appeared in Daniel Berrigan, ed., *For Swords into Plowshares, The Hammer Has to Fall* (Highland Park, NJ: Plowshares Press, 1984).

LETTER FROM NEWPORT NEWS CITY JAIL

Kathy Boylan Shields

I am a mother of five sons. Many years ago, I saw a poster of a mother pushing a baby carriage through a beautiful park, but just beneath the lush grass, thousands of nuclear missiles pointed skyward. It had a powerful impact on me because I identified with the poster. All I was doing for my children would be meaningless if I didn't act to dismantle the weapons threatening all humanity.

We've all watched in horror the tragedy of Waco, Texas, but the world is the Waco compound and preparations are complete for the incineration of the planet. Humanity is held hostage, especially the children. The plowshares act is an attempt to disarm our compound. It is an invitation to everyone to do the same.

I am haunted by the question, "What would I have done to stop the Holocaust?" Would I have refused to pay taxes to Hitler, or blocked the trains, or hidden the victims and would I have cut the fence at Auschwitz, crossed the yard and tried to disarm the gas chamber? I hope so.

Dorothy Day, co-founder of the Catholic Worker movement, called nuclear weapons "gas chambers without walls." The Tucson (fast-attack submarine) will launch the chambers killing millions of people. The weapons must be dismantled.

Newport News Shipbuilding builds death machines just like German companies built gas chambers. Private property warnings should not have stopped German citizens from acting to stop the holocaust. They can't stop us today.

The designer of the Holocaust Museum in Washington, D.C. meant his work to be an indictment of acquiescence echoing across half a century to future generations.

I hope I would not have acquiesced to slavery or to Hitler, and I will not acquiesce to the incineration of the planet.

Editors' Note: This was written from the Newport News City Jail in Virginia where Kathy served a four-month jail sentence for her involvement in the Good News Plowshares action in 1993.

STATEMENT OF JUBILEE PLOWSHARES

Jesus Came to Declare: "The Spirit of the Lord is upon me, because God has anointed me to preach good news to the poor. God has sent me to proclaim freedom for the prisoners and recovery of sight to the blind, to release the oppressed, to proclaim the year of the Lord's favor." (Lk. 4:18-19) No longer are victims to wait fifty or even seven years for justice.

In the spirit of the liberating Christ, the Jubilee Plowshares join with other peacemakers across the country to declare the time of the Lord's favor for the poor. Our faith commands us to disarm and transform the swords of our time into plowshares. Today, August 7, 1995, we expose with our blood the genocidal nature of the nuclear-capable fast-attack submarine and the Trident-II D5 missile built at Newport News Shipbuilding in Virginia and Lockheed-Martin Corporation in Sunnyvale, California, respectively. With hammers we symbolically transform these instruments of death into life-giving technology.

We begin this by enacting the words of the prophet Isaiah:

"They shall beat their swords into plowshares,
and their spears into pruning hooks.
Nation shall not take up sword against nation,
nor shall they train for war anymore."

The period of August 6 through 9 marks the 50th anniversary of nuclear destruction of Hiroshima and Nagasaki, Japan. These horrendous acts robbed us of any legitimate claim to morality. Since August 1945 the entire world, led by the United States, has been held hostage by nuclearism and the exponential rise of military violence. This violence permeates every level of society.

With blind insanity we have amassed enough weaponry to eliminate all life on the planet many times over. In the past 50 years, over $13 trillion U.S. dollars have been wasted on weapons research, development, and deployment. Meanwhile, more than 50,000 children world-wide die every year from hunger-related causes.

Disarmament is the necessary first step to Christ's Jubilee. We refuse to see violence as inevitable, injustice as the order of the day, and death-dealing as the only way of life.

Join us in this declaration for disarmament to announce the Jubilee for the poor, relief for the children, and peace for all.

Editor's Note: On August 7, 1995, The Jubilee Plowshares consisting of four peace activists from the east coast (Michele Naar-Obed, Erin Sieber, Rick Sieber and Amy Moose) and two from the west (Susan Crane and Steve Kelly) carried out the biblical prophecy of Isaiah by beating swords into plowshares at Newport News Shipyard, Virginia, and at Lockheed-Martin Corporation, California. See "Plowshares Chronology" for more information about these actions.

CONFRONTING THE COURTS

DISARMAMENT ON TRIAL

ELMER MAAS

When we are brought to trial for Plowshares and disarmament actions, we try to speak about what we have done and why, focusing attention upon the urgent need for people to take personal responsibility for the disarmament of nuclear weapons, the swords of our time. Yet we are indicted by the court with criminal charges including trespass, destruction to property, and damage to the national defense. How do we answer these charges and, at the same time, speak clearly about the real issues?

The courts have consistently disallowed explanations of motive and purpose during trial and have closed their doors to nearly all efforts to raise defenses that would address matters most relevant to the Plowshares actions.[1] Relying on legal precedents or citing the lack of any legal precedent at all, judges have restricted testimony to facts that would substantiate criminal charges, and they have threatened defendants with contempt of court and immediate imprisonment for speaking about nuclear weapons, the peril that the weapons pose, and other facts that might communicate to juries the true motive for and purpose of the actions.

Despite this repressive atmosphere, those on trial try to say as much as they can: In taking the witness stand they speak very simply of their own lives and of what has brought them to a decision to enact the biblical imperative of the Old Testament prophet Isaiah, "to beat swords into plowshares." Beginning a step-by-step narrative of the action itself, they tell of entering factories where nuclear weapons are made, silo launching pads where the Minuteman II missiles are housed, Air Force bases where cruise missiles are being retrofitted into B-52 bombers, and shipbuilding factories where Trident submarines are docked. They speak of how they carried hammers and their own blood to these places and describe beating upon the weapons and pouring their own blood to symbolically and directly disarm components of the first-strike nuclear arsenal.

The defendants explain that they have acted to save and protect human life, that in this time of nuclear peril the saving and protecting of life has two distinct parts: the sounding of a warning and the direct destruction of the instruments of violence that threaten all lives on earth. As in the story of the shepherd in the book of Ezekiel, those who have knowledge of a danger or threat to the lives of others are culpable if they do not make that danger known; the blood of the victims is on the hands of those who fail to sound the alarm.

The destruction of the weapons, in turn, becomes a direct fulfillment and personal enactment of the biblical imperative: "They shall beat their swords into plowshares and their spears into pruning hooks; nation shall not lift up sword against nation, neither shall they study war any more." (Is. 2:4) The particular swords of our time addressed in the Plowshares actions are the components of the first-strike nuclear arsenal. Far from serving as a deterrent to war, this war-initiating system makes every moment of our lives a potential flashpoint of nuclear incineration.

The victimization brought about by the bomb is all-pervasive, therefore the "beating of swords into plowshares" considers as well the growing number of present victims of cancer, leukemia, and other diseases, whose sufferings have been traced to nuclear radiation caused by weapons testing, nuclear reactors, and various parts of the cycle of uranium mining and processing. The total number of deaths to date caused by nuclear testing alone has been estimated at 16 million.

Also among the nuclear victims are the poor. As human services are reduced, as increasing numbers of people throughout the world live in conditions of poverty and repression, and as an increasing portion of the human family endures hunger and starvation, the Pentagon has asked for and budgeted two trillion dollars for a five-year nuclear build-up, including the Strategic Defense Initiative and a functional capability for winning a protracted nuclear war.

Juries, of course, rarely hear very much, if anything at all, about nuclear weapons during the personal testimony of defendants. Any mention of the weapons or the first-strike system usually brings immediate objections from the prosecution that are sustained by the judge. The judge often explains that "nuclear weapons are not on trial" and that the "courtroom is not a forum for political debate." The judge then tells the jury to disregard anything that might be interpreted as motive or purpose. Judges have even gone so far as to instruct the jury shortly before time of deliberation that any consideration on their part of motive or purpose would be in violation of their sworn oath as jurors. There is no hint made by the court of the jury's power as the conscience of the community to render an independent verdict based upon its own assessment of the merits of the case.

Yet speaking the truth about the weapons is an important part of the act of "beating swords into plowshares." It is an important part of the action statement and of one's statement at trial. So that some of the facts and issues regarding details of the nuclear peril can be placed before the court and so that jurors might be able to deliberate on matters more closely attuned to the real facts and circumstances of the case than otherwise made available to them, defendants often prepare and present what are called affirmative legal defenses.

A defense of necessity or justification, for example, is available when one performs an action that under ordinary circumstances would be illegal, but under special emergency conditions is justified. (An example would be breaking into a burning building to save a child.) For the defense of necessity to be raised one must usually show that the danger is imminent, that there are no legal alternatives available, and that a causal relation exists between the action one undertakes and the abatement of the harm one seeks to avoid.

Through their own testimony and through the testimony of invited witnesses with expertise in nuclear weapons, nuclear physics, medicine, history, and other fields, evidence has been presented in a number of Plowshares trials exposing the immediate and omnipresent danger of nuclear war and its potential catastrophic consequences. Testimony has been offered explaining why legal alternatives to the course of action undertaken by the defendants are not available. Recognized historians have testified that acts of conscience such as those undertaken by the defendants are necessary to abate the threat of nuclear war.

While some judges preclude the availability of the justification defense before the defense case begins and others hear testimony with the jury excluded from the courtroom, much testimony regarding the nature of the first-strike weapons systems and the immediate peril of nuclear war has been presented before some juries. However, most judges in Plowshares and disarmament trials have instructed jurors that they may not consider justification or other affirmative defenses in their deliberations.[2] Judges have taken it upon themselves to decide that insufficient evidence is presented to enable the jury to make up its own mind with regard to necessity. One judge in particular ruled that he could not conceive of any evidence that the defendants might present through expert witnesses that would meet the burden of the justification defense.[3] In light of such comments, at least one appellate panel has ruled that the matter of justification should be a jury question.[4] This ruling, however, was appealed by the prosecution and overturned in a recent State Supreme Court decision.

In addition to raising the defense of necessity, defendants often point out that under principles established by the Nuremberg tribunal following World War II, individual citizens are responsible for crimes of war undertaken in their name by their governments and that citizens not only have a right but an obligation to interfere with and stop these crimes. With special reference to National Security Decision Document #13 of the Reagan administration authorizing a five-year plan to adapt the U.S. strategic nuclear arsenal to a capability for fighting and winning a protracted nuclear war, defendants have presented briefs based on the Nuremberg principles and other principles of international law. They have attempted to raise defenses that would enumerate before the court and jury the defendants' rights and obligations in the face of these and other developments in U.S. nuclear planning, including the Strategic Defense Initiative. Defendants have been denied the opportunity to even raise this defense or present witnesses.

Defendants at trial have attempted to raise closely related issues by addressing the matter of criminal intent. Recognizing that the prosecution must prove criminal intent, defendants have often argued that evidence should be presented showing that their actions were not based on criminal intentions, that indeed they acted to save life in the face of preparations for nuclear war, such preparations themselves being crimes of unprecedented magnitude. But, once again, the courts have denied such efforts, ruling that criminal intent be narrowly defined and reducible to only whether or not the defendants intended to enter the missile factory in question and hammer on the weapons, knowing that they would be in violation of specific state or national laws.

Some Plowshares defendants, in reflecting upon the court's systematic denial of efforts to speak about nuclear weapons and to raise affirmative defenses that would attempt to keep the focus on the real issues, have seen this pattern of denials as symptomatic of a larger denial within our society.

It is specifically the denial of one's personal responsibility for questioning what has become the absolute authority of the bomb, of nuclear weapons. They see the unquestioned authority of the weapons as part of what is clearly a growing state religion, a state religion of nuclearism. The weapons have become gods of metal, and the state acts to punish those who would disarm or damage these idols with charges of trespass, damage to property, or damage to the national defense. A number of Plowshares groups have raised this issue in a pretrial brief elaborating upon the unconstitutionally established state religion of nuclearism. They have moved for dismissal of all charges inasmuch as the laws, as applied in these cases, are used to protect this unconstitutional state religion. These motions have been denied.

Consistent with the pattern of denials that have suppressed defendants' efforts to speak to the real issues during trial, the judges' instructions to juries have limited jurors to considering only evidence that would substantiate specific charges of trespass, damage to property, and so on. Defendants try nevertheless to remind jurors that as the conscience of the community they have the power to act on their conscience, even independently of the instructions of the judge. After all, they need be answerable to no one for their verdict. Such suggestions to juries by defendants, however, elicit sharp reprimands to defendants by the judge, who often threatens defendants with contempt of court when they continue to inform the jury of its power.

On occasion, defendants do continue to speak, not only to inform the jury of what it is in fact able to do, but also as a nonviolent protest of the court's consistent effort to suppress the truth.

At other times as well, defendants nonviolently witness to the illegality of court proceedings by continuing to speak truths that should be heard, and these defendants have been immediately jailed for contempt of court. (Some defendants have also received contempt of court charges and additional jail sentences for not answering questions put by the prosecution that might implicate others.) Other defendants have chosen not to participate in the proceedings at all and, with the exception of a short statement before the jury or at time of sentencing, allow their silence and noncooperation to witness to the absence of legitimacy within the court process. Others, having attempted to testify and raise what issues they can, choose a point when the court has definitively refused to deal with the real issues and stand quietly with their backs to the court as a public witness to the absence of truth and justice in the halls of justice. Some have left the court during trial or on the day of sentencing to return to the location where their action originally occurred, to say that "here" is where and how the truth can be spoken.

In each of the Plowshares and disarmament trials to date, juries have returned verdicts of guilty and prison sentences have become increasingly harsh. But the community of disarmament continues to expand in the spirit of Isaiah and Micah as the enactment of their ancient prophecies becomes a source of light and hope for our times.

NOTES

1. The generalities and observations in this chapter are based on experiences of Plowshares defendants on trial. In each case groups or individuals have been brought to trial for beating swords into plowshares and for symbolically destroying weapons. In each case charges of damage to property have been brought against the defendants. While there are similar patterns in court rulings on admissible evidence for jury consideration in Plowshares trials and trials for nonviolent resistance that have not involved property damage, the patterns have not been identical.

2. The exception in this case is the judge in the trial of the Sperry Software Pair, Judge Miles Lord. Even though the jury returned a guilty verdict, Judge Lord, in his instructions to the jury, outlined the elements of the justification defense and granted its availability to the jury in their deliberations. (See p. 125 for excerpts of Judge Lord's instructions to the jury and comments at time of sentencing.)

3. In the 1981 trial of the Plowshares Eight in Norristown, Pennsylvania, Judge Samuel Salus precluded the testimony of Robert Aldridge and other experts on nuclear weapons on the grounds that none of the evidence these witnesses might offer would be relevant to a justification defense. A short excerpt from the trial transcripts might be helpful:

> **The Court (Judge Salus):** I will allow to be put on the record the name of the witness that you called, Mr. Aldridge. And I said his testimony is not relevant to the issues at hand.
>
> **Mr. Schuchardt:** You don't know what his testimony is.
>
> **Mr. Philip Berrigan:** I thought the jury was to decide the facts.
>
> **The Court:** The jury does decide the facts. I decide the law and relevance. And that is a matter of law.

(Transcript of Notes of Testimony, Comm. of Pennsylvania vs. Daniel Berrigan et al., March 4 1981, 132.)

Similar rulings preventing jurors from hearing any expert testimony at all on nuclear weapons have been made during Plowshares trials in Connecticut, Florida, and Rhode Island.

4. When the Plowshares Eight conviction was appealed and overturned by an appeal panel, Judge Spaeth, in writing a concurring opinion, observed:

Nor is the [nuclear] peril confined to those who will be "irradiated, burned, blasted." It extends much farther, to our survival as a species. If only a small fraction of the nuclear missiles now able to be fired, either by us or the Soviet Union, are fired, a "dark nuclear winter" will occur: a cloud of debris will block off our sunlight; temperatures will plunge; and our death by freezing or starvation will follow. Scientists have identified a 100 megaton explosion as the "nuclear threshold" that once crossed will lead to such a global catastrophe. See "After Atomic War: Doom in the Dark," Philadelphia Inquirer, November 1, 1993,

It is in the light of this peril that the reasonableness of appellants' belief is judged.

Perhaps a jury will discount evidence that our situation is as desperate as authorities I have alluded to believe. Or perhaps a jury will regard appellants conduct as mere bravado. On either of these views, appellants' plea of justification will fail. But we must leave such appraisals to a jury. For we are not entitled hold, "as a matter of law," as the dissent would, that a jury could not find that our situation is as desperate as appellants offered to prove, and then, proceeding that finding, could not go on to decide that appellants' conduct, however unlikely of success, represented a reasonable response. I admit that for my part — and here at least I suppose that the dissenters and I are not far apart — I am skeptical of the appellants' conduct. I believe there are better ways, the bishops' among them. But that is what trial by jury is all about: to ensure that the defendant is not judged by a skeptical judge but by his peers.

(Comm. of Pa. v. Rev. Daniel Berrigan et al., Appeal from the Judgment of Sentence in the court of Common Pleas of Montgomery County, Criminal, No. 2647-80, Concurring opinion by Judge Spaeth, February 17, 1984.)

This appellate panel ruling was overturned by the Pennsylvania Supreme Court in the Fall of 1985.

ON OBEDIENCE TO GOD AND GOD'S LAW:
AN EXCERPT FROM THE GRIFFISS PLOWSHARES TRIAL BRIEF

Editors' Note: *This brief was proffered at the trial of the Griffiss Plowshares who, on Thanksgiving Day, 1983, entered Griffiss Air Force Base in Rome, New York, and hammered and poured blood on a B-52 bomber converted to carry cruise missiles.*

We state with clear conscience that our action at Griffiss Air Force Base was an act of obedience to the law of God, indeed an act of religion and worship of God. It is our conviction, which we will seek to prove, that such action is protected by the First Amendment to the U.S. Constitution, which states the "Congress shall make no law respecting an establishment of religion, or prohibiting the free exercise thereof . . ."

We went to Griffiss Air Force Base and we come into this court because we are Judeo-Christians (biblical people) seeking in our lives to be faithful to God's law. Our responsibilities/duties as biblical people have been the subject of careful study and reflection among us. In the course of this study and reflection, we find our religious faith and practice (which should be protected by the Constitution) in conflict with the conduct of our government, especially as regards its sanctions of nuclear war preparations, and the monies, the resources, the trust it puts in them. In short, we are compelled by this government into a stance of false worship of its weapons unless we act against them as we have sought to do.

Three articles from the Decalogue, the Law of God, are especially germane in this regard, as is the mandate from Micah. We wish to cite them and demonstrate how our lives in nuclear America are twisted into disregard of these laws and of the God of the Bible.

A.

"I am the Lord your God who brought you out of the land of Egypt, out of the land of slavery. You shall have no other gods to set against me."

(Dt. 5:6-7, *NEB*)

"You shall demolish their [reference to 'pagan peoples' inhabiting the lands of Canaan] alters, smash their sacred pillars and cut down their sacred poles. You shall not prostrate yourselves to any other god. . . ."

(Ex. 34:13-14, *NEB*)

B.

"You shall not make carved image[s] for yourself . . . you shall not bow down to worship them." (Dt. 5:8-9, *NEB*)

"You shall not make yourself gods of cast metal." (Ex. 34:17, *NEB*)

C.

"You shall not commit murder." (Dt. 5:17, *NEB*)

D.

"They shall beat their swords into plowshares and their spears into pruning hooks; nation shall not lift sword against nation nor ever again be trained for war." (Mi. 4:3, *NEB*)

A. *"You Shall Have No Other Gods to Set Against Me."*

While the Constitution claims that "Congress shall make no law respecting an establishment of religion, or prohibiting the free exercise thereof. . . ." (Amendment i), a religion has been established in and by this country that violates the conscience of its citizens.

The cult of national sovereignty is the major religion. This cult, as we will show, has all the dimensions of a religion, and worship of the imperial god is required of all. The nation-state/empire has become our god. For when one analyzes the implications of sovereignty (as in national sovereignty), it means divinity and nothing less.

We do not quarrel with patriotism, with love for one's own country. We do not quarrel with the need to respect — and require respect for — one's real needs as a country. Our difficulties are rooted in the reality that, in these days, we are citizens of a country with imperial claims, policies, and weapons. And the more imperial a nation seeks to become, the more it threatens religious freedom, because in its lust to be number one, it does not stop at usurping the authority, even, of God.

It may be truthfully argued that the United States does not make overt claims that our nation or its leaders are gods. (Such would be too unsophisticated.) Still, our country and its leadership (as well as other "imperialist" countries and their leaderships — the Soviet Union, China, etc.) see themselves as the "engine of history." McGeorge Bundy called the United States "the locomotive at the head of mankind [sic] pulling the caboose of humanity along behind." Any engine-of-history outlook requires the displacement of the one who is the Lord of History.

People are lured into this absolutizing of the state. We live in a situation analogous to the ancient attempt to have God and "other gods." And the people today seek to give God and the nation-state each its just due. But the "just due" required by the nation-state is full allegiance and support of its military purpose. Such is not possible. The God of the Bible describes himself as a jealous God. He will not take his place alongside family, country, occupation. Nor is the nation-state content to exist alongside God or "other gods." It demands preeminence and so propels us into conflict. We live in a situation where we must exercise our consciences and choose the sovereignty of God *or* the sovereignty of nation.

B. *"You Shall Not Make Carved Images for Yourself or Worship Gods of Metal."*

The gods of the nations are idols of silver and gold
    made by the hands of men.
They have mouths that cannot speak
    and eyes that cannot see.
They have ears that do not hear
    and there is no breath in their nostrils.
Their makers grow like them
    and so do all that trust in them.

(Ps. 135:15-17, *NEB*)

We assert that the nation-state as "god" has created idols that all its citizens, in the name of loyalty and patriotism, are required to worship and to trust in. This is a violation of our freedom of religion and worship.

In July 1945 at the "Trinity" (so-called) test at Alamogordo, J. Robert

Oppenheimer was amazed and confounded by the bomb's demonstration of "godlike" power. At the dawn of the atomic age physicists assumed a mythic (religious) standing in the public imagination. It was thought that they had achieved the godlike knowledge of the primal serpent's promise. In turn, the weapons were named for gods: Poseidon, Titan, Trident — "Devil Gods!"

That these weapons are the object of worship is demonstrated by the awe with which they are regarded. Enter the Air and Space Museum in Washington, D.C., to see this enfleshed, or attend one of the many air shows or arms bazaars at military installations and hotels across the country and experience the "worship" offered this technology.

Then, we are required to trust in the security these weapons offer us and our way of life — not to trust in God as the Bible requires. (This is verified in the daily pronouncements of our president, our military, arms manufacturers, and media people). And they demand more and more of the resources of our country and its people at the expense of the real needs — the needs of justice, of men and women and children at home and abroad. (Forty-two thousand children die daily from hunger-related causes while we spend billions yearly on arms.)

The Psalm quoted above warns: "Their makers shall grow like them and so do all who trust in them." We assert that these weapons were created out of a spirit of insensitivity to the humanity of their victims. The weapons themselves — the bombs, missiles, and their carriers — have no feeling, no conscience, no imaginative sensitivity toward those against whom they are targeted. So, in imitation of our "gods," the nation (and other nuclear powers as well) has given way under an enveloping insensitivity, hardness, emptiness. There is in the nation and its weapons a gravitational field that draws people to itself and absorbs them into that senselessness whose ultimate fulfillment would be nuclear obliteration.

Part of the meaning of war, we are convinced, lies in its being the chief ritual of our national religion. In war, we find all the elements common to religious worship:

The scene of war is the altar. Radio and TV (modern technology in general) enable millions to worship at the altar. Technology enables the state to become totalitarian, to absorb completely the lives of citizens. (Note the attention the news media gives to any so-called national emergency: the Korean jetliner, the invasion of Grenada, etc.

The original meaning of "victim" was one sacrificed to a deity. Victims still fall within that little remembered etymological meaning. Even, in this regard, with the term "holocaust" or "whole burnt offering," we look eye to eye at human sacrifice on a scale one cannot begin to imagine.

And war has its priests and high priests, its fire, smoke, ash, its blood, and song.

When we think of it, nuclear holocaust becomes a terrible parody of Pentecost with its mighty wind, its tongues of fire, although in the instance of war, they reach from earth to heaven rather than heaven to earth.

Then, we reflect, a liturgy of worship is often envisioned and enacted in order to help heal the wounds of division within a community of worship. Again we see the parody repeated in this country (and, we must assume, in other countries) where wars have been used to conceal, evade, and cover up the wounds, divisions, injustices within the nation — to create a false unity. Wars have more often than not been used to rescue presidents from declining domestic support.

The worship required by the God of the Bible who compels our lives is not only different, but is also opposed to the worship the nation-state requires of its citizens. For example, hear these words of our God about the offering he requires (Is. 58:7-11, *NEB*):

> Is it not sharing your food with the hungry, taking the homeless poor into your house, clothing the naked when you meet them and never evading a duty to your kinsfolk? Then shall your light break forth like the dawn and soon you will grow healthy like a wound newly healed; your own righteousness shall be your vanguard and the glory of the Lord your rearguard.
>
> Then, if you call, the Lord will answer; If you cry to him, he will say, "Here I am." If you cease to pervert justice to point the accusing finger and lay false charges, if you feed the hungry from your own plenty and satisfy the needs of the wretched then your light will rise like dawn out of darkness and your dusk will be like noonday; the Lord will be your guide continually and will satisfy your needs in the shimmering heat.

Clearly, we are told, to know God, to worship God requires that we practice justice to one another and especially to those most needy. Clearly, we are told, while there is injustice among people, their worship and prayer cannot have God as their object. So Jesus says in Matthew 5:23-24 (*NEB*): "If, when you are bringing your gift to the altar, you remember that your brother has a grievance against you, leave your gift where it is and first go and make peace with your brother. Only then come back and offer your gift."

The injustice upon which nuclear weapons are based, the weapons we are asked by our nation-state to worship, are suggested by former president Dwight David Eisenhower: "Every weapon that is made, every warship that is launched is a theft from those who hunger."

C. *"Thou Shalt Not Kill."*

God enjoins us against killing other human beings. Genesis 9:5-6 established this even before the covenant was made with Moses:

"I will require satisfaction for the death of a fellow-man . . . for in the image of God has God made man." Human beings are the one image of God the Bible allows. Human beings, all created in the image of God, must not destroy the image of God incarnate in another. Nor does God allow us (i.e., human beings) to avenge murder; it is God who requires satisfaction for murder. "Your brother's blood . . . is crying out to me from the ground." (Gn. 4:10, *NEB*)

"So the Lord put a mark on Cain in order that anyone meeting him should not kill him." (Gen. 4:15, *NEB*)

The command against killing includes the preparation for killing. Even the law makes the intent to commit a crime equivalent to the crime itself. We find the killing of human beings in war and preparations for war to be against God's command, and so we are commanded to resist war preparations to be obedient to God. We believe that war is the key issue for coming to grips with who we are before God.

Why the killing, why the mass disregard of the sacredness of human life created in the image of God? To the degree that each of us tends to proceed as if we were the center of the universe (individually or collectively, i.e., as a nation-state), we find that whatever is not in our immediate experience (the dimensions of the suffering of other human beings, for example) remains abstract or remote. A biblical word for this absorption in self is blindness, which is closely related to murder and which brings on the furies of war.

With the cruise missile and other weapons of our first-strike arsenal, we face mega-kill — a ghastliness of intent for murder hundreds of million fold. An intimation of hell is found in the lack of feeling, the petrification with which this murder is viewed by our leadership, the military, and the general public. In truth, in the nuclear arms buildup what has happened is that the general public has granted to our government the authority to enter into immense sacrificial destruction of our right to life, liberty, and the pursuit of happiness.

We believe that this idolatry of patriotism must be unveiled not when it leads to open warfare, but when that possibility has been accepted by the government itself (that is, now, when first-strike capability is lauded, planned for; when the policies to justify it are promulgated; when we develop and deploy first-strike weapons in Europe as well as here at home) because it is not so much the killing that is the deepest sin of militarism.

In all of this, we have, as Paul warns in Romans 1:25, "given up the truth of God for a lie."

D. *"Beat Swords into Plowshares. . ."*

The context in Micah in which this command is addressed to us is the context of a courtroom in which God stands as a witness against us: "Listen you peoples . . . That the Lord your God . . . may bear witness against you . . . ." (Mi. 1:2, *NEB*) Above all, this is the court and judgment that we fear. The crimes for which God testifies against us are as follows:

"They covet land and take it by force; if they want a house, they seize it; they rob a man of his home and steal every man's inheritance." (Mi. 2:2, *NEB*)

"But you are no people for me, rising up as my enemy to my face, to strip the cloak from one that was safe and take away the confidence of returning warriors, to drive the women of my people from their pleasant homes and rob the children of my glory forever . . . you that . . . would commit any mischief, mischief however cruel." (Mi. 2:8-10, *NEB*)

"Listen you leaders of Jacob, rulers of Israel, should you not know what is right? You hate good and love evil, you flay men alive . . . you devour the flesh of my people." (Mi. 32:1-2, *NEB*)

"Listen to this, leaders of Jacob . . . you who make justice hateful and wrest it from its straight course, building Zion in bloodshed and Jerusalem in iniquity. Her rulers sell justice, her priests give direction in return for a bribe, her prophets take money for their divination." (Mi. 3:9-11, *NEB*)

The words "Listen" and "Hear" are addressed to us. A deeper listening is incumbent upon us; we are compelled to listen, and this listening has its roots in obedience. We cannot listen and conclude that these crimes were the crimes of Israel, crimes in which we have no part. We, in this nation and culture, must recognize that our megatons are in existence because we "covet land," "rise up as enemy of God . . . and drive women from their homes . . . rob children of God's glory," and "make justice hateful . . . build our cities in bloodshed and iniquity."

God calls us out of this infidelity and back into obedience. His judgment has as its aim not punishment but redemption. The injunction follows — it is the path to restoration: "They shall beat swords into plowshares and their spears into pruning hooks; nation shall not lift sword against nation nor ever again be trained for war." It is clear. Justice and peace will be available, but not until there is disarmament. "On that day, says the Lord, I will gather all who are lost." (Mi. 4:6, *NEB*) In short, then will come the restoration, the passover into a new sense of justice.

In our act at Griffiss, we were seeking to listen to and receive God's judgment, to act in obedience to God's will and (we believe) the deep longing in the human heart for justice. We know that that is impossible as long as these weapons exist — between us as people as well as over the heads/lives of all people.

Our action at Griffiss Air Force Base was a simple act of obedience, of religion, and of worship.

NOT GUILTY

Shelley Douglass

On June 21, 1985, we listened to the court clerk say "not guilty" 19 times. Something special had happened in Kitsap County, Washington — for the first time in a jury trial related to the Trident submarine base at Bangor, a jury had brought back a "not guilty" verdict.

The verdict represented years of waiting and communicating, years of involvement in the Trident campaign. People had resisted the building of the Trident base, the arrival of the first Trident submarine, the transportation of missile motors for the Trident missiles. Since 1983 there had been many people on the tracks in front of the White (Nuclear) Train as it carried hydrogen bombs into the base to be loaded onto Trident submarines.

There had been other trials before this one, trials that prepared the way for this verdict of "not guilty." Ted Dzielak, Lynn Greiner, and John Midgley, members of the National Lawyers Guild, had for several years worked faithfully with Ground Zero, and later with the Agape Community, trying to bring the truth about the arms race into the courtroom. They had tried to create an opening for international law to gain a hearing and for the jury to render a verdict based on the fullness of the law.

Seeds grow unnoticed, silently. The seeds planted through the years since the Trident campaign first began and the faith of the people who planted them bore fruit on June 21, 1985, when a jury in Kitsap County found 19 people who had sat or knelt in front of a train carrying hydrogen bombs to the Trident submarine base at Bangor on February 22, 1985, not guilty of a crime.

The defendants had been charged not only with trespass but also with conspiracy to commit trespass. Four other people who were not on the tracks in front of the train were charged with conspiracy to commit trespass for the part they played in preparations for meeting the train. These people had represented the Puget Sound Agape Community in meetings with Pat Jones and Chuck Wheeler from the Kitsap County Sheriff's Department and Tom Lawson and Don Roetering from Burlington Northern Railroad.

The defendants believed the conspiracy charge was an infringement of their First Amendment rights and an attempt at intimidation. In a pretrial hearing Judge W. Daniel Phillips ruled that the conspiracy charges should be dismissed since the meetings held with the authorities were not conspiratorial but for peaceful purposes and since the state's case had no substantial grounds for conspiracy.

When the trial began on June 18, Judge Phillips ruled that a defense based on necessity and international law would not be permitted. However, since the charge of criminal trespass contains within the statute the words "knowingly enters or remains unlawfully," the defendants were able to testify as to what they knew, what they did knowingly. In other words, they testified as to their state of mind.

Because many of the defendants were knowledgeable about the Trident submarine and weapons system, the U.S. policy regarding nuclear weapons, the route of the train, the function of the Pantex plant in relation to nuclear weapons in this country, and many other facts, they were able to communicate a great deal of information to the jury. They were also able to convince the jury that they were not guilty of any crime. They sat or knelt on the tracks because they could not do otherwise; they were there to uphold moral and international law.

Some expert witnesses were able to testify to corroborate a particular defendant's state of mind: Mary Fujita, who is a victim of the atomic bombing at Hiroshima; Daniel Ellsberg, who spent years planning American strategies for nuclear war; Sam Keen, who has studied the psychology of enemy making and seen its effects on our spirits; and Mona Seehale, who left her job at the Strategic Weapons Facility Pacific at Bangor and testified that she did so because of the witness of people like the defendants, people who acted on their consciences and challenged her to do the same. Robert McAfee Brown, a theologian who would have addressed moral law, and Richard Falk, Professor of International Law at Princeton University, were not permitted to testify.

During the months of preparation for trial, the 19 defendants and the lawyers who worked with them became a community. The trial lawyers,

Kate Pflaumer, Bill Bender, Mike Fox, and Russ Hauge, exhibited a flexibility, creativity, and expertise that was reflective of the larger "behind the scenes" legal team as well. During the trial it was clear that defendants and lawyers were speaking as one and that they deeply shared two things in common: a love and reverence for life and a profound need to defend it by nonviolent means.

After all the testimony was heard, the jury deliberated for 2 1/2 hours, returning a verdict of "not guilty" for each of the defendants. Sallie Shawl, one of those acquitted, wrote later, "In February the train was stopped by love manifested in the relationship between the Puget Sound Agape Community, Burlington Northern security personnel, and the Kitsap County Sheriff's Department; in June the train was stopped by the truth as heard and then spoken by a jury in Kitsap County."

UNITED STATES V. LAFORGE AND KATT

Editors' Note: *On August 10, 1984, John LaForge and Barbara Katt gained entry to the Sperry Defense Systems Division plant near St. Paul, Minnesota and, with hammers, damaged a Trident submarine guidance system. They were arrested and ultimately convicted of destroying government property. Maximum sentence for the $36,000 damage was 10 years in prison and a $5,000 fine. The judge sentenced each defendant to six months in jail and then suspended that sentence on condition of six months probation.*

Excerpts from Jury Instructions and Sentencing Statement of U.S. Judge Miles Lord

At trial, defendants were allowed a necessity defense and the court instructed the jury as follows:

During their case in chief, the defendants have been allowed to attempt assert a defense in this case which has been variously referred to as the defense of necessity or justification. The defense of necessity or justification requires evidence of each and every one of the following essential elements:

1) That the criminal conduct of which the defendants stand accused was taken to prevent a greater harm to themselves or others, which was imminent to occur;

2) That there was no effective legal alternative method or course of action available to them that could be taken to avert this so-called harm, and;

3) That there was a direct causal relationship between the criminal conduct

taken and the avoidance of the alleged harm. It is not necessary that the steps be completely effective in order to use this defense; in other words, it wouldn't be necessary that they destroyed all nuclear weapons, but that they had an effect upon them.[1]

Defendants were found guilty by the jury. At sentencing Judge Miles Lord made a lengthy statement, excerpts from which follow: It is the allegation of these young people that they committed the acts here complained of as a desperate plea to the American people and its government to stop the military madness which they sincerely believe will destroy us all, friend and enemy alike. ... Can it be that those of us who build weapons to kill are engaged in a more sanctified endeavor than those who would counsel moderation and mediation as an alternative method of settling disputes?

Why are we so fascinated by a power so great that we cannot comprehend its magnitude? What is so sacred about a bomb, so romantic about a missile? Why do we condemn and hang individual killers, while extolling the virtue of warmongers? What is the fatal fascination which attracts us to the thought of mass destruction of our brethren in another country? ... Have we given thought that, in executing that decree, we will also die? ... Have we so little faith in our system of free enterprise, our capitalism, and the fundamental concepts that are taught us in our constitutions and in our several bibles that we must, in order to protect ourselves from the spread of foreign ideologies, be prepared to die at our own hands? ... I would here in this instance, attempt in some way to force the government ... to remove the halo — which it seems to hold over any device which can kill — and, instead, to place thereon a shroud, the shroud of death, destruction, mutilation, disease, and debilitation.[2]

NOTES

1. No CR 4-84-66, U.S. District Court, Minnesota, partial Transcript of Proceedings, Portion of the Court's Final Jury Instructions, November 8, 1984.

2. Id. Transcript of Sentencing, November 8, 1984. (Source: Robert Aldridge and Virginia Stark, "Nuclear War, Citizen Intervention and the Necessity Defense," Santa Clara Law Review 26, no. 2 [Spring 1986], pp. 322,323.)

THE NECESSITY DEFENSE
A REPORT
Thomas Lumpkin

Civil disobedience acts of conscience have, in the measure of their truthfulness, an inherent power that in no way depends upon the various judgments made by judges and juries. Nevertheless, on a number of occasions in recent years nuclear resisters . . . have claimed a legal justification for their acts. Most often they have presented their cases as clear and obvious applications of what is known in U.S. civil law as the defense of necessity or duress. In response, some judges have simply refused the claim. In several instances, however, a defense of necessity was allowed in theory, but in fact a judge or jury imposed so narrow an interpretation on its meaning that it was inapplicable to the acts of resistance. In a very few cases the necessity defense has been the basis for sane and heartening judicial statements and decisions of acquittal. It is my pleasure to report one such instance of my own experience.

On December 28, 1984, a commemoration of the Holy Innocents feast was held at the headquarters of the Williams International Corporation in Walled Lake, Michigan. Williams is responsible for the small fanjet engines that are an essential component of modern U.S. cruise missiles. During the service Dan Lagrou was arrested for pouring his blood upon the company's fence and charged with malicious destruction. Marietta Jaeger and I were among four arrested and charged with trespassing. Upon our arraignment in District Court in Walled Lake, the three of us entered pleas of "not guilty." We were set for trial on March 22, 1985 before Judge Martin Boyle, one of the court's three judges. None of us requested lawyers, preferring to make our own defense.

Initially we had asked for a jury trial. By having a jury, Dan and Marietta hoped their testimonies would educate and convert (in the best sense of both words) seven more people to the realities of the cruise missile and their local corporation's involvement with it. I was inclined to make a legal case for our innocence using the necessity defense.

In the weeks preceding our trial, I realized that only one of the half dozen previous Williams civil disobedience cases had come before Judge Boyle, and it had been a jury trial. Judge Boyle remained the only one of the three district court judges who had not yet ruled himself on the actions at Williams on the basis of the necessity defense. I thought we should give him the opportunity. Dan and Marietta agreed and we collectively changed our request for a jury trial to a bench trial about a week before our scheduled court date.

My understanding of the necessity defense is that the defendants must show, first, there is a situation posing a serious and imminent danger to life and limb; second, they believe their act of breaking civil law is a necessary and effective remedy to that situation; and third, they were compelled, or under duress, to so act.

To substantiate the first requirement, we called upon two expert witnesses, a physicist at the University of Michigan and a political scientist at Wayne State University. Professor Daniel Axelrod from the University of Michigan testified on the nature of modem-day cruise missiles, the critical role of Williams International in their development, and the role of the cruise missile in U.S. nuclear strategy. Professor Maurice Waters from Wayne State testified on the particularly destabilizing impact of the cruise on arms control.

Our argument for the second requirement was a historical and sociological one, and we made it ourselves. (We had sought expert witnesses in these areas but none were available on our short notice.) We claimed no reasonable and effective remedy exists to the present and imminent danger posed by the cruise missile that does not include acts of civil disobedience. We argued that, historically, no significant social change in our nation's past had occurred without elements of civil disobedience (e.g., the right of workers to organize, of women and blacks to vote, the curtailment of the Vietnam draft). Sociologically, we argued that public opinion has an impact on U.S. public policy, and civil disobedience has been a sociologically significant component in determining public opinion.

To substantiate compulsion, each of us simply explained the motives that led us to civil disobedience. We spoke of moral rather than physical compulsion. We were not physically compelled to go to Williams (i.e., we acted in full and free command of our faculties) but, because of who we were and what we knew, we (to use Dan Berrigan's phrase) could not not do what we did.

At the trial's conclusion, Judge Boyle began by taking up Dan's charge of malicious destruction. He focused on the "malicious" requirement of the law and found himself convinced that no malicious intent existed:

> His testimony is clear and convincing that he did not act out of malice. He may have acted wrongfully. He certainly acted willfully but in the eyes the law he did not act maliciously. . . . We can't go beyond the language of the statute, and the court would have to find Mr. Lagrou not guilty for that reason.

Turning to the trespass charges against Marietta and myself, he said:

> Now with respect to the other two, answers are not so easy. Again, there's no question they trespassed. . . . The Prosecutor suggests that there's some inconsistency in their conduct as to suggest they did not act under duress and that their . . . testimony from the witness stand [does] not support that conclusion either. Well, of course, the defense of duress is not often used in this context. . . . But in the commentary of the standard jury instructions it's stated that there's a meagerness of case law on this subject . . . so just because it's never been applied to a circumstance such as this doesn't mean that it can't be.

Judge Boyle went on to respond to our arguments:

> Now the defenses listed in the jury instructions provide first that the threatening conduct must have been sufficient to create in the mind of a responsible person the fear of death or serious bodily harm . . . I don't think anybody would deny the risk of nuclear annihilation exists. It's been expressed by the President of the United States, and politicians talk about it more than they act upon it, and one has to be almost totally ignorant not to be aware of it. . . . It's not unreasonable to believe that Ms. Jaeger and Mr. Lumpkin have a reasonable fear of death. Now they didn't express that so much for themselves. They expressed it for the children . . . for society, but . . . the fear of death for society, it seems to me, would justify a defense of duress a whole lot quicker than the fear of death for an individual.
>
> And they must have committed the act to avoid the threatened harm. Perhaps that's the most difficult standard to establish in this circumstance because, as the prosecutor's questions suggest, how futile must their action be when one or two persons stand against the kind of power we're talking

about.... But these defendants are of a mind that political persuasion, while it may be helpful, is not going to be effective. They cite experiences in the history of this country, and we're all familiar with them, and they're not only of recent history. They run through the course of our history, and sometimes the defendants of yesterday are the heroes of today.... Can two people stop the nuclear arms race? Probably not, but they suggest that they do this in the hope that others will join them. There can't be any question that if enough people take their side, the nuclear arms race is going to end.... There are some who say that there is absolutely no prospect of the administration or the Congress ... bring[ing] this matter to a successful conclusion and that the track record proves it and that the only possibility, however remote, the only possibility of survival lies in protest. If people believe that, who can say they are wrong? These people in my opinion believe that, and I don't judge anyone else who goes out there and enters upon the property until I've heard them explain themselves.

By now it was clear Marietta and I were also going to be acquitted. Judge Boyle made a few more observations before concluding with his verdict:

And I don't propose to respond to the suggestion that such a defense cannot be accepted if we are to have any control in society. Do we have any control in society now when we have 50,000 nuclear arms?

How is Williams to operate if their property is not protected? Well ... if we have to surround our nuclear weapons plants with military personnel, that's the price we'll have to pay for nuclear arms. If we have to turn the military against the people, that's the price we'll have to pay ... if enough people feel like Ms. Jaeger and Mr. Lumpkin.

These people have acted in good faith. They've acted out of compulsion. ... While what they do presents a problem for the order of society, it does not constitute a criminal offense. I accept their defense and find each of them not guilty.

Needless to say, it was a great feeling to be acquitted (for once!). Yet it must be obvious that the necessity defense (and certainly "not guilty" verdicts) is incidental rather than essential to the work of civil resistance. Our trial appearances are just one part of a witness that begins with the act of civil disobedience itself and often extends to jail and/or prison time: with various kinds of support work carried on throughout. The necessity defense is simply one way to be considered within the entire spectrum of ways to witness in court.

THE NECESSITY DEFENSE ALLOWED:
DEFENDANTS FOUND NOT GUILTY BY JURY

On November 13, 1984, 22 people were arrested for blocking the entrance to the Great Lakes Naval Training Center in Wake Forest, Illinois. The purpose for the demonstration was two-fold: to protest U.S. naval activities in Central America and to protest the Navy's part in nuclear weapons proliferation, such as stationing nuclear submarines in the Caribbean and supplying artillery with nuclear capability to the Central American region.

All of the 22 were charged with mob action — a sort of misdemeanor conspiracy charge that involves knowingly assembling with one or more people to break the law. About half were charged with resisting arrest because they did not get up and walk when arrested. Sixteen of those arrested went to trial, but charges against eight were subsequently dropped and a ninth was dismissed. The seven remaining were allowed to present a defense based on the principle of necessity.

After a one-week trial defendants were found "not guilty" by the jury. In his charge to the jury, the judge instructed them to find the defendants guilty of either mob action or resisting arrest if the prosecution proved that they did not act out of necessity.

In addition, the judge gave the following instruction to the jury regarding international law:

"International law is binding on the United States and on the State of Illinois.

"The use or threat of use of nuclear weapons is a war crime or an attempted war crime because such use would violate international law by causing unnecessary suffering, failure to distinguish between combatants and noncombatants, and poisoning targets by radiation."[1]

NOTES
1. People v. Ann Jarka. Nos. 002196-2212, 002214, 002236-2238, Circuit Court of Lake City, IL, April 1985. (Source: Robert Aldridge and Virginia Stark, "Nuclear War, Citizen Intervention, and the Necessity Defense," Santa Clara Law Review 26, no. 2 [Spring 1986], pp. 324-325.)

ACTING ON BEHALF OF THE HOMELESS:
A LETTER TO THE COURT
Felton Davis

To the Court:

Enclosed is a copy of the court order which I received on February 20th, after being found guilty of Disorderly Conduct for attempting to block a bulldozer that was in the process of destroying the shacks of homeless people on East 3rd Street. I was ordered to pay a fine of $65 by March 14th. This is my response to the decision of the Court, and I ask that it be made part of the official transcript of the case.

For the past several years, we have seen a series of large-scale evictions of homeless people, from subway and train stations, from city parks, and also from empty lots and abandoned buildings. Massive contingents of police, fire and sanitation department workers descend on a site and push everyone out, destroying makeshift dwellings and erecting fences or installing barricades.

I think if anyone of us would look deeply into the eyes of the homeless people as they watched their shacks being leveled by a bulldozer, there would be no need for me to offer any verbal explanation. The wrongness of it would become an immediately felt quality, rather than something arrived at after a chain of inferences, a concrete perception and premise, not an abstract, intellectual conclusion. I draw the court's attention to this crucial distinction, because so often in court we become involved in lengthy arguments and forget that morality and the perception of morality is behind the law and prior to it.... Wrongness as an intellectual conclusion may remain in the mind of the beholder and not give birth to any action, but wrongness as a concrete perception demands a commensurate response.

In 1990, when the city started evicting homeless people out of Penn Station, my friends and I lay down on the floor of the station and got arrested.

In 1991, when the city closed down Tompkins Square Park, I tried to cut down the chain link fence with a boltcutter and got arrested.

In 1992, when the city bulldozed homeless people out of the empty lots on 8th Street and 9th Street, I sat down in front of the bulldozers and got arrested.

In 1993, when the city bulldozed homeless people out of the Manhattan Bridge encampment, I sat down in front of the bulldozer and got arrested.

And on December 15, 1993, as the city bulldozed homeless people out of an empty lot on East 3rd Street, I refused to leave the area and that resulted in the charge which led to the fine which we are considering this morning.

It must be noted that in terms of earthly outcome, all of these acts of protests were failures. We failed to stop the city from kicking people out of Penn Station. We failed to stop the closing and destruction of the old Tompkins Square Park. We failed to stop the city from arresting people who squeegee cars. We failed to stop the city from arresting people who panhandle. And we are failing to stop the destruction of shantytowns and encampments.

So people ask me, in light of this near constant record of failure, how is it that some of us are able to keep on protesting, to keep on accepting the inevitable arrests and convictions and the occasional periods of incarceration.

For myself the answer is simple: I am able to keep on because I believe that one day justice will triumph. One day all the people who have been pushed out, locked out, kicked out, bulldozed, swept up and locked up, will come forth and enter a place prepared for them since the beginning of creation. Not a single bit of injustice has gone unnoticed. Not a single poke of the nightstick has gone unrecorded. Not a single shove . . . not a single word . . . not a single close of a door.

Here in this courtroom, in large letters on the wall above the judge's bench it is inscribed, "IN GOD WE TRUST," to which I say, "Amen!" I trust in God, and I believe that, as it is so eloquently promised in the last pages of the Bible, God will "wipe away every tear" (Rv. 21:1-4) from the eyes of the victims. On that day, all the sources of discord and division that plague this world, will disappear. There will be no more rich against poor, no more white against black, no more straight against gay, no more men against women, no more young against old, no more country against another, and no more one culture against another. The "old order of things" will pass away, and those who are ready will step into the new order and see things undreamt of in this world.

What is a few days in jail next to this ultimate promise? How do the small sacrifices stand when viewed in the light of such a comprehensive vision? Where is the scale by which we can measure what we must do to prepare ourselves for participation in the new heaven and the new earth? Where must we place our mortal bodies, in front of what obstacles, in the path of what engines of death, so that when the whole nightmare of this world is over, we will rise with the new dawn and greet the new day with joy?

These are my questions, and I place them before the court in lieu of payment. These questions are all I have to offer today. Their elucidation is the extent of my compliance. I will not offer any money to this court, whether for fine, or court costs, or compensation. If anybody is to be compensated for what happened on December 15th, it should be the homeless people whose shacks were destroyed. . . .

Editors' Note: Excerpted from a longer "Letter to the Court" by Felton Davis.

Opening Statement of the Pax Christi – Spirit of Life Plowshares

U.S. District Court, Elizabeth City, N.C., February 15, 1994 —

Good morning jurists, friends and supporters, members of the press, court officials, Judge Boyle. It is my privilege this morning to present the statement of the Pax Christi – Spirit of Life Plowshares on behalf of Phil Berrigan, John Dear, Bruce Friedrich, and myself, Lynn Fredriksson.

On December 7, 1993 the four of us walked onto the Seymour Johnson Air Force Base in Goldsboro, N.C. to nonviolently disarm one F-15E Strike Eagle, a nuclear-capable fighter bomber which has already been used notably in the massacre of Iraqis during the Gulf War. We poured our own blood on one bomber to expose the bloody warmaking of the entire U.S. military; we hammered on that bomber to begin the process of disassembly and conversion. We acted in the Spirit of Life and the peace of Christ to fulfill the words of the prophet Isaiah: "They shall beat their swords into plowshares, and their spears into pruning hooks; nation shall not lift up sword against nation; neither shall they train for war anymore."

Each year, 40 million people starve to death while the people of the U.S., who make up 4.6 percent of the world's population, consume half of the world's resources. One F-15E costs $40 million just to build. And the United States devotes over $500 billion to warmaking — a sum that virtually bankrupts the economy.

We are not guilty of committing any crime. The real crimes have been committed by institutions, corporations and the U.S. government and its military and covert forces that develop, construct, stockpile, and deploy genocidal weapons. It is no coincidence that we acted on "Pearl Harbor Day." The nuclearism (and racist imperialism) of the U.S. government has surpassed even the murderous psychosis of Nazi fascism.

Lest you feel isolated from the truth of this reality, lest you feel safe from this madness as you sit in this courtroom, consider closely what is really taking place. The so-called criminal justice system, which includes this very court, offers legal sanction to the high crimes of government and its military, for example the "turkey shoot" in Iraq. The court indicts peace activists for a felony, while utterly ignoring those who make nuclear hostages of the whole world.

The criminal justice system and the nuclear strike force are two sides of the same coin, the coin which threatens our planet's survival. This court, like all others, protects the interests of the national security state and uses its illegitimate power to suppress the truth and to discourage further acts of resistance.

To be more specific, the four of us have been denied basic rights, supposedly guaranteed by the criminal justice system. We have been denied means to represent ourselves. We have been denied meetings with our attorney advisor. We have been denied meetings together to prepare a mutual defense. The date and location of the trial have been manipulated, making it more difficult for our families and friends to attend.

This court has made a fair trial impossible. From this point on, we will not participate in this travesty against justice. From this point on, we four will remain silent and will nonviolently noncooperate with these proceedings. We invite all of our friends here in the courtroom to join us if they wish in standing and turning our backs in witness against it.

Editors' Note: As Lynn began reading this statement, Judge Boyle ordered her to stop. When she continued, a U.S. Marshal grabbed the statement from her. Bruce, and then John, continued reading the opening statement, but U.S. Marshals grabbed each of their copies of the statement. The four then turned their backs to the court along with about 20 supporters and said the Lord's prayer and sang peace songs. Lynn, John and Bruce were found in contempt of court as well as seven supporters. One supporter was assaulted by U.S. Marshals and he, in turn, was charged with assault. That afternoon, the judge declared a mistrial stating the jury had been "contaminated."

PRISON WITNESS

LETTER FROM ROBESON COUNTY JAIL

Phil Berrigan

I recall an intense discussion 10 years ago. The question in the air went something like this: How do we remain faithful to the gospel in a climate of nuclear terrorism, military interventions and public confusion and indifference? Around the circle, people had their say. Finally, a woman, legendary for her 30 years of anti-war resistance, for numerous demonstrations and jailings, offered this: "We must risk jail without, of course, seeking it. Then we must ponder the value of being there. As far as I can understand, things are that simple."

Our friend was confirming Gandhi's observations that "the truth seeker should go to jail even as a bridegroom enters the bridal chamber; that social betterment never comes from parliaments or pulpits, but from direct action in the streets, from the courts, jails and sometimes even the gallows." Or Dorothy Day's statement that "if Christians seek a better life for the poor and relief from the tyranny of nuclear weapons, they must fill up the jails."

Dorothy's "filling up the jails" is her translation of the nonviolent revolution of the gospel. One accepts jail as a consequence of resistance; then the jailed one reaps a paradox benefit. As Tom Lewis puts it, "I have to be free enough to go to jail."

"Filling up the jails" also clarifies the struggle, as St. Paul reminds us, not against flesh and blood but against principalities and powers. The struggle is for possession of our own soul and the souls of others. It is a bill of divorcement drawn up against false gods. It offers deliverance to the poor, something quite other than feeding and housing them. It pits the realm of God against the murderous deceits of the technocratic state. Its character, finally, is a quest for liberation. Paul again: "It was for freedom that Christ has set us free."

Christians of every age are confronted by the question of Christ: "And you — who do you say that I am?" Much depends on our answer, much more than we are commonly prepared to admit. And whether our image of Christ is of the Suffering Servant, the Man of Sorrows or the one who refused the sword in favor of the cross, the same imperative follows on the answer, whatever form it takes: "Follow me."

The "following" becomes the fundamental problem. He leads, and we so often renege. We are slow to follow Jesus in living the gospel and building community; slow to follow, resisting, as he resisted, illegitimate power; slow to follow into jail as he was jailed. Slow and then a halt. Follow him in torture and death?

I write this from jail. On Dec. 7, 1993, four of us — Lynn Fredriksson, Jesuit Father John Dear, Bruce Friedrich and I — disarmed an F-15E fighter-bomber at Seymour Johnson Air Force Base in North Carolina. The F-15E was the winged workhorse of the Iraqi war. It brought death to thousands. More, it is, as the jargon has it, "nuclear-capable."

In consequence of our crime, the government refuses to set bail. According to the judge, we are a "danger to the community." So in all likelihood, we will remain in jail until trial — and undoubtedly afterward.

From the standpoint of most, jail is irksome, boring and absurd. But we have another view. Jail for us is a way of subverting a society that needs more and more jails. Jail is a way of disarming a society that builds nuclear weapons and indulges in perpetual war-making. Jail unites us with the poor, confronting a society that manufactures destitution and homelessness. Jail is subversive of a society that in one way or another manages to shackle the conscience of even its favorites.

Mark declares at the beginning of his gospel that social change comes from "the wilderness." John the Baptizer emerges from that unlikely setting, as did Jesus. Today the "wilderness" could well be translated as the ghettos and slums of our cities. Out of them emerges an unlikely hope, such spirits as Dorothy Day and the communities that continue to serve the destitute. "Wilderness" also includes the jails and prisons across the land; there resisters appeal to the hearts and minds of others, whether in or out, and testify against the criminality of public authority.

Let me briefly describe our present "housing." The Robeson County Jail is one of the worst ever. Dust thou art. We are lodged in a dustbin where it is all but impossible to obtain a book or a change of clothing. Lynn did three weeks in solitary, unable to bear the heavy smoking of the women's cell block. She is now in a smoke-free block. We three men are blessed in being together for Bible reflection and good talk, weirdly isolated as we are from TV, the culture at top volume, at once violent and soporific.

No one of us likes jail. No one in right mind would seek it. But God's word and the strenuous work of community are sufficient for us. We transcend this pit of misery, we shrug, grin and bear it. In measure, we help humanize it.

Meantime, in the so-called real world, the Clinton Administration sounds the war tocsin against North Korea. According to this august hypocritical exercise, the vast American nuclear arsenal and the considerable nuclear development of South Korea are equally beside the point.

What then is the point? A perennial worldwide search is on for that all but vanished species, a veritable Loch Ness monster, "the enemy." Purportedly, in some mirage or other, Cuba and Libya together with desolated Iraq have been sighted by the mad clairvoyants.

As for slavish concessions to the Pentagon, President Clinton outpaces former President Bush by a mile — in arms sales, fiscal support, new weapons systems and a belligerent ideology to match. The rich are reassured. The weapons are in place. The great democratic hope has lately been hailed as the "best Republican in memory."

In this morally polluted atmosphere, we believe that imprisonment could hardly be more to the point. We shudder under the blows of a society permanently mobilized against peace. Duplicity, propaganda, media indifference, institutional betrayal mark our plight. Our people are confused and hopeless.

Let us not give up hope. Let us continue to nourish one another by consistent and prayerful presence at military installations, in courts and in lockups.

Indeed, we need to be free enough to go to jail. We need to fill up the jails.

Nonviolent revolution will come out of the wilderness, as it always has.

And be assured, dear friends, one formidable wilderness today is an American prison.

Spiritual Power Behind Bars

Anne Montgomery, R.S.C.J.

A time to plant and a time to uproot. . . .
A time to seek and a time to lose. . . .

Many people understand political action, public demonstration, even "civil disobedience" — what we would name "divine obedience" — but consider the consequences of such action — jail to be a stumbling block, a waste of time when they might otherwise be continuing their work for peace and for the poor on the streets. Paradoxically, just as crossing the line in action clarifies one's vision, so the experience of the non-action, the seemingly, useless life of prison, reveals a level of truth-force difficult to perceive from the "outside." There is a good reason for this difficulty. The center of power that can be reached in any imprisoned life is as hidden as the buried seed. "For you have died, and your life is hidden with Christ in God." (Col. 3:3)

This is not to say that prison is a good place. It is not the desert of the hermits who fled a corrupt Roman Empire. Rather, this "desert" encapsulates some of the most dehumanizing and debilitating aspects of our modem "empire." Prison is a repression of the freedom and creativity crucial to productive life and action. It is an expression of the fear and violence that undermine our "free" institutions, the fear and violence that seek to secure weapons, to control and punish, and it concretizes that violence in a way that we who accept the consequences of our actions cannot avoid.

We do not choose prison. We choose, rather, to resist the forces of death within and without and to entrust the fruits of our truth telling to God. But here there is an opportunity to live out the essence of our action: to meet violence in its petty, institutionalized forms outside ourselves, to meet it again in our own reactions, and in both situations to allow the transforming power of love to work in and around us.

Most obvious at first, however, is the helplessness, the loss of control, the reinforcement of all that is degrading to human dignity and self-respect. We come with a sense of peace, of celebration even, buoyed by our recent act of resistance. But then we find ourselves instant criminals — we are strip-searched, fingerprinted, numbered. Worse, we meet and compare experiences with those for whom prison is not the result of an act of resistance but of its opposite — a further rejection by a society that provides little help or sympathy for the marginalized, whether the problem stems from drugs, economic need, or abuse. Our own "ineffectiveness" to change anything is all too obvious — a seeming confirmation of the words of mainstream critics.

It is in this most adverse situation, however, that the power of God can be released, because any illusions we might have had about "justice" are shattered and our hands are sometimes literally bound. The promise stands that "God works for good with those who love him" (Rm 8:28) in all things — not just in the good situations but also in the midst of evil ones, the mistakes and the results of our sin. This is our faith.

Jim Douglass has called prisons the "monasteries of the future" because of this emptying process and the need to depend entirely on God. This prediction has been criticized because prison is an environment so inimical to the human development that is the foundation of a healthy contemplative life. But is this criticism valid in the world as we know it, where the majority of its population lives in scarcely human conditions or under repressive governments? If the contemplative spirit flows from the Spirit of Christ, it can only be strengthened by identification with the poor, the oppressed, and the marginalized. We, who can never lose the privilege of our education, inner resources, or the free act that landed us in prison in the first place, can still become more grounded in reality by touching the lives of so many unfortunate sisters and brothers by experiencing something of their inability to choose the next meal or to find a measure of silence and solitude, something seemingly so essential to contemplation. Prayer must be as simple as breathing — not as an exercise or a method, but as the movement of the Spirit breathing within the whole of creation.

Life in prison is part of a continuing "experiment in truth." Actions of divine obedience are moments in this continuum of prayer and community building, of witness and of its deepening in the life that follows. This is a truly creative process, never perfected but always full of new possibilities.

LIBERATION IN CAPTIVITY:
A FABLE
John Bach

There was once a prison that ran pretty well. It encircled the lives of some 800 men, all of whom would have preferred being someplace else. It ran as well as it did because it employed the carrot and the stick, the iron fist and velvet glove, and a Skinnerian method of behavior reinforcement. It managed somehow to keep the eight-hundred men emotionally apart in spite of the fact that they lived on top of each other. It succeeded in large measure because it succeeded in instilling the following lessons: do your own time; go along and get along; don't make waves; look out for number one; don't get involved; make acquaintances not friends; and so forth. Since these were the same lessons that the men had been taught all their lives, they were easily applied here and were not questioned for the most part. The men became suspicious, macho, abusive, lustful, envious, and thus they kept each other in line.

The prison ran pretty well because it not only kept the inmates apart; it kept them at each other's throats. Favoritism was bestowed; racism was practiced and provoked; classism was reinforced; big and small manipulations took place; inalienable rights were doled out to the well-heeled as privileges. Prisoners were encouraged to become like the prison that enslaved them. Violence among inmates was, according to the situation, either punished, overlooked, or rewarded. The prison figured that everyone had his price, and for the most part the price was shamefully crumb-sized.

The prison ran pretty well, like the larger society it reflected. There was more emphasis on proper working order than on people. Yet, sometimes in fables, as well as in real life, goodness happens for no apparent reason — at least not for reasons that most people understand or accept. And such was the case in this prison, which had always run pretty well.

Things began to happen, things not unlike the occasional weedy flowers that grew out of cracks in the concrete walls. It happened that a handful of prisoners recognized each other as brothers, and they organized to stop rape within the prison. This was not as hard as they had thought. They went further. They encouraged others to share, not horde, to open up, not close off or shut down. They read books together and discussed them; they shared their life histories. Slowly walls came tumbling down as they began to trust each other. They did favors for each other without thought of recompense. Birthdays were celebrated; contraband cakes were baked; musical reviews were written and performed. An underground paper (The Shit-House Press) was published and circulated. "Stay strong" was a common parting. Smiles and grins, like the weedy flowers, began splitting the concrete. The oasis began crowding out the desert.

The men looked out for each other, stood up for each other, occasionally went on hunger strikes and work strikes, were transferred across the country, were put in the hole, lost good time and parole dates. It didn't matter. A sense of responsibility and resistance evolved, and as long as that endured and prevailed, it gave the men a sense of freedom that mere physical imprisonment could not take away. It no longer mattered so much to the men which side of the wall they were on. Their sentences were not just so much time out of their lives, but time of their lives that could be just as worthy a period of growing and living as any other. People who had never cottoned much to the notion of miracles (like the person who is writing this) had to rethink their beliefs on the subject. It was all a dream, and it was real.

All of this was like sand in the grinding cogs, and the prison, which was no longer running pretty well, responded, as one might suppose, with small-mindedness and brutality. It went too far though and did not discover until too late that it was no longer dealing with 800 self-serving individuals, but with a community of related people who had tasted a better way of life and who were not willing to wipe that out of their lives.

A strike was organized. Black, Hispanic, and white inmates worked together. This was a rare occurrence indeed, and the prison was — horrified. It pressured some men, bribed others, but nothing worked; it was like threatening Brier Rabbit with the briarpatch.

One Monday morning, the prison that for years and years had run pretty well didn't run at all. A nonviolent work strike surrounded the prison which surrounded the 800 lives. Thousands of dollars of revenue were lost as the prison industry shut down its defense department, war, profiteering work. Inmates took control of their lives, had meetings, discussed central issues, took risks. Even during the next tense nine days there was still no violence, no destruction of property, no abusive language, no vamping or exploitation, which in the past had pretty much been the order of the day. What there was was a truly human community in the face of great adversity.

The prison that wasn't running at all eventually got back to running pretty well. The prison broke the strike, and to its way of thinking it had been a decisive victory for the bleak forces of lock and key. But all the inmates knew, and the prison knew too, in the lifeless marrow of its bones, that what had happened was not something the prison could ever take away or deny or belittle or disrespect or not live in fear of, for it was the life force moving toward liberation, which is the working of goodness among people. It was a remarkable progression of consciousness: It was liberation because of and in spite of jail.

This fable really happened at the federal prison in Danbury, Connecticut in the spring of 1972, and I was there. Since then, I've returned there and other places like it that run pretty well, and the scene has changed a lot. Like community, this sense of liberation in captivity is a gift, and sometimes you just can't make it happen beyond an individual level. But in every case the victory is in the struggle and as long as the flame of resistance remains unextinguished, there is no defeat or dishonor or even imprisonment of the spirit.

Other examples of this abound in the ongoing examples of witness around us. It surfaces in the dozens of origami paper cranes strung from the bars of a jail cell and in the look of joy and freedom on a grandmother's face as she is led to a police van after her first arrest. It is reflected in the small acts of daily heroism done in anonymity and most clearly (and joyfully) in the continuing Plowshares actions, despite long-prison terms. This notion of liberation in captivity comes alive in the willingness of people to take risks and suffer to turn the consequences into positive experiences as they endeavor to build a better world. Just that. Life itself, to the fullest.

EXPOSING THE INJUSTICE

Judith Beaumont

The spirit of the Lord has been given to me, for he has anointed me. He has sent me to bring the good news to the poor, to proclaim liberty to captives and to the blind new sight, to set the downtrodden free, to proclaim the Lord's year of favor.

Luke 4:18

Reflection on this passage in which Jesus identifies himself with the mission of the prophet in Isaiah 61 has inspired countless responses by the Christian community over the centuries. In a small way the passage has been fulfilled once again by a community in Connecticut — primarily women and not all Christian — who confronted the unjust conditions in the Connecticut Correctional institution for Women in Niantic.

Following the Trident Nein Plowshares action at Electric Boat Company in Groton, Connecticut on July 5, 1982, Anne Montgomery, Anne Bennis, and I were held on bond for about seven weeks in the pre-trial unit of the only women's prison in the state. Convinced in our hearts that Trident must be disarmed, we knew when we chose to act that we would have to spend time in prison. Prison is not a good place to be, but the opportunities for ministry are abundant, as we were to find out.

Although the facility as a whole was considered minimum security, the pre-trial unit where we were held was at least medium security. Our first days were spent rejoicing in our symbolic act of disarming the U.S.S. Florida Trident submarine and two sonar spheres for other beasts of mass destruction. Messages of support from friends and strangers began arriving, and even some of our sister inmates could appreciate what we had done. As we settled in to the daily routine of inactivity, we began to be aware of conditions at the prison. Gradually we got to know other women and heard about the situations that angered them and the conditions that violated their own ethic of fairness.

The absence of planned activities — no classes, no craft projects, little outdoor recreation — was perhaps the worst circumstance we identified. Personally I didn't mind so much at first because I welcomed the time to pray, read, and answer letters. But for most women the time hung heavy. There were few books available and no magazines or newspapers. The color TV in the dayroom and the radio in the laundry were the only media available. We longed to get out in the small yard, but all of us were cooped up inside for days. Summer was given as the excuse for school not being in session.

The facility was quite dirty and poorly lit — terrible light for reading. The overall sanitation was awful. There were moldy shower curtains, broken plumbing, and the usual cockroaches in the toaster. Inmates were locked in rooms without toilets at night. To use the facilities we had to bang hard on the bedroom door or shout to be heard by a correctional officer who might be downstairs and out of earshot. This was especially hard on the pregnant women, who also suffered from an inadequate diet. Some women resorted to "piss cans" — one pound coffee cans they had confiscated from the kitchen garbage.

One of the more disturbing policies of the prison was the one allowing male officers to be assigned to the sleeping areas. They could lock and unlock the doors of bedrooms and bathrooms at any time of the day or night, peering through them at the times the women were most likely to be dressing or undressing.

There were frequent complaints about the quality of medical attention and length of time it took to see a doctor. We heard the cries and moans of the drug addicts detoxing "cold turkey" without medication or supervision.

As we listened to the complaints and saw this dehumanization for ourselves, we began to realize our need to liberate these women and ourselves from these oppressive conditions. We began by telling our friends who came to visit about them. Some of them encouraged us to write about what we had experienced. Letters were sent to friends and former co-workers, who in turn sent the letters to others who might share our concerns. Letters were written to the prison ombudsman, who came to listen to our concerns.

As time went on our increasing awareness of the problems led us to realize the institutional violence of the criminal justice system. Most of the women I met were primarily victims rather than criminals. They had been abused and victimized by racism, poverty, poor education, male violence and sexual exploitation. They were not bad people. They were the victims of a society that idolizes nuclear weapons as its human-made god of safety and that pours billions of dollars into coffers for their continued production.

For their "crimes" these women were warehoused in overcrowded facilities where only a very few were given the opportunity to change their lives. It is only fair to say also that there were good people working in corrections, and the occasional exposure to their genuine concern was a treasured moment.

Each time we went to court, it was a joy to get outside the prison and to be with the six Trident Nein men and our growing support group. But upon returning to Niantic, like all the other women, we were subjected to a vaginal search for contraband. Our legal advisor appealed to the judge to sign an order prohibiting these searches. Predictably the judge refused, so the searches continued.

About two weeks before trial we were released rather unexpectedly and once on the outside had even more opportunities to relate our experiences to others who shared our concern. During the weeks we were on trial, two women from among our supporters also acted at Electric Boat and were held at Niantic as "Jane Does." As part of their non-cooperation they refused the vaginal search upon return from court and were placed in the detention unit, which also houses the mentally ill inmates and those who are suicidal. They were able to gather information about that unit and the absence of treatment and care for those with the most severe problems.

As soon as our trial ended, a meeting was called to hear about Niantic and to decide if something could be done to remedy the unacceptable conditions. Social workers, educators, lawyers, and community activists came to listen and decided that something must be done. After further meetings the Connecticut Coalition for Women in Prison was formed to address the problems we had identified. Three tactics were selected: negotiation, legislation, and litigation. The work was parceled out to different groups and individuals. Over a period of several months, research was done and new groups and individuals, including former inmates, were contacted. Members of the coalition met with prison officials and were given a tour. Finding that not much could be accomplished by negotiation, the coalition focused on legislation and litigation. One bill to fund the mental health unit was introduced through the efforts of a coalition member. Some of us testified at committee hearings. This bill did get passed.

Preparation began for the filing of a class action suit on behalf of all the Niantic inmates and their children. Anne Montgomery was in Niantic at the time for her part in Trident Nein, as were the women from Plowshares Number Four. They all were talking with other inmates about conditions and about the need for plaintiffs.

In the midst of all this I returned to Niantic myself. Having refused to pay restitution to Electric Boat, I was sentenced to one year. Knowing that much work needed to be done inside, I went with some eagerness. I hoped to confront the body cavity search regulation. My opportunity came when I went to court for a sentence reduction hearing. It was denied as expected, but I returned from court determined to resist the search we all found to be so offensive, humiliating, and painful. When I refused to submit to it I was taken to the locked unit and placed in a room with only an iron bed with a thin mattress, toilet, and sink. I would be locked up for 23 hours a day until I submitted to the search.

I was allowed a phone call to the coalition attorneys who were prepared to act. The next morning a call came from the lawyer informing me that she was hand-delivering a letter to the Assistant Attorney General asking for a change in the search regulation and for my release. By lunchtime I was back in the general population and the word was out that there would be no more body cavity searches for court returnees unless probable cause could be shown. The news was received by the inmates with disbelief and rejoicing. The timing could not have been better. This was just the encouragement the women needed to continue working on the lawsuit.

Several inmates had agreed to meet with the lawyers and law students. After a number of interviews, the named plaintiffs were selected and the suit was filed in federal court. After many hearings the Department of Correction agreed to a settlement without going to trial. On most counts the plaintiffs can claim victory. However, it remains to be seen whether the Department of Correction will comply as they have agreed. It will be necessary for inmates to keep close watch on conditions and to speak up when they find themselves unfairly treated. Let us hope that the prison resistance can be maintained and that periodic visits by civil disobedients (divine obedients) will be occasions not only to resist the war preparations going on in

Connecticut, but also to gather information about current conditions and the identity of inmates willing to challenge the unjust conditions found.

Prison conditions cannot be changed by resisters alone, but with a hard-working support community on the outside the "system" can be challenged and made to conform to what is more right and just and liberating.

Resisters blessed with different gifts have engaged in other forms of witness in prison. Some have been teachers or tutors; others have done counseling or led Bible study groups. Some have chosen to carry on their resistance by refusing to do any prison jobs. While in prison, resisters have come to know sisters and brothers, learn of their struggles, and share their dreams and hopes for a better life.

All of us have received a great deal from those we have met in prison. In our times of loneliness and frustration there have been sisters and brothers there who understood, who cracked a joke at the right moment, who shared the little they had: tea bags, pencils, crochet hooks — little things on the outside but so much more on the inside.

Many acts of resistance have grown out of works for justice. In prison we become intimately connected to the work for justice as we live and work with those people who are the victims of the arms race. We learn compassion, work for small changes, struggle in ways we've never dreamed of and long for a world in which liberty is proclaimed and prisons will be no more.

PRISON POETRY AND PROSE

EARTH DAY
by Art Laffin

Mother Earth,
 once teaming with such splendor and beauty
  now groans in travail
   crying out to humankind:
    STOP THE ASSAULT!

Humankind,
 in your thoughtless pursuit of what you think is progress,
  can't you see,
   you are poisoning me!

Don't you realize
 that as you desecrate me,
  you destroy yourselves, too!

I have seen with sorrow-filled eyes:
 cratered, contaminated earth at the Nevada Test Site -
  home of the Shoshone Indians;
   forever changed radioactive landscapes at Rocky Flats
    and the Savannah River Weapons Plant,
     scorched earth in El Salvador by U.S. napalm,
      a Trident sub desecrating the serene Atlantic Ocean,
       a bulldozed, once majestic mountainside in Scotland -
        converted into a tomb of bunkers to store nuclear warheads,
        a Minuteman missile silo, buried deep into the heart
        of a wheat field in Missouri,
         rivers contaminated by toxic chemicals.

I have choked breathing polluted air.

I have witnessed
 I have complicity in the destruction of you, Mother Earth.

Forgive me, forgive humanity, O God
for treating your creation with such arrogance and disdain.
O Holy One, help me, help all your people
to revere the earth as sacred.

There is still time to save the ozone;
there is still time, humankind,
to save Mother Earth -
if we relinquish our consumer addictions,
live simply and responsibly steward the earth's resources.
And realize every day is Earth Day!

Come, Holy Spirit, fill me and all your people
with your Divine love,
so that we may renew the face of the earth.

(Written in Danbury, CT Federal Prison, Earth Day, April 22, 1990)

Dream
by Roger Ludwig

I saw all the singers
refusing to sing
until. . .

I saw all the dancers
refusing to dance
until. . .

I saw all the preachers
and politicians
gagged for refusing
to shut up
until. . .

I saw all the world
refusing to go
being world without end
until. . .

everyone was fed
and unafraid
and free of the dark cloud
that had hung overhead
for so long,
so long.

I saw all the weapons
gone!

(Written in Rhode Island State Prison, Nov. 1985)

FROM ALDERSON: LENT, 1985
by Anne Montgomery

I walk the road,
  one mile, more or less,
up the hill to view
  Outside
these sun-tipped hills;
  mocking? hollowed to hold death?
  or are they cradles of spring's
    birth, echoing our longing?

and Inside:
A distorted mirror of worldwide
  pain:
    hospital -
    razor-wired detention -
    drug unit -
then downhill to the valley of our
  ordinary
  mind-numbing
  daily
  come and go.

and yet Inward
  to face another mirror - darkened -
  someone walking long ago
    in small space
      and time
    but made a difference -
      how?

The "how" our hope
  not big numbers
    big names
    big news
but its very substance-self
  discounted
  forgotten
  discontinued
  lost and buried
and, behold,
  alive:
the Oneness
- we can name the Name -
good news for all,
  breathed deep
  into the soil of our
    here
      and
        now

(Written in Alderson Federal Correctional Institution, Spring 1985)

Thoughts on Deterrence
(In Season and out of Season)
by Anne Montgomery

The leaves are past their turning,
  like the road that curves between the trees
     and stops,
  dead at the door,
  deterred perhaps
    but only from going back -
      denying or forgetting
        that it must lose its boundaries,
          all sign secure in shape and color,
  and tunnel deep.

And so the leaves,
  dropping now,
  their last clinging to color and form
  cut short by an arbitrary win.
They fall -
  a platitudinous lesson for slow learners:
  all about dying to live,
    losing to find -
  the fallow season of creation
    when seeds, in the darkness of this rotting place,
      gather strength from broken soil,
        drink deep from hidden springs,
    turn upwards,
      and
  in that push towards light,
    resist.

(Written in Connecticut Correctional Institution for Women, Niantic, CT, Fall 1982)

FOR MARTIN LUTHER KING
by Art Laffin

Dear brother,
  servant of justice,
  you showed America how
  to walk in the light,
  to tell the truth,
to create the beloved community.

  Like Gandhi,
  you conspired
to nonviolently resist injustice-
  to overcome evil with good!

  Minister and Peacemaker,
  prisoner for Jesus,
you challenged America
to break its addiction to the triple evils:
  racism,
  materialism,
  militarism.

  You called us forth,
    to follow the way of Jesus,
      to renounce violence,
      resist war,
to break down the walls of prejudice,
  to embrace peace.

The powers that be
threatened by justice,
  killed you -
  but not your message.

You live, dear brother,
  your life -- a beacon of hope!
  The beloved community
  is still being forged.
  Death will not have
  the last word.

    Love will overcome!

(Written in Rappahannock Jail, Fredricksburg, VA, Martin Luther King Day 1994)

THIS PARADISE EARTH
by Roger Ludwig

This paradise earth
  we turn into a wasteland
    of trivial pursuit,
battlefield of petty differences,
  prison of dire necessity
    devoid of meaning and miracle.

O come recover
  paradise with me,
    with any sister, any brother
in the love of the Risen One
  who joins us in our hands joined.

O come and wed
  this wealth in poverty,
    this patience so full of promise.

O come and die
  and live in this constant
    ending and beginning again.

(Written in the Adult Correctional Institution, Cranston, R I, Spring 1985)

FOR THE SILO PRUNING HOOKS
by Helen Dery Woodson

Forgetful earth
by human treachery now damned
her creatures' modest need neglect
gives but a grudging portion for her children's fill
and in unfruitful labor thus
anticipates the sterile scape of death.
Her victims sprung like rotting teeth from dragon's horny jaw
their eyes scratched senseless in the stony waste
seek answer from her barren breast.
And will you give a million tons of fire
instead of bread? How long
O Lord?
How long?
Where still unshattered sacred voices fly
where martyr's
copious blood yet feeds
the fragrant soil
our hammers rang with urgent song
may hardened steel be bent
in mercy's grasp
and concrete split beneath perduring truth.
May earth again redolent
pungent, sweet
revoke her mindless curse
and yielding to her Lord's unceasing love
let peace and justice sear her bleeding heart.

(Written in the Jackson County Jail, Kansas City, Missouri, November, 1984.)

The Acts of Midwest Resisters
According to Carl Kabat, O.M.I.
(Based on the Acts of the Apostles According to Luke)

God had planned that the Silo Pruning Hooks: Helen, Whitefeather, Paul and Carl, would be arrested and sentenced and that everyone will be baptized in the Holy Spirit.

Later they arrested Jean and Joe and put them in jail and everyone knew that these two were ordinary people.

Do you think that God wants us to obey you or to obey God. We do not obey people, we obey God. All of them were happy because God considered them worthy to suffer. They later grabbed Jerry Zawada and dragged him in. "You stubborn and hard headed people, you are always fighting against the Holy Spirit. Is there one prophet that you have not mistreated?"

It is true that none of them received a fair trial. Many were frightened and no longer acted. When they saw these arrests pleased the system they had Angie and others arrested.

It is true that you have to suffer a lot before you can get into God's Kin-dom.

Then they grabbed Bonnie, Barb, Jeff and John and brought them into court. "They are upsetting E.L.F. They break the laws of the empire, so they put them into jail." They later grabbed Sam and Mike who had come with Carl.

All admit that "We don't know what will happen but we must obey God's Spirit. The Holy Spirit tells us that we will be put in jail and will be in trouble, but we do not care what happens to us as long as we do the work that God wants.

It is true that none of these are guilty of anything for which they should be put in jail, but they have been imprisoned.

The courts want to do the empire a favor so they kept them in jail.

What we are saying is true and makes sense.

We know that many of you will listen and listen but never understand. You will look and look but never see.

NO MORE NUCLEAR WEAPONS.

Note: Reprinted from *Year One*, Summer 1994

RESISTANCE TO WAR TAXES

WAR TAX RESISTANCE:
A CHRISTIAN RESPONSE TO THE DEMONS AROUND US
William Durland

Editors' Note: *This article, which appeared in the first edition of* Swords into Plowshares, *was revised in 1993.*

Prophetically, Philip Berrigan saw Americans at a highpoint in demonism in the early 80s, possessed by the bomb and in slavish complicity with it in a lockstep toward our nuclear doom.[1] One effort to break out of that lockstep was the refusal by thousands of Christians to pay for war by withholding that part of their tax money designated for military expenditures. In 1986, 64 percent of defense fund outlays was so designated. As of 1993, the percentage has dropped to about 55 percent, a small reduction considering the end of the Cold War. Following the example of the earliest Christians, these people of conscience have formed part of what has been referred to as "the Resistance Church."

The religious tax resistance movement is not restricted to the United States, however, but appears in other countries as well. To date, there are about 30 countries in which war tax resistance is practiced. In Japan, for example, the movement is led by an organization called COMIT — Conscientious Objectors to Military Income Tax. Mennonites, Quakers, Catholics, and other members of other denominations band together with Buddhists and people of no church affiliation to witness to the illegality of military preparedness.

Article Nine of the Japanese Constitution prohibits war-making, but that nation violates its own laws nonetheless. Japan is not unlike the United States and other superpowers, which have set the pace for violations of international agreements since 1945. While the Nuremberg Principles call it a crime against peace to plan or to prepare "a war of aggression, or a war in violation of international treaties, or (to participate) in a common plan for the accomplishment of any of the foregoing,"[2] the nations continue such violations. "First-strike" military policy continues to be a part of U.S. security plans.[3]

Individuals are left to choose between violating national law requiring the payment of taxes for such purposes and complying with international law prohibiting such preparations. The Nuremberg Principles also state that individual responsibility attaches to such crimes.[4] It is not an excuse to say that one was following orders as long as a moral choice exists.[5] Further, the United Nations Charter recognizes the obligation to refrain from "the threat or use of force."[6] While the political powers continue to play dangerously in Iraq, Palestine, Somalia, Haiti, Russia and Bosnia, it is commonly recognized that military threats are a violation of the United Nations Charter. And, for Christians, the threat to kill is as evil as the killing itself, for sins are born in the heart. The early Christians knew too well that the only moral choice is to refuse Caesar what is God's.

In A.D. 70, Christians refused to pay the tax appropriated for Caesar's pagan temple in Rome and became the first Christians to resist paying tax for reasons of religious conscience. [7]

> Christian disobedience under persecution was regularly defended on the broad ground of the supremacy of God's law to man's. . . . It is important to notice that this doctrine of disobedience is a principle perfectly general. The law of God, which the Christians put over against the law of the state, embraced a good deal more than the prohibition of idolatry and polytheism. It embraced a whole Christian ethic. . . . Numerous instances of this obstinate and avowed disobedience to government orders are mentioned in the literature of the period.[8]

The foremost historical record of early Christian belief and practice, C.J. Cadoux's *The Early Church in the World*, describes the common stance of active resistance and protest:

> The martyr-acts frequently speak of the prosecuting officials in terms of strong censure. . . . The words, "I am a Christian," were persistently repeated, sometimes in reply to questions from the magistrate perhaps on quite other points, sometimes on the speaker's own initiative, and in reply to no question at all. . . . It seems not to have been uncommon for Christians

attending the trials of their co-religionists to protest boldly in open court against the condemnation of innocent persons, and by thus disclosing their own faith to draw the death sentence upon themselves also.[9]

The paradigm for Christian obedience and disobedience is found in the Gospels and the Old Testament. Matthew 12 is perhaps the best example of Jesus disobeying the religious (theocractic) authorities. In respect to the civil authorities, Richard Cassidy in his book *Jesus, Politics, and Society* writes: "If large numbers came to adopt his (Jesus') stance toward the ruling political authorities, the Roman Empire (or indeed, any other similarly-based social order) could not have continued."[10]

In his book *The Trial of Jesus*, Walter Chandler concludes that Jesus was guilty of sedition under the Roman law of the time.[11]

The Christian philosopher, Lactantius, wrote in his *Divine Institutes*: (Chapter 18, c. 300 A.D.)

> When men command us to act in opposition to the law of God, and in opposition to justice, we should be deterred by no threats or punishments from preferring the command of God to the command of man. . . . When compelled to desert God and betray our faith, we should prefer to undergo death and should defend our liberty against the foolish and senseless violence of those who cannot govern themselves, and with fortitude of spirit we should challenge all the threats and terrors of the world.

There is no doubt of the legitimacy of civil disobedience, including tax resistance or of the imperative for Christians to witness in this way. Throughout history a remnant of Christians in each generation has understood its relationship to secular authorities and cultural norms in essentially this way.

Colonial America experienced John Woolman's forceful presence against slavery and war. Woolman was a pacifist Quaker who refused to pay taxes that were used to finance the French and Indian War. His journal tells us, "I besought the Lord to enable me to give up all, so that I might follow him wheresoever he was pleased to lead me. Under this exercise I went to our Yearly Meeting at Philadelphia in the year 1755."[12]

There he presented his scruple to other Friends who, at length, drew up an epistle supporting his resistance. By 1795 many members of the Religious Society of Friends had suffered for their civil disobedience, and a letter from one of them, relative to the conscientious scrupulousness of its members to bear arms, is worth noting. It says, in respect to the reasons Quakers could not bide with killing and war: "It is inconsistent with Christianity to resort to arms — one crime will not justify another. The *Lex Talionis* is not a part of the Christian religion; and the using of arms, to resist an attack, is returning violence for violence, and opposing force with force, involving ourselves in the like criminality, and making ourselves as deserving of chastisement as they are on whom we inflict it. . . ."[13]

The modern religious war tax resistance movement began during World War II with the witness of people like Ammon Hennacy, a Catholic layperson, and Rev. Ernest Bromley, a Protestant minister. Bromley was prosecuted and imprisoned. Dorothy Day and others paved the way for organizations like the War Resisters League, the Peacemakers, the Catholic Worker and the Committee for Nonviolent Action.

Since World War II we have entered the nuclear age, and the nature of history, and therefore of Christian responsibility, is radically changed. In 1952, A.J. Muste, a war tax resister, minister, labor leader, pacifist, and veteran Quaker peace crusader, evolved a position of absolute conscientious objection. His *Of Holy Disobedience* was published in 1952. It called for total noncooperation with any preparation for war. Going to prison, Muste argued, is less damaging to the soul than participating in war or cooperating with war preparations.[14] As the Vietnam War intensified, the anti-war movement was coupled with another movement, with equal political and domestic immediacy — telephone tax resistance.

At one point during the Vietnam War there were estimated to be 200,000 telephone tax resisters and many thousands of income tax resisters. But only as an exception and not as a general rule were people criminally prosecuted and convicted. The exceptions during the 1960s and early 1970s included Juanita Nelson, Rev. Maurice McCracken, and Karl Meyer.

After the Vietnam War ended, the movement slowed. In Philadelphia, lawyer John Egnal was a mainstay during those years aiding Rev. David Gracie, an Episcopal priest and Robin Harper, a Quaker, in their cases against the IRS, which sought to collect unpaid taxes with penalties and interest.

A new era began in 1978 with the birth of the National Center on Law and Pacifism. Four cases were brought to the Supreme Court of the United States using various legal *and* theological arguments. The cases were designed to draw the highest court's attention to three things: the retained rights of citizens under the Ninth Amendment to the U.S. Constitution, international law violations by governments, and the free exercise and disestablishment of religion guaranteed by the First Amendment. Each case emphasized how the religious morals and conscience of the individual citizen are affected by violations of these amendments and the forced obligation to pay war taxes in complicity with them.

In *Anthony v. Commissioner of Internal Revenue*, 436 U.S. 904 (1978), Robert Anthony petitioned the Supreme Court to hear his argument in favor of his conscientious objection to the payment of military taxes under the free exercise and establishment clauses of the First Amendment. Anthony, a Quaker, argued that forcing him to pay for war was the same as forcing him to shoot a gun and that interfered with his higher obligation to worship as a Quaker, such worship consisting of living pacifism as a way of life. Not to live that pacifism would force him to accept a form of worship foreign to his conviction, a type of civil religion normative to America — the so-called just war. Anthony was denied his rights before the U.S. Supreme Court.

Bruce and Ruth Graves followed Anthony in 1979 in *Graves v. Commissioner of Internal Revenue*, 1140 U.S. 946 (1979), and based their case on the free-exercise clause also, arguing that a constitutional right takes precedence over an IRS regulation and that "only the gravest abuses endangering paramount interests give occasion for permissible limitation" of the free exercise of religion. No such occasion existed. The Court denied the Graves' case too, upholding an IRS regulation over the free-exercise clause.

The Rev. Howard Lull (an Episcopal priest), his wife, Barbara, and Peter Herby, a Roman Catholic peace activist, brought the Ninth Amendment argument to the U.S. Supreme Court in *Lull & Herby v. Commissioner of Internal Revenue*, 62 L.Ed. 643 (1980). They argued the retained rights under that amendment that prohibit government subversion of conscience. The early Christian church, they said, "forbade the receipt of money for magistrates polluted by war." James Madison's Ninth Amendment was composed for just this sort of matter — the state should not have the power to take away one's retained freedom to choose not to kill. The Supreme Court again denied the case.

Finally, Charles Purvis brought the fourth case in the series, *Purvis v. Commissioner of Internal Revenue*, 450 U.S. 997 (1981), arguing the violations of international law under many treaties to which the United States is signatory concerning wars of mass destruction. Purvis established that he was caught on the horns of a dilemma — either he would be in violation of international law by paying his war taxes or by not paying his war taxes he would be punishable under the domestic law of this country, the IRS Code. He chose not to pay, along with Anthony, the Graveses, the Lulls and Peter Herby. And he suffered the same fate. U.S. courts acted illegally in refusing to prohibit the executive and legislative branches from further infractions of the law of nations.

Although the Supreme Court would not listen to the arguments of Christian conscience firmly supported in constitutional principle, the movement grew. The Peace Church of the Brethren in Portland, Oregon, responded by letter to the IRS in this way:

> Peace Church of the Brethren has been ordered to pay the Internal Revenue Service for income taxes owed by our pastor, Rick Ukena, and his wife, Twyla Wallace. Rick and Twyla have withheld the approximate portion of their tax liability devoted to military purposes as an act of moral and spiritual dissent to participation in and preparation for war. We, as a body of Christian believers, have thoroughly and prayerfully examined the levy issued against us, and have found no grounds consistent with our collective conscience and understanding of Christ's message, on which we can offer payment in their stead. . . . Our reasons for taking this stand are twofold. First, the church's intercession would negate Rick and Twyla's conscientious act of civil disobedience and would violate their right to personally bear the consequences of their decision, which they have accepted as their responsibility for choosing to affirm life. Second, as a body of Christian believers, we are compelled by the same biblical teachings and example of Jesus Christ, to implement our faith and refuse to participate in the making of war. We cannot perform corporately that which violates our Christian duty as individuals. . . . We have been placed in a position where a choice must be made between compliance with human laws aimed at destroying life and a higher order which commands us to love one another, even our enemies. We have no alternative but to obey God's law.

Another example of church resistance was that of Tom Cordaro and St. Thomas Aquinas Church in Ames, Iowa. Cordaro, a lay campus minister and peace and justice coordinator, decided in 1979 that he could not in conscience pay federal income taxes that would be used to fund the nuclear arms race. Given his understanding of the gospel message of unconditional love, the statements of popes, Vatican II, and individual bishops denouncing the threat of nuclear war, Cordaro came to see his own participation, however unwilling, as greatly evil. He determined to resist paying war taxes, even if it would cost him time in prison.

In the fall of 1981, the IRS moved to collect Cordaro's back taxes. Since he had neither property nor bank account, they served a levy on the parish demanding that his salary be garnished to pay the debt. Rather than complying automatically, a pastoral team brought the matter to the December parish council meeting. After discussion, the council unanimously resolved to refuse to pay the IRS levy and directed the administrator to write a letter to the IRS so stating, because they were not a tax collecting agency and because they saw underlying moral implications they had not had time to explore.

In April 1982, the Department of Justice wrote to Archbishop Byrne, urging him to secure the compliance of the parish within two weeks or a lawsuit would be filed against them. The council voted to engage counsel to contact the IRS, indicating the parish would go to court over the issue. But Archbishop Byrne decided otherwise. After the parish administrator protested the order to write a check for the tax debt, the archbishop asked to be sent a blank check so that he could write it. Archbishop Byrne issued a press release that contained no theological or pastoral comment upon the moral merits of the case, simply a statement of the legal situation, with the conclusion, "Accordingly, as president of St. Thomas Aquinas Church, I have instructed the officers to honor the levy to the extent authorized by law." While the parish administrator agonized over the final details of how to deal with the directorate and order in a way least destructive to his own conscience, he was informed that several parishioners had gathered the money to pay the debt anonymously.

Arthur Jones in "An Alternative Pastoral Letter," which appeared in *The National Catholic Reporter* of April 14, 1983, suggested that the National Conference of Catholic Bishops and the U.S. Catholic Conference develop "the groundwork and material for a regular and sustained campaign for nonviolent civil disobedience to continue on a regular basis until abolition (of nuclear weapons) is achieved. It is likely that such a campaign will include the refusal to pay taxes, with that money instead going directly to the poor."

The hierarchy did not act.

In summer 1983, a "Resolution on Faithful Action Towards Tax Withholding" was brought for decision before the General Conference Mennonite Church in Bethlehem, Pennsylvania. The resolution was passed and the GCMC was the first denomination to take the step called for in the resolution.

The resolution asked delegates of the conference to authorize the conference officers to test the constitutionality of the tax-withholding requirements of the United States and to assert the higher claim of Christ's law of love by refusing to serve as tax collectors in cases where individual employees have asked that their federal income taxes be withheld from their wages so that they may conscientiously refuse to pay for war preparations.

The witness of Charles Purvis on international law was taken a step further in 1983 when Catholics Eugene and Mary Doyle took their case to the Second Circuit Court of Appeals in New York on the grounds that Section 7852(d) of the IRS Code prohibits the assessment and collection of income taxes in violation of any treaty obligation of the United States in effect as of August 6, 1954. Such treaty obligations make it a violation of international law to plan or prepare for wars of mass destruction or threaten the use of such force. The Doyles' motivation was their loyalty to the gospel imperatives. The court stopped just short of declaring their arguments of conscience "frivolous." Their public prayer in the courtroom as the judge entered may have contributed to that view by the court.

"Frivolity" is the government's name for refusing to pay war taxes for reasons of conscience. In late 1982, the administration added new penalties to many existing ones. Bringing a case to the U.S. Tax Court that proves to be "frivolous" (i.e., the subject matter has been before the court at a previous time) will cost the plaintiff a $5,000 penalty. To file an incorrect tax return, (i.e., for war tax resisters to claim a "war tax deduction" that is not legal) constitutes a $500 fine. Hundreds of such fines have been levied since 1983. The war tax resisters' efforts have not been deterred even though the government resorted to seizures of cars and even homes.

In May of 1982, the National War Tax Resistance Coordinating Committee, a grass-roots organization, was formed, sponsored by the National Center on Law and Pacifism, the War Resisters League, the Peacemakers and the Conscience and Military Tax Campaign. (The latter organization is dedicated to the passage of the Peace Tax Fund, which would legalize war tax conscientious objection.) A clearinghouse was created for war tax information and counseling and to coordinate local organizations.

Following the witness of Tom Cordaro and the St. Thomas Aquinas Church, a Roman Catholic church council in Indianapolis refused to comply with an IRS demand to pay federal taxes owed by its priest, the Rev. Cosmo Raimondi, based on "the sacredness of conscience."

In New Haven, Connecticut, the Summerfield United Methodist Church refused to hand over records relating to its pastor, the Rev. Carl Lundborg, a war tax resister. The IRS also ordered that church to withhold his salary, but the church did not comply.

In Cleveland, a Presbyterian church sided with its minister, Charles Hurst, when the IRS ordered a levy of that pastor's salary. They wrote:

> This levy is not an attempt to collect taxes. It is an attempt to collect a penalty or fine sought to be levied against Charles Hurst solely because of his expression of conscience with reference to payment of taxes for military purposes. We know our pastor. We know his deeply held conviction based upon his religious faith. It would border on blasphemy for us to cooperate in treating his action as frivolous.

By the mid 1980s the movement, originating through the witness of individual Christian resisters and thereafter developing to include church support for such resistance, began to express a corporate church position on war tax resistance. Sojourners Community and its magazine, *Sojourners*, were leaders in this respect. Some of the examples of this transition are as follows: the Philadelphia Yearly Meeting of the Religious Society of Friends passed a statement saying that, "Friends are ready to give strong support to members led to refuse payment of taxes for military purposes."[15]

In 1984 the Lutheran Peace Fellowship issued a call to Lutherans for war tax resistance. They said: "We who abhor the devastation of modern warfare, pledge our resistance at the place where preparation for war must most directly intersect our lives, in our payment of taxes."[16] The statement entitled "Half Century After Barman," referring to the 50th anniversary of the Barman Declaration and the beginning of the Confessing Church movement in Nazi Germany in 1934, remembered the joining together of Lutherans, Reformed and United Churches at the town of Barman to issue a declaration that became one of the few public denunciations of Nazism at the time. The Lutheran Peace Fellowship call invited Lutherans to join "in some form of tax protest or tax resistance as a witness of faith against the false lordship of nuclear weapons and other instruments of mass destruction."[17]

In 1985 at a gathering of 200 top military leaders at the National War College a revealing statement was made by a high-ranking general. "The greatest challenge to all that we do now comes from within the churches," he said. "A whole new way of thinking is developing in the churches and we have to know what to do with it."[18]

The demons did not go away in the late 80s and early 90s. Ronald Reagan made the most blasphemous statement of any president when he paid tribute to the nation's military personnel as "the ultimate guardians of our freedom . . . our final protection against those who wish us ill . . . they are prepared if need be to make the ultimate sacrifice for our nation."[19] He quoted the Bible to support his military budget and labelled pacifism as simple-minded folly and wishful thinking[20] and referred to the anti-nuclear peace movement as "modern hype and theatrics."[21] Meanwhile, the military budget rose to its greatest heights with George Bush, only beginning to level off as the Clinton administration took over. Nevertheless, new nonviolent applications of war tax resistance have arisen elsewhere, such as in the Intifada in Palestine.

In 1989, the IRS auctioned the home of Randy Kehler and Betsy Corner in Massachusetts, and Don Mosley and Max Rice of Jubilee Partners in Georgia were jailed for contempt. 1990-91 saw Alternative Revenue Service campaigns commence. Hundreds of activists circulated the EZ Peace Form, a "parody" of IRS form 1040EZ.[22] And tax day 1992 marked the arrest of Bill Ramsey, whose appeal was handled by noted war tax attorney Peter Goldberger.

The *Willets News* wrote on April 17, 1991: "Every minute fifteen children in the world die for want of essential food and inexpensive vaccines. And every minute the world's military machine takes another $1.9 million from the public treasury."[23] But Jesus urged us to give life to the children.

"Let the children come to me, do not hinder them; for to such belongs the kingdom of God . . . and he took them in his arms and blessed them." (Mk. 10:14-16 *RSV*).

The demons are still around in 1993 but our children who receive the greatest harm from this world turned upside-down are also part of the holy witness. Our son, Christian, became a war tax resister at age eight. Later, impressed by the events in Panama, he expressed to the IRS that a reason for his withholding the military taxes owed from a savings account we placed in his name was that he felt in so doing he might have saved a life in the invasion of Panama.

The children are the future. They will outlast the demons in the end and peace will surely come *as promised* for those who endure!

NOTES

1. Philip Berrigan, "We Are One Family," *Catholic Agitator*, January 1982, p. 2.
2. *The Charter of the International Military Tribunal* of August 8, 1945, Art. 6(c). See also William Durland, *The Illegality of War* (Colorado Springs: National Center on Law and Pacifism, 1983), p. 4.
3. See Robert Aldridge, *First Strike* (Boston: South End, 1983) and Durland, *The Illegality of War*, pp. 11-12.
4. *The Charter of the International Military Tribunal*, Art., p. 6.
5. Ibid, Art., p. 7.
6. *United Nations Charter*, Art. 2, p. 1037.
7. Donald Kaufman, *What Belongs to Caesar?* (Scottsdale, PA: Herald, 1969), p. 21.
8. C. J. Cadoux, *The Early Church and the World* (Edinburgh: Clark, 1925), pp. 251, 351, 354.
9. Ibid., pp. 252-53, 351, 354.
10. Richard Cassidy, *Jesus, Politics, and Society* (Maryknoll, NY: Orbis, 1980), p. 79. For examples in the Hebrew Scriptures see Exodus 1:15; 2:11-4:17, Jeremiah 27:5, Daniel 6, and Isaiah 40-55. See also Millard Lind, "Is There a Biblical Case for Civil Disobedience?" (Elkhart, IN: Associated Mennonite Biblical Seminaries, 1979).
11. Walter Chandler, *The Trial of Jesus* (Harrison, 1975), pp. 71, 72, 79.
12. *The Journal of John Woolman* (Secaucus, NJ: Citadel Press, 1972), p. 75.
13. Durland, *Conscience and the Law* (Cokedale, Colorado: Center Peace Publishers, 1982), p. 12.
14. Durland, *God or Nations* (Baltimore, MD: Fortkamp, 1989), p. 233.
15. *Philadelphia Yearly Meeting News*, vol. 23, no. 4, May 1984, p. 2.
16. Ibid., p. 1.
17. Ibid.
18. Jim Wallis, "The Rise of Christian Conscience," *Sojourners Magazine* Vol. 14, no. 1, January 1985, p. 12.
19. "Reagan Lauds Military," *Colorado Springs Sun*, May 16, 1982, p. 4a.
20. "Reagan Says Grenada Was Turning Point for America," *The Pueblo Chieftain*, October 24, 1984.
21. Ibid.
22. See Hedeman, *War Tax Resistance* (New York, NY: War Resisters League, 1992), pp. 27, 28. This complete guide is the best source for war tax information.
23. Ibid., p. 113.

COLRAIN WAR TAX WITNESS
Randy Kehler

My wife Betsy Corner and I have been withholding the full amount of our federal income tax liability since 1977, the year after we were married and the first year we had a taxable income. I had been withholding the federal telephone tax since the late 60s. Our tax refusal has always been motivated by our moral opposition to this country's obscene military expenditures which result in death, suffering, and deprivation for so many people in other countries and here at home. We have focused particularly on expenditures for nuclear and other weapons of mass destruction, and on military interventions in places like Vietnam, Lebanon, Grenada, Panama, Libya, Central America, and the Persian Gulf.

For many years we placed our withheld war taxes in an escrow account operated by the New England War Tax Resistance Alternative Fund. Beginning in 1987, however, we decided to give away the accumulated total plus each year's additional taxes — half to organizations that assist victims of U.S. war-making abroad and half to groups helping the poor here in Western Massachusetts.

In March of 1989, after many years of sending us forms, taking money from our bank account (which we finally closed), garnishing our wages (until we became self-employed), and placing liens on our property, the IRS seized our home in Colrain. That is, they seized our small, 90-year-old farmhouse and the lease rights to the land under and around it. The land itself was, and still is, owned by the Valley Community Land Trust, which had been leasing the land to us. Within 48 hours of receiving the seizure notice, over 50 people gathered in our living room and the War Tax Refusers Support Committee was off and running.

Over 500 people participated in a silent vigil outside the Greenfield IRS office on July 19, 1989, to protest the IRS's sealed-bid auction of our home. They set the minimum bid at $5,100, although the house alone was worth $50,000-$75,000. Close to a hundred bids were received, but none was monetary — the bids consisted of free massages for IRS employees, nonviolence training, flowers, trips to Nicaragua, and one joint bid of $30,000 worth of community service pledges and donated food for the poor. The latter was stacked up in front of the IRS office and later given to our local food bank. After rejecting these bids, an IRS official announced that the U.S. government itself would buy the property, for $5,100. The crowd broke into chorus after chorus of "We Shall Not Be Moved" — which, in succeeding months, became our anthem — and we declared victory.

Two months later, however, the IRS announced that they were seizing another home — that belonging to our WTR neighbors and fellow land trusters, Bob Bady and Pat Morse. So another auction was set, this one for November. Once again, hundreds of supporters gathered. While outside the IRS office $8,000 of refused war taxes was given to local human service groups, inside, the IRS managed to come up with one lone bidder who purchased Bob and Pat's house and lease rights for $4,800 (also a fraction of the real value).

Both of our families were given 180 days from the date of our auctions to leave the premises and both, needless to say, refused. The Support Committee, meanwhile, formulated elaborate plans for nonviolently blocking the take-over of either home. But upon the expiration of the 180-day "redemption" period, nothing happened in either case. Bob and Pat tried to communicate with the purchaser of their home, but to no avail, and to this date that person, though clearly not a supporter, has not tried to claim what she allegedly purchased — and Bob, Pat, and Pat's son Casey continue to live there as before.

In our case, the U.S. government filed a civil suit against us in May of 1990, charging us with illegal possession of government property. With the help of pro-bono lawyers, we attempted to put the government on trial by charging selective prosecution (why us versus all the big-time corporate tax evaders?) and, more importantly, U.S. violations of international law. Our hope was to get a jury trial and argue that our tax refusal was consistent with international law, including the Nuremberg Principles, and therefore the government wrongfully seized our home. As it happened, the federal district judge (in Springfield, MA) rejected all our arguments without even so much as a hearing, and, in November of 1991, granted summary judgement to the government and ordered us to be out by twelve noon on November 22nd.

The deadline came and went, and we didn't budge. Then, on the night of December 2nd, we got tipped off that federal marshals would be showing up the next morning to arrest us. Betsy and I had decided that one of us would stay and face arrest and the other would leave that night with our 12-year old daughter Lillian. I ended up being the one to stay, and early the next morning, December 3rd, in the middle of a blizzard, federal marshals accompanied by state and local police surrounded the house and hauled me off. My sentence was six months for "contempt" of the court order to leave our home. Judge Freedman refused to let me speak in court that day.

The following day, December 4th, 1991 marked the beginning of what has been perhaps the longest and certainly one of the most remarkable war tax protests in U.S. history. According to plan, a 15-member "Morning After Team," cheered on by a couple hundred supporters, dismantled the locks the marshals had put on the house and moved in to occupy it. No law enforcement people showed up and so the next day the first of close to 20 affinity groups — this one calling itself the "Colrain Neighbors" — replaced the Morning After Team and began a week's residence in the house.

Still no arrests and so the next week it was the "Roots and Branches" affinity group from the nearby town of Wendell. And they were followed by the "Grimkes" from Brattleboro, VT, and then the "Companeros" from Deerfield, MA, and on and on, group after group, week after week, from all over New England plus New York City, New Jersey, Washington, D.C., and St. Louis. Each group handed the proverbial baton to the next one at a weekly ceremony called "the Changing of the Guardians" — usually a well-attended event complete with poetry, song, moving testimonials, and plenty of laughter.

This routine continued until February 12, 1992, when the IRS tried a second time to auction our home. As before, the Support Committee advertised prior to the auction, explaining our war tax refusal, urging people not to bid on the house, and warning them that Betsy and I would not cooperate with eviction and that the land belonged to the Land Trust. This time, however, there was no minimum bid and it was held in Springfield, about an hour's drive south. Hundreds gathered to protest, despite sub-zero wind chill temperatures, and the IRS received a handful of bids. The winning bid was for $5,400, made by a 22-year-old, part-time Greenfield, MA, policeman and his fiancee. The couple later told us that they had seen our ads, but figured that if they didn't enter the winning bid and proceed to evict us, someone else would. They said it was just too good a deal to turn down.

In order to be able to sell the house empty, federal marshals showed up that morning, arrested seven members of the "Flowing River" affinity group, and had a crew of movers cart away all of Betsy's and my belongings. As soon as the auction was over, though, the seven were released, and so was I. The feds claimed that the whole thing was now out of their hands and it was up to the people who bought the house, with the help of local and state authorities, to deal with us. Naturally, the rotating occupation of the house continued, barely skipping a beat.

In the next couple months we made various attempts to talk with the young couple who made the winning bid, Danny and Terry. We offered to help them find other housing, and to help them sue the IRS for not telling them all the circumstances (with lawyer friends of ours offering to provide free legal representation if they wanted to sue). Later down the road, we also proposed that they join with us in a cooperative home-building project that would construct, Habitat for Humanity-style, homes for them and other families unable to afford housing on the conventional market. Unfortunately there were never any real signs of interest, and before long, perhaps due to the urging of their attorney, they stopped speaking to us altogether and became openly hostile.

Then, on April 15, 1992, while most of us were in Greenfield engaging in a Tax Day demonstration, Danny, Terry, and a group of their male friends barged into the house and proceeded to lock the doors and nail shut the windows. Three members of a Boston affinity group who were in the house at the time and refused to leave were denied food, water, and bathroom facilities for the next five days. On Easter Sunday they finally left, joining the 24-hour-a-day vigil that we had begun just outside the house.

For the next 14 months, the vigil continued, through snow, sleet, driving rain, and blistering sun. Our banner read, "It's wrong to confiscate homes to force people to pay for war," and the affinity groups kept coming. For the first six months, there was a good deal of off-and-on harassment, both by Danny and Terry's immediate family and friends, and also from passersby. Tents were destroyed, headlights smashed, signs and banners stolen, vigilers assaulted. Tensions ran very high. By late fall, however, when vigilers moved into a mobile vigil structure for the winter, the situation calmed down.

In the meantime, the Valley Community Land Trust filed a civil suit against Danny and Terry for being on Trust land without a valid lease, and Danny and Terry's attorney counter-sued the Trust and all the rest of us for depriving Danny, Terry, and their young son Ephraim of their right to "quiet enjoyment" of their property. Both cases are still languishing in the Massachusetts court system, allegedly because no one wants to deal with this political "hot potato." At the same time, however, in June of 1993, a superior court judge issued a criminal injunction forbidding us from vigiling on the disputed property. Though the maximum sentence for violating the injunction is two-and-a-half years and/or a $5000 fine, over 60 people have been arrested for continuing the vigil as of September 1993 with most spending 10 to 15 days in jail, often fasting. The few who have been sentenced have been given suspended sentences or time served. It seems clear that the local authorities do not want us clogging up, or vigiling outside, their over-crowded jail or courtrooms.

Finally, amidst weekly arrests, jailhouse vigils, and pre-trial court appearances, a part of the support community has launched a spin-off project called "Building Our Swords into Plowshares." When Danny and Terry rejected our home-building proposal last year, a number of us decided that we should go ahead with it anyway, as a community demonstration project focusing on the need to use our resources for nurturing life rather than destroying it. So, last month, on August 17, we had a festive groundbreaking on a vacant lot in south Greenfield, and as of mid-September, the foundation has been poured, framing has begun, and we are busy soliciting contributions of labor, materials, and money. So far, a sizeable fraction of the money has come from alternative funds set up by war tax resistance groups around the country.

Endorsed by 19 local organizations, the project will result in an ecologically-designed, energy-efficient duplex that will house two needy families in the area. We like to think of this in the Gandhian sense, as the "constructive program" that goes hand in hand with our nonviolent resistance.

While it's still not clear whether we will ever get our home back, Betsy and I have no regrets about having initiated this whole chain of events. The community that has formed around the action has been wonderfully inspired and deeply inspiring, and the issue of paying for war has been raised in these parts as never before. For sure there have been enormous stresses for us, for our Land Trust neighbors in Colrain, and for the support community as a whole. Not the least of these stresses has been our own strenuous disagreements with each other over tactics and strategy.

As the action has progressed, some folks have pulled out and others have joined in. But the core community has remained solid, based on the principle of mutual respect for what each person feels called upon to do and not do.

The conflict with Danny and Terry has been sad for all of us, but we recognize that conflict is inevitable and that the real issue is how we engage in it. As a community, we have tried our best to engage in this conflict according to what we perceive to be the dictates of nonviolence. No doubt we've made mistakes, but on the whole I think we've done well. And certainly the effort has enriched us all.

Editors' Note: In late December 1993 a settlement was negotiated and the Franklins moved out of the house after selling it to the Valley Community Land Trust for an undisclosed amount.

U.S. Military Invasion of the Western Shoshone Nation and Resistance at the Nevada Test Site

For thousands of years the Shoshone have survived without destroying their surroundings. Respect for nature and the land and living in harmony with their environment have been central tenets of the Western Shoshone religion. The Western Shoshone Council, which dates back to time immemorial, continues to be dedicated to the preservation of their ancestral lands, culture and tradition.

The federal government recognized the Shoshone title to this ancestral territory, known as New Sogobia, in 1863 when it solemnly signed a treaty of peace and friendship known as the Treaty of Ruby Valley. This treaty has never been modified or abrogated. It still stands as a form of domestic and international law. But what began as an act of Western Shoshone goodwill to facilitate travel to California has been perverted by the federal government. As trustees who are supposed to protect Western Shoshone interests, the U.S government has taken advantage of its controlling position as trustee and has contaminated Shoshone lands, exploited precious resources and have endangered the Shoshone way of life. In 1979 the U.S. government even attempted to buy their land (26 million acres), which has never been for sale, at $1.15 per acre.

The building of military bases and the testing of nuclear weapons at the Nevada Test Site continues to be the greatest crime committed by the U.S. government against the Shoshone. The Shoshone people, along with many other supporters, have resisted U.S. expropriation of their land for military and commercial purposes. They continue to struggle to protect their native land and resources and to hope that future meetings with the U.S. government will end the exploitation of their land, of Mother Earth.

Resistance at the Nevada Test Site

In the late 1950s and 60s several small groups of people came to the Nevada Test Site to protest atmospheric nuclear weapons testing. With the passage of the Limited Test Ban Treaty in 1963, active resistance diminished for a time, though testing continued. In the late 1970s the Franciscan community in Las Vegas began holding vigils at the test site.

In 1982, to celebrate the 800th anniversary of the birth of St. Francis of Assisi, the Franciscan community of Las Vegas sponsored a Lenten vigil which brought people from varied religious communities across the U.S. to protest at the site. In 1984, the Nevada Desert Experience (NDE) was formed and still continues to sponsor annual retreats and nonviolent actions at the test site commemorating the bombings of Hiroshima and Nagasaki (Aug. 6-9) and during Lent.

Since the early 1980s Greenpeace, the now disbanded American Peace Test, NDE, women's peace groups and host of other groups have organized numerous protests at the test site, which have resulted in thousands of arrests. Shoshone Indians have been an integral part of this resistance, giving enthusiastic permission to resisters to be on their land to resist testing. On a number of occasions, members of the Shoshone Nation have been arrested for going onto the test site — their own land — to demand an end to nuclear testing.

The NDE and many other peace groups continue to work arduously for an end to nuclear testing and the passing of Comprehensive Test Ban Treaty.

Local Campaigns

Faith, Hope, and a Nonviolent Campaign

Molly Rush

Imagine a world without nuclear weapons. It's difficult. Nuclear bombs exist and are real; the threat of extinction is real. This reality, which seems to cancel out any future, is so overwhelming that it forces us into passive resignation — call it psychic numbing, a sense of helplessness, or despair. We put the blame on God, saying, "It's all in Revelation." Or we hope that God won't let it finally happen. In any case, we feel that nothing can be done. Even some resistance efforts suggest an attitude of righteous futility instead of Christian hope grounded in a loving but tough-minded realism.

Could anything be changed? We knew we had already been changed by having to confront the reality of the bomb in our lives. Fear, conscience, imagination, hope — these all cause us to make new decisions and to change. Could we entertain the audacious idea that acts of nonviolent resistance at two local producers of components for first-strike nuclear weapons, Rockwell International and Westinghouse, could change anything?

About four years ago a small group in Pittsburgh began meeting to pray about and discuss the nuclear threat, a threat that seemed — and often still seems — overwhelming, remote, and beyond our grasp. We couldn't see the weapons; they were built in plants in Ohio, Maryland, and California as a result of the decisions made at the corporate headquarters in Pittsburgh. The assembly process took place mysteriously, out of sight, if not entirely out of mind. Our months of thought and prayer led to a written proposal that formed the basis for the River City Nonviolent Resistance Campaign. We sent copies of the proposal to both Rockwell and Westinghouse, which informed them that we would leaflet weekly, alternating from one company to the other. We would from time to time engage in "graduated provocations," by which we meant civil disobedience. We would also continue to meet and pray each week and we would invite other community and religious groups to share in our activities. We would always proceed openly, notifying the corporations of our plans, hand-delivering our weekly leaflet to the front offices, and warning them when acts of civil disobedience were imminent.

Over the weeks, months, and years during which we've distributed nearly a hundred thousand leaflets, we have experienced a wide range of feelings. Sometimes our efforts have seemed futile. Apathy more than hostility can enrage anyone trying to make a dent in what seems a nearly impervious surface. Sometimes an insult has brought tears. Cold has numbed fingers and toes. We have often come to our weekly meetings feeling discouraged, but in the sharing of experiences we usually found ways to lighten up, to come up with a new idea, or to laugh together over our foibles.

On the other hand, once in a while we have received a "Thank you for doing this" or a friendly smile. And we've come to find out that corporations are not monoliths beyond human judgment and decision; they are made up of people, and many are people we know: colleagues in the civil rights movement, former students, fellow students, neighbors, or members of churches supporting our vigils. We know a few executives' wives who are involved in peace work. And we've come to know the security people. We invited them to our nonviolent training sessions — and they came! In the spring of 1985, we met with four Westinghouse officials. It was the second meeting of an "ongoing dialogue" agreed to by top management following nine days of civil disobedience in their lobby in March and April. During those nine days, 18 people were arrested as they carried messages in the form of homemade banners, sang songs, or gave speeches on the company's production of first-strike weapons parts. Eighty people later showed up in support of those arrested. The building manager then convinced the corporation, to which he is very loyal, that good security required discussion with us. His own views had undergone a real change in the preceding years.

In that meeting, River City member Liane Norman gave an impressive presentation outlining just what first-strike capability meant. It was a careful, lucid picture, without rhetoric or moral posturing, of the direction weapons developments are taking. Norman pointed out that both the United States and the Soviet Union base their policies on capabilities, which they can see, rather than on intentions, which are invisible. "First-strike" does not so much describe particular weapons as it does a system capable of destroying enemy weapons and communications command control centers with accuracy, coordination, simultaneity, and unanswerability. She pointed out that the Soviet response to a system perceived to give the United States a first-strike capability might well lead to their adoption of a launch-on-warning posture. The safety of the world would then be tied to the reliability of Soviet computers. Norman asked the Westinghouse officials to keep in mind the question, "Do you, as individuals and as members of a corporation, consent to the acquisition of a first-strike capability?"

In the discussion that followed, one official incredulously but courteously asked, "What do you expect us to do, stop making nuclear weapons?" Our answer was yes! But we pointed out that the arms race will end one step at a time, as it began. And Westinghouse can end its contribution one step at a time as well. If it's impossible to imagine a world without nuclear weapons all at once, perhaps one can imagine a gradual reduction. Westinghouse could refuse one new contract, which would be a public first step away from involvement with first-strike weapons.

We discussed the psychological impact such a decision might have. It might encourage others to take similar steps. Perhaps we and Westinghouse might lobby together for peaceful production alternatives in which their technical expertise might be used to solve pressing environmental problems. The question arose about stockholders. We imagined an educational program designed to create a base of support among employees and shareholders for new and safer policies. An educational precedent does exist: in 1960, after Westinghouse pleaded guilty to criminal price-fixing, Westinghouse devised a series of seminars on sound business ethics for its employees. This series continues to this day. Our discussions with corporate officials have forced River City Campaign members to come up with a concrete vision of steps leading toward a future without nuclear weapons.

While only two of the original members of River City Campaign remain, new people have joined us. Currently there are eight or ten regular participants. While our lives differ, we have come to care deeply for one another. One member is a young mother and artist, another a philosophy student, another a lawyer. We have one member who says she previously cared only about giving dinner parties and decorating her house; she considers her current work far more important. Another member is a teacher who drives an hour each way. Two members have changed careers from college professor and corporate worker to staff members of a peace institute. Other members are grandmothers. As we've shared hopes and fears, a bond has developed.

A similar bond has developed with the Westinghouse executives we've come to know. When I spoke to them of my experiences of psychic numbing, their eyes reflected a shared experience. They have eagerly agreed to talk about their own feelings at future meetings. Also on the agenda for the future is a discussion of options for action; we know that we're still very far apart on that one. Our blunt discussion of individual employees' criminal liability under international law raised hackles, as we knew it would. But the Westinghouse executives listen, and they tell us reports on these meetings go to top management. Four years ago our wildest dreams would not have included such a response from these corporate officials.

A few years ago a senior vice-president of Westinghouse looked on in red-faced horror as we trespassed in his lobby. It was Nagasaki Day, 1983. Several of us took turns naming — at the top of our lungs — the first-strike weapons components Westinghouse makes. After each piece we named, for example, "radar for bombers that will drop nuclear bombs," we chanted, "Hear the voice of conscience. Know what you do." As a result, two of us spent a week in jail. A few weeks ago I spoke in the backyard of the angry man's home as part of a neighborhood nuclear weapons study group! One Westinghouse employee contradicted me at a meeting with, "Do you really think our experiences are so different, Molly?" I do. In many ways. But we share a great deal too, and that is the basis for my sense that change is possible.

Sometimes we are skeptical. The Campaign's checking account is down to a few dollars. Can we really persuade Westinghouse to give up lucrative contracts in today's business climate? Maybe we're being conned by a clever public relations department with these meetings, in hopes that we'll eventually go away. But we believe we have no grounds for hope unless we are able to make a leap, replacing our natural suspicion with trust — trust based not so much on present realities or as a result of simple naivete or gullibility, but on a vision we have to imagine, shape, and flesh out. Unless we act on the realistic expectation that Westinghouse employees can respond to the truth of what we say with their own version of the truth — which may include some things missing from our own vision — we can't really expect any kind of change. If we allow cynicism to prevail, then any hope we may have to end the arms race is a pipe dream or fantasy.

An early meeting with Westinghouse employees was largely a public relations effort: one man claimed that they did not make nuclear weapons. This, we agreed, was true. No one makes nuclear weapons. Companies make components; these are shipped to Texas, where they are assembled at the Pantex plant in Amarillo. No one person makes a nuclear weapon, and so no one person feels responsible. We tried to explain then that we had come to Westinghouse to take on the responsibility for these weapons and to invite Westinghouse employees to do the same.

Now this man recalls that statement. It made an impression. Another employee now admits our campaign has changed his thinking. He is the one who got the corporation to commit to ongoing discussion.

We have no way of knowing, except for these glimpses, what is understood, what is remembered, what, if anything, works on the hearts, the minds, the consciences of the people we confront. We only know that our own lives have changed, that we have been brought to places we never thought we would be, and this has often happened because of another person who affected our thinking, helped us to understand.

In imagining how Westinghouse might change by taking steps that, linked to other steps around the world, could help back us out of the arms race, we've found that something unexpected has happened to us. The questions we are asking ourselves about our own nonviolence are deeper. We're recognizing more fully our own need for tougher spiritual roots. As militarism increases around us, we ask if we are ready to face consequences more serious than our previous brushes with lost jobs, despair, and jail.

We're beginning to see that the most important change is not up to others, but up to us as a community of individuals seeking to be peacemakers. Not only must we say "no" with our lives, but we must be willing to imagine possible alternatives to the evils that beset us, taking a leap of faith to do so. It is clear that the arms race does not exist apart from us; it will not magically end itself, nor can we end it by ourselves. We need the help of our adversaries. We also need to find practical, nonviolent ways to struggle for and defend freedom and justice.

There is little in our society that provides support and sustenance for what is essentially a spiritual task. Our understanding is based on the spiritual concept that we and all of creation are profoundly connected. We have no security in a system of deterrence that is based on a credible threat to destroy millions of our brothers and sisters, literally all of creation.

Neither can we reasonably expect to see immediate or effective results when the task is so great that it requires millions of people to respond. Yet our hope is based on the faith that the world can be changed and that it is God's will that we are being called to respond to in our resistance.

We must develop that "revolutionary patience" (in Dorothee Solle's words) that aims at the transformation of the world by remaining faithful, even when we see no results at all, knowing that it is in so doing that we will hold on to our humanity, living most fully that life which is gift, spirit, love.

The powerful lessons in nonviolence I learned from the River City Campaign (which is no longer active) have forever changed my view of peacemaking. A recent call from a former employee will, I hope, expose the existence of a now-unreported radioactive waste dump a few miles from here. The whistleblower referred to the Berrigans in a subsequent letter to me. Most recently, I've seen the hopelessness that draws young people into gangs begin to dissolve through the efforts of the Gang Peace Council of Western Pennsylvania, a faith-based effort begun by former gang members. I am more convinced than ever that when we seek common ground with our adversaries as we challenge our own and their assumptions, miracles happen.

NORTHERN LIGHTS DISPEL NUCLEAR DARKNESS

John LaForge and Mike Miles

Hidden deep in the beautiful Chequamagnon Forest in north-central Wisconsin, the U.S. Navy operates a gigantic transmitter system called "Project ELF." Designed to send secret one-way orders to submerged missile-firing submarines, Project ELF has been the object of fierce opposition since it was proposed in the early 1960s.

The acronym stands for extremely low frequency (ELF) electromagnetic radiation (EMR) — the very same EMR often associated with human health hazards, especially childhood leukemia. Project ELF's two huge generator-transmitters — a second operates in Upper Michigan — create enough electromagnetic radiation to continuously encircle the Earth with weak ELF waves. These signals are bounced between the earth's surface and a layer of atmospheric particles called the ionosphere, and they penetrate soil and sea water "several hundred feet," according to the Navy.

Even though the system is powered by millions of watts of electricity at the source, its signals are ultimately so weak at sea, that ELF can only 'blip' a single 3-letter code every 15 minutes to the submarine fleet. ELF's signals are so slow that the submarines with receivers can be used 'effectively' only if they are pre-positioned for a first-strike attack. The 24 highly accurate Trident II (D-5)missiles — with up to eight warheads each — carried by Trident submarines are designed to attack 'hardened targets,' i.e., to destroy (former Soviet) missiles before they are launched. ELF's 'starter pistol' nickname comes from this function.

With active opposition spanning 27 years, it should be no surprise that resistance to Project ELF would manifest itself in a variety of ways.

Differences in philosophies, tactics, personnel, energies, as well as historical influences, have brought the campaign through various stages including legal challenges, educational opportunities, and mobilizing participation by individuals. The end of the Cold War brought about a revitalized Stop Project ELF Coalition — over 40 nationwide peace and environmental groups — which has succeeded in bringing about a long overdue federal re-evaluation of this nuclear war fighting system. Letter writing, student organizing, and public speaking against the system have raised public awareness, but the most dramatic and effective attention brought to bear against Project ELF has been direct action at the two sites in northern Wisconsin and Michigan's upper peninsula.

During the dark era of the 1980s, a remnant of activists continued the resistance at the ELF sites in Wisconsin and Michigan. Their witness included efforts to educate the public, vigils, "tresspass" actions at the ELF sites, and a number of disarmament actions. Nearly seven years of jail and prison time was served by activists during this time.

A full blown campaign of civil resistance was initiated in November 1991, with the coalition organizing ongoing nonviolent occupations or blockades of the secluded facilities resulting in over 300 arrests. Generally charged with "trespass" and given a $175 citation, 38 of the people arrested have served nearly 30 months in the Ashland County jail for refusing to pay. Sentences have ranged from six days to eight months depending on the mood of the judge. Others have faced suspension of their driving privileges by the Wisconsin Department of Transportation for up to five years, a constitutionally questionable yet chilling technique to leverage payment of fines. Penalties are completely arbitrary, following no pattern save the whim of the court. Michigan courts have for the most part chosen not to prosecute fearing adverse publicity.

Because of this continuous pressure, several serious challenges to the Navy have been mounted. In 1983, the State of Wisconsin brought a federal suit against the Navy. The suit alleged that the Navy ignored Project ELF's health threats, and violated the National Environmental Policy Act. Senior U.S. District Judge Barbara Crabb found that the Navy had unlawfully disregarded data showing the possibility of biological and ecological harm from long-term exposure to Project ELF's electromagnetic radiation. In 1984, Judge Crabb issued an injunction halting Project ELF's construction. The Navy appealed to the U.S. Court of Appeals which sided with the Navy and lifted the injunction. It found in effect that the "Soviet Threat" was more dangerous than Project ELF's threat of possible cancers. The U.S. Supreme Court let the decision stand and ELF began transmitting in 1988.

The campaign to Stop Project ELF has recently been boosted by the formal condemnation of the system by state and federal officials, including both Wisconsin's U.S. Senators Russ Feingold and Herb Kohl and Representative Dave Obey in whose district Wisconsin ELF is located. The Duluth *News Tribune* noticed all the attention and in a May 5, 1993 editorial said: "Being against Project ELF . . . is getting so fashionable it's starting to attract major league politicians." In 1995, Michigan's U.S. Senator Carl Levin and Rep. Bart Stupack joined the ranks of federal officials calling for ELF's closure. Also in 1995, the Milwaukee *Journal-Sentinel*, the Ashland *Daily Press*, the Wausau *Daily Herald* and the Eau Claire *Leader-Telegram* all called for closing Project ELF.

After meeting with representatives of the Coalition, Senators Feingold and Kohl have pursued a cornucopia of legislative paths to shut down Project ELF. Calling it a "relic of the Cold War," Feingold introduced bills in both 1993 and 1995 to cut funding for the project. After being rebuked by their colleagues, the Senators and six other members of Congress urged the Base Closure Commission (BRAC) to include the ELF transmitters in its 1995 list of bases to be eliminated. Even overwhelming public input could not sway BRAC and again civilian control of the military (an alleged touchstone of American democracy) was thwarted.

Feingold and Kohl finally hit paydirt as they got an amendment to cut funding attached to the 1995 Recision Bill, a measure that cuts funding for previously financed programs. The full Senate voted to kill funds for Project ELF only to be overturned in a joint conference committee. An eleventh hour secret briefing by the Pentagon *on the wrong weapons system (EHF-an experimental Air Force project in Alaska)* turned the conferees around and Project ELF survived the budget ax. However, the uniqueness of so many legislators actually trying to *close* a military base attracted the attention of Jack Anderson who blasted the blatant pork-barreling in two nationally syndicated columns.

Feingold and Kohl continued to look for opportunities to pull the plug on the controversial transmitter and six months later they scored again. An amendment that any funds appropriated for Project ELF in 1996 could only be used to dismantle the facility passed the full Senate as part of the Defense

Appropriations Bill. Before the bill even made it to conference, eight Senators — the so-called "submarine caucus" because of their vested economic interests in construction and operations of the submarine fleet — sent a letter to the chair of the Senate Defense Appropriations Committee urging that the vote be reversed. It was. So for the second time in six months Project ELF survived a 'no' vote by the full Senate thanks to back room maneuvering.

The Center for Defense Information was called on by the Coalition to issue a statement and they agreed that ". . . Project ELF no longer has a valid military mission. . . ."

Only time will tell if the campaign finally succeeds or if it will once again be reduced to "a voice crying out in the wilderness." It is not likely that such persistent opposition to nuclearism in the North Woods will be silenced no matter the outcome.

REFLECTIONS ON A LENTEN FAST AND PUBLIC WITNESS

Art Laffin

In mid-January 1995, I woke one night from a fitful sleep, consumed by the nightmare of violence in our society, especially the gun-violence claiming so many youth. I felt overwhelmed by the horrifying reality that we live in a culture where nuclear weapons endanger all life; where the U.S. is the world's #1 arms dealer; where a ruthless war is being waged by the rich against the poor; where gun-violence has become a public health emergency. It dawned on me that everyone is a potential target of violence. I began to pray about what more I could do to help stop the epidemic of killing, violence and injustice that is destroying our society. With Lent approaching, I thought of Jesus' 40-day fast in the wilderness. I thought, too, of the transforming power of Gandhi's fasts. I felt that this Lent I should make a greater effort to disarm my own heart and, with others, call on the nation to choose God's way of nonviolence and justice. Hence the idea of a 40-day fast and vigils at places responsible for so much death and suffering.

It has been a great blessing to undertake this 40-day fast with Anne Tucker, Lynn Fredriksson, Michael Walli, and Jean Chapman and Patrick O'Neill, both of whom fasted in North Carolina. The Spirit also moved over 75 people from eight different states to fast for part of Lent. Many others participated in vigils and supported this witness, especially my community at Dorothy Day House. What a great gift to be in the company of so many wonderful justice-seeking people. It is amazing to see how, through this witness, new bonds of community and solidarity have been created.

In reflecting on this fast and the numerous vigils we held, the question arises: What did we accomplish? I can only say that the main hope of this witness was to be as faithful as possible to the truth and to somehow be a voice for the victims. Yes, our society is still marred with the same ills as when the fast started. Yet, somehow, through the grace of God, I know I have been changed by this witness, and I know others have too. I know that in each of our vigils — at the Pentagon, the White House, the D.O.E., the Republican and Democratic National Committee headquarters, the U.S. Capitol, the N.R.A., Beretta-USA, Lockheed Martin, General Dynamics, and at area gun shops — we tried to say as clearly as possible: "Stop the Killing," "Disarm," "Stop the War Against the Poor," "Beat Swords into Plowshares," "Save Our Kids," and "Choose Nonviolence." We acted in faith and humility, sowing seeds, leaving the final results in God's hands.

During our vigils we talked with countless people, including gun shop employees, as we passed out some 3,000 leaflets. At one gun shop in Alexandria, The Old Town Armory, a number of people told us that they had walked by this shop numerous times without ever realizing it sold guns. Bothered by our witness, Old Town Armory passed out their own leaflet to counteract our protest.

Throughout these vigils we sought to expose and resist the violence of our society. We received support from some and criticism and indifference from many others. We were told numerous times to "get a job" and "get a life." We tried our best to speak the truth with each person we encountered, and we invited them to join with us in creating a world without weapons.

As I write, it's day 38 of the fast — with two more days to go. This has been a very challenging time for me, a time to confront more acutely personal and societal demons. I must confess that I wasn't sure I could fast the whole 40 days. Like most people, I do like to eat! Yet, I knew that if I just got beyond my own compulsiveness and trusted in God, I just might be able to follow the leading of the Holy Spirit. Thus I was able to take this "leap of faith." I realize now, more than ever, how much I can do without and how essential the nourishment of God's word, friendship and community are for my spiritual and physical survival.

As the fast draws to a close, I am more keenly aware of the preciousness of life as well as the victims of greed in our world. During those moments when I craved a sumptuous meal, I think of what it must be like for the over 35,000 children who die daily from hunger or preventable diseases. While

I know that I can eat in a few days, these sisters and brothers cannot. God have mercy on me and on our world for allowing this scandal of hunger!

Living in an empire where violence and killing are the norm, we must "keep our eyes on the prize" and seek with all our being to live justly and nonviolently. Certainly this is a task that calls us to make sacrifices and life-changing decisions.

I know I have a long way to go to become nonviolent. I believe that every prayer, every word, and every act we take for peace and justice does make a difference. Gandhi declared: "My optimism rests on my belief in the infinite possibilities of the individual to develop nonviolence. The more you develop it in your own being, the more infectious it becomes." Thus, a nonviolent society can only come about if we daily strive to become nonviolent people — that is, people who embrace the command "Thou Shalt Not Kill," who hunger and thirst for justice, who practice compassion and forgiveness, who are responsible stewards of resources, and who resist all forms of state-sanctioned violence.

During this time when we remember the passion, crucifixion and resurrection of Jesus, let us commit ourselves to following the nonviolent example of Jesus. Let us be filled with the hope of Easter because Jesus, through the power of nonviolent love, has overcome the forces of death in our world!

October 1992: Protest by Atlantic Life Community at the White House, part of the "Vote with your Life" campaign.

PART II

FROM THE PEACE ARMY TO CRY FOR JUSTICE:
A SHORT HISTORY OF NONGOVERNMENTAL NONVIOLENT CRISIS INTERVENTION

Yeshua Moser

Editors' Note: *Parts of this article have been excerpted and slightly edited from the original. This article comes from the author's forthcoming book,* Recurrent Visions: A History of Citizen Peacekeeping Actions.

Today's headlines are captured by the attempts of governments to intervene in armed conflicts and civil wars by sending military troops under United Nations auspices to "help." U.N. Peacekeeping is sliding dangerously into Peace Enforcement, which is simply a euphemism for war. As soldiers and global strategic thinkers show themselves inept at developing new ways to deal with conflict, there are calls for the development of a nonviolent alternative.

There is a long and rich history of nongovernmental efforts at sending peace missions. Known as Peace Brigades, Peace Teams or Peace Armies, these ad hoc citizens efforts have been sent out since the time of the League of Nations. In total there have been more such citizen's missions than U.N. Peacekeeping missions. These people's actions, however, are not as well known. They are under-funded and minimally staffed, which often leaves them invisible to global media. They have been, for the most part, ad hoc efforts instead of issuing from central authority. We have no single word for describing the concept, and for the purpose of this brief overview I will call them citizen based nonviolent conflict intervention initiatives.

1932-1939 — The Peace Army (PA)

The Peace Army, proposed to intervene in the fighting between Japan and Chinese in Shanghai, was mobilized in Britain by Anglican minister Maude Royden. Ms. Rauden was inspired by Gandhi's description of a "Living Wall" of unarmed national defenders standing against external aggression. The force was offered to the League of Nations who did not give it any substantial support.

The Peace Army failed to raise enough recruits and finances to intervene before the crisis in Shanghai passed. The organization did follow-up with a few less ambitious proposals including eventually fielding a team of volunteers in Palestine for a couple years. At the outbreak of WWII the Peace Army was shelved because most of its proponents began working on the Pacifist Service Corps, an alternative to armed service in the British Forces during WWII.

1959-1960 — Sahara Protest Action (SPA)

The SPA attempted to interrupt the first French nuclear weapons test scheduled to be held in Africa. A multi-national group of Africans, Europeans and Americans gathered in Ghana. From there it sent three teams across the desert to enter French West Africa to interrupt the test. All were apprehended by French military forces. This action had the support of several neighboring African nations and peace action organizations in Britain and the U.S. Supporters in France publicized the actions of these teams, and organized public pressure in Paris. An all-Africa conference to coordinate nonviolent action to stop the tests was called Accra, which established a center for "positive action" against French nuclear tests and led to the freezing of French assets in Ghana by the government there.

1960-1961 — San Francisco to Moscow Walk

Taking the people's voice to end nuclear testing to three nuclear capitals, a multi-national group walked across North America, West and East Europe to Russia. The group managed to organize the first "uncontrolled" demonstration in Red Square. It is included here as an act of intervention in the Cold War — an act that was bold and international in perspective. The Walk was organized by the Committee for Nonviolent Action (CNVA), which organized several boats to the U.S. South Pacific nuclear test sites and an international protest within Vietnam.

1961-1964 — The World Peace Brigade

The World Peace Brigade was proposed at the War Resisters meeting in India in 1960 to "internationalize the Shanti Sena idea." Many westerners present at this meeting were inspired by the work of the Shanti Sena (lit. Peace Army) manifested by Gandhi's followers in India. The Shanti Sena's work in riot prevention and the disarming of bandits was particularly spectacular. The WPB was founded at a meeting in Lebanon in 1961, and had three sections: Asian (India), European (Britain) and American (U.S.). Each section was to coordinate the formation of small brigades to be sent jointly to intervene in an international conflict. The organization then became focused on a few immediate projects. The WPB established a training center in Dar es salaam, Tanganyika (1962), where it attempted to coordinate an international freedom march into Northern Rhodesia to support nonviolent calls for independence from British rule. The march became unnecessary due to changing political events which turned the tide in favor of the pro-independence movement. The last action officially undertaken by the WPB involved sailing a boat to Leningrad and the arctic sea to protest Soviet nuclear testing.

Several WPB veterans were instrumental in establishing and maintaining a cease-fire between the Indian government and Nagaland independence activists. The WFB drifted into oblivion by the mid 1960s without fulfilling the goal of regionally-developed crisis response teams.

1966 — Nonviolent Action Vietnam (NVAV)

A British-based initiative to intervene in the U.S. war with Vietnam proposed sending hundreds of nonviolent volunteers to North Vietnam in an attempt to halt the bombing. The effort proceeded, although without the support of the North Vietnamese government, and was able to send only a token team of about 20 people. NVAV never got further than Cambodia in its trek to put a presence in Vietnam. After losing their original goal, some of the NVAV team stayed in Asia to stage a protest outside the a U.S. airbase in Thailand.

1968 — Czechoslovakia Support Actions (CSA)

The War Resisters International coordinated this ad hoc effort to support the "Prague Spring" and to protest the Russian invasion of Czechoslovakia. The CSA "intervention" was at the level of information and authority challenge. They set out to "put into practice precisely those freedoms which the Czechoslovaks were attempting to defend" according to the organizers. CSA sent volunteers to leaflet in most Eastern Bloc capitals in an act of solidarity with both Czechs and local protesters in East Berlin, Moscow and Leningrad. Seven different nationalities were represented in the teams of volunteers carrying out this action.

1966-1971 — A Quaker Action Group (AQAG)

A group of U.S. nonviolent activists, including some former members of WFB, AQAG mobilized volunteers to complete several small overseas actions. One such action supported people displaced, harassed and sometimes wounded by a new U.S. military target range set up on the Island of Cuelbra, Puerto Rico. The Puerto Rican Independence Party called for citizens to engage in "pacific militancy" or nonviolent action. Over 600 of the 730 inhabitants of the island part in these actions. When the people of the island attempted to rebuild a former Chapel, AQAG sent a team to help them, and to provide a foreign presence for several months. Later, AQAG team members carried a model of this chapel around embassies in Washington, D.C. to publicize the islanders plight.

The struggle was ultimately successful.

AQAG also sailed the Phoenix to Vietnam in 1967 in attempts to deliver medical supplies to noncombatants in both North and South Vietnam. In all, three different voyages to Vietnam were attempted. All three were both acts of aid and intervention. AQAG volunteers were arrested by South Vietnamese naval forces when they attempted to breach a blockade of Danang Harbor.

In 1971 AQAG also sent a team to Panama in protest of U.S. support for counter-insurgency strikes in South America.

1971-1973 — Operation Omega (OO)

The organizers of this multi-lateral action were Indian Gandhians, the WRI in Britain, and Philadelphia Quakers. Participants of this adhoc effort also included some former WPB and NVAV activists. In India, Shanti Sena met with a number of refugees to organize a 50,000 strong column of refugees to return to the country as a "nonviolent liberation force." International volunteers to join the column were sought. The march was stopped by the beginning of the Indo-Pakistan war. Meanwhile, the international and local volunteer groups who organized under WRI's initiative attempted to take relief supplies directly into East Bengal (later Bangladesh). They had two trucks full of relief supplies, but no visas. One group was arrested by the Pakistani army, but the other group got through with its relief supplies well ahead of established aid agencies working through official channels. Some of these OO volunteers stayed on working within the country until 1973.

1975 — Cyprus Resettlement Project (CRP)

The CRP set out to respond to the needs of people displaced by the communal fighting between Turkish and greek Cypriots. This program was put together by several WPB veterans and others with support from the International Peace Academy. . . . The CRP succeeded in negotiations between Greek and Turkish communities where even the U.N. had failed. Several communities had joined together under the international presence and encouragement of the CRP to rebuild and resettle their communities before the project was brought to a halt by two major political events: the coup in Greece followed by a Turkish military invasion of the island.

1981-Present — Peace Brigades International (PBI)

Peace Brigades International was founded at a meeting in Canada as a second attempt by many former WPB activists and others inspired by the idea of an "International Shanti Sena." PBI has now grown into an international organization with 15 country sections. Each section produces newsletters, seeks funds and recruits and trains volunteers to serve on one of PBI's current projects. PBI is the most successful effort to date in creating and sustaining multinational peace teams in conflict situations.

PBI's first action was in Nicaragua along the border in Honduras, where PBI placed an international monitoring contingent. In August of 1981, tension was high with the expectation of an imminent invasion by U.S. and Contra forces. After the period of high crisis had passed, PBI's border presence was followed by Witness for Peace.

In 1983 a PBI peace team was sent to Guatemala and has maintained a presence up to today. The team developed what is PBI's most distinctive feature: international protective accompaniment of local human rights activists living under threat of abduction or assassination. Shortly after their arrival in Guatemala the PBI team witnessed that members of the directorate of a Guatemalan organization seeking the whereabouts of disappeared family members were being systematically assassinated. The Team members moved into apartments and offices of the remaining directorate members and discovered that when this immediate presence was initiated, assassinations against the directorate stopped.

PBI has since carried out similar projects in El Salvador (1987-1992) and Sri Lanka (1989 - now). PBI has mobilized short-term teams to accompany returning refugees in Honduras and Southern Mexico. PBI also had a project in Israel/Palestine (1989) and, until the change in government in 1990, was cooperating with the government of Nicaragua to develop a program of nonviolent, civilian based defense. In 1992 the North American Project opened to provide support for native communities facing external violence in North America. In late october 1993, PBI sent a team to Haiti. Currently exploratory teams have been sent to Columbia, Croatia and Chad in response to requests from local activists.

1981-Present — Witness for Peace (WFP)

WFP organized a permanent border and conflict monitoring program on Nicaragua's borders and brought teams of previously trained U.S. citizens for short-term tours of duty. Each group was coordinated so that after it left, another group took its place, providing continuous foreign presence. This was a U.S.-based initiative, and only accepted a few volunteers of other nationalities. The program was administered in several U.S. offices and a permanent office in Managua. WFP has the dual focus of: 1) providing a foreign observer presence; and 2) continue increasing the number of American citizens with direct experience of the results of U.S. foreign policy in Nicaragua. After their return home, participants are expected to organize domestic resistance demanding a change of U.S. policy in Nicaragua.

In 1989 WFP succumbed to pressures to expand their focus beyond Nicaragua. WFP has begun accompaniment of Guatemala refugees from Southern Mexico. In 1990, with IFOR, WFP sent a team to the Mid-East. This helped to develop what later became an independent organization, Mid-East Witness. . . .

1990-1992 — Mid-East Witness (MEW)

MEW, a U.S.-based program, provided teams based on the WFP model and received much of its initial support and expertise from WFP. MEW volunteers lived with Palestinians in the occupied territories. MEW folded due to lack of both money and volunteers.

1990-Present — Christian Peacemaker Teams (CPT)

Although first chartered in 1984 at the U.S. General Conference of the Mennonite and Brethren Churches, CPT was not mobilized in the U.S. until late 1987 when its activities focused on training and disarmament issues. CPT began its activities abroad by seeking hostage release in Iraq in 1990. Since then, CPT has sent teams to the Gaza Strip on a frequent basis, and to Haiti as part of the Cry for Justice coalition. In October 1993 CPT launched the Christian Peacemaker Corp, a ready reserve of people trained and standing by to enter into situations of conflict quickly.

1991-1992 — Peace Mission to East Timor (PMET)

This Portuguese-based effort was mobilized in response to the Dili funeral killings in East Timor. Organizers sent a ship with students from 21 nations in an attempt to land without Indonesian visas to challenge Indonesian sovereignty land claims to East Timor. The ship did consciousness-raising during it's voyage to Indonesian territorial waters and made it to within sight of Timor Island before being forced to turn back by Indonesian navy warships. Although questions of Portuguese political motives and corporate sponsorship marred the initiative, it still succeeded in publicly challenging Indonesian authority.

1991 — Memorial Human Rights Observer Missions (MHRS)

Memorial has trained and sent observers to several areas of conflict in the former Soviet Union to provide an outside nonpartisan observer presence. Set up by the human rights section of the organization Memorial, it is primarily a Russian initiative, but with members in several other, now independent, Republics.

Formerly a dissident organization in the Soviet Union, Memorial was dedicated to the social reinstatement of former political prisoners and the victims of Stalin. . . . MHRS has brought together social reformers from Armenia and Azerbaijan to promote "reconciliation from below." MHRS openly publishes its observations

of conflicts within the CIS and their causes, in Russian and foreign journals....
MHRS continues to send missions, especially to the volatile trans-Caucaus region.

1993 — Mira Sada (MS)

A joint effort of an Italian faith-based group, We Share One Peace, and a French aid delivery initiative, Equilibre, MS set up an international peace encampment in Sarajevo. MS hoped to place as many noncombatants as possible (Equilibre publicly called for 50,000-100,000) in Bosnia in an attempt to stop aggression through third-party interposition. MS did manage to get an international team of Italian, French, other Europeans and volunteers of a few other nationalities to the town of Prozor in Southern Bosnia before the project collapsed due to unforeseen political changes, disagreements within the group and stress.

1993-1994 — Cry for Justice (CFJ)

CFJ sent its first team to maintain a nonviolent presence in Haiti in late September of 1993, the anniversary of the 1991 coup. CFJ is a coalition of groups pooling resources and volunteers to put together this presence during the current political crisis. Originally this program hoped to ease internal fear due to an increase in repression prior to the scheduled return of former president Aristide. Now CFJ provides a foreign presence near rural grassroots organizations who are suffering increased attacks upon their members while the U.N. program has been sidetracked, the military maintains its hold on power and Aristide's ability to return is in question. More than 20 U.S.-based groups along with PBI coordinated the CFJ.

1994-The Future — The Balkan Peace Team (BPT)

The BPT now has its first volunteers in Croatia and has begun interviewing and recruiting more volunteers to be placed in Croatia. An exploratory team goes to Kosovo in November. The BPT is a German-based initiative organized with the support of WRI and BUND (Federation for Social Defense) and several other international organizations.

The World Peace and Relief Teams, mobilized out of Austria, has escorted some aid convoys into the former Yugoslavia, and also seeks volunteers to do reconstruction in Iraq.

The Future

The Global Peace Service is in the formative stages and Christian Peacemaker Corps continues its important work. PBI and WFP continue to operate, with peace team volunteers in international service and facing dangers 24 hours around the clock.

Each of these efforts are plagued by chronic lack of resources, both financial and personnel. Inadequate infrastructure, poor communications, and limited training opportunities are major impediments to manifesting a large-scale effort. Minimum public exposure in the mass media combined with little popular understanding of the dynamics and history of this manifestation of nonviolent action has also hindered growth.

The movement has, however, gained from the experience of past efforts. Better organization, more public exposure and more thorough volunteer and project preparation we will eventually move past these obstacles and put forward a peoples peace action plan to challenge the U.N.'s military-based "Agenda for Peace."

Editors' Note: We want to make note of two other groups involved in direct nonviolent citizen intervention work:

IFCO/Pastors for Peace coordinates the U.S./Cuba Friendshipment Caravan to Cuba. They have organized six shipments of humanitarian aid to Cuba in defiance of the U.S. embargo. During a caravan on January 31, 1996, members were roughly treated by customs agents, equipment was seized and 14 people were arrested and now face prosecution.

Voices in the Wilderness Campaign began in January 1996. The aim of the campaign is to break the immoral sanctions against the people of Iraq by soliciting medical aid to deliver to Iraq. As of February 1996, about 90 people have endorsed the campaign. Due to U.S./U.N. sanctions, over 1 million Iraqi children suffer from malnutrition and illnesses because sanctions make standard medicines impossible to get. The U.S. Treasury Dept. has threatened the group with a maximum penalty of 12 years in prison and $1 million fine if U.S. laws to enforce the sanctions are violated.

RESISTANCE TO U.S. MASSACRE IN IRAQ

1) REFLECTIONS ON THE GULF PEACE TEAM WITNESS
Anne Montgomery

What do the 90s mean for those who wish to beat swords into plowshares? First, they call for gratitude to the courageous women and men who nonviolently toppled dictators and tumbled walls. But these times also require a faith-directed response to the new-old "order": a world of economic rivalry, deep-rooted regional conflict, and the military dominance of the one remaining superpower, with its researching new weapons of mass destruction even as it focuses on "security" risks from Third World nations not always willing to support our interests before their own.

The Gulf War, in its high-tech overkill and its deliberate destruction of the civilian infrastructure of Iraq, points to an alarming future even as it concretizes such abstract terms as "discriminate deterrence" and "collateral damage." This Kairos time — a time of crisis and opportunity — challenges us to creativity in our resistance at home and nonviolent intervention abroad. One such creative response was that of the Gulf Peace Team.

In October, 1990, faced with the growing military presence in the Persian Gulf, a group of peace activists met in London to plan a nonviolent presence between the Iraqi army and the United States-led multinational forces. Members of the Gulf Peace Team intended to serve as human shields opposing armed aggression by either side and to bring home to politicians, soldiers and the public the understanding that killing is not "collateral damage" or "fulfilling a mission" or eliminating a depersonalized and demonized enemy, but the murder of ordinary, loving, frightened, caring human beings and neighbors.

On November 16, Pat Arrowsmith, Jean Dreze, Bella Bhatia, Sa'ad Allah Atrib, Bassam Pattal, Richard Crump and John Steel went to Iraq to negotiate the establishment of a camp. The hope was to have a presence on both sides of the border, but the Saudi authorities gave permission neither for that nor for campers to travel through their territory. One important condition firmly maintained by the advance team and finally accepted by Iraq was the strict neutrality of the camp and non-interference by the authorities, with the understanding that the Gulf Peace Team opposed aggression and violation of human rights by any party.

Finally, on December 24, 29 people from 11 different countries and ranging in age from 22 to 78 arrived at Wadi Ar'Ar, close to the Iraq/Saudi border. Significantly, the camp site was a place where pilgrims to Mecca laid down their arms. Word of the camp spread quickly so that by January 15, 1991, people from 21 countries had arrived, some of them committed to remain through the deadline. All who volunteered agreed to a policy statement:

> We are an international multicultural team working for peace and opposing any form of armed aggression, past, present, or future, by any party in the Gulf. . . . Our object will be to withstand nonviolently any armed aggression by any party in the present Gulf dispute.
>
> We as a team do not take sides in this dispute and will distance ourselves from all the parties involved, none of whom we consider blameless. As peace-minded people, we deplore any human rights violations that have already occurred in the area and urge that they cease forthwith. We recognize the intense suffering, death and environmental devastation that would occur in the area (and beyond) were the war to escalate, and we consider any nonviolent action to prevent such a catastrophe to be of paramount importance. . . .

As a member of the Gulf Peace Team, I found this time a Kairos moment, indeed, and the desert a place of learning.

On January 4, 1991, I flew to Amman with two other New Yorkers to join the Gulf Peace Team Camp on the Iraq/Saudi border. Since its opening on Christmas Eve, the camp had included over 150 activists, with a good proportion of women, over 60. Our group, joined by one from Germany, arrived in Baghdad on the Feast of the Epiphany — our own search for wisdom.

The next day we saw the human face of the embargo in the children's hospital: 40 babies dying daily for lack of milk and simple medications, the mothers holding them like a collective vision of the Mother of Sorrows. Children like these are now dead and mutilated from the bombing.

On January 8 our busload drove the 400 kilometers to join the 11 campers left in the large concrete-paved compound where most of us remained until evacuation on January 27. The advance team had set up Bedouin tents, rather primitive cooking arrangements, and trailers for washing facilities. That section of desert contained unromantic dirt and rocks with a few scraggly bushes nourishing a flock of sheep tended by a single soldier beyond the fence. The night cold was intensified at times by rain and wind, usually relieved in the morning by the sun.

And so, isolated behind a fence, within sight of the border station, and sharing food and our soccer ball with the border guards, we began the task of building a peace community in a war zone. The first days were filled with meetings (endless), workshops (informative), and the necessary cleaning, cooking and washing, (inventive). At 8:00 a.m., January 16, 1991 (deadline, Iraqi time), when the last bus to Baghdad had gone, there were 73 campers from 16 nations, West and East.

Between 2:00 and 3:00 A.M. the next morning we woke to the sound of bombers and rushed outside to huddle around our short-wave radio, the only source of news. At the same time, some of our friends in Baghdad were lying in the mud by the Tigris, on the receiving end of the bombs. The camp was on the corridor between allied air fields and Baghdad, so the waves of bombers continued, night after night: a call to prayer for the victims as well as for the young pilots caught up in the work of technological killing.

From that moment until evacuation on January 27, we worked through many decisions in our affinity groups: practical matters like conserving food or policy decisions concerning possible attempts to evacuate us. As it turned out, the Iraqis, who all along had shown concern for our safety and welfare, ordered us out just before their own sortie into Saudi Arabia. It was a difficult and tearful moment. A small group of campers sat in the middle of the compound. They refused to leave, and had to be carried to buses by their drivers when the soldiers refused to do so. My reaction was disappointment that we were moved at a moment when 73 strong-minded culturally and spiritually diverse peace activists were relating and working together in a new way. This was and is the basic work of creating peace in a war-making world.

In Baghdad, we joined other internationals who had been gathered for safety in the Al-Rasheed Hotel where luxurious surroundings contrasted with unlit halls and once-a-day cold water. But the spirit of the people on the streets was strong and their welcome to us humbling. We had time to visit a hospital and bombed milk factory: an experimental factory converting milk powder into baby formula, not only for Iraq, but also for neighboring regions.

Early on January 31, the buses arrived again to take us to the Jordanian border along the bombed road and around craters where civilian trucks still burned. After two hours at the crowded border post, the Jordanians met us and brought us to Amman.

But this was not the end. There was a week of meeting Jordanians and Palestinians, of discussing future projects with government officials and United Nations personnel, of talking to ordinary people in the market, of joining 2,000 children as they demonstrated for Iraqi and Palestinian children, the latter under strict curfew in Israel. A working group remained in Amman to accompany shipments of medicine on the bombed road to Baghdad and discuss other plans.

What did all this mean to me? To be between two armies seemed the right place at a time when we had the opportunity to stop a war before it began. It was the right place afterwards, too: the presence of people striving to be a community of peace in solidarity with those who could not escape, especially women and children. We believed ordinary people could create peace in spite of the powerful interests behind governmental war-making. The desert also spoke to me: of an emptiness where it is easier to shed the materialism of our culture and touch reality; of the biblical call to insecurity and trust in the power of God; of the search for the path revealed to the humble and the duty to "prepare the way of the Lord," to seek a conversion of heart to solidarity with the dispossessed.

I returned home with this sense of "no-home" unless it is "on the way" with people as loving and forgiving as those we met.

2) Resistance in the U.S. to Iraqi Massacre

Overview of Resistance

Resistance to the Gulf War was widespread and under-reported. According to *The Nuclear Resister* (April 24, 1991), in the United States and Canada, in at least 80 different cities and towns, in 28 states, there were over 6,000 anti-war arrests from August, 1990 through mid-April, 1991. In Washington, D.C. the White House was the focus of continual vigils and demonstrations.

On December 30, 1990, 11 members of the Atlantic Life Community Faith and Resistance Retreat climbed over the White House fence — the "Leap of Faith" action. Five people poured blood and red dye in the North Lawn fountain while others prayed and hung a banner on the fence: U.S. Foreign Policy – A Fountain of Blood. Thou Shalt Not Kill. Unfortunately the prophetic warning went unheeded:

> President Bush has the world well on the way to war. He has shown blatant disregard for diplomatic options offered by other national leaders, he will not hear the words of caution from religious leaders, he will not heed the advice of former diplomatic and military experts. He falsely tells us that Iraq will soon have the capability to make one nuclear bomb while he sends ship after ship and plane after plane to the Persian Gulf armed with hundreds of nuclear bombs. Soon he will devastate the Middle-East in order to "save" it, and the blood of the innocent will flow.

ANZUS Peace Force Plowshares Disarm B-52 System

On January 1, 1991, Moana Cole, Susan Frankel, Ciaron O'Reilly, and Bill Streit, calling themselves the ANZUS Peace Force Plowshares (Australia, New Zealand, United States), disarmed a nuclear weapons system at Griffiss Air Force Base, Rome, New York.

To begin the new year with an act of peace, the four entered Griffiss and damaged the runway and a B-52 nuclear-armed bomber. The B-52 was used in bombing targets in Vietnam and in the Persian Gulf. As a peace force, they came to Griffiss with the belief that the force of nonviolent active love is stronger than the violence of the Air Force, more powerful than the "deadly force zones" which protect the B-52s, and that such acts of disarmament represent the only way to peace.

The four appeared before Magistrate Scanlon in U.S. District Court in Syracuse, New York, on January 2 where they faced charges of destruction of government property and sabotage — charges carrying a maximum of 10 years imprisonment and/or $250,000 fine. The magistrate offered to release the four on their promise to return for trial. Each defendant, a member of the Catholic Worker movement, explained to the court that, in good conscience s/he could not accept the conditions for release. They would feel it necessary to return to Griffiss to continue their disarmament efforts. So the magistrate reluctantly sent them back to jail.

Before returning to jail, the defendants presented the court with their indictment of the U.S. government for war crimes and international law violations. Specifically, they explained that they were guided by the Nuremberg Principles to not remain silent when the U.S. government violates the law. They went to Griffiss, they said, to disarm a weapon of mass destruction, in this case, a B-52 nuclear armed bomber.

In their statement they declared:

> The New Year's resolution of our President and of the United Nations seems to be WAR; they threaten the destruction of thousands of children, of millions of soldiers, of whole cities, of our already precariously balanced environmental system — in the end, of all life. We cannot sit by and watch such wanton irresponsibility. We have just celebrated the advent of Christ, who came to reconcile all people to each other, to bring true peace, and to remind us that the way to peace is to place our allegiance in God alone and to lay down our own lives in nonviolent confrontation of injustice and oppression.

(See "Plowshares Chronology" for more information.)

YOLANDA HUET-VAUGHN

Perhaps the most impressive resistance to the Gulf War came from the military itself. Many of its members opposed it, and over 1,500 filed for conscientious objector status, many of them speaking out publicly and many accepting the consequences of court martial, harassment and prison.

Captain Yolanda Huet-Vaughn, MD, 39, arrested on December 30, 1990 for failing to report for active duty in the Gulf, made the following statement:

> I, Yolanda Huet-Vaughn, MD, am a board certified family physician, a wife, a mother of three children. I am also a member since 1980 of Physicians for Social Responsibility, the U.S. affiliate of the International Physicians for the Prevention of Nuclear War.
>
> I am a captain in the U.S. Army Reserve Medical Corps. In connection with the Gulf crisis I was called to active duty service in December 1990.
>
> I am refusing orders to be an accomplice in what I consider an immoral, inhumane and unconstitutional act, namely, an offensive military mobilization in the Middle East. My oath as a citizen-soldier to defend the Constitution, my oath as a physician to preserve life and prevent disease, and my responsibility as a human being to the preservation of this planet, would be violated if I cooperate with Operation Desert Shield. . . .
>
> I consider myself as a patriot and have taken these actions in support of American troops who have been deployed in the Gulf region, in support of

the American people, and in support of the children, both here and in the Middle East, who have no voice. I hope that in some way my act of conscience will help promote a peaceful resolution of the Gulf crisis.

Dr. Huet-Vaughn paid the price for her patriotism in prison, separated from her young children.

3) GROUND WAR — WHOSE ORDER?
by Jeanne Clark, OP

The order is very old
It smells.
Not only stale,
It smells like death,
Flesh corrupting.
Stale blood seeped out not only thru the days of air strikes
But thru centuries of innocence sacrificed for greed.

The order is very old
Kill the poor.
Take charge.
Might makes right, macho.
The weapons are new, need testing, experimentation.
So too the soldiers, some new, young, inexperienced.
But the motives are old,
Seizing land for resources native to our country.
Our means of solving conflict ancient, barbarian.
As if we had no voice to speak, no mind or reason
    for negotiation, no patience,
Just fists like bullies in a schoolyard fight,

The fists are now high tech and cause much more than nosebleeds
But blood unseen is tolerable and good for TV viewing.
The order is very old.

The new was breaking ground
Seed bursting forth with hope.
Many had discovered that war was obsolete

The world was one
And even animals and plants part of our community.
Minds were changing and actions following suit.
Peace through justice though fragile seemed possible.
A new world order was emerging where the poor would have a
place and the environment took precedence over money.

Intolerable to some this new world order.
The weapons makers felt insecure.
Centers of power shifting
Things turning upside down, inside out, side by side
Towers and pinnacles changing into circles
Loss of control, liberation.

They would crush this new world order being born
And in their darkness would attempt abortion
Offering instead their skeleton child as new.
They would even use God's name
And ask for prayers and sacrifice to old idols
Many would not see thorough their deception
And would join in choruses of hymns to a god who blesses
        bombs and death.
The order is very old.
But not as old as God
Not of her creation.

Some are still, silent
Knowing how deep they have to go
How far back to God
To discover again the child not aborted but
        silenced, gagged, imprisoned
By a technology that has no ears or eyes or heart to know
        the human.
They must continue to speak the truth
Now drowned out by shouts and jeers and messages of hatred
  wrapped in a flag of stripes and stars.

They know how deep they have to go
How long the journey.
They know too a rage that only a God of mercy could
        understand.

They go with tears
Loving those who look at them with hatred or disbelief that
    they could be so "unamerican".
A God incarnate journeys with them
Her voice is like a gentle breeze, quite still and soft.

The new world order of the nightly news is very old
An invention of doublespeak, a lie.
Turn off the set and enter into the community of silence.
The child is waiting there alive to be given voice and words
        and tune to sing.
We'll join in chorus loud and clear one day.
The order will be truly new
And every living thing will be at home.
But now the time is dark
And we are passing through the desert trying to be faithful.

4) SOLIDARITY WITH THE VICTIMS: RETURN TRIP TO IRAQ
Anne Montgomery

Editors' Note: *The following was written in Autumn 1992.*

In this year of remembrance, as we attempt to recognize very divergent visions of the conquest of the Americas, it is important to see it as but one in a series of imperial adventures, like the endless reflections in a house of mirrors, the house built by the old world order, now the new one.

We need to focus certain images, to hold them steady in the face of the ever shifting mind-and-heart-numbing media barrage. For me, the past 20 months have deepened some of these images to symbols of the intentions and choices, actions, and consequences of our current principalities and powers. It became yet clearer to me in my third journey to Iraq since January, 1991, that, even in the midst of so much world-wide warfare and impoverishment, the Gulf War, perpetuated in the sanctions, stands as the crucial violent event of our time as the deliberate setting of a future pattern.

The nature of the war and its effects have been analyzed by U.N. and independent teams: Bombing "surgically" designed to reduce a progressive — and therefore threatening — nation to a Third World economy and dependency; an embargo to continue that destabilizing and weakening process. Violence is an old story, but the weapons are the product of our time: the fuel-air bomb — the poor person's nuclear weapon. Behind it, the threat of the real thing in the Gulf; the biological weapon of pinpoint bombing of electric, water and sewage plants; the subversion of the U.N. through bribes and threats. All this points to a world order that small nations might understandably reject.

That is the reality reflected in the faces and questions of the people in the streets and hospitals of Baghdad and Mosul, in the refugee camps of Gaza, the villages of Upper Egypt. Last summer a doctor in Karbala spoke of burn cases: mishaps resulting from the unaccustomed use of kerosene stoves after the bombing of electrical power station. This summer I held children at a burn clinic in a small Egyptian village — burned feet, burned hands, burned bodies too young to understand that our "way of life" has much to do with theirs; that their half-built houses, which could have had proper stoves, were "bombed," too, with the job opportunities in Iraq.

Fire smoldered in the eyes of young teens in Gaza, filled with frustration and a learned hatred, a need to throw stones, perhaps because that is what they have been offered instead of the bread of opportunity. Their parents echoed the question of the Iraqis: "Why are you punishing the people if Kuwait was the problem?" and "Why the selective enforcement of U.N. resolutions?"

Other images suggest their Gospel opposites: wheat fields burned by American pilots, who, after bombing Mosul, could then make a cross in the sky: seeds of hatred sown so that Moslems in Egypt attack Christians — because Christians have killed Moslems in Iraq. Yet, in the Christian village of Karakush, the Dominican sisters daily handed out 4,000 loaves of bread (baked from grain "unfit for humans") to Christian and Moslem alike, to families who took refugees into their own homes until there were 40 to a room. And, back in Baghdad, young lay Dominicans had formed a community of the destitute, "holding all things in common," in a graveyard — the safest place available.

In a Mosul hospital, a Moslem farmer of 80 could only pray: "My heart is too full to speak," as the beads slipped through his fingers. His younger companion voiced another repeated theme: "You are a large country; we are a small one. Why have we been hurt? We are farmers, ordinary people; tell Americans we are like them." A woman specialist later echoed him and described the young especially as "put in a cage without food or water or dreams for the future." The psychological damage evident here, and in those who still heard "bombs" and saw "soldiers" or who could not speak at all, was a reminder of one of the most diabolical effects of terror and malnutrition: a generation of hurt children, many physically or mentally handicapped, all with grim memories, even the baby whose first word was not "abuna" but "bomb."

But there are other vivid memories pointing to the sources of hope: the children of Karakush crowded on old school benches in July heat, still eager to learn, singing to us; handicapped children in Baghdad, secure in the love of the Missionaries of Charity, learning to dance to their own music; the rebuilt Jumhuriya Bridge, a tribute to the energy and creativity of a people concerned about rebuilding the spirit of a city where once there were few thieves and fewer beggars.

Most impressive perhaps was the ever-present "Welcome," the offer of tea or even a free shoe-shine — that to Americans. This summer, even more than last, Iraqis seemed determined to make a distinction between "people" (them and us) and "governments" (the great powers that war on the innocent and their own government that does not share the suffering). Paradoxically, the sanctions and the sense of victimization have created a greater sense of unity and determination, even, as one cleric put it, "a new Iraqi personality": creative and hard-working where once everything could be bought from abroad.

But no amount of creativity can replace what *must* come from elsewhere: medicine for leukemia and diabetes, anesthesia, and on and on, to say nothing of milk for babies who die if they cannot be breast-fed by undernourished and traumatized mothers. The frustration and anger of doctors were encapsulated in the words of one: "I would like to help Somalia." Iraq could do so if the embargo were lifted. How to live with a national disaster for which a simple answer is simply refused?

In our own sense of helplessness we can at least "watch," refuse to flee awareness, pray to maintain faith in the Way of nonviolence, and actively resist the powers. They do not grasp the weapons of love, of forgiveness, the refusal to hate enemies or to place an embargo on the human spirit. Jesus did more than build bridges; he literally took the place of the enemy, the one scapegoated. One Iraqi painting shows two faces: an Iraqi and a U.S. soldier, with the words "I Am You."

Finally, the story of Jonah becomes a symbol for our own inner conflict as a rebellious people unable to accept God the Merciful, that in asking pardon we might receive the power to forgive ourselves and others. We need to risk repentance, admit, "I know it is my fault that this great storm has come upon you." (Jon. 1:12) We must allow ourselves to be thrown into the depths of the sea, the belly of the whale to rise again to the surface of the reality we have plumbed, one with ourselves and our sisters and brothers. And then we must walk from end to end of our imperial city, ourselves clothed in the sackcloth of self-knowledge, one with the "enemy." "I Am You."

5) PSALTER:
THE SECOND WATCH
by Anne Montgomery

The heavens declared the river of God;
   the sun stepped forth from its tent of clouds
     where light and darkness, wed at night,
         gave birth once more
            to hope.

And silver wings across the dawn
  or banked, silent, against the crimson sunset
seemed as graceful as home-bound geese,
      until we remembered when,
        in the moon's darkness,
        we first woke to the sound of bombers.

Each evening they return, the mighty nations,
and prowl the darkness;
they snarl like dogs across the sky:
they howl for their prey:
    the city
    its children,

their mothers.

Have pity, 0 God, have pity,
   for in the shadow of your wings
     we gather them for refuge
       'til harm pass by,
        'til the hounds of death run to their kennel,
          wave upon wave.

Awake, 0 my soul, watch and pray,
     remember:
Ours is the desert
   but theirs is the city of death.
 Watch with the watchman;
   dream of the garden:
   and awake the dawn of his rising.

Then shall we not fear the terror of the night,
   nor the missile that flies by day,
     God's pinions our cover,
     our only shelter
       trust in the Almighty.

When faithfulness looks up from the earth
   and justice down from the heavens,
     God proclaims Peace,
      The Merciful,
      The Advocate
      The Restorer.

BOSNIA PEACE WITNESS

1) BRIDGE BETWEEN TWO CITIES
Anne Montgomery

On December 15, 1993, as two of us from Sjeme Mira talked with workers in an office of the War Presidency of East Mostar, I was distracted by a constant tapping on the wall, a strange reminder of the recurring insanity of the ex-Bastille prisoner and shoemaker in *A Tale of Two Cities*. That vision was quickly transformed when we were invited next door by an artist in military camouflage painstakingly creating a wooden mosaic of the destroyed Turkish bridge over the Neretva River: the tragic symbol not of two cities, but of one divided by ethnic cleansing and increasing non-communication and enmity.

Bridges are old, but still powerful symbols, intimately linked as they are to both the building and breaking of civilizations and to what, on a deeper level, makes us human or inhuman in our relationships. The Nobel Prize winner Ivo Andric centers his chronicle of Bosnian history on the Turkish bridge over the Drina, a bridge built by an ex-Christian slave, grand Vizier of the Ottoman Empire, in the 16th century and destroyed by the 20th century war. The Turkish bridge in Mostar, preserved in lovingly crafted mosaic and the detailed records of an engineer, is a similar symbol as seemingly strong in its power to unite, but as vulnerable to the powers of hatred and division.

An hour before we saw the mosaic, our guide had led us, sometimes running across open spaces, sometimes against crushed walls, to within a few yards of the Neretva and a remaining pillar of the bridge. Nearby, in constant danger from snipers, women and men waited in line for water in a city also lacking electricity and gas: a scene reminiscent of Sarajevo where citizens, vulnerable to snipers on the adjoining mountain, precariously carried water bottles while walking over a bridge's remaining steel beam. But the bridges of Sarajevo, damaged as they were, still symbolized a city united in spirit, in the determination not to let "the aggressor" or the media define it as divided by religion or ethnic origin, still determined to name themselves only as "Bosnian." In Mostar the river had become more like a wall blocking communication and understanding as well as material aid. To reach the west side of the river we needed permission from the Croatian authorities, but we could travel in our own vans. We never received group permission to enter the east side but depended on empty places in a UNHCR vehicle, possible only because the regional director wanted us to see and communicate the situation.

And I saw the situation: rubble filled buildings and smashed windows, the barricades, the guns. But even more in the faces, sometimes visible only by candlelight: the faces of children looming out of the dark in a basement "safe place." I saw it in the crowded bedroom of 13 families; in the sad faces of nurses in a darkened hospital basement, speaking of co-workers killed; in the faces of wounded soldiers, a speechless but smiling woman, a boy lying patiently in a busy corridor; in the welcoming faces of people on the streets reading our leaflet. Their message, heard so often before, was, in essence, "Stop the war; then we won't need humanitarian aid."

We heard identical words in West Mostar, but many on one side found it difficult to believe that people on the other side spoke the same message. The tragedy of broken bridges and broken cities is most evident when one must travel miles and negotiate psychological as well as military checkpoints rather than simply cross a river to meet friends and family members.

I remember another city — broken by our own bombs — and a bridge, the Jumhuriya, laboriously rebuilt by the time of my last visit to Baghdad in the Spring of 1993. This bridge tells another story, constructed as it was from local materials by a creative and determined people. It joins a city within itself but not to the outside world whose embargo isolates a population that needs, beyond the necessities of medicine and food, human dialogue and cultural exchange.

So how can we, in our own powerlessness, help rebuild the brokenness that is so evident everywhere, in the divisions between rich and poor, "aggressor" and "victim" in our own cities as well as in the crisis centers of the world? The warning of an Imam in Sarajevo echoes: "You see yourself when you see Sarajevo. . . . The problem of Sarajevo is the problem of the world." And the words of several others become a theme: "If it can happen here, it can happen anywhere."

In December, 20 internationals attempted an experiment in truth, an effort to spread "seeds of peace" through our own vulnerable presence and the appeal of a leaflet to both sides of the Mostar bridge and also to the Serbs. The internationals walked to the Stolac checkpoint, this last venture blocked by the HVO: the occupying Croatian army. We will never know how "effective" we were, but perhaps each of those almost 3000 leaflets touched more than one person and planted the seed of possibility that there is another way besides armed aggression or submission born of despair. Certainly we all need to be open to "impossible" transformation and empowerment if more than bridges of stone and steel are to be rebuilt. If, according to the Scriptural promise (Ez. 36:26) our hearts of stone will be replaced by hearts of flesh, we can, in the power of the Spirit, become living stones in living bridges. Active and faith-filled nonviolence can support the hope of the future, of the children who still say: "We in this class [Croats, Muslims, Serbs] are very good friends," and "I want peace to all the people of the world." They, in turn, can renew our faith that the love of the weak and vulnerable is stronger than violence, fear, and enmity and will renew the face of the earth.

2) SJEME MIRA (SEEDS OF PEACE) LEAFLET

Editors' Note: *Sjeme Mira, Seeds of Peace, was an effort in December, 1993 of an international peace group to enter both the eastern and western sides of Mostar in the Neretva River valley of Bosnia. As the main organizer, Scott Schaeffer-Duffy, reported:*

> We were not able to stop the Bosnian war, but we were able to plant many seeds toward that end. We offered a Jewish, Muslim, Christian and Buddhist prayer in New York City at the U.N., in Rome at St. Peter's Basilica, in Croatia and throughout Bosnia. We distributed nearly 3,000 leaflets calling all parties to embrace nonviolence. We brought our entire group safely to the west side of the war-torn Bosnian city of Mostar. We even managed to send five of our group into the far more dangerous eastern side. We delivered over $5,000 worth of medical supplies to both the Croatian and Muslim hospitals in Mostar. We met hundreds of people: civilians, soldiers, clergy, doctors, teachers and U.N. personnel. . . . We can second guess our time here forever, but I believe that we did our best for peace.

The following is the leaflet Sjeme Mira distributed in Bosnia.

We are here from many countries because we could not stay in the relative peacefulness of our homes and watch while yours are destroyed. We are believers in peace who are deeply disturbed by the war that is going on in the former Yugoslavia. It grieves us to see your people being displaced, injured and killed, and your beautiful towns and cities destroyed.

We represent several religions and philosophies. The majority of us believe in God, but several do not. All of us believe that truth and love are supreme values and that nonviolent resistance, rather than military force, is the best way to pursue justice and peace. We are inspired by peacemakers like Mohandus Gandhi who said: "For the nonviolent person, the whole world is one family." In this sense, you are siblings, children and parents. How could we not come to your aid?

We come hoping to talk with people on all sides of the conflict here and to help relieve the suffering. We do not take sides, in the sense of believing that someone is completely right and someone else is completely wrong. We believe that, over the centuries, injustices have been perpetrated by all sides in former Yugoslavia (and in our own countries for that matter). We believe that these injustices have occurred largely because all sides have tried to gain their way by military force. In indiscriminately killing and otherwise hurting people and destroying valued property, war always violates truth, perpetrates injustice and generates hatred. We believe it is impossible to build lasting peace on a foundation of war.

We ask all the people in the former Yugoslavia to abandon military force as the means by which you struggle for freedom and justice. We ask you to adopt nonviolent resistance as your means of struggle. We know that nonviolent action, like military force, involves sacrifice and the risk of suffering and even death. But it does not do irreversible harm and generate hatred, and it will win approval and support of most of the people in the world. It can end the cycle of violence, vengeance, and destruction in former Yugoslavia. It can enable the children of this land to grow up free of hatred and able to see their dreams for a better life realized. It can make this land a place that people throughout the world would like to visit and enjoy.

We try to come without a sense of self-righteousness. In our own countries there is injustice and violence. We are painfully aware that we have been unable to overcome these evils. We welcome suggestions that you may have to improve our own societies.

We are not armed. We will not retaliate against anyone who may attack us. We do not seek the armed protection of any nation or combination of nations. We come with the conviction that, in a world of increasingly destructive weapons, if the human family is to exist much longer, people must give up military violence and use nonviolent means in their quest for freedom and justice.

PART III

SOLIDARITY WITH LATIN AMERICA AND INDIGENOUS PEOPLE

JOURNEY TO FORT BENNING

Larry Rosebaugh

Editors' Note: *On July 30 and 31, 1983, Roy Bourgeois, Linda Ventimiglia, and Larry Rosebaugh were apprehended and given "ban and bar" letters at Fort Benning, Georgia for leafletting Salvadoran soldiers. On August 9, 1983, the three ignored this order and entered a wooded area at Fort Benning, across from the restricted barracks area where 530 Salvadoran soldiers lived. They scaled a tall pine tree and broadcast a message taped by the martyred Salvadoran archbishop Oscar Romero via a large portable tape recorder. After half an hour, they were apprehended by military police and were charged with criminal trespass and impersonating officers. In addition, Roy was charged with simple assault. They were expelled from the base at 2 a.m.*

Two days later, they were taken into custody by the FBI and imprisoned. During this time they began a 40-day liquid fast to appeal for an end to the training of Salvadoran soldiers at Fort Benning. They were subsequently tried and convicted in federal court and received 18-month and 15-month prison sentences.

This article was written at La Tuna Federal prison in Texas in October 1983 while Larry Rosebaugh was serving a 15-month sentence.

The people of Brazil sing a song entitled "Hoje e Domingo o dia de Senor" — "Today is Sunday, the day of the Lord." It is a joyful, spirited song that depicts the true meaning of Sunday. It is the one day of the week in Latin America that is waited for, anticipated, and planned for by all.

Even when torn by war and hunger and broken spirits, they do not forget "Domingo," the Lord's day. To the people of Guatemala, El Salvador, Nicaragua, Peru, Bolivia, Brazil, and all the countries of Central and South

America, a sense of family, community, faith, and hope persists that cannot be destroyed. And in the heart, if not in the village church, "Domingo" remains the day set apart to give thanks and praise to God.

It is no coincidence, then, that such thoughts come to me today on a bright sunny Sunday morning. The setting in which I write, however, is a federal prison located on a tract of desert land 30 miles outside the city limits of El Paso, Texas. But Sunday does not lose its meaning within these walls for giving thanks cannot be limited by concrete walls and barbed wire fencing.

Two and a half months ago, Fr. Roy Bourgeois, Linda Ventimiglia, and I were arrested by FBI agents and charged with criminal trespass for entering the Fort Benning military base in Columbus, Georgia. Our concern was the 530 Salvadoran officers being trained at Fort Benning. Once trained, they would return to their country to continue the massacre that has already claimed the lives of over 45,000 civilians in less than four years.

No one craves taking up residence as a guest of the federal government. However, I am thankful for the opportunity to have been "called" to Fort Benning, thankful for the opportunity, along with many others locally and across the country, to march, to vigil, to fast, and to proclaim our "No" to U.S. military intervention in El Salvador. And finally I am thankful for the chance to plead in the words of the martyred Archbishop Romero to the Salvadorans in training at Fort Benning: "I beg you, I beseech you, I order you in the name of God, stop the killing. Lay down your arms now. Stop the killing of your sisters and brothers and accept the asylum we offer you!"

Roy, Linda, and I sit in three different federal prisons presently. We are thankful for the chance to join sisters and brothers everywhere in a conscious effort to end the insanity our government wages in our name. The following is some personal background that may help shed light on why I, in this case, am now where I am.

In 1974, I found myself setting out from my parents' home in St. Louis, Missouri. Destination: Recife, Brazil. I was ordained a Catholic priest in 1963 after five years of study in Pass Christian, Mississippi, with the Oblates of Mary Immaculate, a missionary order founded to work and live among those abandoned the world over.

Active in civil rights work, the peace movement of the 1960s, and various forms of service in the inner cities of Chicago and Milwaukee, I felt it time to follow my Order's call to serve the poor in Recife. It followed, too, to hitchhike across Mexico, Central, and South America. To hop a plane and arrive in Brazil in 14 hours seemed to go against the notion of identification with the poor to whom, by vow, I had committed my life. I was accustomed to hitchhiking, and it would give me a chance to acquaint myself with the conditions and culture of the people.

The two-month trip to Rio de Janeiro has left lasting impressions on me. After settling in Brazil, it was possible to understand even better the suffering and misery I observed on my trip across Latin America.

I spent the first several months in Recife walking the railroad tracks or, more properly, the government property that extends 15 yards on either side of the tracks. By law it was not permissible to buy or sell this land. Despite the hazardous living conditions for children and adults alike, the poor had no other choice but to settle here. Their shacks were lined up for miles, just feet apart from each other. Even though they lived with open sewers, faulty electricity, and often times bad water, my newly acquired friends welcomed me warmly.

The kids helped me a lot with my Portuguese and introduced me to the rest of their families. The adults loved to talk for hours over a cup of coffee and would share whatever little they had to eat. "How many children do you have?" I would ask. The reply was always, "four, five, six, here" — meaning still alive — and "at least that many more who had died before the age of five," they would add.

One day I was paying a visit to Jose and Maria and their 10 children. They lived in one room with only two beds. As I approached, I noticed a group of men, women, and children coming up the embankment in front of their house. Leading the group were three or four persons carrying a wooden casket that measured about four and a half feet long. The night before, Maria and Jose's nine-year-old boy was rushed to the hospital with stomach cramps. He died that same night. Diagnosis: death from malnutrition. When I entered the house, Maria was sitting cuddling her six-week-old daughter, Fatima. Smiling, she looked up and greeted me.

Early in the 1960s, Archbishop Dom Helder Camara, of Recife, Brazil, renowned spokesperson for the rights of the poor, and others introduced the notion of the small Christian "base community" among the poor in Brazil. For centuries, religion had taught the poor that poverty was something to be endured as God's will and for the salvation of one's soul. But now this notion would change. Meeting with their neighbors, people would come together to reflect on the Scriptures in light of the reality around them. They would soon realize the root causes of their oppression and how to liberate themselves from its bind.

These base communities were not a concept that could be put into practice easily. Lay leaders, men and women, young and old were chosen, trained, and sent back to their communities. The communities began to take shape. People were taught to see their struggle as one between the "haves" and "have-nots," between themselves and those 2 percent who own 70 percent of the land, between themselves and the owners of the giant corporations, foreign and home-based, who drive them off their land forcing them into the large cities where jobs are nonexistent and their human misery is only intensified.

In their newly formed communities, people also learned that the Sunday Eucharist was a place to celebrate their common struggle and future hopes. Their music spoke of the long hot hours in the fields, of young children cutting sugar cane along with their parents, of pitiful wages.

Before the "base communities" existed, few men attended church services in Latin America. However, when religion came to be seen as an integral part of daily life and gave hope to a more humane and decent future, men began to surface in the churches. Prayer and action based on faith in Jesus Christ was seen as worth living and dying for.

At the heart of the "base community" is the notion of nonviolence. In the countryside of northeastern Brazil, whole villages of campesinos schooled in nonviolence and the concept of the "base community" gather to voice their absolute "no" when government officials arrive to claim the land for cattle grazing. Accompanying the poor on horseback are often the local priest, nuns, lay leaders, and the bishop, who comes as an added strength during these confrontations.

Over the years members of these "base communities," sisters, and priests, have disappeared and been tortured and killed. Yet the people recognize this as the price to be paid for their eventual liberation.

Today in Brazil, there are as many as 80,000 Christian "base communities" and 500,000 are estimated to exist across Central and South America. In 1968 the Catholic Conference of Bishops of Latin America met in Medellin, Columbia, and chose to make a "preferential option for the poor" the primary objective of the church in Latin America. Ten years later in Pueblo, Mexico, this option for the poor was reinforced with more vision and clarity.

In the 1960s, Dom Helder Camara stood as the main figure in the struggle for justice in Brazil. His voice, which continued to cry out in defense of the poor, was soon silenced. Between 1968 and 1978 he could not be heard on radio or seen on television. His name could not be mentioned in the Brazilian press, so much was he feared by the powerful. However, this personal persecution only fostered the rise of other church leaders, Protestant and Catholic.

Today, it is the united voices of the bishops and church leaders in Brazil who are first to be heard when injustice is incurred. It is the church in Brazil, Catholic and Protestant, and its commitment to the poor that threatens the government the most. Bishops, clergy, religious, and lay members of the Christian community are called "Communists" and "subversives" and accused of homosexual activities on the front page of the newspapers. In other countries of Latin America, the story runs much the same.

In Nicaragua, it was the men and women of the "base communities" who rose up to lead the struggle against the tyrannical regime of Somoza. In El Salvador, Archbishop Oscar Romero was assassinated three weeks after writing President Carter demanding that all U.S. military aid be prohibited from entering El Salvador. He believed in the people's right to determine their own destiny and that outside military intervention only prolongs the oppression of the people.

Fr. Miguel d'Escoto, Maryknoll priest and Sandinista Minister of Foreign Affairs in Nicaragua, says that the armed revolution that occurred in Nicaragua could have been prevented had the bishops been united in their condemnation of the Somoza dynasty. However, in Latin America, bishops are often chosen from the ruling class, who for centuries have determined the direction of the church. With the bishop's conferences of Medellin and Pueblo, things are changing, but slowly. Despite the disappearance, torture, and death within the "base communities," the people continue meeting to pray and reflect on the gospel. The Acts of the Apostles, with the accounts of imprisonment and persecution, reads as an existing reality to the people of Latin America.

Big corporations, foreign and native, are being condemned by the church for their exploitive and deplorable practices. Coca-Cola in Guatemala was condemned for its hazardous working conditions and unjust wages. The people have come to see the exportation of coffee, cattle, and sugar cane to North America and Europe as a grave and fatal social sin that must be resisted.

We went to Fort Benning to be a voice for the poor and voiceless of Central America. We went to plead on behalf of the Salvadoran people in the words of their own Archbishop Romero: "Lay down your arms, stop the killing, and cease the oppression once and for all."

The cry of Communism is once again heralded by the U.S. government as an excuse to protect the interests of the rich at the expense of the poor in Central America. The cry of Communism legitimizes the killing of an innocent people.

Let us listen to our own people returning from Latin America after years of service and identification with the poor. Let us discover the truth of what is really happening from those who have shared the true spirit of Christianity with members of the "base communities," who strive to make the gospel a reality in their lives today.

Confinement now for the three of us is a time when we sit longer and chew the words of world realities more thoroughly. We begin to feel the conditions we hear of in the Philippines, Grenada, Lebanon, Honduras, and all of Central America. And we ask "why" even more intensely!

We see our brothers and sisters confined to meaningless existences, and our blood begins to stir. Each news item of torture or disappearance deeply touches our nervous system. We know an identification not before sensed, between the imprisoned here and with sisters and brothers everywhere. The Third World is obviously not confined to existence outside our own borders.

Sometimes the most important thing we can do is merely to share the experience of being imprisoned. It is not so much in doing, meeting, and solving problems, but in being with, and being without, and, most significant, in just being.

The poor and oppressed of our own cities, of the rural areas of Appalachia, of Native American reservations across the United States have much to teach us. We must listen and share in their oppression. By doing this, we join hands with sisters and brothers the world over.

Note: SOA Watch, a public education and nonviolent action campaign to shut down the School of the Americas (SOA), based at Ft. Benning, GA, was founded in 1990 by Fr. Roy Bourgeois. Roy, Pat Liteky and Charlie Liteky poured blood on the SOA on the first anniversary of the murders of the six Jesuits and two women who were killed on November 16, 1989 at the University of Central America in El Salvador. Roy served an 18-month prison sentence while Pat and Charlie each served 6-month prison sentences. As this book goes to press, others are awaiting trial for recent protests and a bill has been introduced in the U.S. House of Representatives that would drastically alter the mission of SOA. For more information contact: SOA Watch, PO Box 3330, Columbus, GA 31903, (706)682-5369

THE CONSPIRACY OF SANCTUARY
Stacey Lynn Merkt

Editors' Note: *This article was written in early 1985 shortly before Stacey Lynn Merkt was sentenced for conspiring to transport undocumented Salvadoran refugees.*

What speaks to us today as we live our lives in the face of hunger and plenty, the homeless and the mansions, the welcomed and the unwelcomed? To whom or to what do we listen to make decisions about how to live responsibly? I cannot begin to list here the biblical passages that try to teach of the sanctity, the gift of life. I cannot begin to list the passages that exhort us to rout out injustice. It's our task to affirm life and in so doing denounce injustice.

Sanctuary offers protection to the refugee in our midst and publicly speaks out against our U.S. policies in El Salvador that have helped create a war there and thus refugees. More important, sanctuary is a faith response of God's people to injustice and those in need. Let's begin with a glimpse of why there is such a need for sanctuary.

El Salvador is a country the size of Massachusetts with a population of approximately five million. A small elite of 14 families, along with the military, dominate land ownership, banking, commerce, and industry. That leaves 70 percent of the population living in poverty with malnutrition, disease, illiteracy, early death, and no recourse. Throughout the last 50 years, numerous peoples' organizations have called for an end to these social injustices and the establishment of a true democracy. But these attempts to bring about change have been thwarted by the oligarchy and military. Seeing armed struggle as the last option available to bring about social reform, some of the major opposition groups banded together over the last eight years to form the Farabundo Marti Liberation Front/Democratic Revolutionary Front (FMLN/FDR). The armed conflict between the Salvadoran government and the FMLN/FDR continues to intensify.

In an attempt to crush all domestic opposition, the Salvadoran government has recently escalated its war against the FMLN/FDR and has repressed all popular dissent. It has labeled as subversives not only those directly affiliated with the FMLN/FDR, but also any group or individual advocating human rights and social change. This includes leaders and members of unions, teachers, students, doctors, nurses, clergy, religious, and those who help the poor. To be labeled subversive in El Salvador means to be labeled "communist," making you free game for the death squads. The death squads, known to be connected to the military, have carried out countless assassinations and are responsible for the disappearances of thousands. Those who "disappear" later turn up dead with obvious signs of torture.

The war against these "subversives" extends to the campesinos, the civilians. Women are seen as factories that produce guerrillas and therefore need to be eliminated. Children are seen as seeds of the guerrillas and therefore need to be eliminated. Currently, the increased bombings of the countryside are killing these civilians.

This is why people are fleeing El Salvador. Men, women, and children are risking the journey through Mexico every day. Already there are 500,000 refugees from El Salvador in the United States. What happens to the refugees once they are in the United States? If they are picked up by the border patrol (the police branch of the Immigration and Naturalization Service), their deportation process begins. The vast majority are indeed deported and face possible death. Why? One reason is that they no longer have their cedula, their I.D. The border patrol keeps it. Without a cedula, a person cannot prove that he or she is not a guerrilla and is thus killed by government forces.

Political asylum is supposed to be an option for the refugee who flees a country and is unable to return because of a well-founded fear of persecution for reasons of race, religion, nationality, or membership in a particular social or political group. Unfortunately, political asylum is not available for Salvadorans and Guatemalans. Less than 3 percent of the Salvadorans who apply for it are granted it. Extended voluntary departure (a stay on deportations while investigations in El Salvador would take place) has been pending in Congress for a year and a half. This status has been granted to nationals from 11 other countries in the past and is now in effect for nationals leaving Poland, Afghanistan, and Ethiopia. But it's not available to Salvadorans. That is because it does not coincide with our foreign policy. The United States has chosen to support the current, repressive government and thus does not support the thousands who flee that government.

I began working at Casa Romero, a hospitality house for Central American refugees, located in San Benito, Texas, in 1984. During the first 27 months after the house opened, more than 2,800 refugees passed through. Comparatively speaking, this is a small number of refugees. But what this small number does for me is put names and faces on what we read as statistics. I have seen the hungry, the homeless, the stranger. And I have seen Christ. "Lord, when did we see you hungry and feed you; or thirsty and give you drink? When did we see you a stranger and make you welcome, naked and clothe you; sick or in prison and go to see you?" And the King will answer, "I tell you solemnly, in so far as you did this to one of the least of these brothers [and sisters] of mine, you did it to me." (Mt. 25:38-40 *JB*)

My response to the refugees comes out of a deep-down spot inside of me that sometimes seems pretty foolish and simplistic. I believe in a God of love, a God of justice. The Greatest Commandment tells me that I am to "love the Lord my God with all my heart, soul, and mind and to love my neighbor as myself." Love is an active choice, not some weak, pansy feeling. Love must be visible in my life. So when I see my sister or my brother in need, I cannot turn my face. My sister of El Salvador or of the Soviet Union. My brother who lives next door. We are one community.

Sanctuary is a faith response to these sisters and brothers in need. It has Old Testament roots. In Exodus, Moses was chosen by God to lead the Israelites out of slavery and exploitation into the promised land. This was no easy task! As they entered into Canaan, God commanded them to set aside six cities of refuge. (Nb. 35) It was God's order to protect from further violence persons who accidently killed. It was a way of saying, "Stop! The violence stops here." The sanctuary is where the authority of God, the Giver of Life, is recognized as ultimate.

Today the need for sanctuary once again exists. Recognizing that the people fleeing El Salvador and Guatemala are fleeing for their lives, realizing that the U.S. policy of sending rifles, bombs, planes, advisers, and training creates the refugees, we, the church as a body without borders, must take a stand. Sanctuary's goals are twofold: to offer protection to the fleeing refugees and to offer a platform from which the voiceless can speak, so that the truth will be told and U.S. policy and involvement will be challenged. Currently over 200 churches of various denominations have made public declarations of sanctuary, officially stating their intention to directly assist refugees and to publicly speak out against the causes of the war in El Salvador.

What is the administration's response to people trying to assist refugees? Indictments. I've come through two trials. In the first trial in March 1984 I was convicted of conspiracy to transport and of transporting Mauricio Valle and Brenda Sanchez Gallan. Their crime? Fleeing for their lives to seek refuge in the United States. In the second trial I was found innocent of transporting two refugees to the bus station, but guilty of conspiring to commit that "crime." In this same trial Jack Elder, the director of Casa Romero, was convicted on six counts of charges ranging from conspiracy to bringing in, landing, and transporting refugees. In January 1985 he was acquitted by a Corpus Christi jury of transporting three refugees to a bus station.

What do we have in common? We are called "church workers." We are regular people who have heard of the atrocities in El Salvador. We have heard too much, seen too much. And we can't keep quiet when our God reminds us that "when an alien resides with you in your land, do not molest him [or her]. You shall treat the alien who resides with you no differently than the natives born among you; have the same love for them as for yourself; for you too were once aliens in the land of Egypt. I, the Lord, am your God." (Lv. 19:33-34 *NAB*)

Living faithfully is becoming subversive. I think people of faith in the United States have a unique opportunity. We are being asked to love by standing with the oppressed and confronting the oppressor, all the while realizing those fine lines within ourselves. The violence of war, the violence of the underlying causes of war, the injustices of hunger, disease, the few having all while the majority have none, we of the United States have the luxury of addressing these violences without dying. The costs for us are courtrooms (and their injustices) and prison time. I do not take either of those things lightly. But the cost of doing nothing, sitting idly by is too high. If I examined Scripture in light of today's realities in Central America and the United States and do not act in some small way, I would not sleep at night. My hope lies in the ripples that come from one small insignificant person seeing her task and doing it. The hope has already been born, killed, resurrected. We are witness to that.

The following was my reflection as I awaited my probation hearing on March 26, 1985, and my sentencing on March 27, 1985:

"He has nothing on!" cries the little boy as the Emperor swaggers down the road in the parade. It's a children's story (an adult's parable) by Hans Christian Andersen, "The Emperor's New Clothes." It's the story of two weavers (liars) who come to the Emperor offering to weave the finest cloth ever seen, so fine that the only ones who couldn't see it were either stupid or didn't know their job. The rules are set. It is mandatory for everyone to see these nonexistent clothes. And so though no one sees the clothes, everyone lives within the set rules, too afraid to question or speak out. Everyone sees the clothes — until the boy's cry. The cry turns into a murmur. The crowd turns it into a shout.

So many parallels jump out of this story for me. The people held on to their lies. They were afraid. The rules were set. Their decision to see clothes when there were none was based on the fear of not conforming, of not being able to speak out for the truth.

What does this have to do with refugees? The fine cloth we are given by this administration is nonexistent. We are told that the Salvadoran government does not make war on its people; it only quells a few Communists. Our role in this war is minimal: we send economic rather than military aid. And the refugees that continue keeping Casa Romero overflowing are economic refugees, not people fleeing war. Political asylum continues to be a fruitless recourse, but the only one offered.

The days between conviction and sentencing have been full ones for me. Full ones inside me. I think I have felt every feeling known to exist but anger, fear, hurt, and depression are my top four. In a nutshell, anger comes from the lies and injustices; fear factors down to being afraid of the unknown; hurt stems from being continually attacked by the U.S. government; and depression occurs because of the sameness of the situation. When will it change? For me it has become a time of letting go, of relaxing and accepting. It is a time for loosening my grip on what we've called our security. In letting go, I return. What I seek to return to is the faithful loving God that I have known for years, the God of Hosea who woos his straying people time and time again to say: "I will break bow, sword and battle in the country and make her sleep secure. I will betroth you to myself forever, betroth you with integrity and justice, with tenderness and love; I will betroth you to myself with faithfulness and you will come to know Yahweh. . . . I will love the Unloved. I will say to No-People-of-Mine, 'You are my people,' and they will answer, 'You are my God.' " (Hos. 2:18-23 *JB*)

We take a stand, risk, and face consequences not so that our commitment or faithfulness to God can be seen, but so God's faithfulness and commitment to us can be seen. I've come full circle. We love because God first loved us. There is hope . . . the hope that sustains me. I remember the God who is faithful to God's people. I act in community with the thousands of people who, propelled by faith, give assistance to the refugees. I and all of us here do not act alone. Our community begins with our brothers and sisters of El Salvador and Guatemala. If I go to prison, I do not go alone.

The truth is spreading. Just before the trial in Houston a bipartisan Congressional committee accused the government of misinformation about our involvement in El Salvador. We have more "advisers" in that country than the limit of 55 we have admitted to. And sometimes they do more than advise. Much of the supposed economic aid we send is really military aid, which means we feed the war, not the people.

The fabric is ripping. There are rips that we can see and tiny tears not yet visible. The seeds that have been sown with blood in El Salvador spring up here as we stand up for justice, love, people. My choice is to persevere. Let's remember the words of Archbishop Oscar Romero: "To each one of us Christ is saying: If you want your life and mission to be fruitful like mine, do like me. Be converted into a seed that lets itself be buried. Let yourself be killed. Do not be afraid. Those who shun suffering will remain alone. No one is more alone than the selfish. . . . Do not fear death or threats. The Lord goes with you."

Editors' Note: In June 1985, the Fifth Circuit Court of Appeals overturned Stacey's first trial conviction and remanded that case for a retrial. On June 2, 1986, U.S. Judge Ricardo Hinojosa dismissed Stacey's indictment after the U.S. prosecutor motioned to dismiss the case claiming that there was difficulty in obtaining witnesses.

Stacy's second trial, with Jack Elder, resulted in her conviction on a single count of conspiracy. On March 27, 1985, U.S. Judge Silemon Vela sentenced her to 179 days in jail and three years on probation. A condition of her probation is that she not live at Casa Romero. Her conviction was affirmed on her initial appeal.

In the same case, Jack Elder was convicted on six counts of conspiracy and was sentenced to one-year in prison for each conviction and three years on probation with the same condition that he not live at Casa Romero. After telling the judge that he would not abide by that probation condition, he was re-sentenced to 5 1/2 months in a halfway house instead of three years on probation.

Meanwhile, in a separate case, Lornita R. Thomas, who replaced Jack Elder as director of Casa Romero, was sentenced to two years in prison after being convicted of transporting illegal Central American refugees. She was scheduled to be released from prison in December 1986.

In another landmark case, 11 people were federally indicted on various charges relating to sanctuary work. On May 1, 1986, after a six-month jury trial in Federal Court in Tucson, Arizona, eight of the 11 defendants were convicted of conspiracy and smuggling undocumented Central American refugees. Six of these people were sentenced to five years probation, and two were sentenced to three years probation. The other three people were acquitted.

In July 1986 there were estimated to be about 300 sanctuary churches and synagogues in the United States, 19 sanctuary cities, 20 sanctuary universities, and one sanctuary state — New Mexico.

INDEPENDENCE FOR CAPTIVE STATES WITNESS

On September 14, 1988, 16 religious peace activists carried out simultaneous nonviolent actions at the U.S. Embassy in Honduras and Palmerola Military Base in Honduras and at the U.S. Embassy in Guatemala to demand an end to U.S. military intervention in Central America.

In Tegucigalpa, Honduras, Teri Allen, John Bach, Patricia McCallum and Mark Fryer, peacefully blockaded the U.S. Embassy for three hours. Simultaneously, Elmer Maas, Judith Williams, Kathy Boylan, Mary Jane Helrich, Gail Presbey, Bob Simpson, Brian Terrell and Art Laffin nonviolently blocked the main entrance to the Palmerola Base for one hour. This base, located 50 miles outside of Tegucigalpa, serves as a central U.S. military base where more than 1,000 U.S. troops are stationed at any time, ready to intervene, to direct and support acts of terrorism against the people of El Salvador, Nicaragua, and Guatemala. Both groups, along with Andres Thomas, who was taking photographs of the Palmerola blockade, were detained and held in a Tegucigalpa jail, incommunicado, for 65 hours before being deported.

In Guatemala, Charlie Liteky, Sarah Story, Dale Ashers-Davis and John Schuchardt poured blood on and chained themselves to the U.S. Embassy gate in Guatemala City, where they were able to maintain a prayer vigil and fast for nine days. Each day scores of people joined them in their prayer vigil. They returned to the U.S. on their own on September 23, 1988.

What follows is the Statement of Conscience which the group, "Independence for Captive States," issued at the time of their action:

We journey to Central America as people of faith, citizens of the world and U.S. citizens to stand with the oppressed people of Central America and to resist nonviolently U.S. military aggression against our Central American sisters and brothers.

We are People of Faith. Our spirituality is the framework of our resistance. Our faith tells us that we are all interconnected: What hurts one of us hurts all of us. Our faith also tells that we are mandated to uphold the Divine Command "Thou Shalt Not Kill" and to resist actively all forms of violence and killing. We vehemently deplore the violence, killing and economic exploitation carried out by the U.S. government against the Central American people because such policies violate God's law.

We are Citizens of the World. We have come to Central America in a spirit of faith-based solidarity and nonviolent resistance against bloody U.S. policies which kill Central Americans and violate international law. The continued courageous witness of our Central American sisters and brothers is an inspiration. Our consciences and our bodies cannot remain unmoved.

We are United States Citizens. As U.S. citizens we abhor the way our government has violated the U.S. Constitution by militarily intervening in the affairs of sovereign nations as well as by deliberately subverting the Esquipulas II Peace Accords. Governments exist to protect the rights of all their people. Our Declaration Of Independence states: ". . . Whenever any form of government becomes destructive of these ends, it is the right of the people to alter or to abolish it, and to institute a new government. . . ." We are deeply saddened by and denounce the ignorance, the arrogance and the hard hearts displayed by the U.S. government toward the democratic aspirations of Central Americans. As members of various U.S. peace groups, we have protested these policies at home. Our government does not speak for us in this matter. We cannot be in silent complicity with the death and destruction of human life wreaked by such policies.

On This Day Remembering Central American Independence from Spain, we have come to join with Central Americans in declaring their independence from U.S. domination. Such independence means an end to:

* immoral/illegal U.S. policies which aid governments controlled by the military, as well as mercenary contra forces who kill Nicaraguans;

* the neo-colonization of Guatemala, El Salvador, Honduras and Panama;

* the displacement and forced relocation of tens of thousands of Central American people;

* the disappearance of individuals by governments controlled by the military and with sanction of the U.S. government;

* a U.S. military policy of "Escalation Dominance" which centers a first-strike nuclear weapons policy to reinforce military intervention and low intensity

conflict in most of the world;

* money spent on the military which robs the poor, homeless and hungry in the U.S. and around the world of scarce resources that could be used for their needs.

We Have Come to Express Solidarity with those in Central America who struggle daily for peace, sovereignty, and dignity. Their determination, courage, hope and vision echo our sentiment: "We are one in the Spirit."

Editors' Note: The Committee of Honduran Women for Peace — Visitacion Padilla — have held periodic nonviolent protests at the Palmerola Military Base demanding that it be shut down. For example: from Sept. 11-13, 1990 they organized a "Peace Camp" outside the base. Also in April-May 1994 a coalition of groups organized a hunger strike to end forced military recruitment in Honduras.

THE PEOPLES FAST FOR JUSTICE AND PEACE IN THE AMERICAS

Editors' Note: *Following a three-month journey to Latin America where they met with numerous people from popular movements, Brian Willson, Karen Fogliatti and Scott Rutherford initiated the "Peoples Fast for Justice and Peace in the Americas."*

On September 1, 1992, 12 people began their intended 42-day water-only penitential fast on the steps of the Capitol in Washington, D.C. to mark the end of the first 500 years of the "Columbus Enterprise" and to honor 500 years of resistance by indigenous peoples. Seven other people joined in the fast at the Capitol for shorter periods of time, and many others were involved in support fasts around the U.S. During each day of the fast, except Sunday, a vigil was held on the East Capitol steps from 2:00 - 7:00 p.m. Throughout the fast, speakers active in the struggle for nonviolent transformation from North and South America gave powerful testimony; fasters met people from 33 countries. With several hundred supporters present, the fast ended with a special ceremony on the Capitol steps on October 12, 1992. What follows are excerpts of a statement by the fasters explaining the purpose of the fast.

The fast is a penitential reflection to mark the end of the first 500 years of the "Columbus Enterprise" — 500 years of domination, exploitation and genocide by the European invaders that continue to this day under the "New World Order."

We are also fasting to honor the 500 years of transforming resistance by the intended victims of the Columbus Enterprise — the indigenous, the African Americans, the mestizos, the poor and oppressed who would not be broken.

The fast, which begins on the fifth anniversary of the assault on Brian Willson by the U.S. Navy munitions train, (during a nonviolent act of civil disobedience at the Concord Naval Weapons Station, Brian was run over by a munitions train and lost both legs and sustained other serious injuries) will provide those of us who are beneficiaries of the Conquest with an appropriate culminating activity for the quincentennary and opportunity to prepare for the difficult task of transformation that lies ahead.

We have chosen to fast as part of our struggle for a radical transformation of values and conscience in this country and for a world based on justice and compassion, a world understood in terms of the interconnectedness of all life. We have concluded that we are quite inept on this journey but that is no reason to hold back, simply a reason to be humble. . . .

All of us who are fasting concur in the findings of Brian, Karen and Scott during their recent three-month trip to Latin America:

* Our government violates the sovereignty of other nations at will.

* The Andean initiative — the war on drugs — involves the U.S. in a counter-insurgency campaign marked by widespread human rights violations, including assassinations, disappearances, torture and massacres.

* Our neo-colonial economic policies are an extension of low intensity warfare. Our efforts to collect the foreign debt are pushing the poor to the margins of their societies — to squatter towns, to lives of misery and fear, not unlike the lives of the people who recently rose up in Los Angeles. Marginalized and unable to participate in the modern sector of their economies, they are considered expendable.

* Yet even in the face of the Conquest, people throughout Latin America offer our world hope and inspiration. Their life-risking and transforming struggle to liberate themselves from injustice and oppression strives to be democratic and collective and is conducted with a spirit of self-sacrifice. It transforms the people and their relationship to one another even as it transforms their relationship to the state and to the society. At its core it is nonviolent and prophetic.

All of our lives have been affected profoundly by our encounters with the people of North, South and Central America as well as with others who have carried the burden of the Columbus Enterprise. We have accepted their struggle for liberation as our own, a struggle being waged in our own land by the Native Americans, African-Americans, Latinos, women, the people of Appalachia and the "rust belt," workers everywhere.

We invite all who mourn 500 years of injustice and oppression to participate in this penitential reflection on the Columbus Enterprise and its legacy, the New World Order. We invite especially our brothers and sisters who have suffered from and resisted the Conquest to gift us with their presence. Let us share our stories and together envision a more just and humane world — a Peoples World Order.

Good Friday, April 1, 1994: During his Good Friday — April Fools Plowshares, Fr. Carl Kabat, OMI, dressed as a clown, hammers on the lid of a Minuteman III missile silo lid in North Dakota.

PART IV

Human, Spiritual and Environmental Consequences of the U.S. Nuclear Weapons Build-up and Military Policy

The Human and Environmental Cost of Nuclear Technology, Militarism and Ongoing Weapons Production

Art Laffin

If the world were a global village of 100 people, 20 of them would be rich or of moderate income. These 20 would have over four-fifths of the world's annual income: 150 times the income of the poorest 20 people. These 20 people would consume 60 percent of the food, 70 percent of the energy, 75 percent of the metals, and 80 percent of the wood. The one richest person would have more wealth than the poorest 50.

The poorest 25 people would live every day in "absolute poverty," subsisting on less than the required caloric intake for basic bodily functioning; and 45 would live on less than $500 per year. Twenty-five people would be chronically ill, and 50 would not have access to clean water. Thirty would be unable to read and only one would have a college education.

If the world were a global village of 100 people, five of them would live in the U.S. These five would have over one-fourth of the wealth, and the other 95 people would subsist on the remaining three-fourths. How could these wealthy five live in peace with their neighbors? Surely they would be driven to arm themselves against the other 95 — perhaps even to spend, as the United States does, as much on militarism as the rest of the world combined.[1]

The threat of nuclear violence and the use of military force have clearly become the chief means of maintaining U.S. control over much of the earth's global village and enhancing worldwide economic and political interests.[2] The end result of this means of control has been exploitation, suffering, and death for countless people worldwide.

The Human Cost of Militarism and Weapons

Presently, the nations of the world, led by the U.S., spend nearly $1 trillion annually on military purposes. The world produces enough food to adequately feed more than the current population. Yet, over 1 billion people are chronically malnourished and seriously ill and some 2 billion people suffer from "hidden hunger" because of diets lacking essential nutrients and vitamins.[3] About 40 million people worldwide die each year from starvation and preventable diseases.[4] This includes 250,000 child deaths a week and over 12 million a year. As the 1993 UNICEF State of the World's Children Report states: ". . . no famine, no flood, no earthquake, no war has ever claimed so many lives in a single week."[5] Over 60 percent of these deaths are caused by pneumonia, diarrhoeal diseases, or vaccine-preventable diseases or some combination of the three. In sub-Saharan Africa, where the situation is even more dismal, 10 million children die every year of causes that are easily and inexpensively preventable.[6] UNICEF estimates that it would cost about $25 billion a year to end child malnutrition, disease and illiteracy by the end of the decade.

Also, one out of every eight people worldwide lives on an income of less than $300 per year: a state of destitution so total that it constitutes a silent genocide.[7] In regions of Southeast Asia, nearly 40 percent of the population is afflicted with malaria, measles, diarrhea and respiratory disease in addition to hunger. Over the last decade, women have increasingly become victims of this dehumanizing poverty. The term "feminization of poverty" has been used to describe the reality that over 60 percent of the world's poor are women.

For me, these horrifying figures of suffering and death are not abstractions. In my visits to Central America, I have met sisters and brothers who live in utter deprivation. I have held Salvadoran children dying from malnutrition-related illness and gazed into their pain-filled eyes. I have witnessed how poverty kills! The tragic reality of our day is that the violence of hunger and poverty has become acceptable — while the nations of the world continue to devote increasingly more resources for weaponry and war. Hence, even if weapons are never used, by their cost alone, armaments kill the poor.[8]

It is not only in Third World countries that the needs of millions are sacrificed at the expense of sustaining weapons production and war-fighting efforts. In the U.S., over 36 million people live below the official poverty line and millions more live just above it. One in every four children under age six is poor, nearly 10 million children are without adequate health care, and 5.5 million suffer from hunger.[9] According to the Children's Defense Fund 1991 Report, every 32 seconds a baby is born into poverty in the U.S. and every 14 minutes a baby dies. Furthermore, 33 percent of African-Americans and 29 percent of Hispanic Americans live below the poverty line.[10] In Washington, D.C., 50 percent of all children are living in poverty.[11] It is estimated that up to 7 million are homeless, and nearly one-quarter of poor families live in housing officially classified as inadequate. About 25 million people in the U.S. are illiterate and 37 million are without health insurance.

Despite this litany of dehumanizing poverty, the U.S. has invested over $3 trillion dollars during the last decade on the military budget, or $45,500 for each U.S. family.[12] And the situation continues to worsen as elements of the "Contract with [on] America" are enacted and as legislation is proposed to severely cut and, in some cases, eliminate urgently needed social programs for the poor.

Since 1945, it is estimated that the U.S. has spent some $12.8 trillion on the military budget.[13] And after a 12-year $3 trillion plus military spending binge by Presidents Reagan and Bush, the $500 billion Savings and Loan rip-off, and the profiteering of military contractors and other big businesses, no wonder the federal government is near bankrupt. Despite a $4 trillion national debt and a projected $200 billion budget deficit, the Clinton Administration, Congress and the Pentagon will still spend well over $1.3 trillion over the next four years on the military budget. The official budget category for national defense understates the full magnitude of military spending. By adding other costs generated by national security programs — such as the military share of interest on the national debt, veterans costs, military aid to other countries, the military share of the U.S. space program and the Department of Energy — would bring military-related outlays to $426 billion in FY 1995.[14]

Not one major weapons program was terminated in the first Clinton budget which contained billions of dollars for new weapons.[15] Contrary to Clinton's disarmament rhetoric, the commitment to worldwide nuclear/military superiority is unwavering. This excessive military spending only serves to perpetuate a permanent war economy at the expense of the health and welfare of millions of people.[16] And because of its excessive military expenditures spanning four decades, countries of the former Soviet Union will continue to experience this economic deprivation as well.

Ironically, U.S. officials have encouraged and assisted military industries in the former Soviet Union to convert to non-military production, but have failed to promote a serious conversion program at home. Just think how society would benefit if the billions of dollars currently spent to build weapons were spent instead to retrain workers to make solar energy cells, housing units, mass transit systems, and technologies to clean up the environment? Economic conversion would also create more jobs. A 1993 Congressional Research Service Report shows that spending $3 billion on state and local government services would create 12,000 more jobs than spending the same amount on the military. Rather than embrace conversion, Clinton and the Congress have pursued dual-use (civilian-military) programs, most of which have a military mission.[17]

Meanwhile, as certain companies have been forced to close, diversify, or lay-off workers due to changing military priorities, weapons contractors like Lockheed Martin, General Dynamics and McDonnell Douglas continue to reap huge profits from their weapons programs.

Economic conversion and the demilitarization of our society is possible. Certainly, there exists the technical know-how to convert weapons industries into socially useful facilities. What is lacking is the will and heart to make it happen.

The Deadly Legacy of Nuclear Technology

Reliance on nuclear technology by the U.S. and other nations has caused untold environmental destruction and continues to claim a host of innocent victims. In her article "Early Crimes of World War III," published in 1984, Dr. Rosalie Bertell conservatively estimates that the global victims of fallout from nuclear testing number almost 16 million, with genetic damage being passed on from generation to generation until each family dies out. Dr. Bertell also claims that the past 40 years of weapons production have created some 2.3 million radiation victims. Moreover, she contends that between 36,700 and 78,300 new victims are generated each year by nuclear weapons production; by the "routine" pollution of uranium mining, refining and enrichment; and by nuclear power plants' reprocessing, transportation, and waste disposal activities.[18] The Center for Defense Information asserts that those in the U.S. exposed to risk of injury or illness as a direct result of the bomb include: nearly 600,000 individuals who have worked in the weapons complex since its inception, 250,000 U.S. military personnel who were present in high fallout zones where nuclear weapons were tested, and millions of residents of communities surrounding weapons facilities and test sites. Furthermore, radiation exposure from past atmospheric nuclear tests will occur over thousands of years as "delayed fallout" continues to settle over the earth's surface.[19]

In the 1970s and 1980s when Bertell and other experts on nuclear radiation were releasing information about the damages of nuclear technology, they were largely ignored by the public and discredited by the government. But recent disclosures by the Department of Energy of over 200 secret U.S. nuclear tests since the late 1940s and secret radiation experiments on tens of thousands of individuals between 1944 and the mid-1970s, including the mentally retarded, pregnant women, and prison inmates confirm the findings of Bertell and others and also expose an even greater crisis than first thought.[20] Given the number of above ground tests that took place in the 1940s and 50s, will it ever be possible to determine how many people died premature deaths or contracted cancer or leukemia as a result of nuclear testing? Just one of those secret nuclear tests in 1949 released 100 times the amount of radiation emitted at Three Mile Island! What about the nuclear tests that took place in the Pacific region during the 1950's and the effects on the peoples of the Marshall Islands, Australia and even Asia? And what about the ongoing secret releases of nuclear radiation from the Hanford Nuclear Facility? As recently as 1986 Hanford secretly released a cloud of radioactive iodine-131 carrying hundreds (or perhaps thousands) of times more radiation than that emitted at Three Mile Island.[21]

Radiation exposure has been linked to cancer, leukemia, brain tumors, miscarriages, thyroid problems, etc. As little as .000001 ounce of plutonium-239, the radioisotope of plutonium used to fuel nuclear weapons, may be sufficient to cause lung cancer if inhaled in fine particles.[22]

Nuclear accidents like those at Three Mile Island in March 1979 and Chernobyl in April 1986 have clearly underscored the fallibility of nuclear technology and the great peril nuclear radiation fallout poses for life. And as we know from the Chernobyl accident, radiation knows no territorial boundaries — it can affect people thousands of miles away. According to a 1993 Department of Energy (DOE) report, "the likelihood of a (nuclear) disaster is high."[23] Thus, as long as this lethal nuclear technology exists, accidents will occur and more people will needlessly suffer and die.

Pollution created by the DOE and the Department of Defense (DOD) has left and will continue to leave a horrifying legacy of environmental damage. The nuclear weapons production complex is plagued by radioactive contamination, toxic chemical contamination, and the absence of facilities for disposal of radioactive and mixed (radioactive and chemical) waste. According to the Worldwatch Institute's State of the World 1991 Report, the U.S. military generates a half-million tons of toxic waste annually, "more than the top five U.S. chemical companies combined." More than 4,500 contaminated sites of nuclear weapons facilities have been identified as having soil contamination, water contamination or both. Another 17,400 sites at 1,850 Pentagon installations have been identified as having toxic chemical contamination.[24] The Department of Energy estimates that it will cost more than $230 billion and take over 75 years to contain or clean up the current mess created in the U.S. by nuclear arms production. The situation in the former Soviet Union is just as bad.[25]

The final cost of the Cold War has yet to be tallied, but it has cost us much more than just money: Our obsession with national security is obliterating the poor, the children and our sacred earth!

NOTES

1. Adapted by Bruce Friedrich from Simple Living Collective, American Friends Service Committee, San Francisco, *Taking Charge: Personal and Political Change Through Simple Living* (New York, NY: Bantam Books, 1977), p. 340. Sources: *World Military and Social Expenditures*, 1993, *Washington Post*, Mar. 7, 1995 and Mar. 13, 1995; NCCB, "The Harvest of Justice is Sown in Peace," Nov. 1993; *The Prism*, October 1994; *Nation*, Dec. 19, 1994.

2. For a more comprehensive examination of how U.S. power has been asserted in the world to protect its economic interests, see Noam Chomsky, *Turning the Tide* (Boston: South End Press, 1985). Noam Chomsky, et al., *The Washington Connection and Third World Fascism* (Boston: South End Press, 1979); Richard

Barnet, *Roots of War* (New York: Penguin, 1971); Richard Barnet and Ronald E. Muller, *Global Reach* (New York: Simon and Schuster, 1974); and Howard Zinn, *A People's History of the United States* (San Francisco: Harper and Row, 1980); and Susan George, *The Debt Boomerang - How Third World Debt Harms Us All* (Boulder: Westview Press, 1992).

3. Ruth Leger Sivard, *World Military and Social Expenditures*, 1993, World Priorities, Washington, D.C., p. 28.

4. Jack Nelson-Pallmeyer, *War Against the Poor* (Maryknoll, NY: Orbis Books, 1989), p. 10.

5. *The State Of The World's Children — 1993*, UNICEF Report, p. 57.

6. Sivard, *World Military and Social Expenditures*, 1991, p. 3.

7. Ibid.

8. "A Plea for Disarmament," Osservatore Romano, June 1976.

9. Sivard, *World Military and Social Expenditures*, 1991, (see Priorities USA, section on poverty). Also see: *Wasting Americas Future: The Children's Defense Fund Report on the Costs of Child Poverty* (Boston: Beacon Press, 1994). For more information on children in poverty contact: Children's Defense Fund, 25 E Street, Washington, DC 20001.

10. *Washington Post*, October 5, 1993.

11. *Washington Post*, May 25, 1995.

12. Sivard, *World Military and Social Expenditures*, 1991.

13. *Center for Defense Information Military Almanac*, 1995, p. 17.

14. *Center for Defense Information Military Almanac*, 1995, p. 16. The War Resisters League, in their fact sheet: "Where Your Income Tax Money Really Goes," estimated that the 1993 overall Military Budget was about $602 billion. This breaks down to $317 billion for the current military budget and $285 for past military outlays. The $285 billion figure is broken down into two categories: Veterans Benefits - $33 billion; and interest on National Debt (80% estimated to be created by military spending) - $252 billion.

15. *The Defense Monitor*, Vol. XXII, Number 4, 1993.

16. See Seymour Melman's *The Permanent War Economy*, (New York, NY: Simon and Schuster, 1974).

17. Governments are intent on protecting, not dismantling, their "defense industrial base." The adjustment to lower military spending is largely left to the market, resulting in mergers, plant closures and job loss. In the U.S. Clinton budgeted nearly $20 billion from 1994-1997 as an economic adjustment to lower military spending. This amount, however is deceiving. More than a third of this amount is funding for

a variety of high-tech initiatives but not targeted for conversion. Another 30 percent is devoted to so-called dual-use projects (military and civilian), most of which have a military mission. Only one-third of the dual-use funds are civilian-oriented. See Lester Brown, et. al., *State of the World*, New York: W.W. Norton, 1995, p. 163.

18. See Daniel Berrigan, ed., *For Swords into Plowshares, The Hammer Has To Fall*, (Highland Park, NJ: Plowshares Press, 1984), p. 26. For further information about the history of the nuclear industry and the deadly effects of nuclear radiation see Dr. Rosalie Bertell, *No Immediate Danger: Prognosis for a Radioactive Earth*, (Summertown, TN: The Book Publishing Company, 1985).

19. *The Defense Monitor*, Vol. XXIV, Number 8, October/November 1995. Since 1945 over 1,900 nuclear weapons tests (atmospheric, underground and underwater) have occurred worldwide, with over 1,000 tests in the U.S.

20. Source for nuclear experiments on human beings is taken from the Advisory Committee on Human Radiation Experiments, cited in the *Washington Post*, October 3, 1995.

21. Newsweek Magazine, "America's Nuclear Secrets," December 27, 1993.

22. *The Defense Monitor*, Vol. XXIV, Number 8, Oct./Nov. 1995.

23. *The Defense Monitor*, XXIII, Number 2, 1993.

24. *The Defense Monitor*, Vol. XX, Number 6, 1991.

25. *The Defense Monitor*, Volume XX, Number 1, 1993.

THE U.S. WEAPONS BUILD-UP AND NUCLEAR AND INTERVENTIONARY POLICY — PAST AND PRESENT

Art Laffin

"The unleashed power of the atom has changed everything save our mode of thinking and we thus drift toward unparalleled catastrophes."

Albert Einstein

With the advent of the Nuclear Age in 1945, Einstein, who had been instrumental in persuading President Roosevelt to build the atomic bomb, knew that for the first time ever, humans possessed the capability to destroy the world. However, over the last five decades the U.S. and other nuclear powers have ignored his advice (and that of many others) and consequently our world spirals toward catastrophe.

With the end of the Cold War, the threat of nuclear war between the U.S. and Russia has greatly diminished. Nevertheless, U.S. reliance on nuclear weapons and other weapons of mass destruction continues and as more countries acquire nuclear technology, the likelihood that nuclear weapons could be used somewhere in the world increases.

Meanwhile, since World War II, some 125 wars and conflicts in the developing world have resulted in over 40 million deaths.[1] And UNICEF estimates that in the 1980s alone 1.5 million children were killed in conventional wars worldwide.[2] What more horrifying evidence is needed to conclude that we must rid our world of weapons and abolish war?

We must begin the process of repentance and real disarmament. If we are to truly heed Einstein's advice to ban nuclear weapons, we must acknowledge what really happened at Hiroshima and Nagasaki. We also need to confront and hold accountable the U.S. government, which for the past 50 years has pursued a policy of nuclear terror and global domination. This chapter reviews this policy of terror.

The Bombings of Hiroshima and Nagasaki and the Nuclear Arms Race

On August 6, 1945, at 8:16 a.m., the United States dropped the first atomic bomb, made of uranium, over the city of Hiroshima, Japan. Nine seconds later, Hiroshima was destroyed, over 100,000 civilians were killed and over 100,000 more were maimed and eventually died from the effects of the bomb's radiation. Sixty-five hours later, the U.S. government used a second nuclear weapon, a plutonium bomb, on the Japanese city of Nagasaki. Many *hibakusha* — the Japanese term for A-Bomb survivors — continue to suffer and die prematurely from their exposure to the nuclear radiation released by these bombs.

We live with the myth that the atomic bomb had to be used to save American lives and end WWII; however there is convincing evidence to the contrary. Many historians now believe that it was not necessary to use the bomb to save lives or end the war. The following summarizes this evidence.

Realizing that Japan was on the verge of surrender as early as July 1945, General Dwight D. Eisenhower, along with Admiral William Leahy, head of the Joint Chiefs of Staff, opposed the use of the bomb. They advised President Harry S. Truman that the Japanese would surrender in several months without the use of the bomb and without invasion. In Leahy's own words: "The use of this barbarous weapon at Hiroshima and Nagasaki was of no material assistance in our war against Japan. The Japanese were already defeated and ready to surrender . . . because of the effective sea blockade and the successful bombing with conventional weapons."[3]

Nuclear weapons were used against the Japanese primarily for two reasons: First, the U.S. wanted to hasten its victory over Japan without the aid of the Soviet Union, who was about to enter the war; second and most importantly, Truman intended to threaten the Russians and warn them not to challenge U.S. plans to organize the post-war world.[4]

Through the use of genocidal weapons against the Japanese, the U.S. set the tone for the already emerging Cold War with the former Soviet Union and made clear its willingness to use the bomb in the future, if need be, to protect its rapidly expanding worldwide corporate interests and its quest for global empire. It is from within this context that the nuclear arms race began.

Historically, the dynamic of the nuclear arms race can be described as an action-reaction cycle between the U.S. and the former Soviet Union. We need only to briefly review the major developments of the nuclear arms race since 1945 to see why this is so. For example, the U.S. was the first to develop the atomic bomb, the intercontinental bomber, the hydrogen bomb, the submarine launched ballistic missile (SLBM), the multiple independently targeted re-entry vehicle (MIRV), the maneuverable reentry vehicle (MARV), and the Cruise, Pershing II, MX and Trident missiles. A few years after each of these developments, the Soviets responded with a comparable weapon. In two exceptions to this pattern, the Soviets first developed the intercontinental ballistic missile (ICBM) in 1957 and the antiballistic missile system (ABM) in 1968. In response, the U.S. developed its own ICBM in 1958 and an ABM in 1972.

During the last 50 years, the U.S. and the former Soviet Union have amassed an arsenal exceeding 48,000 nuclear weapons. According to the Center For Defense Information, these weapons together are over 900,000 times more powerful than the Hiroshima bomb.[5] Collectively, they have the explosive power of 11,700 megatons of TNT — 2.2 tons for each person on the planet.[6]

The money spent by the U.S. to develop and maintain its nuclear arsenal has been colossal. Since the government first began work on the bomb in 1940, the U.S. nuclear arsenal has cost about $4 trillion in 1995 dollars. An additional $500 billion to $1 trillion could be added to this total once all known costs, especially those for operating and maintaining the arsenal, are documented and analyzed. In short, 1/4 to 1/3 of all military spending since World War II has been devoted to nuclear weapons and their infrastructure — far more than the government has ever acknowledged.[7]

An Overview of U.S. Nuclear and Military Strategy

After 1945, the announced nuclear policy of the superpowers had been "deterrence." This policy, also described as Mutually Assured Destruction (MAD), was based on the premise that both superpowers would refrain from firing nuclear missiles first for fear of the massive retaliation that would follow. In the late 1950s, the Pentagon secretly shifted from this defensive policy to an *offensive* nuclear war strategy of "counterforce" or "first-strike."

This strategy relies on deployment of weapons systems capable of executing a pre-emptive, surprise attack against the enemy's strategic weapons and command and control centers, thereby disabling their capacity to retaliate.

Signs of this strategy first emerged when the secret Single Integrated Operational Plan (SIOP) was approved by the Pentagon in January 1962.[8] This strategy was not announced publicly until May 30, 1975, when Secretary of Defense Schlesinger declared that the U.S. must have a "flexible option" of targeting "selective" military sites in the Soviet Union. He also said that the U.S. would consider a "first-use" of nuclear weapons to stop a large-scale Communist advance in Western Europe and South Korea.[9] In August 1980, President Carter officially confirmed this strategy upon issuing his Presidential Directive 59. This directive mandated that precision attack missiles be targeted against key Soviet military installations. It also conceded that the U.S. reserved the right to use nuclear weapons first if its national interests are deemed jeopardized, especially in the Persian Gulf. In the case of a perceived attack, this directive clearly authorizes striking *first* at strategic military targets — land-based missiles, airfields, submarines, command centers, and so on.

The Reagan Administration further advanced this counterforce strategy in 1982 when it issued the "Fiscal Year 1984-1988 Defense Guidance." This document calls for U.S. military forces to be prepared to fight and *win* a limited or protracted full-scale nuclear war. To achieve this goal, the document stated that American forces must be equipped to "render ineffective the total Soviet (and Soviet allied) military and power structure."[10]

To reinforce its first-strike posture, the U.S. has repeatedly refused to support a "no first use" policy of nuclear weapons. To enable the U.S. to carry out a successful "first-strike," the Reagan Administration and Congress authorized the stepped-up production of a new generation of "first-strike" multiple warhead systems that have unprecedented destructive capability as well as the precision accuracy necessary to destroy specific strategic military targets (i.e., missile silos, air bases, etc.). These weapons included the MX missile, the Cruise and Pershing II missiles and the Trident D-5 missile. Moreover, to make these and other nuclear weapon systems invulnerable, over $30 billion during the last 10 years was poured into the research and development of offensive and defensive laser weapons to be used as part of the "Star Wars" program. The Soviets responded by developing similar weapons such as the Typhoon submarine, the Backfire Bomber, and the SS-

20 and SSNX-18 missiles.[11]

Ever since the U.S. used the bomb against the Japanese, nuclear weapons have been the cornerstone of U.S. military and foreign policy. The U.S. government has consistently relied on the threat of using nuclear weapons, primarily as a means to protect its geo-political interests. On over 20 occasions since 1945, U.S. presidents have threatened to use the bomb against other nations. For example, such threats were made against Iran in 1946, Korea in 1953, Vietnam in 1954 and 1968-69, Cuba in 1962, Jordan/Syria in 1970, and during the Iranian crisis in 1980.[12] Military strategists have referred to the strategy behind these nuclear plans as "escalation dominance," which means the ability to threaten or coerce other nations by being capable of dominating the next level of escalation of violence.[13] Thus, as a result of its credible nuclear threat, the U.S. is able to carry out its interventionist policies and deter its political opponents. This policy also enables the U.S. to control close to 50 percent of the world's resources for its own consumption. George Kennan, a chief policy-crafter of the Cold War, sums up U.S. foreign policy in a statement made in 1948: "We have about 50 percent of the world's wealth, but only 6 percent of its population. . . . Our real task in the coming period is to devise a pattern of relationships which will permit us to maintain this disparity. . . . We should see to it that [poor nations] remain in hands that we can control and rely on. . . ."[14]

During the Reagan/Bush era, the Pentagon also employed a military strategy of "low intensity conflict" in Nicaragua and El Salvador which caused untold suffering and death in these countries. Borrowed from counterinsurgency techniques used during the Vietnam War, low intensity conflict uses "active" and "preventive" political, economic, military and psychological aggression designed to wear down a political opponent. The U.S. also actively supported repressive regimes in Guatemala and Honduras, pouring military aid into these countries. According to the document "Kairos Central America," 200,000 Central Americans died violently during the 1980s — victims of a policy of terror and counterinsurgency.[15]

U.S. Arming the World

Today, there are numerous wars being waged worldwide in which the U.S. has vested interests. And the U.S. helps to fuel most of these wars through weapons sales. According to a report, "U.S Weapons at War: U.S. Arms Deliveries to Regions of Conflict," published by the World Policy Institute at the New School, U.S.-supplied weaponry is involved in 90 percent of the world's most significant ethnic and territorial conflicts. Of the 50 largest ethnic and territorial conflicts under way during 1993-94, 45 involved one or more parties that obtained U.S. weaponry or military technology in the period leading up to the outbreak of the war. This report also provides new documentation on the "boomerang effect" — the leakage of U.S.-supplied weaponry into the hands of U.S. adversaries. The report gives a detailed history of U.S. weapons supplies to Panama, Iraq, Somalia and Haiti in the periods leading up to U.S. intervention in those nations.[16]

Over the last decade, the U.S. exported weapons valued at $135 billion to countries worldwide. From 1979 to 1989, nations in Africa purchased $82 billion of U.S. weapons and suffered over 2 million deaths. During this same period Latin American governments bought $41 billion worth of arms from the U.S. War-related deaths totaled some 222,000.[17] Also from 1988 to 1992 the U.S. exported over $214 million of arms to the Mexican government. In the wake of the Zapatista uprising in Chiapas and national elections in 1994, Clinton authorized a $64 million arms export package to Mexico.[18]

The group Demilitarization for Democracy found that non-democratic governments received 85 percent of the $55 billion of arms transferred to developing nations in 1991-94.[19] The U.S. currently provides weapons to 59 authoritarian governments. In 1991 the U.S. authorized the sale of a staggering $63 billion worth of weapons, military construction and training to 142 nations.[20] And in 1992, the U.S. approved over $32 billion in new arms sales to eight countries in the Middle East. Even as Israel was discussing the prospects for peace with its Arab neighbors, Israel was proceeding with plans to buy $2 billion of combat aircraft from the U.S.[21] In keeping with its past weapons sales, U.S. defense firms secured $32.4 billion in overseas weapons sales in 1993, thanks to a surge in orders from the Middle East and Asia.[22] According to the Congressional Research Service, since 1990, the U.S. has accounted for over 56 percent of all the world's arms transfer agreements.[23] In 1993 the U.S. was responsible for 73 percent of all arms transfers agreements to the Third World.[24] Although Clinton issued Presidential Directive 34, a policy that promotes "restraint" on the part of the U.S. and other suppliers in the transfer of weapons systems, the Pentagon forecasts that the U.S. share of the world's arms market will increase from about 50 percent to 63 percent by the year 2000.[25]

As long as the U.S. and other arms merchants continues to flood the Middle East, Africa, Asia and Latin America with weapons, regional conflicts will continue and a just and lasting peace will not be attained in the war-torn regions of our world.

Post Cold-War U.S. Nuclear/Military Strategy

As the U.S. has sought to adapt its military strategies to a changing post-Cold War world, several government commissions have proffered recommendations for the U.S. military over the next 20 years (some of which we are now seeing implemented). In January 1988, the Commission on Integrated Long-Term Strategy, whose members include Henry Kissinger and Zbigniew Brzezinski, devised the strategy of "Discriminate Deterrence." The Commission recommends the following:

> *Our strategy must also be integrated. We should not decide in isolation questions about new technology, force structure, mobility and bases, conventional and nuclear arms, extreme threats, and Third World conflicts, from the lowest intensity and highest probability to the most apocalyptic and least likely.[26]

> *We must diversify and strengthen our ability to bring discriminating, non-nuclear force where needed in time to defeat aggression. To this end, we and our allies need to exploit emerging technologies of precision, control, and intelligence that can provide our conventional forces with more selective and more effective capabilities for destroying military targets.[27]

> *Both our conventional and nuclear posture should be based on a mix of offensive and defensive systems. . . . In a conventional war, our space capabilities — critical for communications, intelligence, and control of our forces — must be made survivable or replaceable. . . . We will need capabilities for discriminate nuclear strikes to deter nuclear attack on allied or U.S. forces and, if necessary, to stop a massive invasion.[28]

> *In the past 40 years all the wars in which the U.S. has been involved have occurred in the Third World. . . . Given future trends in the diffusion of technology and military power, the U.S. needs a clear understanding of its interests and military role in these regions. . . . In the coming decades the U.S. will need to be better prepared to deal with conflicts in the Third World.[29]

Thus, "discriminate deterrence" calls for a more aggressive global military policy, especially toward the Third World, which includes rapid military intervention backed up by nuclear forces. Jim Douglass succinctly sums up this strategy: "'Discriminate Deterrence' means enforcing U.S. dominance over other countries by a variety of threats, from covert intervention to the use of accurate, long-range 'smart' bombs, as were used with conventional warheads to destroy the infrastructure of Iraq during the Persian Gulf War. A flexible deterrent, with weapons appropriate to any and every conceivable challenge, is required for the maintenance of U.S. power." [30]

Building on the "discriminate deterrence" strategy, a military advisory panel of 21 nuclear experts responded to the breakup of the Soviet Union by issuing a new nuclear targeting strategy report which was leaked to the *Washington Post* and published on January 6, 1992. This 44-page report was prepared by the Joint Strategic Target Planning Staff Advisory Group for Air Force General Lee Butler, the commander in chief of U.S. strategic forces and director of U.S. nuclear targeting. According to several panel members, this plan calls for the most sweeping revision of U.S. strategic targeting since the dawn of the nuclear age. The panel rejects any notion that the sole remaining purpose of nuclear arms is to deter a strategic nuclear attack against U.S. territory, as some experts claim. The nation "must keep nuclear weapons to protect its fundamental interests . . . [including] a healthy and growing U.S. economy," panel chairman Thomas Reed, a secretary of the Air Force under President Reagan, advised General Butler after the reports completion. "If the U.S. moves from superpower to being an equal, others may decide to become equals as well." The panel recommends the following objectives:[31]

*Have the U.S. strategic nuclear arsenal target roughly 5,000 nuclear weapons at its potential foes — a level substantially below the START I Treaty. Further cuts may eventually be warranted (especially under new START II provisions), but the U.S. arsenal should remain larger than the total number of French, British and Chinese nuclear arms.

*Stop using SWIPE, which contains myriad options for detonating nuclear warheads specifically on formerly Soviet territory. Instead, [adopt] five separate plans emphasizing strikes against "every reasonable adversary" around the globe with either nuclear or non-nuclear weapons. . . .

*Abandon the 1979 U.S. pledge not to use nuclear arms against Third World countries. Target nuclear weapons at Third World countries in order to deter them from developing nuclear weapons, from using chemical weapons, or from taking hostile action.

*Create a "Nuclear Expeditionary Force" armed with a handful of bomber-launched and submarine-launched weapons as well as tactical arms, primarily for use against China or Third World targets.

Finally, excerpts from a February 1992 draft of the Pentagon's "Defense Planning Guidance for Fiscal Years 1994-1999," which was leaked to the *New York Times*, underscores the Pentagon's commitment to enhancing a U.S. system of military domination and economic exploitation throughout the world. In this broad policy statement the Pentagon asserts that America's political and military mission in the post cold-war era will be to insure that no rival superpower is allowed to emerge in Western Europe, Asia or the territory of the former Soviet Union. This classified document makes the case for a world dominated by one superpower which would have sufficient military might to deter any nation or group of nations from challenging U.S. primacy. The document asserts the following:

*Our first objective is to prevent the reemergence of a new rival . . . that poses a threat on the order of that posed by the Soviet Union. This is a dominant consideration underlying the new regional defense strategy and requires that we endeavor to prevent any hostile power from dominating a region whose resources would, under consolidated control, be sufficient to generate global power."[32]

*. . . "We will retain the pre-eminent responsibility for addressing selectively those wrongs which threaten not only our interests, but those of our allies or friends, or which could seriously unsettle international relations. Various types of U.S. interests may be involved in such instances: access to vital raw materials, primarily Persian Gulf Oil, proliferation of weapons of mass destruction and ballistic missiles, threats to U.S. citizens from terrorism or regional and local conflict, and threats to the U.S. from narcotics trafficking."[33]

Regarding the role of nuclear weapons in this policy, the report states: "Our nuclear forces also provide an important deterrent hedge against the possibility of a revitalized or unforeseen global threat, while at the same time, helping to deter third party use of weapons of mass destruction through the threat of retaliation."[34]

In reviewing future threats, the document places great emphasis on how "the actual use of weapons of mass destruction, even in conflicts that otherwise do not directly engage U.S. interests, could spur further proliferation which in turn would threaten world order. . . . The U.S. may be faced with the question of whether to take military steps to prevent the development or use of weapons of mass destruction [by other countries]." The document notes that those steps could include pre-empting an impending attack with nuclear, chemical or biological weapons "or punishing the attackers or threatening punishment of aggressors through a variety of means," including attacks on the plants that manufacture such weapons.[35] It is important to note that U.S. military planners considered using nuclear weapons to destroy 18 Iraqi biological weapons sites during the Iraqi massacre.[36] Also, U.S. threats against North Korea to endorse the Nuclear Nonproliferation Treaty is another example of the above stated policy.

In the official Pentagon mission statement of 1992 the Joint Chiefs further articulated the nation's military strategy toward developing countries. The U.S. must be prepared to intervene with military force in Third World nations to "deter aggression, counter terrorism, reduce flow of illegal drugs, ensure access to foreign markets for energy, oil, and minerals, maintain regional balances of power, and combat threats to democracies from aggression, coercion, insurgencies, subversion, terrorism and illicit drug trafficking."[37] Whatever the pretext, this intervention policy violates the U.N. Charter concerning a nation's right to self-determination and gives a green light to military actions which have historically resulted in the gross victimization of the poor.

To carry out its future interventionary policies, the Pentagon, following the warmaking strategy employed against Iraq, is increasingly relying on the use of precision-guided weapons and advanced computer simulations to project its military capabilities. "Two years ago we were still talking about sorties per day. . . . Now we are talking not so much about sorties [military missions] per day but targets per sortie in our ability to project power ashore. This is a fundamental shift in the way we measure how effective we are," Rear Admiral Brent Bennitt, director of the Navy's air warfare division stated in March 1994.[38] This military shift in thinking and technology, which has now changed the nature of warfare, has paved the way for a new generation of smart weapons in the Pentagon's arsenal. These new weapons include improved versions of the Army Tactical Missile System and an extended-range version of the Standoff Land Attack Missile.

Thus, in this changing post-Cold War world the Pentagon continues to develop weapons and refine its military strategies to suit the different kinds of conflicts it expects to encounter in the future. If the U.S. military is to be successful in the future it must, according to Paul Nitze, embrace this premise: "Don't make the wars fit the military, make the military fit the wars."[39] This kind of thinking not only fosters the belief that the U.S. must continue to wage wars, but also that the U.S. must continue to develop sophisticated weapons which ensure military and nuclear superiority — regardless of the cost to human life.

U.S. Foreign and Military Policy in the Clinton Era

Since the end of the Cold War, the U.S. has sought to shape the world to suit to its own imperial design and political and economic interests. Accordingly, U.S. foreign and military policy has been, and still is, carefully crafted to advance the wealth and power aspirations of the U.S. empire.

In response to critics of the Clinton Administration, Anthony Lake and Warren Christopher gave several major speeches in the Fall of 1993 which clearly articulated the Administration's foreign policy objectives. In September 1993, Lake, Clinton's National Security Advisor, asserted that the U.S. is now embracing a strategy of "enlargement" to replace the strategy of "containment" that guided U.S. policies during the Cold War.[40]

This policy of enlargement was expounded on by Secretary of State Christopher in November 1993 as he outlined Clinton's six foreign policy priorities before the Senate Foreign Relations Committee. These priorities are: economic security, reform in Russia, a new framework for NATO, trade relations with the Far East, Middle Eastern Affairs and nuclear nonproliferation.[41] He noted that "our national security is inseparable from our economic security." Regarding its free trade approach to dealings abroad, he said administration goals include opening Japan's markets, implementing NAFTA, successful international talks on tariffs, and promoting APEC (Asian-Pacific Economic Conference) — a NAFTA-like Asian trade organization.[42]

Illustrative of the Clinton Administration's commitment to these goals is the estimated $575,000 it spent in mid-February 1994 to help American military contractors promote their weapons at a major air show in Singapore. Viewing Asia as fertile ground for future weapons sales, the Pentagon dispatched 75 U.S. military personnel and 20 top-of-the-line fighters, bombers and other military aircraft to "Asian Aerospace '94." The Pentagon even diverted an aircraft carrier so that three Navy fighter jets could be shown.[43]

In developing its foreign policy, the Clinton Administration has been careful to keep continuity with Bush's policies. This is clearly evidenced by its Middle East policy as well as by its commitment to fight and win two wars at the same time anywhere in the world. Dubbed "win hold win" by the Pentagon, this military strategy of "medium intensity conflict" calls for first fighting and winning one war while holding the line in another war.[44] The October 1994 deployment of U.S. troops in Haiti and Kuwait foreshadow this new policy.

The U.S. has also engaged in different forms of military intervention (what is called "humanitarian" and "peacekeeping" missions) to help "stabilize" and control troubled regions of the world (i.e. Haiti and Bosnia). Strategic and political interests have primarily dictated the degree of U.S. intervention in each region. This intervention has also served to provide justification for ongoing weapons contracts and exorbitant military spending.

Although in recent years we have heard much about U.S. involvement in limited forms of intervention, government officials have asserted that the military has not changed its primary mission of fighting wars. Regarding the role of U.S. peacekeeping operations, Lake succinctly explained: "Let us be clear: peacekeeping is not at the center of our foreign or defense policy. Our armed forces' primary mission is not to conduct peace operations but to win wars. The bottom-up review of our post-Cold War defense requirements insures that we remain prepared to do that."[45]

Clinton and Nuclear Arms

In October 1993 former Secretary of Defense Les Aspin announced that a comprehensive "bottom-up" review of nuclear policy, doctrine, force structure, operations, safety, security, and arms control would be undertaken.[46] This review included integrating a review already underway by the Bush administration.

In 1989 Secretary of Defense Richard Cheney reviewed U.S. nuclear war plans (SIOP) and discovered that multiple warheads had been programmed inadvertently to strike the same targets. Cheney reduced the number of targets from a Cold War peak of 40,000 to 10,000.[47] General Lee Butler directed a more detailed review from 1991 to 1994 which reduced these targets to 2,500 and led to a smaller flexible plan that would make it possible to for the U.S. to aim nuclear weapons at any threat around the world within

24 hours by the year 2,000.[48] After Aspin was replaced by Secretary of Defense William Perry in January 1994, the scope of the nuclear review was scaled back and key work turned over to military and former Bush administration operatives. Under classified Presidential Decision Directive 31, Clinton authorized a plan that would maintain a strong nuclear capability while ordering some reduction in alert levels and leaving open the option of deeper reductions in the U.S. arsenal. Perry called the new policy "leading and hedging." The U.S. would continue to lead the way toward smaller nuclear arsenals and lower alert levels, but would hedge by maintaining its ability to rebuild forces quickly and by keeping some of its nuclear missiles on "Cold War-style alert." [49]

Clinton also adopted the following specific proposals by the Pentagon (in Presidential Review Directive 34) to chart the direction of U.S. nuclear weapons policy in the next decade: that there be no major changes in key nuclear weapons policies set by the Bush administration; that the U.S. retain a first-use nuclear weapons policy which includes the option of a "last resort" nuclear retaliation after a non-nuclear attack on U.S. forces; that the U.S. keep about 480 nuclear weapons in Europe to deter an attack on U.S. allies; that the U.S. target 2,500 Russian targets with nuclear weapons in the event of an all-out war; and that the U.S. install more accurate, nuclear-tipped missiles on four additional nuclear submarines.[50]

In light of these new policy directives, Clinton called for the restructuring of U.S. nuclear forces to accommodate arms cuts required by the START II treaty which, if implemented, could reduce the U.S. nuclear arsenal over the next 10 years from 20,000 to 8,500 nuclear warheads (3,500 strategic and 5,000 stored and deployed tactical "theater" type weapons).[51] And the former Soviet nuclear arsenal would be reduced to 7,000 warheads (2,000 deployed and 5,000 stored).[52] This includes cutting the Trident program from 18 to 14 submarines, the B-52 strategic bomber forces from 94 to 66 and eliminating 150 of the 450 - 500 Minuteman III missiles.[53]

With respect to the issue of nuclear weapons proliferation, Clinton has maintained a policy of assuring U.S. nuclear supremacy in the world.

At the U.N., 110 members of the non-aligned Movement (N.A.M.), supported by citizens groups like the International Physicians for the Prevention of Nuclear war, sponsored a resolution in November 1993 calling on the World Court to declare nuclear weapons illegal. Fearful of losing their "legitimacy" as world powers, the U.S., Britain, and France waged an intense lobbying campaign and stopped the initiative before it reached the General Assembly. A senior Congressional arms expert who followed the debate closely stated: "We [the U.S.] are refusing to accept as illegal what 98 percent of the world is being asked to accept as illegal — an elite view that we are the only ones who can hold onto nuclear weapons. . . . It makes us look like a double-faced nuclear power, talking one game and playing another. It plays into the hands of the North Koreans' efforts to obtain nuclear weapons, and countries like the Ukraine's efforts to hold on to them."[54]

Furthermore, at the nuclear Non-Proliferation Treaty (NPT) Review Conference held at the U.N. in April-May 1995, the Clinton Administration was able to broker an agreement that indefinitely extends the NPT, thereby ensuring that the U.S. can maintain the most lethal nuclear arsenal in the world. This agreement was attained after months of U.S. pressure on allies, smaller nations, and Arab countries resentful about Israel's refusal to endorse the NPT. Under the treaty, the U.S., Russia, Britain, France and China pledge to gradually dismantle their weapons; the non-nuclear states agree to forego nuclear weapons. The five nuclear powers took no new immediate disarmament steps. However, a set of principles were adopted to bring their arms control efforts under international scrutiny in five conferences in a five year period. To address the concerns of Arab countries, the conference also adopted a consensus resolution calling on Israel — without naming it — to join the treaty. A total of 12 countries have not signed the NPT, but only Israel, Pakistan and India are believed to possess nuclear capability. Finally, the five nuclear powers committed themselves to sign a comprehensive treaty banning all nuclear weapons tests in 1996.

As of February 1996, France, with U.S. support, and China continue nuclear testing. Although the U.S. has stated it will no longer test nuclear weapons underground, the U.S is building new facilities designed to do laser-simulated testing to improve nuclear weapons capabilities. These facilities will, in effect, provide research and simulated testing which can help refine existing nuclear weapons and develop new weapons. Chief among these facilities is the $1.1 billion (the whole project is estimated to cost over $4 billion) National Ignition Facility (NIF) at Lawrence Livermore Labs, which is to be built in 1997 and possibly completed by 2002. Billed as a path to clean, boundless fusion energy (it may take at least 30 years before a fusion reactor could be built), NIF, using superlaser beams, will provide unsurpassed capability for studying nuclear weapons and will supply important data relevant to nuclear weapons in the area of physics and weapons effects.[55] Hence, the main purpose of NIF and other nuclear weapons simulation projects is to keep researching, developing and testing the effects of nuclear weapons in a way that would bypass global arms proliferation treaties.

In a Department of Energy report titled "The Stockpile Stewardship and Management Program," future U.S. commitment to nuclear weapons is clearly articulated. By presidential decision directive and act of Congress (P.L. 103-160), the DOE was directed to establish a program to "ensure preservation and core intellectual and technical competencies of the U.S. in nuclear weapons." This program includes transforming the nation's nuclear weapons laboratories and production facilities and fully supporting a "'science-based' stockpile stewardship and management program which will enable those people responsible for maintaining the U.S. nuclear arsenal stockpile to increase their fundamental understanding of the basic scientific phenomena associated with nuclear weapons."[56] This nuclear weapons science will be advanced at new facilities to be built at Livermore, Sandia, and Los Alamos National Laboratories and at the Nevada Test Site. Large above-ground and underground non-nuclear explosions involving radioactive and other hazardous materials will be conducted (hydrodynamic tests), as well as miniature contained thermonuclear explosions (inertial confinement fusion). Data generated by these experiments will be run through supercomputers. These supercomputers, in the words of Energy Secretary Hazel O'Leary will ". . . unlock the ability to confidently simulate nuclear tests in the laboratory."[57]

During his August 11, 1995 press conference calling for a permanent comprehensive nuclear test ban, Clinton stated that if Department of Energy officials in charge of nuclear weapons labs cannot certify the reliability of nuclear weapons, "I would be prepared, in consultation with Congress, to exercise our supreme national-interest rights under a comprehensive test ban to conduct necessary testing." He further asserted that "the U.S. must and will retain strategic nuclear forces sufficient to deter any hostile foreign leadership with access to strategic nuclear forces from acting against our vital interests and to convince it that seeking a nuclear advantage would be futile."[58]

To make certain the U.S. will maintain its underground nuclear testing capability, the DOE announced on October 27, 1995 that six "subcritical high-explosive experiments with nuclear materials" will be conducted in 1996 and

1997 at the Nevada Test Site. (Bechtel Nevada Corporation was awarded a $1.5 billion five-year contract to manage the Nevada Test Site). The DOE claims that these tests will contain no nuclear chain reaction and no nuclear explosions. However, in light of past government secrecy, it will be difficult to verify what kind of testing actually takes place.

In the end, the U.S. will remain the world's leading nuclear superpower and has no intention of outlawing or abolishing nuclear weapons. This is dangerous because as long as the major powers retain their nuclear weapons, the danger of nuclear proliferation is inevitable.

Despite the end of the Cold War and the prospect of SALT II being implemented (the U.S. Senate ratified the treaty in late January 1996; however, as of February 1996 the Russian Duma [legislative assembly] had not), the Cold War lives on as a reality in Pentagon nuclear weapons programs. The Pentagon spent some $27 billion in 1995 on nuclear war preparations and intends to spend $300 billion over the next 10 years to prepare for nuclear war.[59] And the U.S. will spend $1.3 trillion overall on the military budget over the next four years. The U.S. continues to buy missiles and bombers designed to fight a nuclear war with the (now dissolved) Soviet Union. Furthermore, the Pentagon is pressing the Energy Department to rebuild its nuclear weapons factories so they can resume production of a small number of warheads. Pentagon planning also calls for enough production capacity to "allow additional forces to be reconstituted in the event of a threatening reversal of events."[60]

Contrary to public perception that disarmament is breaking out, the Clinton Administration proceeds with Trident (one more is being built as four older Tridents are retired) NAVSTAR, the Ballistic Missile Defense Organization (BMDO) — a revised version of Star Wars, three Seawolf submarines and the New Attack submarine program, the F-15, F-16, F-18 and F-22 fighter planes, the B-2 stealth bomber, and a new multi-billion nuclear reactor to produce tritium for nuclear warheads.

Other horrific weapons are also in the research and development stages. The 1994 DOE budget provided for advanced study of a third generation-type high-power radio frequency warhead, meant to destroy enemy electronics (and people) with microwaves beamed to earth, and a precision low-yield warhead. The 1995 DOE budget requested money for "engineering development and technology demonstrations of new weapon systems [including an] ICBM replacement warhead, gravity-bomb studies, and enhanced safety warheads for the Navy."[61] Also in the development stage is the "Arsenal Ship." This new warship would essentially be a floating missile barge that would be able to launch 500 missiles within a matter of minutes on targets hundreds of miles away. The ships weapons would include: Tomahawk Cruise Missiles, long-range artillery shells and an assortment of different rockets.[62] Also a new laser is being developed for Navy ships which would be powerful enough to down missiles and jets and flexible enough to fire accurately in all weather and battlefield conditions.[63] And High Frequency Active Auroral Research Project (HAARP), a secret project of antennas capable of transmitting beams of high frequency energy into the Ionosphere as a way to improve military communications and destroy missiles and spacecraft, is also being developed. The use of HAARP could have far reaching damaging effects around the earth for years to come.[64]

These are just some of the new weapons that we know of — there are other "black budget" weapons projects that are considered too secret to be revealed.

From 1945 up to the present U.S. policy remains staunchly dedicated to maintaining worldwide military and nuclear superiority while protecting economic privilege for the power elite. The Clinton Administration's post-Cold War foreign policy and its efforts to restructure the U.S. military and nuclear forces, remains consistent with the major tenets of past U.S. military/nuclear strategy: **to use whatever military force is necessary to protect U.S. economic interests, including the use of nuclear weapons, and to prevent the emergence of another rival military superpower.** As the country moves farther to the right, we can certainly expect an even more aggressive military policy, regardless of who is elected president in 1996.

NOTES

1. See article by Robert McNamara, "The Post Cold War World: Implications for Military Expenditure in the Developing Countries," from proceedings of the World Bank Annual Conference on Development Economics 1991. Published by the International Bank for Reconstruction and Development/The World Bank, 1992.

2. See *The State Of The World's Children - 1993*, UNICEF Report (Oxford, U.K.: Oxford University Press, 1993), p.50.

3. See Gar Alperovitz, *Atomic Diplomacy: Hiroshima to Potsdam* (New York, NY:

Simon and Schuster, 1965), p. 238.

4. For a more in-depth understanding about the U.S. decision to use nuclear weapons against the Japanese, see Gar Alperovitz, *Atomic Diplomacy* (New York, NY: Viking, Penguin, 1985 — updated version of this book by Pluto Press). Also see Gar Alperovitz, *The Decision to Use the Atomic Bomb* (New York, NY: Alfred A. Knopf, 1995). Other books on Hiroshima: Joseph Gerson, *With Hiroshima Eyes*, (Philadelphia: New Society Publishers, 1995). Robert J. Lifton, *Death In Life - Survivors of Hiroshima* (New York: Simon & Schuster, 1967). Robert Lifton and Greg Mitchell, *Hiroshima in America: Fifty Years of Denial* (New York, NY: Grosset/Putnam Books, 1995).

5. See *The Defense Monitor*, Vol. XXII, Number 1, 1993. Published by the Center for Defense Information, Washington, D.C.

6. Ibid.

7. See "Four Trillion Dollars and Counting" by the Nuclear Weapons Cost Study Project Committee. *The Bulletin of the Atomic Scientists*, November/December 1995.

8. Robert Aldridge, *First Strike* (Boston: South End Press, 1983), p. 27.

9. Ibid., p. 33.

10. *New York Times*, August 6, 1980.

11. *New York Times*, May 30, 1982.

12. Daniel Axelrod and Michio Kaku, *To Win A Nuclear War* (Boston: South End Press, 1987), p. 5.

13. Ibid., p. 4.

14. Jack Nelson-Pallmeyer, *War Against the Poor* (Maryknoll, NY: Orbis, 1989), p.5.

15. *Kairos: Central America, A Challenge to the Churches of the World* (New York, NY: Circus Publications, 1988).

16. Taken from "U.S. Weapons at War: United States Arms Deliveries to Regions of Conflict," compiled by William D. Hartung and issued by World Policy Institute at the New School in May 1995. See Peace Action Briefing Paper: "U.S. Weapons at War," October 1995. Also see Hartung, W., *And Weapons for All* (New York, NY: Harper Collins, 1994).

17. *Washington Post*, "The Competition No One Really Wins," by Coleman McCarthy, July 20, 1993.

18. See "Lightning at the End of the Tunnel: U.S. Military Involvement in Mexico's Quagmire Deepens," by Peter Lumsdaine, September 1995. Imported U.S. military aircraft played a decisive role in the January conflict in Mexico when over 400 Indian peasants were killed in 12 days.

19. *Washington Post*, "We Arm the World," by David Isenberg, February 18, 1996.

20. *The Defense Monitor*, Vol. XXI, Number 5, 1992 and "Fact Sheet," The Arms Control Association, October 8, 1992.

21. *Washington Post*, September 11, 1993.

22. *Washington Post*, February 26, 1994.

23. "Corporate Welfare for Arms Merchants," by Project on Government Oversight Reports, p.4., June 1995.

24. See "Bill Clinton's America: Arms Merchants to the Third World," by Lora Lumpe. *The Nonviolent Activist*, May/June 1995. Also see "Hostile Takeover: How the Aerospace Industries Association Gained Control of American Foreign Policy and Doubled Arms Sales to Dictators," A Report by the Project on Demilitarization and Democracy, November 1995.

25. *Washington Post*, "We Arm the World," by David Isenberg, February 18, 1996.

26. *Discriminate Deterrence*, Report of the Commission on Integrated Long-Term Strategy, Fred C. Ikle and Albert Wohlstetter, co-chairmen, et. al. (Washington, D.C.: G.P.O., January, 1988). p.1.

27. Ibid., p. 2.

28. Ibid., p. 2.

29. Ibid., p. 13-14.

30. James W. Douglass, *The Nonviolent Coming of God* (Maryknoll, NY: Orbis Books, 1991), p. 10.

31. *Washington Post*, January 6, 1992.

32. *New York Times*, March 8, 1992.

33. Ibid.

34. Ibid.

35. Ibid.

36. *Washington Post*, July 25, 1993.

37. *The Defense Monitor*, Vol. XXI, Number 4, 1992.

38. *Defense News*, "DOD Eyes 21st Century Now," March 28 - April 3, 1994, p 1.

39. *Washington Post*, July 17, 1994 (p. C4).

40. *Washington Post*, September 22, 1993.

41. *Washington Post*, November 5, 1993.

42. Ibid.

43. *Washington Post*, February 26, 1994.

44. *New York Times*, September 2, 1993.

45. *New York Times*, February 6, 1994.

46. *Washington Post*, September 22, 1994. It is interesting to note that in an early response to this proposed review, such nuclear proponents like Paul Nitze called for a de-emphasis on the role of nuclear weapons and instead recommended a more credible U.S. deterrent based on "strategic, high precision" conventional weapons. This view is based on the recognition that in this post-Cold War era, nuclear threats do not deter so-called rogue states in the way they once did. While certainly not advocating the abandoning of the bomb, some cold warriors now concede that economic sanctions, diplomacy and a reliance on the threat of lethal conventional weapons may be more beneficial to U.S. interests rather than making nuclear threats. See *Defense News*, "U.S. Nuclear Threat Loses Its Value," March 28-April 3, 1994, p. 31.

47. *Washington Post*, April 12, 1995, p. 25.

48. Ibid.

49. Ibid.

50. *Washington Post*, September 22, 1994.

51. *The Defense Monitor*, Vol. XXIV, Number 1, 1995.

52. Ibid. On September 28, 1994 Russian President Yeltsin and President Clinton agreed to speed implementation of the Start II agreement, which calls for the reduction of each nation's arsenal by 2003. Instead of taking the nine years originally allowed, Clinton stated that dismantling will begin as soon as the accord is ratified. Now that START I is in effect, the Clinton administration is pushing for ratification of START II in 1995.

53. *Washington Post*, September 22, 1994.

54. *The Nation*, "Mutiny on the Nuclear Bounty," December 27, 1993.

55. See "The Bomb Tribe," by David Beers. *Mother Jones*, March/April 1995. Also see "NIF-TY Exercise Machine" by Hugh Gusterson, *The Bulletin of the Atomic Scientists*, September/October 1995.

56. "The Stockpile Stewardship and Management Program: Maintaining Confidence in the Safety and Reliability of the Enduring U.S. Nuclear Weapon Stockpile," U.S. Department of Energy Office of Defense Programs, May 1995.

57. *The Washington Times*, August 12, 1995, p.11.

58. *The Defense Monitor*, Vol. XXIV, Number 8, Sept./Oct. 1995 and Vol. XXII, Number 1, 1993.

59. *Washington Post*, September 25, 1993.

60. "The Bomb Tribe," *Mother Jones*, March/April 1995, pg. 48.

61. *New York Times*, September 3, 1995.

62. *The Day*, New London, CT, August 30, 1995. Continuous Electron Beam

Accelerator Facility (CEBAF) in Newport News, VA has been developing this laser.
63. *The Washington Post*, April 4, 1995, article by John Mintz. For more info see section on "Key U.S. Weapons Programs."

Editors' Note: For further info on the U.S. Armed Forces, nuclear and conventional weapons, the military budget, arms treaties, U.S. military deployments worldwide see: *1995 CDI Military Almanac*. Center For Defense Information, 1500 Massachusetts Ave., Washington, D.C. 20005.

IDOLATRY, NUCLEARISM AND THE NATIONAL SECURITY STATE
Art Laffin

Idolatry and Nuclearism

There is a general assumption in the U.S. that despite the colossal threat nuclear weapons pose, they are essential to national security. Even the majority of those who oppose further U.S. nuclear war preparations still favor retaining a small nuclear stockpile as a credible deterrent against foreign aggression. Spawned by deep-seeded violence that, since the beginning of recorded history, has possessed the human heart, nuclear weapons have in fact become an idol in which many people place their trust. The words of the prophet Isaiah describe well this blind allegiance: "Their land is full of silver and gold, and there is no end to their treasures . . . there is no end to their chariots [weapons]. Their land is full of idols and they worship idols made by their own hands." (Is. 2:6-8, *TEV*)

From the launching ceremonies of Trident submarines to victory parades celebrating the U.S. massacre in Iraq and "Arms Bazaars" which display the latest high-tech killing machines; from the Air and Space Museum's exhibit of the Enola Gay to the constant movie and television sanctification of violence, weapons and war are glorified in our culture. In short, the idols of weapons and war are products of a society that has placed its complete trust in military power and material security.

Since the state first developed nuclear weapons, it has consistently propagated the belief that the bomb represents our ultimate security as a nation. This sole dependence on nuclear weapons for our security is what Robert Jay Lifton and Richard Falk describe as "nuclearism." In their book *Indefensible Weapons*, Lifton and Falk define nuclearism as the "psychological, political and military dependence on nuclear weapons, the embrace of the weapons as a solution to a wide variety of human dilemmas, most ironically that of 'security'."[1] For 50 years the state has instilled nuclearism into the American psyche to such a degree that it has become a national religion.

Contrary to God's commands: "Thou shall have no other gods before me" and "Do not bow down to any idol and worship it" (Dt. 5:7,9 *TEV*), the state has placed its authority above God's, demanded absolute loyalty from its citizens and imposed a religion of nuclearism on the nation. As Elizabeth McAlister has succinctly stated:

> There is in the U.S. a fully-developed religion that is state-sponsored and initiated. This religion has many names, but basically it is a religion of national sovereignty or nuclearism. It has its gods, its high priests, its ritual; it is preeminent, and it compels people to acts prohibited by God's law, thus violating our freedom of religion. This national religion compels a loyalty based on our acceptance of the existence of nuclear weapons as a necessity — they are the source of security. We must — to be good citizens — pay for them, thank God for them. The weapons become sacred objects — a worship forbidden by the first commandment of God. Moreover, this religion prohibits the acts of justice required by the law of God: to refrain from killing or preparing to kill, to rescue the victims of murder and to intercede on their behalf. It names these acts as crimes.[2]

Despite the Pentagon's attempt to seduce us into accepting the religion of nuclearism, the truth is that the bomb can only destroy life. And deterrence only serves to perpetuate and to legitimate the ongoing weapons production for the government and for those corporations making huge profits from manufacturing genocidal weapons. However people may try to justify nuclear weapons, or any weapon, it is *immoral* and a *sin* to possess them! True security, according to God's law, can only be found in that which enhances life.

The National Security State: A Web of Unrestrained Power, Secrecy, Deceit

Blind to the truth, the most powerful political, military, scientific and business leaders of our nation consistently invoke "national security" to justify nuclearism. As people have acquiesced to nuclearism, the government has assumed control over every facet of nuclear weapons policy. To "secure" its total control of nuclear weapons, the government has given itself wide-ranging powers including the right to maintain a high level of secrecy regarding its nuclear policy. From the time of the Manhattan Project in 1942, when the government began serious research on nuclear weapons, U.S. nuclear policy has been veiled in a shroud of secrecy.

What has in fact emerged here is a "national security state" created by a political power elite which uses secrecy, surveillance, economic influence and military force to fashion a national and global economic and political system for its own ends. (It remains to be seen how far-reaching new anti-terrorist legislation will be with respect to surveillance of nonviolent dissident groups and the stifling of political dissent). The national security state was institutionalized in 1947 when the Truman Administration, seeking to maintain its control over the post-war world and protect growing U.S. economic and military interests around the world, issued the National Security Act, creating the National Security Council (NSC), the Central Intelligence Agency (CIA), and what is now the Department of Defense (War). The role of the NSC, comprised of the president's top military and political advisers, is to determine for the President all foreign and domestic policies relating to U.S. national security interests. The CIA is responsible for coordinating all governmental intelligence activities. The Department of Defense (War) is responsible for determining U.S. military policy and directing the Armed Forces.

The National Security Act also extended certain emergency powers to the President beyond those given in the U.S. Constitution (the Constitution already gives the president exclusive power to initiate, direct, and enact U.S. military policy). These emergency powers — all pertaining to national security interests — include the prerogative to suspend civil liberties under certain circumstances and to undertake normally illegal covert operations ranging from wiretaps to widespread surveillance. Furthermore, recent presidents, especially Nixon, Reagan and Bush, have interpreted these powers so broadly that they have authorized military actions to destabilize and overthrow governments whose political or ideological orientations are different from those of the U.S. Examples include Vietnam, Chile, Grenada, Nicaragua, Libya and Panama. Such acts of intervention violate the United Nations Charter and are unconstitutional because they interfere with a nation's right to self-determination.

Among other things, the National Security Act gives the president unlimited power to determine when nuclear weapons will be used. There is *no* public participation in any decision to use the bomb. This was made explicit in early 1948 in the first NSC policy document on nuclear war, NSC-30 — "Policy on Atomic Warfare." NSC-30 states, in part, that the ultimate decision on employment of nuclear weapons in the event of war is entrusted solely to the President.[3] It goes on to say that any public debate of the possibility of not using nuclear weapons is unacceptable. Furthermore, the document contends that if there were any public dissent about U.S. nuclear policy, it would only encourage the Russians to think that the U.S. might hesitate to use nuclear weapons and thereby provoke exactly the kind of Soviet aggression the U.S. seeks to avert. The conclusion of NSC-30 makes this point very clear:

> "Were the U.S. to decide against or publicly debate the issue of the atomic bomb on moral grounds, this country might gain the praise of the world's radical fringe and would certainly receive applause from the Soviet bloc, but the U.S. would be thoroughly condemned by every sound citizen in Western Europe, whose enfeebled security this country would obviously be threatening."[4]

Four years after NSC-30, President Truman, in an effort to maintain even greater secrecy surrounding U.S. nuclear/military policy and intelligence activities, issued a memorandum ordering the establishment of an agency to be known as the National Security Agency (NSA). Classified as top secret, this order, which has never been made public, remains the "foundation upon which all past and current communication intelligence activities of the U.S. government are based."[5] The NSA, which has been referred to by different political and military officials as the most secretive member of the intelligence community and as more powerful than the CIA, is the largest U.S. intelligence agency.[6] No law has ever been enacted prohibiting the NSA from engaging in any activity; it is, in fact, the only governmental agency to be exempt from any congressional or legal accountability.

With the NSC, CIA and NSA firmly in place, government officials during the height of the Cold War and the McCarthy era began to invoke "national security" to justify violating the civil rights of people and lying about or withholding from Congress specific information concerning U.S. military and foreign policy matters. The over 200 secret nuclear tests over the last 45 years, the 4,000 radiation experiments conducted on tens of thousands of people from the mid-1940s through the mid-1970s (including some 130 prisoners — most of whom were black, over 700 pregnant women, and mentally handicapped patients), the lies of the "bomber gap" in the 1950s, and the "missile gap" in the 1960s, the lie of using the "domino theory" and the "Communist threat" to justify waging war in Vietnam, Nicaragua and elsewhere, and the lies of high government and military officials surrounding the Iran-Contra affair, are all examples of this governmental deception.[7]

Despite this behavior by the government, the invocation of "national security" to restrict the release of information about "top secret" military matters is rarely challenged. Current examples of this are the restriction of information on the specific military role of the Space Program and the "Black Budget" which funds "classified" weapons programs like the Aurora secret spy plane and covert military operations. The Pentagon reveals little publicly about the black budget, and most in Congress have no access to specific details about it. Referring to the black budget as a "relic" of the Cold War, some senior members of Congress have urged Clinton to make this budget public.[8] In a rare display of congressional disapproval of one agency — the National Reconnaissance Office, which is involved in secret spy satellite programs — Congress will cut some of the (NRO) 1996 budget because the agency hoarded over $1 billion in unspent funds. The NRO budget has been in the $6 billion to $7 billion range over the last several years.[9]

Information leaked about certain black budget programs during the Reagan Administration included: training dolphins as underwater saboteurs and elaborate plans for winning a months-long nuclear war — World War III — and preparing for World War IV. The plans involved robots stalking radioactive battlegrounds, satellites orchestrating nuclear attacks and generals speeding along interstates in lead-lined trucks. The black budget also funds certain secret weapons, covert military units, a fourth of all military research and development and at least 3/4 of the U.S. intelligence community's espionage and covert activities.[10] Over the last eight years over $125 billion has been spent on black budget programs with the Air Force accounting for a large portion of this funding.[11] The black budget for intelligence agencies was estimated to be nearly $28 billion in 1993.[12]

Although information about nuclear weapons and U.S. military policy has become more readily available, the decision-making process about using military force remains removed from the public. We need only to scrutinize the War Powers Resolution (enacted by Congress on November 7, 1973) to underscore this point.[13] According to this resolution, the President can authorize for up to 60 days any military action necessary to protect national security interests. The president is urged to notify Congress before taking such action and is required to do so within 48 hours of authorizing such action. For the President to continue authorizing military action beyond the 60 day period, Congress must have approved a declaration of war, approved the President's use of armed forces, or approved an extension of the President's power to authorize such actions for an additional period of time. In light of this, the power of Congress to limit a presidential order authorizing the use of nuclear weapons is remote. And certainly there would be no public referendum or debate beforehand about a decision to use nuclear weapons.

We, therefore, have a situation today where a president can bomb civilians in Libya, Lebanon, Panama and Iraq, invade Grenada, and mine the harbors of Nicaragua without prior congressional approval, and can authorize the use of nuclear weapons without Congressional approval or public debate. In this post-Cold War era, the decision by Clinton or his successor to use nuclear weapons would be carried out in essentially the same secretive manner as was the decision to first use the bomb against the Japanese.

With respect to the U.S. massacre of Iraq, although George Bush requested congressional approval prior to bombing Iraq in January 1991, decisions had already been covertly made to initiate military action against Iraq. This is clear from "War Plan 1002-90" which was drawn up in 1989 and designated Iraq a threat to the Persian Gulf region.[14] It is also evidenced by the fact that Bush, five days after Iraq invaded Kuwait, deployed 40,000 U.S. troops, without congressional authorization, to defend Saudi Arabia — even though satellite photos showed no Iraqi troops near the Saudi border.[15] Bush's decision to seek congressional approval for the 1991 bombing followed several months of U.S. manipulation and coercion of the U.N. Security Council which passed Resolution 678 in November 1990 authorizing member states of the Security council to "use all necessary means to drive Iraq from Kuwait."[16] With 540,000 U.S. soldiers poised for combat in the Gulf, Congress, on January 11, 1991, voted to endorse Bush's war against Iraq. Over 150,000 Iraqi civilians and at least 125,000 Iraqi soldiers were killed by the U.S. and their allies.[17]

Four years after the bombing of Iraq, the war against the people of Iraq continues. As a result of the destruction of Iraq's infrastructure, including water and waste treatment centers, diseases became rampant. Combined with imposition of U.N. sanctions, which in turn has created massive shortages of food, health services and medicines, this has caused the deaths of as many as 576,000 children over the last five years according to the U.N. Food and Agriculture Organization. Also, in 1994, economic deprivation was so great in Iraq that some people sold their kidneys in order to survive.[18]

The legacy of U.S. weaponry used in Iraq is still claiming innocent lives. In the spring of 1995 French journalists reported the secret use of Depleted Uranium (DU) weapons by the U.S. in the Iraqi war. The dust produced when these munitions struck tanks and other vehicles and ignited them into flames, was radioactive and very toxic. Many civilians who collected spent shells are suffering from serious illnesses. It is estimated 940,000 30 mm shells, each containing 300 grams of depleted uranium, were fired by A-10 Thunderbolt aircraft. And 4000 120 mm shells, each containing one kilogram of uranium, were fired by M1A1 Abrams tanks.[19] Also, a Government Accounting Office Report revealed that most veterans in the Iraqi war did not know that they had been exposed to or were handling DU weapons.[20] It is suspected that exposure to DU may have contributed to various illnesses of Gulf War veterans. Estimates concerning the amount of DU used in Iraq and Kuwait are between 300 and 800 tons.[21]

In response to an alleged plot to assassinate former President Bush during a visit to Kuwait, President Clinton, without consulting Congress beforehand, authorized the use of 23 Tomahawk cruise missiles against an Iraqi intelligence center in Baghdad on June 27, 1993. The attack, which killed and wounded civilians, is another case of unilateral presidential action.

To date Congress has done little to challenge this gross abuse of power. For example, even when the World Court ruled in July 1986 that the Reagan administration violated international law by its military aggression against the people of Nicaragua, Congress failed to take action against the administration's illegal activities. Instead, a majority of both the House and the Senate voted to approve $100 million in military aid to support the terrorist actions of the CIA-backed Contras seeking to overthrow the popularly elected Nicaraguan government. Certainly, the convictions of some of those involved in the Iran-Contra affair was a step forward, but it still fell far short of exposing Reagan and Bush's real role.

Thus ongoing congressional appropriations for nuclear and conventional war preparations and its support of the War Powers Resolution indicates that the overwhelming majority of elected officials, both Democrats and

Republicans, have succumbed to the propaganda of the "national security state."

And U.S. deployment of nuclear weapons remains a clear violation of international law. International law accords ranging from the Hague conferences in 1899 and 1907 and the Geneva Protocol in 1925 to the Nuremberg Charter of 1945 have prohibited weapons of indiscriminate or mass destruction (nuclear weapons inherently fit this definition). And the U.N. General Assembly in 1961 declared the use of nuclear weapons a direct violation of the U.N. Charter and international law. A section of the resolution states: "the use of nuclear weapons would exceed even the scope of war and cause indiscriminate suffering and destruction to humankind and civilization and, as such, is contrary to the rules of international laws and the laws of humanity."

The U.S., by its own Constitution, is supposed to adhere to these international laws. Article VI, paragraph 2 of the U.S. Constitution provides that:
. . . All treaties made, or which shall be made, under the authority of the U.S., shall be the supreme law of the land; and the judges in every state shall be bound thereby, any thing in the Constitution or law of any state to the contrary notwithstanding.

Thus, the numerous treaties and laws drawn up after World War II to which the U.S. is a party, have the complete force of law and applicability in any U.S. court. They are "the supreme law of the land." To not uphold these laws is a direct violation of the U.S. Constitution as well as international law. Simply put, nuclear, chemical, biological and other weapons of mass destruction possessed by the U.S. and all other nations are a crime against humanity and must be outlawed.

NOTES

1. Richard Falk and Robert Lifton, *Indefensible Weapons: The Political and Psychological Case Against Nuclearism* (New York: basic books, 1982), p. ix.
2. Elizabeth McAlister, "Idolatry of the State," *Catholic Agitator* (June 1986).
3. William Arkin and Peter Pringle, *S.I.O.P.: The Secret U.S. Plan for Nuclear War* (New York: Norton, 1983), p. 50-51.
4. Gregg Herken, *Counsels of War* (New York: Knopf, 1985), p. 382.

5. James Bamford, *The Puzzle Palace — A Report on the National Security Agency, America's Most Secret Agency* (Boston: Houghton Mifflin, 1982), p 1.

6. For a more in-depth understanding of the NSA see Bamford, *The Puzzle Palace*.

7. Source for number of human radiation experiments, *Washington Post*, October 3, 1995, referring to the "Advisory Committee on Human Radiation Experiments."

8. *New York Times*, November 25, 1993.

9. *Washington Post*, September 26, 1995.

10. *The Hartford Courant*, February 9, 1987.

11. The Defense Budget Project, "Classified Programs in the FY 1994 Defense Budget Request," June 28, 1993.

12. *New York Times*, November 25, 1993.

13. See War Powers Resolution (Pub. L. 93-148, November 7, 1973, 87 Stat. 555).

14. Ramsey Clark, *The Fire This Time* (New York: Thunder Mouth Press, 1992) p. 11.

15. Ibid. p. 11.

16. Ibid. p. 153-155.

17. Ibid. p. 83.

18. *National Catholic Reporter*, February 11, 1994, pg. 7. Private hospitals in Baghdad were paying about $400 per kidney, which could keep a family alive for one year. These kidneys are either used for foreigners who travel to Iraq seeking transplants or are sold abroad.

19. "The Use of Radioactive Weapons Against the 'Iraqi Enemy'," by Naima Lefkir-Laffitte and Roland Laffitte, Le Monde Diplomatique, April 1995 (Translated by W.E. Griffin).

20. *National Catholic Reporter*, August 25, 1995, "First Use of Depleted Uranium on Battlefield Suspected in Ills of U.S. Troops, Iraqi Children," by Kathryn Casa.

21. Ibid.

Editors' Note: An excellent book on the "New World Order" and the "National Security State" please see Jack Nelson-Pallmeyer, *Brave New World Order* (Maryknoll, N.Y.: Orbis), 1992.

COLLABORATION IN NUCLEAR SECRECY

Samuel H. Day, Jr.

An Omaha television station had some good news to report the other night at nearby Offutt Air Force base, headquarters of the U.S. Strategic Command (StratCom): Offutt had signed a contract with Goodwill Industries, Inc. to employ 85 handicapped people as janitors in its main office building.

The camera showed beaming countenances of the local Goodwill director and an Air Force public relations officer. The TV commentator intoned: "Another example of StratCom's double duty for the good — protecting our national security and providing self-improvement for the physically and mentally disabled."

Protecting national security? Helping the handicapped? I pondered these questions from the vantage point of my cell block in the Douglas County Jail, where I had spent the previous seven weeks for portraying a different U.S. Strategic Command.

I had been arrested, prosecuted, tried, convicted and sentenced to six months in prison for walking onto the Air Base last February to raise the question of what StratCom does.

It's a matter of public record that StratCom's mission is to control the targeting and launching of many thousands of long range warheads, some of them a hundred times more powerful than the bomb that destroyed Hiroshima.

That's no secret. But curtains of secrecy dropped by the Air Force, the Courts, the clergy, and the media shield the public from the impact of that reality.

Guards at the Air Base gate stopped me from distributing leaflets warning military and civilian personnel that an international court could hold StratCom guilty of crimes against humanity for pointing weapons of mass destruction of defenseless cities.

At my trial, three of the guards professed no knowledge of StratCom's mission; the magistrate refused to subpoena the base commander, who could have told of the number of warheads and their yields and the nature of the targets. The court took no notice of the issue of international law.

As for the clergy, Fr. Frank Cordaro of Council Bluffs, Iowa, made an apt point in federal court last October (1994) on his way to six months in prison for the same offense: "Far more priests and ministers have crossed the line at Offutt to dine at the officers' club than to protest the role of StratCom."

And the mass media? Puff stories about helping the handicapped are typical of the Air Force propaganda cheerfully dispensed by Omaha TV and radio stations and its monopoly daily newspaper, The Omaha World Herald.

A handful of local janitorial jobs notwithstanding, how are the nation's handicapped really helped by the siphoning off of billions of dollars in badly needed public service funds into the coffers of corporation and military services that profit from preparing to wage nuclear war?

And how is the Omaha public served by federal "defense" policies that, in the event of a large-scale nuclear war, would leave nothing but a hole in the ground in this city of a quarter of a million?

Such questions are never asked by the mass media here — and seldom elsewhere in the country.

The silence of the courts, the clergy, the media and the political establishment are what make Stratcom a secret tightly held, in effect, as the ovens of Auschwitz and the killing fields of Cambodia. No government that hides such secrets from its people can be called a democracy. No institution that collaborates in the preserving of such secrets deserves respect.

Reprinted from *The Nuclear Resister*

THE MORAL DILEMMA OF DEFENSE WORKERS

Robert Aldridge

When my daughter was going to the University of Santa Clara in the early 1970s, she loaned me the book *The Respectable Murderers* by Monsignor Paul Hanly Furfuy. I would take this book with me to work at Lockheed, sit in the middle of a secret room where the re-entry bodies of warheads for the Poseidon missile were being designed, prop my feet up on the desk, and read. In the book, Furfuy outlines how the church has been co-opted throughout American history by the pervading mores of the day — through the slave trade and the Civil War to World War II and the nuclear bombings.

Furfuy gives what he calls the four mechanisms of moral deception: repression, rationalization, impossibility, and sublimation. These standards helped me to understand what I was doing and why. And once you become aware of how you're using these mechanisms, you can't fool yourself anymore. Then you've got to face the truth.

The first one, repression, is what psychologists call "denial," putting things out of your mind, not thinking unpleasant thoughts — "I don't want to think about that. Forget about it; it's negative. I want to think of something positive." I know that when I was working at Lockheed, I was not interested at all in Hiroshima or Nagasaki. When we were building the MIRV warheads for the Poseidon missile, I put out of my mind the effect the Poseidon would have — the millions of fatalities that would result if that weapon were ever used. I didn't think about all the killing, maiming, mutilating, and orphaning that the missile was made to do. This is repression, putting things out of mind.

But some things eventually become so persistent that it is hard to put them out of mind; they keep coming back. Here we arrive at the second mechanism — rationalization, which involves obviating uncomfortable facts with faulty logic. We do this all the time, telling ourselves, "I can't make a decision here; the experts know more about it than I do. I'm only following orders. I've got to do this to continue my job." A good example of rationalization was given to me by my boss when, in 1973, I told him that I was going to resign. I told him all the reasons. He listened very sympathetically and said, "You know, you might be right. I think about these things all the time too. But I keep telling myself it's just a game we're playing; we're not really going to use them."

Eventually, we get to the point where we recognize our problem and see that we should do something about it, at least theoretically. But then we often excuse ourselves by saying that it's impossible, that our contribution would be nothing. The third mechanism is impossibility. "If I quit, somebody else will do my job," I told myself many times. "I might as well be here and get the salary because it's going to go on. It's not going to stop just because I quit." After I left Lockheed, I wrote an article in a local journal outlining the reasons why I had left. One of my friends was still working there, and he took it into the Engineering Department where I used to work and sent it around to my former colleagues. On the back of the article was a place to leave comments. When the article was returned to me with the comments, I saw that someone had written the following: "What I can do will have no effect at all, so I do nothing. Your ideology seems correct to me, but it must be accepted by the entire world before it would have any real meaning. The question is where to start." He felt that he wanted to do something, but that it would be impossible for him to accomplish anything.

The fourth mechanism is sublimation — lightening the guilt complex by some superficial activity. Before I left Lockheed, I was working in the peace movement against the Vietnam War. The war wasn't too threatening to nuclear weapons work at that time. But it came through to me that I was really just working for peace in my spare time and making bombs for a living. Understanding that mechanism helped me overcome it.

I want to mention just one more stumbling block, as I see it, and that is fear. Before I left Lockheed, I had a lot of fears about leaving. I've often analyzed these fears since then. I recognize now that the fear was mostly fear of the unknown, fear of something that is imagined to happen. When you start imagining all the negative possibilities, it gets very overwhelming. For example, I was in combat in World War II. When I was going through basic training, I was scared stiff; but when I saw combat I was less afraid because I had actual, tangible things to deal with. Similarly, I found out after I left Lockheed that most of my fears about possible starvation, poverty, and so forth didn't materialize, and the few that did usually came one at a time and were relatively easy to deal with. The only good answer to fear is to realize that you are in a moral and spiritual battle. It is only the intangible faith within ourselves that can deal with the intangible fear.

The decision that reverses the arms race is not going to be based on politics or economics or technology. We've been arguing those things for decades and the arguments go on. What will change the arms race is going to be based on a moral, spiritual decision. It will end when a lot of people see that this is the worst situation that could possibly happen and choose to cooperate with it no more.

Editors' Note: This article, which first appeared in slightly different form in the June 1984 issue of the *Catholic Agitator*, was taken from a talk given by Robert Aldridge at Loyola-Marymount University in Los Angeles on April 9, 1984.

WITNESS OF MORDECHAI VANUNU

THE VANUNU STORY

Anne Montgomery

In 1996 Mordechai Vanunu, an Israeli nuclear technician, completes his tenth year of an 18-year term in an Israeli prison for blowing the whistle on his country's secret nuclear weapons program.

One of 11 children of a Moroccan Jewish family that immigrated to Beersheba when he was a child, Vanunu served in the Israeli Army and then went to work as a young man in the nearby Dimona nuclear "research center," which harbored an underground plutonium separation plant operated in strictest secrecy. As the years went by, he grew increasingly troubled about his work in the nuclear bomb program. In 1985, before leaving Dimona, he took extensive photographs inside the plant. He intended to document the truth for the people of his country and the entire world.

Traveling through Asia with the film in his backpack, Vanunu made his way to Australia where he found company in an Anglican Church social justice community with whom he shared the story of his nuclear background. A British newspaper, the *London Sunday Times*, flew him to England, checked his photos and his facts, and persuaded him to go public with the truth. His story, published on October 5, 1986, gave the world its first authoritative confirmation that Israel had become a major nuclear weapons power with material for as many as 200 advanced nuclear warheads.

Israeli agents got early wind of Vanunu's intentions. Even before publication of the story, they had lured him from Britain and abducted him in Italy, and then dumped his drugged body on a freighter bound for Israel. In the following months he was charged with espionage and treason, convicted in a secret trial, and sentenced to 18 years in prison. All legal appeals have been exhausted.

After his arrest and conviction Vanunu was denied contact with all except his guards, his lawyer, a priest, and members of his immediate family, who were allowed to visit him through glass for short periods once or twice a month. Except for brief, solitary exercise periods, he was confined to a cell no more than six by ten feet. Amnesty International condemned the conditions of his confinement as "cruel, inhuman, or degrading."

Vanunu wrote to his brother in London: "My Christianity is my freedom here. To practice my freedom every day is to declare that I am a believer in Christ in a country that calls itself a democratic country." Jim Douglass comments on the Vanunu poem, "I Am Your Spy," that the symbol of stopping and getting off the train "recalls not only the White Train tracks campaign but also the Austrian World War II martyr Franz Jaegerstaetter's dream of a train going to hell. Vanunu, like Jaegerstaetter, has gotten off the train going to hell. Vanunu like Jaegerstaetter, has gotten off the train — and has also suffered the consequences."

Editors' Note: U.S. citizens concerned about human rights and nuclear weapons proliferation have joined thousands worldwide in demanding Vanunu's release. These have included five former Middle East hostages (Terry Anderson, Fr. Lawrence Jenco, Jerry Levin, Charles Glass and Benjamin Weir) who have called on President Ezer Weisman of Israel to exercise his clemency powers and release Vanunu on humanitarian grounds. During 1994-5 there have also been people from the U.S. Campaign to Free Vanunu who have been arrested for nonviolent sit-ins at Israeli consulates in Boston, Philadelphia, New York, Chicago, Los Angeles and Washington, D.C. to bring Vanunu's plight to the attention of the public.

During 1995, Vanunu has written letters to supporters expressing thanks for the many efforts to win his release. He has also exhorted Israel to abolish its nuclear weapons program during the NPT review conference at the U.N. in April 1995. And, in remembrance of the 50th anniversary of the U.S. atomic bombings of Hiroshima and Nagasaki, he called on people everywhere to rid the world of nuclear weapons.

To help win Vanunu's release, please contact **The U.S. Campaign to Free Mordechai Vanunu**, 2206 Fox Ave., Madison WI 53711.

I AM YOUR SPY

by Mordechai Vanunu

I am the clerk, the technician, the mechanic,
  the driver.
They said, Do this, do that, don't look left
  or right,
don't read the text. Don't look at the whole
  machine. You
are only responsible for this one bolt. For this
  one rubber-stamp.
This is your only concern. Don't bother what
  is above you.
Don't try to think for us. Go on, drive. Keep
  going. On, on.
So they thought, the big ones, the smart ones,
  the futurologists.
There is nothing to fear. Not to worry.
Everything's ticking just fine.
Our little clerk is a diligent worker. He's a
  simple mechanic.
He's a little man.
Little men's ears don't hear, their eyes
  don't see.
We have heads, they don't.
Answer them, said he to himself, said the
  little man,
the man with a head of his own. Who is in
  charge? Who knows
where this train is going?
Where is their head? I too have a head.
Why do I see the whole engine.
Why do I see the precipice -
is there a driver on this train?
The clerk driver technician mechanic
  looked up.
He stepped back and saw- what a monster.

WITNESS OF MORDECHAI VANUNU

Can't believe it. Rubbed his eyes and - yes,
it's there all right. I'm all right. I do see
the monster. I'm part of the system.

  I signed this form. Only now I am reading the
      rest of it.
  This bolt is part of a bomb. This bolt is me.

    How
    did I fail to see, and how do the others go on
    fitting bolts. Who else knows?
    Who has seen? Who has heard? - The
      emperor really is naked.
    I see him. Why me? It's not for me. It's too big.
    Rise and cry out. Rise and tell the people.
      You can.
    I, the bolt, the technician, mechanic? -
      Yes, you.
    You are the secret agent of the people. You
      the eyes of the nation.
    Agent-spy, tell us what you've seen. Tell us
      what the insiders, the clever ones, have
      hidden from us.
    Without you, there is only the precipice.
      Only catastrophe.
    I have no choice. I'm a little man, a citizen,
      one of the people,
    but I'll do what I have to. I've heard the voice
      of my conscience
    and there's nowhere to hide.
    The world is small, small for Big Brother.
    I'm on your mission. I'm doing my duty. Take it
      from me.
    Come and see for yourselves. Lighten my
      burden. Stop the train.
    Get off the train. The next stop - nuclear disaster.
    The next book,
    the next machine. No. There is no such thing.

                        written from Ashkelon Prison, Israel

PART V

HISTORICAL OVERVIEW OF NONVIOLENT ACTION

Editors' Note: *Throughout history, individuals and groups have used various forms of nonviolent action in response to both internal and external forces of aggression, state-sanctioned violence and social injustice. In the introduction to the* Power of the People *the editors write: "Nonviolence did not appear in this land with the arrival of European immigrants. Native Americans had a reverence for life, respected human dignity, and understood the interconnection of all things to an extent that has yet to be surpassed."[1] Explaining the origins of the word nonviolence they continue: "The word 'nonviolence' first appeared in the U.S. in the 20th century and the evolution of the concept can be traced through earlier changes in terminology. The word 'nonresistance' was used from the 17th Century through the mid-19th Century; 'passive resistance' and 'moral force' were used by 19th Century abolitionists and labor organizers; and 'nonviolent resistance' appeared in the 1920s. Only after the Second World War did the terms 'revolutionary nonviolence' and 'active nonviolence' begin to be used."[2]*

What follows is a selective historical overview of people and groups who have practiced active nonviolence dating back to biblical times. Most of these examples are taken from Walter Wink's Engaging the Powers[3] and other sources which are noted.

1350 B.C.E.(?): The Hebrew midwives commit the first recorded act of civil disobedience by refusing to carry out Pharaoh's order to kill Hebrew babies.

388 B.C.E.: *Lysistrata,* by Aristophane, depicts women on both sides stopping a war by withholding sex from their husband-soldiers.

167 B.C.E.: The Book of Daniel depicts civil disobedience against the King's edicts. (Chapters 3 and 6)

26 C.E.: Pilate introduces idolatrous Roman standards into Judea. Jews by the thousands prostrate themselves around his house for five days. When Pilate threatens to kill them all, they offer their necks to the sword but will not move. Pilate removes the standard.

ca. 30 C.E.: Through his teachings of unconditional love for all, including enemies; his identification with victims and outcasts, in violation of religious and civil laws; and his call for justice for all who are oppressed, Jesus sets a new standard for nonviolence and is crucified.

30-312: Christians are martyred for refusing to worship the emperor, to serve in the army or engage in war. Based on the writings of Tertullian, Justin Martyr, Origen and others, Christians during the first three centuries disapproved of war and were pacifists. One example is a 21-year-old North African named Maximilian, who was beheaded in 295 because he refused to serve in the Roman army. During his trial he stated: "I cannot fight for any earthly consideration. I am now a Christian . . . and it is unlawful to do evil."[4]

547: St. Benedict begins a religious order in Italy which, among other things, instructs community members to seek peace and not participate in war.

1181-1226: The Franciscan movement is born. St. Francis of Assisi exemplifies a nonviolent life and renounces war.

1400s: Taborites (followers of Jan Hus) practice nonviolence for a time.

1537: Menno Simon founds the Mennonites, a peace church.

1652: George Fox founds the Quakers.

1660: Mary Dyer, a Quaker, is hung on the Boston Common. Fellow Quakers William Robinson and Marmaduke Stephenson are also executed in Massachusetts.[5]

1708: Alexander Roch founds the Brethren peace church.

1765-75: American colonists mount three nonviolent resistance campaigns against British rule resulting in de facto independence by 1775 even before war was declared in 1776.

1780: Quakers start the first American anti-slavery society.

1815: Massachusetts Peace Society proposes a World Court as an alternative to war.

1818: Hospital laundresses in Valencia, Venezuela, strike to demand back pay.

HISTORICAL OVERVIEW OF NONVIOLENT ACTION

1838: William Lloyd Garrison publishes the "Liberator," a pacifist and abolitionist paper. Adin Ballou develops pacifist theory. Both men had great influences on Tolstoy and Gandhi.[6]

1840-60: "Underground Railroad" helps slaves escape to the northern U.S. and Canada.

1846: Henry David Thoreau is jailed overnight for refusing to pay taxes supporting the Mexican-American War.

1850: Hungarian nationalists, led by Francis Deak, engage in nonviolent resistance to Austrian rule and eventually regain self-governance for Hungary as part of an Austro-Hungarian federation.

1871: Women in Paris block cannons and stand between Prussian and Parisian troops.

1890s: Tolstoy's writings on civil disobedience and nonviolence begin to circulate around the world.

1892: Ida B. Wells-Barnett leads first a mass boycott and then a mass exodus from Memphis to northern cities to protest lynchings and discrimination against blacks. Whole congregations leave the city — over two thousand in two months.

1900s: Labor movement (largely nonviolent) uses strikes to secure economic justice.

1901-1905: Finns nonviolently resist Russian oppression and force them to repeal the law imposing conscription.

1906: Gandhi in South Africa lays the foundation of nonviolence on a national scale.

1912: Over 25,000 textile workers strike in Lawrence, Massachusetts.[7]

1914: Fellowship of Reconciliation is founded in England (1915 in the U.S.).

1914-18: Conscientious objection to World War I in the U.S. numbers around 4000. Life sentences were given to 142 men, and 17 were given death sentences which were later commuted. Nobody served more than three years. Brutality and torture was commonplace. The two Hofer brothers died in prison.[8]

1917: The February Russian revolution, largely nonviolent, leads to the collapse of the czarist system.

1917: Police arrest 218 women from 26 states at a Woman's Suffrage demonstration at the White House on May 22 for "obstructing-sidewalk traffic. 97 were imprisoned.[9]

HISTORICAL OVERVIEW OF NONVIOLENT ACTION

1918: U.S. woman's suffrage movement secures a constitutional amendment guaranteeing women the right to vote after a 75 year struggle.

1919-47: Gandhi leads struggle for Indian independence through nonviolent means.

1923: War Resisters League is founded.

1927: Bartolomeo Vanzetti, a fish peddler, and Nicola Sacco, a shoe cutter and C.O. during W.W.I, both committed activists in the anarchist movement in Boston, are arrested for their political beliefs and are wrongly accused of murder. After 5 years of appeals, they were electrocuted on April 23.[10]

1936-37: Palestinians launch a six-month general strike against involuntary displacement and confiscations by Zionists.

1940: On October 16, eight U.S. Divinity Students, including Dave Dellinger, are sentenced to 1 year in prison for refusing to register for the draft.[11]

1940-45: Over 50,000 men apply as Conscientious Objectors to W.W.II and are sent to Civilian Public Service camps while over 6000 others are imprisoned for total noncooperation with draft.[12]

1940-1945: Nonviolent resistance to Nazi occupation in Bulgaria, Norway, Denmark, and Finland.

1943: Austrian Franz Jaegerstaetter, 43 and father of three, is beheaded for refusing to serve in Hitler's army because of his faith in Jesus.[13]

1944: Salvador dictator Maximiliano Hernandez Martinez and dictator Jorge Ubico of Guatemala are ousted as a result of nonviolent insurrections and general strikes. Between 1931 and 1961, 11 Latin American presidents leave office in the wake of civic strikes.

1952-1960: Nonviolent campaign by African National Congress in South Africa.

1955-58: Montgomery bus boycott launches U.S. civil rights movement. A variety of nonviolent methods including boycotts, mass demonstrations, marches, sit-ins and freedom rides lead to passage of the Civil Rights Act in 1964 and the Voting Rights Act in 1965. Countless black children and adults were jailed and many were beaten and killed during this struggle.

1957: Ghana wins independence after a ten year nonviolent struggle.

1961: Amnesty International is founded to document and protest the use of torture and capital punishment.

1963: Atmospheric nuclear test-ban treaty is signed after six years of demonstra-

HISTORICAL OVERVIEW OF NONVIOLENT ACTION

tions and public pressure.

1964-1975: Draft-card burning and draft board protests highlight organized resistance to U.S. military involvement in Vietnam. This is the first direct action campaign in U.S. history to help end a protracted war through nonviolent means.

1965: Ceasar Chavez organizes the United Farm Workers Union and launches grape boycott and subsequent fasts and demonstrations on behalf of farm workers rights across the U.S. The UFW continues this campaign today.

1968: Eight months of nonviolent defiance by the Czechoslovakian people of the Soviet Union is finally crushed by Warsaw Pact armies.

1969: Greenpeace begins nonviolent campaign to protect the environment.

1976: Mairead Corrigan and Betty Williams win Nobel Peace Prize for their efforts at nonviolent reconciliation in Northern Ireland.

Clamshell Alliance organizes mass nonviolent civil disobedience action to protest the Seabrook Nuclear Power Plant in New Hampshire. Over 1400 people are arrested. This action helps catalyze the anti-nuclear power movement in the U.S.

1977-84: Nestle Boycott campaign successfully brings about World Health Organization agreement restricting distribution and sale of infant formula in the Third World. Nestle later violates the agreement and the boycott is resumed.

1980-89: Solidarity Movement is founded in Poland.

1980: Adolfo Perez Esquivel, of Argentina receives Nobel Peace Prize for the work of Servicio Paz y Justicia, which has courageously campaigned for human rights throughout Latin America.

Plowshares Eight carry out the first "plowshares" action at General Electric nuclear weapons plant in King of Prussia, PA.[14]

1982: The Sanctuary Movement begins efforts to protect Central American refugees from deportation by the U.S. by offering them sanctuary in Churches.

1983: On May 11, the Chilean copper miners' union calls a countrywide protest. People respond by banging pots and pans and blowing whistles, and discover for the first time that the vast majority oppose the dictator Pinochet.

1984: The government of New Zealand refuses to allow nuclear ships or ships with nuclear weapons to enter its ports. The U.S. responds by expelling New Zealand from the regional military alliance.

1986: The nonviolent revolution of the Philippines brings down the oppressive Marcos dictatorship.

1987: Palestinian Intifada begins, using primarily nonviolent methods.

1988: Black and White church leaders unite to condemn apartheid and call their churches to active nonviolent resistance in South Africa.

1989: Pittson Coal Strike, Virginia, marking the first time coal miners have consistently used nonviolent methods to secure the first U.S. labor victory in more than a decade.

Nonviolent, pro-democracy movement is suppressed in China.

Hungary, Poland, Czechoslovakia, Bulgaria and East Germany win freedom from Soviet control through essentially nonviolent means.

Nonviolent independence movements among states within the former Soviet Union are launched.

Amazonian rubber tappers, despite the murder of their leader, Francisco Mendez, interpose their bodies before bulldozers and chain saw operators who are denuding the forest; successful 15 out of 45 times.

1990: Disabled demonstrators demanding passage of a bill guaranteeing their civil rights stage a protest at the U.S. Capitol building. 60 crawl out of their wheelchairs and up the steps of the Capitol to make their demands.

1990-: Nonviolent movements concerned with human and civil rights, the protection of the environment, disarmament, social and economic justice and peace continue to grow around the world.

NOTES

1. Robert Cooney and Helen Michalowski, editors, The Power of the People: Active Nonviolence in the United States (Philadelphia, PA: New Society Publishers, 1987) p. 6.
2. Ibid. p. 10.
3. Walter Wink, *Engaging the Powers* (Minneapolis, MN: Augsburg Fortress Publishers, 1992) p. 246 ff.
4. Richard McSorley, *The New Testament Basis of Peacemaking* (Scottdale, PA: Herald Press, 1985) p. 75-77
5. *The Power of the People,* p. 16.
6. Ibid. p. 24-25.
7. Ibid. p. 62.
8. Ibid. p. 44.
9. Ibid. p. 58.

10. Ibid. p. 66
11. Ibid. p. 98.
12. Ibid. p. 95, 101-107.
13. Gordon Zahn, *In Solitary Witness* (Boston, MA: Beacon Press, 1964).
14. See "Plowshares Chronology."

PART VI

CHALLENGES BEFORE US

Art Laffin

Pablo Richard, a Chilean theologian, writes:

The world has changed dramatically at the close of the last decade. . . . But has there been a change in the life and death situation of the poor and oppressed people who make up the majority of the Third World? The Berlin Wall was torn down and the West was elated; but now another gigantic wall is being built to hide the poverty of the Third World. This wall, which is built of lies and misinformation, makes it easier for the First World to forget about the poor of the Third World. It separates the First World from the Third World, so that people of one world will not be disturbed by the poverty of the other: the poor will die in silence and their deaths will go unrecorded in history. . . . We are no longer a Third World but a "Non-World," the cursed world of those who are excluded and condemned to death.[1]

As we reflect on these words by Pablo Richard, countless poor of the Third World continue to needlessly suffer and die as a direct result of a global capitalist system — a system dictated by greed and controlled by the U.S. and other rich nations. This is powerfully evidenced by the way the U.S. and the other Group of Seven (G-7) nations, along with multinational companies and the World Bank, International Monetary Fund and World Trade Organization, maintain economic domination over the Third World. Their web of domination includes an unfair international trade system; unjust trade agreements such as NAFTA, APEC and GATT; corporations which control strategic resources; forced payment of staggering debts with interest; and destructive structural adjustment programs. As of late 1995, the debt of developing nations has reached the intolerable figure of $1.5 trillion.

As the U.S. power structure continues to pursue its imperial quest of being the world's leading military and economic superpower, the poor of our world and society, the majority of whom are women and children, continue to be crucified on a cross built of economic exploitation, militarism and racism. The poor suffer and die in silence, and their deaths go unrecorded!

In discerning the signs of the times, people of faith and conscience in the U.S. face many difficult challenges in the months and years ahead. What further steps can we take to end the war against the poor and stop the U.S. war machine which destroys so many innocent lives and drains our world of vital resources and human talent? How can we stop nuclear weapons proliferation? How can we save our endangered earth and protect the environment? What more is required of us to help establish God's reign of nonviolence, justice and reconciliation on our fragile earth?

In response to these critical challenges and the many urgent life and death concerns facing our human family, a variety of groups and organizations, religious and secular, are engaged in very hopeful and life-giving work. Although, many peace and justice groups have disbanded over the last several years and we do see more widespread public apathy. Now more than ever, we need to deepen our hunger and thirst for justice. We need to continue to build the beloved community and recommit ourselves to what Martin Luther King called "the long and bitter — but beautiful — struggle for a new world." And as we well know, creating a more cohesive nonviolent based multi-cultural movement for social transformation will require developing greater bonds of solidarity with groups committed to nonviolent change, especially those groups with whom we may not normally work. This is already beginning to happen in certain environmental and justice struggles.

As we seek to create with others a genuine movement for social transformation in the U.S., we need to seriously critique where the peace and justice movement has been and clarify where it needs to go. Jim Wallis, among others, has provided important insights in this regard:

> Progressive movements have shown their capacity to critique, but have we shown the creativity and discipline needed for constructing new alternatives? . . . Are we committed to building strong new movements and institutions that have the capacity to change a nation? Are we prepared not only to see the old pass away, but also the new come into being?[2]

These and other vital concerns must be addressed as we pursue our action planning in the period ahead.

In this chapter I reflect on some of the important challenges we face in our journey as peace and justice activists. I also reflect on the faith and hope we need for sustenance over the long haul.

The Challenge of Nonviolence, Resistance and Disarmament

While we all desire a world of peace and justice, most people, including myself, fear the changes we might have to make in our lives to bring it about. We shudder at the thought of reorienting our careers, relinquishing certain comforts and addictions, or struggling through a relationship with a loved one with whom we might have moral and political differences. We are overwhelmed by the prospect of prison should we engage in certain acts of resistance. Yet, we know that if peace and justice are to become a reality, we have to make sacrifices in our lives. In *No Bars to Manhood*, written shortly after the Catonsville Nine trial and sentencing in 1970, Daniel Berrigan addresses this point:

> We have assumed the name peacemakers, but we seem, by and large, unwilling to pay any significant price. And because we want peace with half a heart and half a life and will, the war, of course, continues, because the waging of war, by its very nature, is total — but the waging of peace, by our own cowardice, is partial. So a whole will and a whole heart and a whole national life bent toward war prevail over the velleities of peace. . . .
>
> 'Of course, let us have peace,' we cry, 'but at the same time let us have normalcy, let us lose nothing, let our lives stand intact, let us know neither prison nor ill repute nor disruption of ties.'[3]

Dorothy Day, co-founder of the Catholic Worker, wrote in 1975:

> The peace movement knows there is something fundamentally evil about this society. Kent State and the killing of students. All the years of killing in Vietnam. All the murderous weapons sold throughout the world. All the endured violence of the Civil Rights struggles and the freedom rides and sit-ins. Through all this one comes to know the seriousness of the situation and to realize it's not going to be changed just by demonstrations. It's a question of risking one's life. It's a question of living one's life in drastically different ways.[4]

As we seek to respond to the peril of nuclear weapons and other weapons of terror, to state sanctioned violence, to the destruction of the environment and to the sins of racism and sexism, we must be willing to change the very way we think and live. For me, this means recognizing, first and foremost, that all of life is a miracle, that we are all created by the same God, that each human being is created in God's image and likeness, and that all life is interconnected. Thus, we are mandated by God to uphold the command "Thou Shalt Not Kill," to treat one another justly and nonviolently, and to honor the earth. The 12th Precept of Buddhist Order of Interbeing sums up well our duty to stand for life: "Do not kill. Do not let others kill. Find whatever means possible to protect life and to prevent war."[5]

So we need to weed out from our lives and institutions (including churches) the seeds of violence, fear, greed, racism, sexism and homophobia and all else that divides us as human beings. We also need to examine how we can become better stewards of God's earth, live simply, and embrace a "consistent life ethic" whereby we uphold the sacredness of all life, including the unborn and those who are most vulnerable. For a growing number of people, taking a vow of nonviolence has been an important first step toward cultivating a nonviolent way of life.[6]

What are some of the implications should churches and the wider society embrace radical nonviolence? Christians and other people of faith and conscience would be required to take the following actions:

*Refuse to work in any job that involves weapons/gun production, or is harmful to humans and nature. Do not invest in companies that deprive others of their chance to life;[7]

*Call for a comprehensive program to convert all weapons industries into places which make products that serve life;

*Refuse to participate in military service;

*Work to end military recruiting and ROTC programs in all schools and universities and promote peace studies and conflict resolution curriculum's.

*Practice war-tax resistance. Do not pay taxes which finances state sanctioned oppression, violence, weapons and war (see articles by Kehler and Durland on war-tax resistance).

Embracing nonviolence will also require that we engage in active nonviolent resistance. In our nation — which legally sanctions certain acts of indiscriminate murder (such as occurred in Hiroshima and Nagasaki, Vietnam, Central America and Iraq), where nuclear war preparations continue, which continues to be the world's chief arms exporter and where the military is the world's leading environmental polluter, where the public is virtually excluded from the decision-making process and is constantly deceived by the government about nuclear/military policy, where the government and mass media wage a misinformation campaign and censor news — people of faith and conscience must nonviolently resist all deliberate acts of violence, genocidal war preparations and deception. Also, The Nuremberg Charter imposes on citizens the duty to violate domestic laws to prevent crimes against peace and humanity from occurring.[8]

To prevent the U.S. government, described by Martin Luther King, Jr. as the greatest purveyor of violence in the world, from killing more innocent people worldwide, we must learn from and build on the last several decades of resistance both within and outside the U.S. Since 1980, over 47,000 people from across the U.S. and Canada were arrested for anti-nuclear resistance during 1,800 protests at more than 250 sites.[9] Many hundreds more were arrested for protesting U.S. intervention in Central America throughout the 1980s and during the U.S. war against Iraq.

In 1995, hundreds of people in towns and cities across the U.S. participated in nonviolent actions commemorating the 50th anniversary of the U.S. atomic bombings of Hiroshima and Nagasaki. In June 1995, nearly 30 people were arrested in Washington, DC at the opening of the National Air and Space Museum's Enola Gay Exhibit. Between July 17 and August 9, 1995, over 300 North Americans converged on the Pentagon for a nonviolent campaign of resistance resulting in 106 arrests.

If there is to be true disarmament and demilitarization of our society, we must assume personal responsibility to bring it about. Thus, plowshares actions and other locally based nonviolent actions at weapons facilities, military bases and other key sites of the military-industrial-political-academic complex must continue. These actions have helped sow important seeds of nonviolence at the local level and have fostered a consciousness that there are ordinary people who deeply care about peace and are willing to nonviolently resist the crimes of government, even if it means breaking the law and going to prison.

Over the years, many have come to see that acts of nonviolent resistance must be creative and must always seek to clearly communicate our YES to life as well as our NO to the evil we are resisting. Many have also come to see that our resistance should not just be to a particular weapons system, law, or policy, but must also address the web of violence, greed and fear which underlies the U.S. system and which also lies in the very depths of our own hearts. In response to the violence and lies perpetrated by the state, I believe we must always seek to incarnate into our resistance and peacemaking efforts the self-emptying love of Jesus and the "truth-force" of Gandhi.

In a culture where "peace through strength" is the norm and weapons are synonymous with security, advocating total disarmament and nonviolence is viewed as impractical and foolish. If we disarm, the argument goes, we will be subject to attack. Further, how will we assert our power, protect our wealth and respond to foreign aggression? As people of faith, we are called to trust in God, not in weapons and possessions, for our security. God calls us to serve, not to seek power. And Jesus calls us to love our enemies and pray for our persecutors. Choosing the path of love and active nonviolence to resist evil is the only way we can truly disarm our opponents and foster peace.

The 20th Century has been the most violent in history (over 100 million people have died in wars this century). We urgently need to create alternatives to war and to the use of armed force to resolve conflict. One such alternative is to create a civilian-based defense or peace force.[10] This peace force would consist of people prepared to nonviolently respond to conflict and aggression, even at the risk of suffering and death — a risk identical to that taken by people in the military. The difference is that this peace force would refuse to kill under any circumstance. Strategies utilized by this peace force would include human blockades of advancing military forces (i.e. the Philippines), human shields protecting threatened individuals (see Peace Brigades International, p. 196), and mediation to resolve conflict and create an atmosphere conducive to reconciliation.

Regarding the issue of nuclear proliferation, the U.S. continues to practice a double standard of preaching non-proliferation while maintaining the most lethal nuclear arsenal in the world. If the U.S. is really serious about stopping the spread of nuclear weapons worldwide, it should declare all nuclear technology illegal, immediately abolish its own nuclear arsenal, and call upon existing and prospective nuclear nations to do the same.

In light of U.S. nuclear and interventionary realities, we should be engaged in ongoing analysis of and resistance to this pervasive militarism and not just be reactive when certain acts of U.S. intervention take place.

It is very hopeful to note that there are peace and justice groups around the U.S. which continue to engage in sustained nonviolent action campaigns. Many of these groups, using the liturgical and peace calendars as a timeframe for action, have found the model of the "Faith and Resistance Retreats" to be extremely important in helping to facilitate community building and nonviolent resistance.[11] For example, such retreats are organized during the year in the Midwest by the Lakes and Prairies Life Community and in Washington, D.C. by Jonah House, Dorothy Day Catholic Worker and members of the Atlantic Life Community. In Washington, these retreats take place during Holy Week, August 5-9 (Anniversary of the Hiroshima and Nagasaki bombings) and December 27-30 (the Feast of the Holy Innocents). They involve communal prayer, biblical reflection, political analysis and creative acts of nonviolent resistance at the Pentagon, the White House, the Department of Energy, the World Bank and International Monetary Fund and at other sites. This kind of ongoing reflection and analysis, community building and action is essential to our peace and justice work because it enables us to better grasp the culture of violence in which we live and the faith-filled resistance that is needed to bring about radical personal and societal transformation.

As imprisoned plowshares activists, other prisoners of conscience and political prisoners in the U.S. and around the world remind us, our choice to resist evil in the name of life, justice and peace will inevitably require us to make greater sacrifices and endure persecution. But, ultimately, such redemptive suffering will bring about a new creation. In "The Road to Damascus" Third World Christians write:

> Because of our faith in Jesus, we are bold enough to hope for something that fulfills and transcends the reign of God. . .
>
> The disciple cannot be greater than the master, and we are following the path of the crucified Christ. Whatever twists and turns the road might take, be firm and steadfast. The pain we undergo is part of the birthpangs of a new creation.[12]

The Challenge of Solidarity with the Third World, Nonviolent Crisis Intervention and the Hope of Nonviolent Action

The witness of the countless martyrs who gave their lives and others who have been persecuted for the sake of justice throughout the Third World have been, and continue to be, powerful signs of hope and resurrection. They have called people of faith and conscience in the First World to radical conversion and greater solidarity.

As we seek to deepen these bonds of solidarity with our Third World sisters and brothers, we will also need to deepen our resistance here in the

U.S. to the military, economic and political forces which dominate the poor of the Third World (and of the U.S.). We will also need to support and participate, where possible, in bold peacemaking initiatives to resist war and aggression by the U.S. government. Some of these recent courageous nonviolent initiatives have included the Witness for Peace presence in Nicaragua, the Gulf Peace Team on the Iraq/Saudi border and the Cry For Justice nonviolent witness in Haiti and *Sjeme Mira* (Seeds of Peace) nonviolent presence in Bosnia. Groups involved in nonviolent crisis intervention work like Peace Brigades International, Christian Peacemaker Teams, Witness For Peace, and Nonviolence International must be supported now more than ever.

We must also realize that "humanitarian" military intervention is designed to serve U.S. geo-political interests, and in the case of Somalia translated into more death and suffering for innocent people there. Humanitarian intervention accompanied by guns and bombs is really military intervention which must be unequivocally opposed by pacifists and all people concerned about genuine peace.

To address specific crises that emerge within and between certain countries, be it in Rwanda or the former Yugoslavia, we must find new and creative nonviolent and diplomatic alternatives to replace military solutions. Nonviolent and just options could be found and applied in any given conflict if those groups already involved and trained in nonviolent crisis intervention work, churches and religious leaders, and existing peace and human rights groups within a given nation, were called upon to help as mediators by the conflicted parties and the U.N. at the onset of a crisis. This kind of collaborative effort is being pursued, albeit on a very small scale, in such places as Bosnia and Palestine and must continue to be supported. (See "The Crisis in Bosnia: What Can Pacifists Say?" by David McReynolds, *The Nonviolent Activist,* Jan.-Feb 1996.)

In addition, the weapons that are used to fight the numerous wars being waged around the world must be banned. If the U.S. and other arms exporting nations stopped producing and exporting weapons — from high-tech weapons to landmines to spare parts — it stands to reason that wars could be averted and countless lives could be saved.

We must also question the value of economic sanctions as a means to resolve a given foreign crisis, for they take a devastating toll on the poor of the sanctioned country. While there may be certain exceptions where sanctions may be helpful to bring about an end to a repressive regime such as in South Africa, we must be very careful about how sanctions are ultimately going to effect those already victimized. In the case of Iraq, thousands of people, especially children, have been victimized by U.S. and U.N. initiated sanctions. Since 1991, it is estimated that some 500,000 Iraqis have died as a direct result of the sanctions.

Another critical issue we face is the specter of growing terrorism carried out by political and religious groups in retaliation for acts of aggression and injustice perpetrated by the U.S. and allied states. The U.S. government, itself guilty of such terrorist acts as the indiscriminate bombing of Iraq, ironically invokes the term "terrorist" for any group or government that militantly oppose its interests. As long as the U.S. continue its exploitative policies toward the Third World, we will continue to witness such tragic incidents as the World Trade Center bombing. Moreover, the threat is compounded by "black market" trade in weapons-grade plutonium. Last year German authorities seized small amounts of plutonium which were smuggled into that country.

Our best protection against future terrorist attacks is for U.S. citizens to demand that our government and corporations cease their imperial ventures and exploitative practices, seek forgiveness for past transgressions, and treat the peoples of the Third World with compassion and justice.

Despite the fact that the U.S. and other governments often resort to repressive and violent means to have their way, it is inspiring to note the increasing use of nonviolent action in many countries to resist this violence — from the Philippines to parts of the former Soviet Union to South Africa. Walter Wink writes:

> If we add all the countries touched by major nonviolent actions since 1986 . . . and the other nonviolent struggles of our century — the independence movements of India and Ghana, the overthrow of the Shah in Iran, the struggle against authoritarian governments and landowners in Argentina and Mexico, and the civil rights, United Farm Worker, anti-Vietnam and antinuclear movements in the U.S. — the figure reaches 3,337,400,000: a staggering 64 percent of humanity! . . . All this in the teeth of the assertion, endlessly repeated, that nonviolence does not work in the 'real' world.[13]

These powerful signs of nonviolence are cause for great hope for they not only confirm the transforming power of nonviolence to bring about social change, but also show that nonviolence is really the only force available to bring about true peace to our violent, war-plagued world.

The Challenge of Dismantling Racism and Confronting National Violence

As we strive to be peacemakers and seek true liberation, White North Americans need to learn from our Native American, African American, Hispanic and Chicano sisters and brothers who during the 1990s are celebrating 500 years of resistance to ruthless domination and exploitation. The origins of the U.S. are blood-stained, replete with unspeakable crimes that most white people refuse to confront. For in confronting these crimes a shocking truth is revealed: The U.S. government is illegitimate because native peoples were invaded and their land, which they called Turtle Island, was stolen. White North Americans are beneficiaries of this legacy. If we truthfully confront our origins in this empire, we discover that we are guests on Turtle Island.

We desperately need to understand that the liberation and peace we long for cannot come to pass until white North Americans confront what Ched Myers calls our "origin myths" — until we come to terms with the legacy of European colonization: the genocide, slavery and exploitation of hundreds of millions of Native Americans and Africans.[14]

As we struggle for justice and peace in our North American context, we must deepen our bonds of solidarity with Native peoples and with all people of color. Several important steps toward this end would be: changing Columbus Day to "Indigenous Peoples' Day"; working for the release of Leonard Peltier, a Chippewa/Lakota Indian who in 1975 was sentenced to life in prison for a crime he did not commit; and upholding all treaties effecting Natives Americans which the U.S. government has refused to honor.

Protests and other events held by Native American and solidarity groups throughout 1992, new anti-immigration laws and the historic Million Man March in October 1995 powerfully underscore the need for white America to honestly come to terms with its racist history and with the pervasive racism which is causing so much divisiveness and suffering in our society today. White Americans must repent personally and collectively for the sins committed against Native Americans and African Americans so that true healing can begin and unity and peace among races can be achieved.[15]

Another challenge before us is confronting the violence that plagues our cities and neighborhoods. I submit that the racist and inherently oppressive nature of the present political and economic system, the massive amount of resources diverted away from our cities and human needs in favor of the Pentagon and of corporate America, and the destructive attitudes men have toward women — which have led to increased rape, abuse and harassment of women — are principal factors which have contributed to an increase in national violence and crime.

It is no coincidence that gun violence and the epidemic of drug abuse, which has escalated across the U.S. over the last decade, began to spiral following massive cutbacks in social services by the Reagan and Bush Administrations. Thus, as the poverty level for millions has increased, so too has crime. And the results are troubling: There are now nearly 1.5 million prisoners in U.S. prisons and jails and one-third of African American males are either in jail or on probation.

Still, Instead of dealing with the root causes of national violence, we are told by Democrats, Republicans, the Religious Right and the mass media that the solution to street crime is building more jails (in 1995 California spent $21 billion constructing new prisons), passing tougher laws and increasing the use of the death penalty (there are over 3,000 people on death row in the U.S.)!

What if, instead, the billions that are now earmarked for existing and new weapons programs were scrapped and spent instead to help our youth, to clean up the environment and to fund drug rehabilitation programs and job-training programs for all the unemployed? What if this money was used to guarantee a college education for all lower to middle income students — and a meaningful socially useful job once they finished school? As more and more young adults continue to end up in jail and prisons, might we not see a drastic reversal of this colossal tragedy if we really gave our youth a hopeful alternative to drugs and crime, instead of locking them up?

Biblical justice demands that we confront this unjust system and employ nonviolent and just solutions. We need to move away from a "retributive" justice system based on vengeance and punishment to a "restorative" justice model where the offender is held accountable to repair the emotional and material damage done by him/her and seeks to restore harmony to the community.

Thus, the primary crime which must be confronted is the oppressive and racist economic and political system which dehumanizes and destroys people. Until the root causes of poverty are addressed and alleviated, street crime and violence will continue to escalate. And unless new economic and political paradigms are developed which place people before profit and which justly represent and respond to the needs of all people, future uprisings, like those in Los Angeles, will be inevitable.[16]

A powerful sign of hope emerged in the wake of the Los Angeles uprising: the National Gang Summit in Kansas City in April/May 1993 which called for a truce among gangs across the U.S, an end to urban violence, and economic justice for the poor.[17] This summit has since spurred the creation of a church-based anti-violence network across the U.S. focused on working with youth organizations to end violence in their neighborhoods and to create positive economic development as an alternative to drug-dealing.[18] This effort and many other similar efforts must be actively supported if true peace and justice are to come to our inner city neighborhoods.

With respect to gun violence, which is the number one killer of youth and which claims over 20,000 lives a year in the U.S., we must remember that this "public health emergency" cannot be addressed apart from the way the U.S. government uses "big guns" and force to resolve its problems nationally (i.e. Waco) and abroad. How can we expect to stop gun violence on the streets or avert domestic terrorist acts (i.e. the Oklahoma bombing) when the government uses big guns and force to impose its will on other nations (i.e. Iraq)? As Phil Berrigan points out, there can't be one moral code for the government and another for the people. Promoting an ethic of nonviolence on the streets will prove to be difficult as long as the government (as well as the media and other institutions) remains committed to the use of violence as the primary means to resolve conflict.

And how can we possibly end gun violence and prevent future tragedies like the Oklahoma bombing so long as it is legal to manufacture weapons, weapons materials and handguns? It is a good first step to ban assault weapons, but this is only a beginning. We must outlaw the manufacturing of all weapons, guns and bullets just as we advocate on a global and national level for the abolition of all nuclear, conventional, chemical and biological weapons.

Faith and Hope for the Short and Long Haul

Walter Wink asserts:

Faith does not wait for God's sovereignty to be established on earth; it behaves as if that sovereignty already holds full sway. Like the Psalmists, the early Christians declared as fact what existed only in the imagination. Like God in the creation, faith calls into being what does not yet exist, and races ahead to form something new that never was before.[19]

It is this kind of faith and creativity that we need to cultivate in our justice and peacemaking efforts. Our hearts can be disarmed of fear and violence and the powers of this world can be overcome if we as individuals and communities can enflesh more deeply the revolutionary power of nonviolent love. For once we translate that love into life-affirming action, conversion can begin and radical transformation can occur. If the Berlin Wall and apartheid can fall, so, too, can the wall of poverty. True disarmament and social justice can be achieved. War can be abolished. "With God all things are possible." (Mk. 10:27)

The miracle of true justice and peace will not emerge through the "national security state" and the present political system dominated as it is by a white male power elite concerned about maintaining a system of power, profit and control. It will not come through a president, politicians, the Religious Right or anyone else the corporate-controlled mass media deems worthy of idolization. True peace and justice will come when more people avail themselves of the power of nonviolent love and commit themselves to resisting the evil before them in the same way people of faith and conscience resisted slavery in the 19th Century and, more recently, racial discrimination and the Vietnam War. It will happen when more people personally come to know the victims of our society and create deeper bonds of solidarity with those nonviolently resisting injustice and war today across the world, many at the cost of their freedom and their lives.

As we ponder the challenges of staying faithful for the long haul, how can we avoid burn-out and stay spiritually sustained? How can we stay faithful amidst the inevitable setbacks and disappointing results that we encounter along the way? While I don't pretend to have the definitive answers to these questions, I do have some insights which may prove helpful.

I believe we first need to deepen our prayer life. St. Paul goes so far as to encourage us to "pray without ceasing." (1 Th. 5:17) If our lives are rooted in prayer and meditation — anchored in the word and promise of God — God assures us that we will be able to withstand the difficulties and challenges that come our way. Prayer enables us confront personal and societal demons and helps us to overcome our "unbelief." Prayer also enables us to discern God's will, to attain the faith and courage necessary to act for justice and peace, and to practice peace in our daily lives.

The practice of "mindfulness" meditation — keeping one's consciousness alive to the present moment — is also essential, I believe, for our spiritual survival.[20] Mindfulness meditation can help us to be more aware of the miracle of life and to become more attentive and compassionate in our daily relationships. Meditation is also key in enabling us to acquire inner peace and to truly practice nonviolence in our work for peace. Thich Nhat Hanh, Zen Master and peacemaker, offers some important advise on this point:

> If we cannot smile, we cannot help other people smile. . . . If we are not peaceful, then we cannot contribute to the peace movement.
>
> That is why it is so important for us to practice meditation, to acquire the capacity to look, to see, to understand. . . . Peace work means, first of all, being peace. . . . We rely on each other. Our children are relying on us in order for them to have a future.[21]

Thus, we must never forget that prayer, meditation and action are a reciprocal process and that prayer must be at the heart of our peacemaking efforts.

As we seek to maintain our physical and mental well-being and to lead a more conscientious integrated life, many have come to realize how crucial it is to be more environmentally responsible, to garden and recycle, to be more careful about what we consume, to nurture our artistic talents, and to sing, dance, and recreate. Practicing yoga and participating in Twelve Step programs have also become increasingly vital disciplines and spiritually sustaining for many. We must continue to utilize the creative talents and spiritual resources God has blessed us with as we seek personal healing and wholeness and as we strive to bring hope to our broken world.

Activists have increasingly come to the realization that if we are to embrace more deeply the way of nonviolence, resistance, and peacemaking and stay spiritually sustained for the long haul, we must be connected in some way to a community and/or group. Through such a community or group we can most authentically confront our fears and weaknesses as well as experience the hope, joy and freedom to which we are called. In my experience, the changes we seek for our own life and for our world can best come to fruition within the context of a faith community committed to nonviolence, prayer, meditation, peacemaking, resistance, sharing, the works of mercy and celebration.

Community is not easy; it goes against the grain of our self-centered, consumer-oriented culture. Community requires us to become vulnerable, to confront those personal and cultural addictions we've grown so accustomed to, and to practice sharing, patience and forgiveness.

Also, there is no faith-based community that I know of which has been exempt from internal struggles and difficulties. Here it is helpful to remember that even Jesus' community experienced such difficulties and failure. Liz McAlister and Phil Berrigan, who have lived at the Jonah House Community for over 20 years, speak of the hope and struggle of community:

> But the most profound symbol of all, we believe, is the community itself. On what ground do we enter an Exodus, a Covenant, a life of displacement, loss, risk and hope? Surely we cannot count on ourselves or our own resources to live so deep a commitment. Rather we begin with the person of God holding empty hands before the abundance of gifts that the Lord bestows upon us. The greatest gift, as we have come to know, is a loving unity, a sign of God's presence and a source of the new creation God wills to bring into being through us.
>
> Community remains a beacon and a burden to us. We seem incapable of living in community and incapable of living without it. Perhaps our double mind stems from a dread of trusting God and one another. We try to build a faithful community. Only by beginning with the absolute fidelity who is God can other fidelities (such as in community or in marriage) become possible for us.[22]

Finally, I'm sure many can resonate with the words of Dorothy Day concerning community: "We have all known the long loneliness and we have learned that the only solution is love and that love comes with community."[23]

Another essential aspect of staying sustained in our commitment as peacemakers has to do with personal relationships. For me, the friendships that I have made with people across the country are invaluable and continue to be the greatest source of grace I've received since becoming active in the movement for peace and justice. I'm sure that many who read this will agree that the bonds of friendship we make are key to all the organizing and community building we do. Without creating such loving and nurturing relationships, it is hard to see how any community or movement will last very long. I wholeheartedly agree with Thomas Merton that "in the end, it's the reality of personal relationships that saves everything."[24]

As we try to grasp the meaning of faithfulness, especially in a culture so obsessed with expediency and quick results, Dorothy Day, I believe, has a profound insight to offer:

> What we do is very little, it is like the little boy with a few loaves and a few fishes. Christ took that little and increased it. He will do the rest. What we do is so little we may seem to be constantly failing. But so did he fail. He met with apparent failure on the Cross. But unless the seed fall into the earth and die, there is no harvest. And why must we see results? Our work is to sow. Another generation will be reaping the harvest.[25]

If what we do is truly done in faith, Jesus assures us that our work will bear fruit, not necessarily on our time but, for sure, on God's time. In short, Jesus cautions us not to base our actions on cultural effectiveness or opinion polls, but on being as faithful as we can to the truth — while leaving the final results in God's hands. Merton offers some sound advice on this point:

> The real hope then is not in something we think we can do, but in God who is making something good out of it in some way we cannot see. If we can do God's will, we will be helping in the process. But we will not necessarily know about it beforehand.[26]

If we consider Jesus' life by the world's standards, his life was an apparent failure. He was a poor man, rejected by his own people, betrayed by most of his community and executed by the State. Yet the Scriptures tell us that because he resisted the powers and principalities of this world at the cost of giving his life, God raised him from the dead and granted him eternal life. And so, Jesus, acting in faith and obedience to God, overcame death and the powers of this world and has forever changed the course of human history. Thus, when we look at Jesus' life by God's standards, Jesus is ultimately victorious. The Good News is that this victory is ours if we, like Jesus, can remain faithful.

We live in a time of Kairos, a new moment of truth, a time of grace, an opportunity for deeper conversion to the way of love and justice. We also live in a time of Jubilee where God calls us to proclaim liberty throughout the land (Lv. 25:9,10), and where Jesus declares "release for the captives, recovery of site for the blind, and freedom for the oppressed." (Lk. 4:18,19)[27]

We are called by God to offer a new vision for our world: For where there is no vision, the people perish. (Pr. 29:18) This new vision is deeply rooted in the Scriptures and calls for each person to labor for a society based on nonviolence and compassion, economic and social justice, and respect for the earth. Therefore, as we approach a new millennium, let us commit ourselves to building what Peter Maurin called "a new society in the shell of the old." Let us create a world where all wealth and resources are justly distributed and the debts of the poor are forgiven, where swords are beaten into plowshares, where all weapons — from handguns to nuclear weapons — are abolished, where war is eradicated, where all conflicts are resolved fairly and nonviolently, where reparations are made to all victims of aggression and exploitation. Let us work for a world where the rights of all people, regardless of their race, sex, religion or sexual orientation, are upheld; where the unborn, the children, refugees and the undocumented are welcomed and cherished; where the sick and addicted are adequately cared for; and where individuals and families victimized by poverty, violence and war are supported.

This vision is not outside our reach; it is already being realized through the lives and actions of countless sisters and brothers throughout the world. As Jim Douglass states:

> We can live out the imperative of transformation by acting in a faith in the nonviolent coming of God. Our Nonviolent God initiates the changes we have not yet fully chosen. Yet our transformation is underway; it is our deepest reality, it is beginning to surface in nonviolent movements everywhere. We can see peacemakers, justice-makers, giving their lives to God, in earth encircling Love that will transform even the carnage of the Persian Gulf War. We do have the capacity to destroy ourselves. But our very freedom is so profoundly an expression of Compassionate Love, as in the people born from Mother Intifada, that we can have faith in our ultimately choosing the beloved community.... In the nuclear age that kingdom where we resist evil nonviolently and realize transformation through our enemy, must come. It will come. It is coming now.[28]

Though the future is filled with great uncertainty, the God of history is with us. Therefore, guided by the cloud of witnesses who have gone before us, let us persevere in hope and keep our eyes on the prize, mindful that if we remain faithful to the truth and seek to do God's will, God will transform our life-affirming acts into a harvest of justice, peace and reconciliation.

NOTES

1. Pablo Richard, "Hope for the Third World," *Challenge*, Publication of EPICA, Volume II, Number II, Summer 1991.
2. Jim Wallis, "Lessons From the Celebration," *Sojourners*, August, 1994.
3. Daniel Berrigan, *No Bars To Manhood* (New York: Bantam, 1971), pp. 48-49.
4. Robert Cooney and Helen Michalowski, *The Power of the People: Active Nonviolence in the U.S.* (Philadelphia: New Society Publishers, 1987), p. 127.
5. Thich Nhat Hanh, *Being Peace*, p.98.
6. Some people have taken the Pax Christi "Vow of Nonviolence." For a copy of the vow, contact Pax Chtisti, U.S.A. (see "Organizations"). Also see the "Five Wonderful Precepts of Buddhism" in *Touching Peace*, Thich Nhat Hanh (Berkeley: Parallax Books), 1992. Chapter 8.
7. Thich Nhat Hanh, *Being Peace*, p, 97.
8. Telford Taylor (U.S. Chief Counsel at Nuremberg referring to the trial of the major war criminals before the Military Tribunal). *Nuremberg and Vietnam: An American Tragedy* (Chicago: Quadrangle Books, Inc., 1970), p.84.
9. *The Nuclear Resister*, Jack and Felice Cohen-Joppa, eds. July 7, 1995 #101, p.2.
10. See Gene Sharp, *Making Europe Unconquerable: The Potential for Civilian-Based Deterrence and Defense* (Cambridge, MA: Ballinger), 1985. Also, *National Security Through Civilian-Based Defense*, Omaha, NE: Association for Transarmament Studies, 1985.
11. For further reading on the connections between the liturgical calendar and nonviolent resistance and faith and politics see: Bill Wylie-Kellerman, *Seasons of Faith and Conscience* (Maryknoll, NY: Orbis Books, 1991).
12. *The Road to Damascus: Kairos and Conversion.* A document signed by Third World Christians from El Salvador, Guatemala, Korea, Namibia, Nicaragua, the Philippines and South Africa. Published by Center of Concern, Washington, D.C., 1989, p. 27-28.
13. Walter Wink, *Engaging the Powers* (Minneapolis: Augsburg Fortress Publishers, 1992), p. 264.

For further reading on the how nonviolent action has been used successfully in different social movements throughout history and up to the present see: Gene Sharp, *The Politics of Nonviolent Action* (three volumes) (Boston: Porter Sargent, 1973). Ronald Sider, *Nonviolence* (Dallas: Word Publishing, 1989). Robert Cooney and Helen Michalowski, *The Power of the People: Active Nonviolence in the U.S.* (Philadelphia, PA: New Society Publishers, 1987).

14. Ched Myers, "We're All In the Same Boat," *Sojourners*, October 1991.

15. See "America's Original Sin: A Study Guide on White Racism," *Sojourners*, 1988.

16. For an excellent resource on economic justice see "Who is My Neighbor: Economics As If Values Matter," a 180 pg. booklet and study guide produced by Sojourners magazine. Features articles by nationally known economists, theologians and activists.

17. See special report on the "Gang Summit" by Jim Wallis in the August 1993 issue of *Sojourners*.

18. Jim Wallis, "Worth Fighting For," *Sojourners*, February/March 1994. For more information about the anti-violence network contact Sojourners.

19. Walter Wink, *Engaging the Powers*, p. 323-324.

20. Thich Nhat Hanh, *Touching Peace: The Art Of Mindful Living* (Berkeley: Parallax Press), 1992.

21. Thich Nhat Hanh, *Being Peace* (Berkeley: Parallax Press, 1987), p. 79-80.

22. For excellent reading on community and resistance see: Philip Berrigan and Liz McAlister, *The Time's Discipline: The Beatitudes and Nuclear Resistance* (Baltimore: Fortkamp Publishing, 1989), p. 111

23. Robert Ellsberg, ed. *Dorothy Day: Selected Writings* (Maryknoll, NY: Orbis Books, 1992), p. 363.

24. Gerald Twomey, *Thomas Merton: Prophet in the Belly of a Paradox* (New York: Paulist Press, 1978), p. 52.

25. Robert Ellsberg, ed., *Dorothy Day: Selected Writings*, p. 92.

26. Twomey, *Thomas Merton: Prophet in the Belly of a Paradox*, p. 53.

27. For an excellent reflection/study on the meaning of Kairos for the U.S. see: *On the Way: From Kairos to Jubilee*, by Kairos/ USA, 1994.

28. James Douglass, *The Nonviolent Coming of God* (Maryknoll, N.Y.: Orbis Books, 1991), p. xii.

December 28, 1980: Omaha sign painters change the sign at the Strategic Air Command Headquarters, Offutt Air Force Base. Sign had read: "Peace is Our Profession," the Strategic Air Command motto. Action carried out by members of Strategies and Actions for Conversion.

APPENDICES

APPENDIX A

U.S. NUCLEAR WEAPONS
Bob Aldridge

Nuclear weapons deployed by the U.S. are relatively easy to determine because they are announced and observable. Nuclear weapons which have been removed from service and stored are not as easy to keep track of. For instance, the INF treaty specified that ground-launched cruise missiles and Pershing-2s removed from Europe were to be destroyed. But the nuclear warheads can be stored or recycled. There is no easy way to determine what warheads are still in the stockpile. In his September 1991 and January 1992 initiatives, President Bush ordered some weapons to stand down from "readiness," and others to be removed from "deployment." Some are to be destroyed and others stored. The status of these weapons is also indeterminable without some sort of civilian verification method. So this chapter will be a best-effort to outline the U.S. nuclear potential.

A. America's Strategic Nuclear Triad

The United States has since the outbreak of the Cold War operated a strategic nuclear triad of weapons which can be launched from land, air, and sea. Today the land and air components of this triad have been ordered to stand down. The sea-based portion, however, remains virtually untouched.

1) ICBMs — The Land Leg:

Silo-based inter-continental ballistic missiles (ICBMS) compose the land leg of the triad. They are broken down to 50 MX missiles (euphemistically dubbed "peacekeeper" by the Reagan administration) and 500 Minuteman-3 missiles.

a. Missile-X (MX): Fifty MX missiles have been deployed in converted Minuteman III silos. Each missile carries 10 Mark-21 MIRVS. Each MIRV carries a 330-kiloton W-87 bomb. Under START II all of these MX missiles will be removed.

b. Minuteman III: 200 Minuteman III ICBMs carry three Mark-12 MIRVs each. Each MIRV encases a 170-kiloton W-62 bomb. The other 300 Minuteman IIIs are fitted with three Mark-12A MIRVs each, and each of these MIRVs hold a

335-kiloton W-78 bomb. Under START II all Minuteman III missiles will have their payload reduced to one warhead each. The 500 Mark-21/W-87 warheads removed from MX missiles will be used for this purpose on Minuteman III missiles because they have advanced safety devices.

2) Bombers and Cruise Missiles — The Air Wing:

Three types of heavy, long-range bombers make up the air wing of the triad — B-52Hs, B-1Bs, and B-2s.

These bombers can carry gravity bombs or air-launched cruise missiles (ALCMs). The new advanced cruise missile (ACM), of which some have been produced, is interchangeable with the older ALCMS.

Per the September 1991 initiatives, strategic bombers have been taken off 24-hour airstrip alert and their weapons stored. Under START II a substantial portion of the strategic bomber force will be converted to primarily conventional use.

a. B-52H High-Altitude Bombers: There are currently 94 B-52H bombers in the strategic forces — all B-52G bombers not retired have been converted to carry conventional weapons. B-52H bombers can carry 20 ALCMs each (12 externally under the wings and eight internally on the rotary launcher). The internal load can be twelve B-53/B-61/B-83 bombs instead of ALCMS.

b. B-1B Supersonic Bombers: B-1B supersonic bombers now number 95. They carry weapons internally only, on three rotary launchers. Their capacity is 24 SRAM-As or 36 B-61/B-83 nuclear bombs. B-1B bombers will all be converted to carry only conventional bombs by 1998.

c. B-2 Stealth Bombers: Original plans for 132 B-2 radar-evading bombers have been reduced to 20 plus one test aircraft (prototype). The B-2 does not fly faster than sound as many believe. It is a slow, lumbering aircraft which is a high-tech resurrection of the flying wing from the 1950s, built by the same company. The first operational B-2 was delivered to Whiteman Air Force Base, Missouri on 17 December 1993. Ten B-2s had been delivered by the end of 1993. All 20 are scheduled to be delivered by the late 1990s. B-2s will be able to carry 24 of the follow-on short-range attack missiles (SRAM-2) or 24 nuclear gravity bombs. SRAM-2s, of course, have now been cancelled. Also, in October 1992, the 4th B-2 made a practice drop of a 2,000 pound Mark-4 bomb — the biggest used in the Persian Gulf war. So a conventional role is also a possibility for the B-2.

3) SLBMs — The Sea Leg:

The sea leg of the U.S. strategic is now made up of Trident I (C-4) and Trident II (D-5) submarine-launched ballistic missiles (SLBMS) carried on 16 Trident submarines. Two more submarines to carry the D-5 missiles will be delivered by 1997. Navy plans are to reduce the strategic submarine force to 14 ships, all carrying D-5 missiles.

a. Trident I (C-4) SLBMS: There are currently 192 Trident I missiles deployed (24 missiles each) in eight Trident submarines based at Bangor, Washington on the West Coast. Four of these submarines are to be deactivated and the remaining four converted to carry Trident II missiles. Plans are to then base seven of the planned 14 submarines on each coast. A Trident I missile can carry up to eight Mark-4/W-76 warheads. Each has 100 kilotons yield. A lesser number can be installed to achieve a greater range.

b. Trident II (D-5) SLBMS: Only about 400 of the 475-kiloton Mark-5/W-88 warheads for Trident II missiles were produced before they were cancelled because of production and safety reasons. They are deployed on Trident II missiles, along with 100-kiloton Mark-4/W-76 warheads, in four of the eight Trident submarines on the east coast — the other subs carrying Trident II missiles are loaded with only Mark-4/W-76 warheads. The Department of Energy, however, completed studies of a replacement SLBM warhead in mid-1994. Any plans to produce this new warhead, if any, have not been made public. A Trident II missile can carry eight of the 475-kiloton Mark-5/W-88 warheads. It has the power to carry 12 to 14 Mark-4/W-76 warheads but the START II Treaty restricts each missile to eight.

B. U.S. Tactical Nuclear Delivery Vehicles

Virtually every military fighter, or attack airplane can deliver nuclear bombs. Such short-range air-delivered nuclear weapons, operated by the US Air Force, have not been curtailed by any treaty or unilateral initiative. Land-based and sea-based tactical nukes, as they are called, have been removed by treaty mandate or unilateral initiative. Some have been destroyed and others stockpiled. Deployed tactical nuclear weapons are now restricted to the B-61 gravity, or free-fall, bomb, which has a tactical version. U.S. aircraft capable of delivering this bomb are the A-4, A-6, A-7, AV-8B, F-4, F-15, F-16, F-18, F-111, and presumably the new F-117 stealth fighter.

Editors' Note: This is taken from the *Trident Resister's Handbook,* September 1995. Used with permission.

COMMUNICATION AND NAVIGATION SYSTEMS FOR NUCLEAR AND GLOBAL-WAR FIGHTING

Compiled by Art Laffin

ELF: (see "Northern Lights Dispel Nuclear Darkness," p. 183)

TACAMO: The U.S. has a network of land-based VLF transmitting stations around the world to provide one-way communication with submarines. These are known as the Fleet Broadcasting System. But since ground-based communications are probably the most vulnerable of military targets, TACAMO (an acronym for "Take Charge and Move Out") was developed as a nuclear-survivable alternative. The submarine would put an antenna close to the surface at prescribed times to receive messages.

Since ELF has been fully deployed, and especially since the Cold war ended, TACAMO gave way to budget pressure and was taken off airborne alert. There used to be two aircraft flying continuously, one over the Pacific ocean and the other over the Atlantic. TACAMO aircraft are now on 24 hour strip alert, ready to take off immediately in a crisis. As MILSTAR (see below) satellites become operational, the ELF-MILSTAR combination could well regulate VLF communications to routine message delivery.

MILSTAR: The MILSTAR (Military Strategic and Tactical Relay) satellite was designed as a communications satellite to relay orders to military forces in the middle of a nuclear war. A new design called MILSTAR 2 will have 100 times the communications capacity of MILSTAR-1. MILSTAR 2 will have a medium data rate to support regional war like Desert Storm. It is said to be the most advanced communication system ever built. Lockheed Missiles and Space Company in November 1992 was awarded a $1.7 billion contract to design and develop MILSTAR-2, upgrade the MILSTAR-1 spacecraft still in production, and build a fourth MILSTAR-2 satellites. Lockheed may build an additional three MILSTAR-2 satellites for a total of seven. The first satellite was slated for delivery in December 1992. On August 2, 1993 the first launch of Milstar from Vandenberg Air Force base ended in an explosion due to a booster failure in the Titan 4 rocket. However on February 7, 1994, this 10,000 pound satellite was successfully launched at Cape Canaveral. . . . Spacecraft number four is scheduled to be completed by early 1998. When three MILSTAR satellites are in orbit the system will be considered fully operational. A transmission from a ground command post, ship or aircraft will be received by the nearest satellite, relayed to the satellite closest to the message's designation, and then transmitted back down to the recipient. Troops on the front line of combat will be able to set up a MILSTAR terminal in a few minutes for communication anywhere in the world. MILSTAR is a dangerous addition which will add to the aggressive posture of U.S. decision-makers. Total cost: Over $17 billion; $692 million requested for 1995.

NAVSTAR: Prior to the 1990's, submarines relied on land-based Omega and Loran-C signals, and Transit navigation satellites for these periodic positional fixes. Now the NAVSTAR global positioning system (GPS) is taking over. NAVSTAR will be available any time, in any weather, at any place on or above the earth. A 30 second fix will give the receiver's position within 30-40 feet in three dimensions, and velocity (speed and direction) within a fraction of a mile per hour. NAVSTAR will also provide precise time within a millionth of a second so that a submarine's atomic clock can be synchronized.

The full NAVSTAR constellation will consist of 24 Block-2 (operational) satellites — 21 functioning and three in-orbit spares. The satellites will be divided equally in six polar-orbital planes. The orbits are approximately (10,898 nautical miles above the earth), which means each satellite completes about two trips per day around the globe. The orbits are inclined 55 degrees to the equator. With this full constellation there will always be five satellites in view. The satellites will have a 7 and one-half year service life. NAVSTAR satellites are now being put into orbit by Delta-2 rockets launched from Cape Canaveral. Falcon Air Force Base in Colorado is the master control station for NAVSTAR.

The first Block-2 was launched on February 14, 1989, the 13th on April 9, 1992. But there were problems and only 12 of 13 were functioning at that time. However, there were three of the older Block-1 (development) satellites working so the mixed constellation was something like 15 NAVSTARs functioning. Air Force plans were to launch a block-2 every 2-3 months on Delta-2 rockets. Full operation capability was scheduled for late 1993 even though the May 10, 1992 disarmament action of Peter Lumsdaine and Keith Kjoller resulted in one NAVSTAR satellite being seriously damaged. Both Trident I and Trident II missiles have received NAVSTAR signals during test flights, purportedly to calibrate the on-board navigation system. NAVSTAR receivers have already been incorporated on cruise missiles and have been designed for use in 155 millimeter artillery shells. Some NAVSTAR receivers are as small as cigarette packages.

NAVSTAR also increasingly provide extremely precise guidance and targeting capabilities to advanced weapons and military assault teams across the planet. Such data will:

* guide Special Forces units and helicopter gunships on counterinsurgency search-and-destroy missions against peasant rebels, refugees and indigenous communities from Kurdestan to Guatemala, Indonesia to Peru, Columbia to the Philippines;
* direct bombers and cruise missiles in destroying the national infrastructure of targeted countries, as NAVSTAR did in Iraq, and may do during future regional wars against other countries.

Recently the civilian use of GPS has been highly publicized. For example the FAA approved use of GPS for commercial airlines and private pilots. And soon compact GPS receivers will be used by trucks, trains and cars. Despite these civilian uses, we must not forget the primary military role of GPS.

Sources for TACAMO, MILSTAR AND NAVSTAR:

Trident Resister's Handbook, by Bob Aldridge, 1992. *Washington Post*, February 8, 1994 (Milstar). Other information for the section on NAVSTAR is taken from: Harriet Tubman - Sarah Connor Brigade NAVSTAR Disarmament Action materials, compiled by Peter Lumsdaine in May 1992. Center for Defense Information, 1993.

OTHER KEY U.S. WEAPONS PROGRAMS

Star Wars (Renamed: Ballistic Missile Defense Organization): After 10 years and $32 billion, Star Wars is alive and well. Clinton and the Congress spent $3.8 billion in 1994 on ballistic missile defenses, the same amount funded by Congress in 1993.

Background

The concept of defending against ballistic missiles was conceived during the 1960s, shortly after missiles were introduced as carriers for nuclear warheads. It became known as ballistic missiles defense (BMD) and the missile used to intercept ballistic missiles was named an anti-ballistic missiles (ABM). After Richard Nixon was inaugurated in 1969, he redirected the BMD effort to defend ICBM silos against a Soviet first strike. This system was named "Safeguard" and was approved for 12 sites. The ABM Treaty and a later protocol limited the U.S. and U.S.S.R. to only one ABM site each. In 1975 Safeguard was terminated. In March 1983 President Reagan issued National Security Directive No. 85 entitled "Eliminating the Threat from Ballistic Missiles." This initiative tied together all BMD activity and past research under the Strategic Defense Initiative (SDI), with all the military forces participating. SDI activities did violate the ABM Treaty by developing and testing components and systems which were air-based and space-based. And it was complemented by theater missile defense activities.

In May 1993 Clinton terminated SDI — in name only. The new name became BMDO. And because the word "strategic" was removed, defense against tactical missiles was also included because all activity under the "new" BMDO does not have to be treaty compliant. Prohibited activity can now be pursued under the heading of tactical or theater.

Current BMD activities focus are along two tracks. One is called the National Missile Defense segment which would protect the U.S. from a limited or accidental attack by ICBMs or SLBM's. It would have missiles and sensors designed to protect U.S. forces overseas, as well as friends and allies, from tactical ballistic missile threats. Both segments are to be integrated by automated computer processing and communication — through a command center element — so that they inter-operate with one another. The National Missile Defense Segment would consist of: Space and Missile Tracking Systems, formerly known as Brilliant Eyes, a network of up to 32 small satellites; Ground-Based Radar, Ground-Based Interceptor, and a special hit to kill interceptor known as Endo-Exoatmospheric Interceptor.

The Theater Missile Defense Segment is currently planned as a two-tier system with a possible boost-phase intercept capability. Longer range interceptors designed to destroy incoming missiles or warheads high in or above the earth's atmosphere would comprise the upper tier. This includes, Theater Missile Defense-Ground Based Radar, THAAD (Theater High Altitude Area Defense launchers), and a Navy Upper tier Defense, including the LEAP warhead — a 20 pound hit-to-kill warhead.

Shorter range ATM's for engaging incoming warheads low in the atmosphere make up the lower tier.

The Clinton administration has also focused on developing Theater Missile Defenses to safeguard U.S. troops abroad against short-to-medium-range missiles. Nearly $400 million has been budgeted for fiscal 1996 to continue development of a homefront missile defense system.

Estimated future costs of BMDO are $30 billion through 1998 and over $100 billion for the total program. About $3 billion is budgeted for 1995. And over $15 billion is estimated to be spent on BMD over the next 5 years.

Sources: Most of the background section is taken "From Star Wars to Scud Busters — A Background Paper on Ballistic Missile Defense," Bob Aldridge, August 19, 1995; *Washington Post*, May 14, 1993; Center for Defense Information 1995 Military Almanac.

Fast Attack Submarines (SSN-688-Class): The primary mission of attack submarines is to find and destroy other submarines, but they can also attack surface ships, conduct reconnaissance, attack land targets and mine waterways. Currently, the Navy has a fleet of 88 nuclear powered attack submarines. 51 of these are the recent Los Angeles (SSN-688) class submarines. The number of these submarines will be reduced to 45-55 by 1999 and to 30 by 2010, according to the Pentagon's bottom-up review. Most of the SSN's are capable of firing nuclear weapons, weather the SURBROC anti-submarine missiles for attacking other submarines, or nuclear-armed Tomahawk attack sea-launched cruise missiles (SLCM) for striking targets on land. These missiles fly low enough to be undetectable by radar and can hit a target at a range of 1500 miles with pinpoint accuracy. Their nuclear warheads carry a destructive force of 200 kilotons, 17 times more powerful than the Hiroshima bomb. Tomahawk SLCMs, carrying conventional warheads, were used extensively during the U.S. massacre of Iraq. The cost of one Attack Sub is $800 million.

Source: CDI, *The Defense Monitor*, Vol. XXII, Number 4, 1993; Neptune Papers No. 2, *Nuclear Warships and Naval Nuclear Weapons: A Complete Inventory*, by William Arkin and Joshua Handler. May 1988).

Seawolf Submarine (SSN-21): This nuclear powered submarine is supposed to run faster, deeper and quieter than the Los Angeles class attack submarines. It will have a higher tactical speed, and carry about 50 missiles, mines and torpedoes. According to the Navy, it will have "three times the mission effectiveness of the improved SSN-688." The Navy originally wanted 29 Seawolfs but, due to budget cuts, have had to scale back the number. Due to cracks found in the hull of the first sub it had to be rebuilt. Two are currently in different stages of production at Electric Boat in Groton, CT and a third will be built. At $2.8 billion apiece, the first Seawolf was launched June 24, 1995.

Sources: CDI, *The Defense Monitor*, Vol. XX, Number 2, 1991 and the *New York Times*, August 9, 1991)

New Attack Submarine (NSSN): In early 1994 the Navy dropped its plan to develop the new Centurion sub which would have been the successor to the Los Angeles Class of Submarines. The Navy is now researching the development of the "New Attack Submarine." While funding for naval procurement is tight, Congress provided the entire $507 million request for the NSSN in 1995. The estimated cost for one NSSN is $1.5 billion and production is to begin at Electric Boat in Groton, CT in 1998.

Source: *Defense News*, Oct. 24, 1994.

AEGIS: Aegis is the battle tracking and naval combat engagement equipment around which the Navy is building its current line of guided-missile cruisers and destroyers. These Aegis warships contain a complex mix of radar (the AN-SPY-1A), computerized fire control and launch systems, all integrated in and through a CIC/combat information center which controls an on board arsenal of SM-2 missiles, 5 in rapid fire guns/Phalanx close-in weapon system, and Tomahawk cruise missiles (nuclear-capable) with vertical launch system (VLS) holding as many as 122 Tomahawks.

According to Navy officials, Aegis is "the most powerful war-fighting system the Navy has today." It is also the Navy's most expensive warship ever — $1.2 billion per Aegis cruiser.

Aegis is designed to track and destroy — with automatic capability "from detection to kill" — as many as 200 moving or stationary targets simultaneously within a radius of 300 miles. Aegis is also key to the coordination of the naval surface battle groups in which a battleship or aircraft carrier operate along with an Aegis cruiser and other surface ships, support and assault aircraft, and fast-attack submarines; the Aegis combat system has the capability for overall force coordination."

Aegis, equipped with the standard Block-4A missile, is the Navy's platform for a sea-based missile defense. One Aegis cruiser or destroyer is a lethal weapon system. The same ship operating with a surface battle group is a command post for the even greater lethality of the entire battle group. Surface battle groups operated throughout the Persian Gulf War. It was an Aegis cruiser, the USS Bunker Hill (CG-52) that fired the first cruise missile into Iraq.

The first Aegis cruiser was commissioned in 1983. More than half of the 27 in the planned cruiser class have been built. A fleet of at least 16 Aegis destroyers — the Ardleigh Burke (DDG) class — is also in production.

Sources: *Navy Fact File*, Dept. of the Navy, *1989; Philadelphia Inquirer*, October, 1990; *New York Times*, Nov., 1990, *Newsweek*, July 13, 1992; Brandywine

Peace Community, Swarthmore, PA.

F-15E "Strike Eagle" Fighter: The most modern fighter plane in the air force arsenal. A supersonic all-weather, nuclear capable strike aircraft, it will augment and eventually replace the F-111 in the theater nuclear role. It was designed specifically to enhance the F-15 C/D's nuclear capabilities. Toward that end, a rear cockpit was added for dropping bombs, including B57 and B61 series nukes. Now it is billed as an excellent long-range, deep interdiction bomber, capable of reaching any point in the world with one refueling. According to Air Force Officials, the F-15E's are being equipped with the AGM-130 rocket powered stand-off missile and HARM anti-radar missiles. The F-15E's were used throughout the Iraqi massacre, often flying as many as 60 sorties a day. There are presently some 200 F-15E's and according to the May 31, 1994 issue of *Defense News*, no new F-15E's are scheduled to be built. Each plane costs $40 million.

Source: Pax Christi-Spirit of Life Plowshares Fact Sheet, December 1993

F-22: New air combat fighter plane that has been in production since 1982. Equipped with "stealth" technology, the Air Force claims the F-22 will be invisible to radar, a claim yet to be validated. The F-22 is eventually supposed to replace the F-15's. As of 1994, $9.3 billion had been spent. Total estimated cost for 442 F-22 Aircraft through 2012: $71.6 billion. $2.5 billion was authorized for the 1995 budget and $2.2 billion is proposed for the 1996 budget.

Source: CDI, *The Defense Monitor*, Vol. XXII, Number 4, 1993 and CDI Fact Sheet, Jan. 27, 1995).

F/A-18 Hornet Attack Plane - E/F version: The F/A-18 is a long range fighter-bomber. Even though the plane is a modified version of the existing F/A-18 aircraft, the cost is expected to be almost $100 million per plane. The purpose of this plane is to add range and carrying capability to the existing F/A-18. The estimated cost for the entire program is $95 billion. $1.3 billion was requested for FY 1995.

Source: *The Defense Monitor*, Vol. XXII, Number 4, 1993).

Landmines

There are over 100 million landmines which contaminate some 60 countries around the world and at least 100 million more are stockpiled in the arsenals of various nations. Landmines — camouflaged explosives made to cripple or kill people, or to destroy weaponry — turn fields, paths, and travel routes into potential death traps for innocent civilians long after conflicts and wars end. For example, fighting parties placed 20 million landmines in Angola during the civil war there, of which about 12 million remain. Estimates of amputees resulting from the inordinate use of landmines worldwide range from 15,000 to 55,000. Landmines kill 800 people every month.

Over 50 countries produce 340 types of antipersonnel landmines. Companies in the U.S. which produce landmines or components for landmines include: Alliant Techsystems, Motorola and Hamilton.

The U.S. passed the first moratorium on the sale and export of landmines. This ban expired in October 1993. The U.S. must support the goals outlined by the International Campaign to Ban Landmines:

* Ban the use, production and proliferation of landmines;
* Create a U.N. fund to clear mine fields and to aid victims;
* and make those that fail to do so contribute to the U.N. fund.

Sources: "Hidden Wars: Landmines," by Jody Williams, *The Nonviolent Activist*, May-June 1994. "Landmines," Fact Sheet by Peace Action, October 1993.

The Nuclear Club and the State of Nuclear Proliferation

The proliferation of nuclear weapons has become a major international security concern. Six countries are acknowledged nuclear states, (not including states within the former Soviet Union) although three others (Israel, India, Pakistan) also possess nuclear weapons capabilities. Several other states are clearly interested in acquiring the ability to produce nuclear weapons. Other states have abandoned their nuclear ambitions and have become full members of the nonproliferation club.

Appendices

Acknowledged Nuclear Weapons States

China
France
Russia
CIS (Commonwealth of Independent States): Belarus, Kazakstan, Ukraine
United Kingdom
United States
South Africa (ended its nuclear weapons program)

States Believed to Have Nuclear Weapons or the Ability to Produce Them on Short Notice

Israel
India
Pakistan

States of Immediate Proliferation Concern

North Korea (agreed to freeze nuclear program in October 1994)
Iraq (Eliminated by Gulf War. Monitored by the International Atomic Energy Agency and by a U.N. Special Commission)

Long-Term Proliferation Threats (The year 2000 and beyond)

Iran
Libya

Recent Converts to Nuclear Nonproliferation

Algeria
Argentina
Belarus*
Brazil
Kazakstan*
South Africa
Ukraine*

*Nuclear weapons deployed in these countries are under Russian control. All acceded to the nuclear Non-Proliferation treaty as non-nuclear weapon states.

Sources: *The Arms Control Assoc. Fact Sheet*, April 1995, other public news sources.

APPENDIX B

NUREMBERG PRINCIPLES

Principles of International Law Recognized in the Charter the Nuremberg Tribunal and in the Judgment of the Tribunal

As formulated by the International Law Commission, June-July 1950.

Principle I

Any person who commits an act which constitutes a crime under international law is responsible therefore and liable to punishment.

Principle II

The fact that internal law does not impose a penalty for an act which constitutes a crime under international law does not relieve the person who committed the act from responsibility under international law.

Principle III

The fact that a person who committed an act which constitutes crime under international law acted as Head of State or responsible government official does not relieve him from responsibility under international law.

Principle IV

The fact that a person acted pursuant to order of his government or of a superior does not relieve him from responsibility under international law, provided a moral choice was in fact possible to him.

Principle V

Any person charged with a crime under international law has the right to a fair trial on the facts and law.

Principle VI

The crimes hereinafter set out are punishable as crimes under international law:
a. Crimes against peace:
(i) Planning, preparation, initiation, or waging of a war of aggression or a war in violation of international treaties, agreements, or assurances;
(ii) Participation in a common plan or conspiracy for the accomplishment of any of the acts mentioned under (i).

b. War crimes:

Violations of the laws or customs of war which include, but are not limited to, murder, ill-treatment or deportation to slave-labor or for any other purpose of civilian population of or in occupied territory, murder or ill-treatment of prisoners of war or persons on the seas, killing of hostages, plunder of public or private property, wanton destruction of cities, towns, or villages, or devastation not justified by military necessity.

c. Crimes against humanity:

Murder, extermination, enslavement, deportation, and other in-human acts done against any civilian population, or persecutions on political, racial, or religious grounds, when such acts are done or such persecutions are carried on in execution of or in connection with any crime against peace or any war crime.

Principle VII

Complicity in the commission of a crime against peace, a war crime, or a crime against humanity as set forth in Principle VI is a crime under international law.

Source: U.N. General Assembly Resolution 95 (i)

THE NUREMBERG PLEDGE OF LAWYERS AND JURISTS

Deeply concerned by the commission of many crimes of state and by the terrible danger of an annihilating nuclear war:

We, the undersigned, pledge to work in our professional roles and as citizens for the effective application of the Nuremberg Principles, that acts in violation of these principles are punishable as crimes whether committed by a head of state or by an ordinary soldier or civilian, whether done under governmental order or not, and that crimes against peace, war crimes, and crimes against humanity are to be condemned, prevented, and prosecuted by the enforcement of international law.

More concretely, we pledge to resist the commission of crimes of state, including especially preparations for war waged with nuclear weapons and seek the establishment of a legal framework in international society to assure the impartial and rigorous application of the Nuremberg Principles.

On this fortieth anniversary of the Nuremberg Judgment we call on lawyers and jurists throughout the world to join us by signing this pledge and we invite members of political, military, scientific, religious, business, and all other professional associations to join us in this struggle on behalf of law and peace by drafting and circulating similar pledges to their colleagues and by playing active roles on behalf of the Nuremberg Principles in the constitutional order of international political life.

The Nuremberg Pledge of Lawyers and Jurists was adopted at Nuremberg on November 24, 1985, by vote of the two thousand participants at the International Association of Democratic Lawyers Conference. (Source: *Ground Zero*, Spring 1986, p.3)

U.N. RESOLUTION ON THE PROHIBITION OF NUCLEAR WEAPONS

The General Assembly,

Mindful of its responsibility under the Charter of the United Nations in the maintenance of international peace and security, as well as in the consideration of principles governing disarmament,

Gravely concerned that, while negotiations on disarmament have not so far achieved satisfactory results, the armaments race, particularly in the nuclear and thermonuclear fields, has reached a dangerous state requiring all possible precautionary measures to protect humanity and civilization from the hazard of nuclear and thermonuclear catastrophe.

Recalling that the use of weapons of mass destruction, causing unnecessary human suffering, was in the past prohibited, as being contrary to the laws of humanity and to the principles of international law, by international declarations and binding agreements, such as the Declaration of St. Petersburg of 1868, the Declaration of the Brussels Conference of 1874, the Conventions of The Hague Peace Conferences of 1888 and 1907, and the Geneva Protocol Of 1925, to which the majority of nations are still parties,

Considering that the use of nuclear and thermonuclear weapons would bring about indiscriminate suffering and destruction to humankind and civilization to an even greater extent than the use of those weapons declared by the aforementioned international declarations and agreements to be contrary to the laws of humanity and a crime under international law,

United Nations Resolution 211

Believing that the use of weapons of mass destruction, such as nuclear and thermonuclear weapons, is a direct negation of the high ideals and objectives which the United Nations has been established to achieve through the protection of succeeding generations from the scourge of war and through the preservation and promotion of their cultures,

I. Declares that:

(a) The use of nuclear and thermonuclear weapons is contrary to the spirit, letter, and aims of the United Nations and, as such, a direct violation of the Charter of the United Nations;

(b) The use of nuclear and thermonuclear weapons would exceed even the scope of war and cause indiscriminate suffering and destruction to humankind and civilization and, as such, is contrary to the rules of international law and to the laws of humanity;

(c) The use of nuclear and thermonuclear weapons is a war directed not against an enemy or enemies alone but also against humankind in general, since the people of the world not involved in such a war will be subjected to all the evils generated by the use of such weapons;

(d) Any State using nuclear and thermonuclear weapons is to be considered as violating the Charter of the United Nations, as acting contrary to the laws of humanity and as committing a crime against mankind and civilization;

II. Requests the Secretary-General to consult the Governments of Member

States to ascertain their views on the possibility of convening a special conference for signing a convention on the prohibition of the use of nuclear and thermonuclear weapons for war purposes and to report on the results of such consultation to the General Assembly at its seventeenth session.

Source: United Nations General Assembly Resolution 1653 (XVI) on the Prohibition of Nuclear Warfare, 1961. Note: The United States voted against this resolution.

WE HAVE BEEN GUILTY
Ulf Panzer

Editors' Note: *On January 12, 1987, 22 judges from throughout West Germany formed a nonviolent blockade of the U.S. air base at Mutlangen, near Stuttgart, where the U.S. had deployed Pershing II nuclear missiles. What follows is a statement by one of the participants, a district court judge from Hamburg.*

Fifty years ago, during the time of Neo-fascism, we judges and prosecutors allegedly did not know anything. By closing our eyes and ears, our hearts and minds, we became a docile instrument of suppression, terror and death. We were silent in the face of injustice; we served injustice by just applying Nazi laws. The judiciary allowed itself to be abused, to legitimize injustice, and many judges, as murderers in black robes, under the cloak of the law, committed the most cruel crimes. We have been guilty.

Today, we are on the way to becoming guilty again, to be abused again. By our passivity, but also by applying democratic laws, we legitimize terror: nuclear terror. And today we do know. We know that we need only the push of the button, and all Germany, Europe, the whole world, will be a radiating desert without human life. Today, in the nuclear age, humankind depends on the good functioning of a Soviet or American computer.

It is because we know that, that we have to act. We are concerned, not only as ordinary citizens, as mothers and fathers who care for the future of their children, but, especially, in our office as judges in a democratic state. Since we are judges, we have a special responsibility not to be silent in face of the ever-growing stockpiles of nuclear arms in East and west, whose power of destruction supersedes all human imagination.

Nuclear arms are not only immoral, they are illegal. It is our office to serve justice and peace. Nuclear arms do not serve justice or peace. They are the ultimate crime. They hold all humankind as hostages.

That is why many of us judges have organized "Judges and Prosecutors for Peace." We have raised our voices in warning against nuclear omnideath. We have worked with local peace groups, we have advertized against the illegality of nuclear armament, we have demonstrated and submitted resolutions to our parliament. We have held two peace conferences in Bonn in the summer of 1983, and in Kassel in November 1985.

Our warnings have died away unheard. That is the reason why we, today, block the U.S. air base in Mutlangen, the place where the Pershing missiles are deployed. We hope that such an action will be heard more loudly than all our futile words before.

We do not break the law. We uphold the law, as we swore to do when entering our office. Of course, we do know that, by the predominant opinion of our peers, such a blockade is a crime. They say it is a form of violence punishable by section 240 of the German Penal Code. If it can be called violent to sit peacefully in the street in front of a Pershing base, what are we then to call a Pershing II missile, with its horrific power of destruction?

We have to put up with the risk of being sentenced by our fellow judges. For we are convinced that there do exist things which have to be denied a place in human civilization. The ovens of Auschwitz were such things. Today, it is nuclear armament.

By our action of civil disobedience (or is it not rather an act of civil obedience?!) we want to make clear that there are members of the judiciary — a profession which, by our Constitution, was granted political power and thus political responsibility — who refuse the madness of nuclear armament. We refuse complicity with this policy of our government which is so despising of humankind.

Our blockade is also an act of solidarity. Solidarity with the many hundreds of fellow citizens who have been prosecuted by our fellow state attorneys, and have been sentenced by our fellow judges because they did the same thing we do today. Solidarity also with the peace-loving people in the Eastern block, who are sentenced very harshly only because they committed the "crime" of standing up for peace and disarmament. Solidarity, finally, with our countless peace-loving friends in the United states of America, who, on any given day, go to prison because they dare to resist the terror of nuclear arms. Some of them have been sentenced with imprisonment up to eighteen years — quite unbelievable for a society which calls itself democratic.

They gave us hope. They gave us courage. Their commitment is a signal and shining example. So, together with them we today say, as loudly and clearly as we can: "NO TO NUCLEAR ARMS!"

APPENDIX C

WEAPONS VS HUMAN NEEDS

For the total projected cost of the ballistic missile defense program ($91 Billion)...

... you could fund the Head Start program at its current funding level and provide early education for 740,000 children for 26 years.

For the total projected cost to build 1,000 F/A-18E/F Hornet attack aircraft ($89 Billion)...

... you could fund the National School Lunch Program at its current funding for 21 years.

For the total projected cost of the NSSN New Attack Submarine program ($58 Billion)...

... you could fund the Office of AIDS Research at its current funding for 43 years.

For the total projected cost to build 523 V-22 Osprey tilt-rotor aircraft ($53 Billion)...

... you could fund either the National Endowment for the Arts or Humanities at their current funding levels for 300 years.

For the cost to build 20 additional B-2 bombers ($31 Billion)...

... you could provide care and treatment for over 250,000 HIV-positive patients from time of infection until death.

For the total projected cost of the MILSTAR communications satellite program ($27 Billion)...

... you could fund the National Cancer Institute at its current funding level for 14 years.

For the amount that a congressional budget resolution would add to the FY 1996 military budget ($7 Billion)...

... you could fund federal summer youth employment and training for 550,000 youths for eight years

For the cost to build a single nuclear aircraft carrier ($4.4 Billion)... ... you could double the annual salaries for 190,000 first-year public school teachers.

For the amount that the Clinton Administration requested for the C-17 transport aircraft program for FY 1996 ($2.6 Billion)... ... you could double the federal funding to replace and rehabilitate unsafe and inadequate bridges.

For the cost of a single B-2 bomber ($2.2. Billion)... ... you could pay the annual health care expenses for about 1.3 million Americans.

For the amount that the Clinton Administration requested for the F-22 fighter program for FY 1996 ($2.1 Billion)... ... you could double federal funding for the Centers for Disease Control and Prevention.

For the amount that the Clinton Administration requested for the Seawolf attack submarine program for FY 1996 ($1.7 Billion)... ... you could provide vocational and adult education for nearly 15 million people or low-income home energy assistance for 5.6 million households for one year.

For the amount the Clinton Administration requested for the B-2 bomber program for FY 1996 ($987 million)... ... you could triple federal funding to promote safe and drug-free schools and communities or funding for research on solar and renewable energy.

Source: Center for Defense Information, Excerpted from *The Defense Monitor*, Vol. XXIV, Number 7, August 1995.

WHERE YOUR INCOME TAX MONEY REALLY GOES

The United States Federal Budget for Fiscal Year 1996

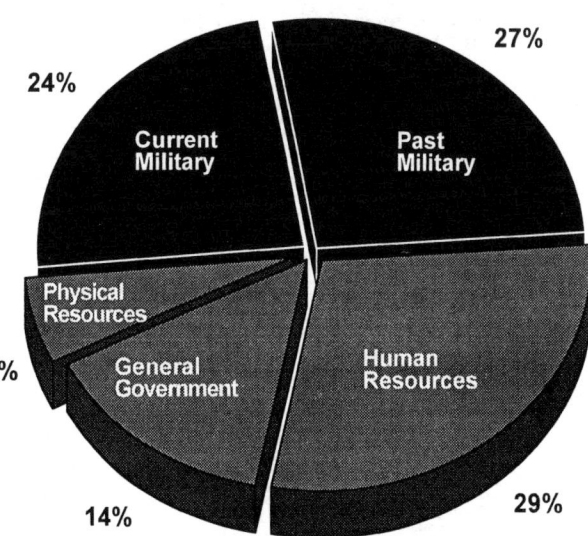

**24% Current Military
$291 Billion**
(Military Personnel $66B, Retired Pay $12B, Operation and Maintenance $91B, Family Housing $4B, Procurement $49B, Research and Development $35B, Construction $6B, DoE Nuclear Weapons $11B, NASA 50% $7B, Coast Guard $4B, plus CIA, President's Funds, International Security Assistance, FEMA)

**27% Past Military
$329 Billion**
Veterans Benefits $38B
Interest on National Debt (80% estimated to be created by military spending) $291B

**29% Human Resources
$358 Billion**
(Education, Health and Human Services, HUD housing subsidies, Labor Department)

**14% General Government
$179 Billion**
(Government, Justice Department, International Affairs, Peace Corps, 20% interest on national debt, civilian portion of NASA)

**6% Physical Resources
$72 Billion**
(Includes Agriculture, Commerce, Energy, HUD administration/community development, Interior Department, Transportation, Environmental Protection)

**100% Total Federal Funds
$1.229 Trillion**

How These Figures Were Determined

All these dollar figures are for fiscal year 1996, as reported in the *Budget of the United States Government, Fiscal Year 1996*. The percentages are Federal Funds, calculated after removing Trust Funds (such as Social Security), which are raised and spent separately from income taxes. What you pay (or don't pay) on April 15 goes only to the Federal Funds portion of the budget. The government practice of combining Trust and Federal Funds (the so-called "Unified Budget") began in the 1960's during the Vietnam War. The government presentation makes the human needs portion of the budget seem larger and the military portion smaller.

"Current military" spending adds together money allocated for the Department of Defense ($251 billion) plus the "defense" portion from other parts of the budget. Spending on nuclear weapons (without their delivery systems) amounts to about 1% of the total budget.

"Past military" is represented by veterans' benefits plus 80% of the interest on the national debt. If there had been no military spending, most (if not all) of the national debt would have been eliminated. Analysts differ on how much of the debt stems from the military; estimates range from 50% to 100%. We felt that 80% may even be conservative.

War Resisters League creates these flyers each year after the President has presented the budget (late January or February). By adding your name to the WRL mailing list, you will receive this information annually.

WAR RESISTERS LEAGUE
339 Lafayette Street, New York, NY 10012

The Government Deception

The pie chart below is the Administration's view of the budget (and similar to the figures you'll see in your IRS booklet or the media). This is a distortion of how our income tax dollars are spent because it includes Trust Funds (e.g., Social Security) and buries the expenses of past military spending in nonmilitary parts of the pie. For a more accurate representation of how your Federal income tax dollar is really spent, see the large chart.

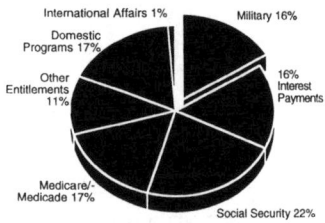

APPENDIX D

GROUPS AND ORGANIZATIONS

ACT for Disarmament, 736 Bathurst St., Toronto, Ont., Canada M5S 2R4.

Alliance for Nonviolent Action, 253 College St., Unit 235, Toronto, Ont., Canada M5T 1R5.

American Friends Service Committee, 1501 Cherry St., Philadelphia, PA 19102.

Anathoth Farm Community, 740 Round Lake Rd., Luck, WI 54853 (Resistance to Project ELF).

Brandywine Peace Community, PO Box 81, Swarthmore, PA 19081.

Christian Peacemaker Teams, 1821 W. Cullerton, Chicago, IL 60608

Citizens for Peace in Space, PO Box 915, Colorado Springs, CO 80903.

Dorothy Day Catholic Worker, 503 Rock Creek Church Rd., NW, Washington, DC 20010 (Resistance at Pentagon, White House and Disarm Bazaar Campaign).

Fellowship of Reconciliation, PO Box 271, Nyack, NY 10960-0271

Jonah House/Atlantic Life Community, 1301 Moreland Ave., Baltimore, MD 21216 (plowshares actions/support).

Lakes and Prairies Life Community, 4924 Chicago Ave., Omaha, NE 68132 (Resistance at Strategic Command Headquarters).

Los Angeles Catholic Worker, 632 N Brittania St., Los Angeles, CA 90033 (Disarmament and anti-intervention focus).

New Call to Peacemaking, PO Box 500, Akron, PA 17501.

Nukewatch, PO Box 2658, Madison, WI 53701 (Watchdog of N-weapons production and N-waste).

Pax Christi, U.S.A., 348 E 10th St., Erie, PA 16503-1110.

School of the Americas Watch, PO Box 3330, Columbus, GA 31903.

Shundahai Network, PO Box 1255, Nevada City, CA 95959 (Native American and environmental issues/nuclear testing).

War Resisters League, 339 Lafayette St., New York, NY 10012.

SELECTED BIBLIOGRAPHY

Aldridge, Bob and Ched Myers, *Resisting the Serpent: Palau's Struggle for Survival* (Baltimore: Fortkamp Publishing Co.), 1990.

Aldridge, Bob and Janet, *Children and Nonviolence* (Pasadena, California: Hope Publishing House), 1987.

Alperovitz, Gar, *Atomic Diplomacy* (New York: Viking/Penguin), 1985.

Berrigan, Daniel, *To Dwell In Peace* (San Francisco: Harper & Row), 1987; *Whereon To Stand: The Acts of the Apostles and Ourselves* (Baltimore: Fortkamp Publishing Co.), 1992.

Cone, James H., *A Black Theology of Liberation* (Maryknoll, NY: Orbis), 1986.

Day, Sam, *Crossing The Line* (Baltimore: Fortkamp Publishing Co.), 1991.

Dellinger, David, *From Yale To Jail* (New York: Pantheon Books), 1993.

Douglass, J., *The Nonviolent Coming of God* (Maryknoll, NY: Orbis Books), 1991.

Durland, W., *God or Nations* (Baltimore: Fortkamp Publishing Co.), 1989.

Gutierrez, Gustavo, *A Theology of Liberation* (Maryknoll, NY: Orbis), 1974.

Matthiessen, Peter, *In the Spirit of Crazy Horse* (NY: Viking), 1983.

McAlister, Elizabeth and Philip Berrigan. *The Times Discipline: The Beatitudes and Nuclear Resistance* (Baltimore: Fortkamp Publishing Co.), 1989.

McSorley, Richard, SJ, *It's a Sin to Build a Nuclear Weapon: Collected Works on War and Christian Peacemaking* (Baltimore: Fortkamp Publishing, Co.), 1991.

Nouwen, Henri, *Love in a Fearful Land: A Guatemalan Story* (Notre Dame, IN: Ave Maria), 1985.

O'Reilly, Ciaron, *Bomber Grounded, Runway Closed* (Marion, SD: Rose Hill Books), 1993.

Schumacher, E.F., *Small Is Beautiful* (New York: Perennial/Harper & Row), 1975.

Silen, Juan A., *We The Puerto Rican People: A Story of Oppression and Resistance* (New York: Monthly Review Press), 1971.

West, Cornell, *Race Matters* (Boston: Beacon Press), 1993.

Zinn, H., *A People's History of the United States* (N.Y.: Harper Colophon), 1980.

PERIODICALS

Articles on the U.S. nuclear/military policy, disarmament, U.S. intervention, nonviolence and resistance can be found in the following publications:

Bulletin of the Atomic Scientists, 1020-24 E. 58th St., Chicago, IL 60637

Catholic Agitator, L.A. Catholic Worker, 632 N. Britania St., Los Angeles, CA 90033

Catholic Worker, 36 E. First St., New York, NY 10003

Central America Report, Religious Task Force on Central America, 1747 Connecticut Ave., NW, Washington, DC 20009-1108

Defense Monitor, Center for Defense Information, 1500 Massachusetts Ave., NW, Washington, DC 20005

Estafeta, (East Timor Support Newsletter), PO Box 1182, White Plains, NY 10602

Fellowship, Fellowship of Reconciliation, Box 271, Nyack, NY 10960

Greenpeace, 1436 U St., NW, Washington, DC 20009

The Little Way, Dorothy Day Catholic Worker, 503 Rock Creek Church Rd., NW, Washington, DC 20010

National Catholic Reporter, P.O. Box 419281, Kansas City, MO 64141

Nonviolent Activist, War Resisters League, 339 Lafayette St., New York, NY 10012

The Nuclear Resister, P.O. Box 43383, Tucson, AZ 85733-3383

The Other Side, 300 W. Apsley St., # 12236, Philadelphia, PA 19144

The Plough, Spring Valley Bruderhoff, Farmington, PA 15743.

Peacework, American Friends Service Committee, 2161 Massachusetts Ave., Cambridge, MA 02140

The Progressive, P.O. Box 421, Mount Morris, IL 61054

Sojourners Magazine, Sojourners, 2401 15th St., NW, Washington, DC 20009

Spirit of Crazy Horse (Newsletter of Leonard Peltier Defense Committee), P.O. Box 583, Lawrence, Kansas 66044

Witness, 1249 Washington Blvd., Suite 3115, Detroit, MI 48226-1822

Year One, Jonah House, 1933 Park Ave., Baltimore, MD 21217

Z Magazine, 116 St. Botolph St., Boston, MA 02115

BIOGRAPHIES

Arthur J. Laffin, a native of Hartford, CT. From 1978 through 1989 he lived in New Haven, CT where he was a founding member of the Covenant Peace Community and Isaiah Peace Ministry. A member of the Atlantic Life Community, he served time in prison for his part in the Trident Nein and Thames River plowshares actions. He has also been involved in numerous nonviolent disarmament, anti-intervention and social justice actions. Since 1990, he has lived in Washington, DC where he has been a member of the Dorothy Day Catholic Worker.

Anne Montgomery is a sister of the Sacred Heart, teacher, and member of the Kairos Community. She has lived in New York for over 20 years. A member of the original Plowshares Eight, she has participated in four other plowshares actions, spending 2 1/2 years in prison for these actions. She was part of the Gulf Peace Team and has travelled numerous times to Iraq to support victims of U.S. bombing and economic sanctions. Anne has also travelled to Bosnia to offer support to victims of war and has recently been part of a peace team presence in Palestine.